CW00494488

ACCESS TO JUSTICE

Building on a series of ESRC-funded seminars, this edited collection of expert papers by academics and practitioners is concerned with access to civil and administrative justice in constitutional democracies, where, for the past decade, governments have reassessed their priorities for funding legal services: embracing 'new technologies' that reconfigure the delivery and very concept of legal services; cutting legal aid budgets; and introducing putative cost-cutting measures for the administration of courts, tribunals and established systems for the delivery of legal advice and assistance. Without underplaying the future potential of technological innovation, or the need for a fair and rational system for the prioritisation and funding of legal services, the book questions whether the absolutist approach to the dictates of austerity and the promise of new technologies that have driven the Coalition Government's policy, can be squared with obligations to protect the fundamental right of access to justice, in the unwritten constitution of the United Kingdom.

Access to Justice

Beyond the Policies and
Politics of Austerity

Edited by
Ellie Palmer
Tom Cornford
Audrey Guinchard
and
Yseult Marique

·HART·
PUBLISHING
OXFORD AND PORTLAND, OREGON
2018

Hart Publishing

An imprint of Bloomsbury Publishing Plc

Hart Publishing Ltd	Bloomsbury Publishing Plc
Kemp House	50 Bedford Square
Chawley Park	London
Cumnor Hill	WC1B 3DP
Oxford OX2 9PH	UK
UK	

www.hartpub.co.uk
www.bloomsbury.com

Published in North America (US and Canada) by
Hart Publishing
c/o International Specialized Book Services
920 NE 58th Avenue, Suite 300
Portland, OR 97213-3786
USA

www.isbs.com

**HART PUBLISHING, the Hart/Stag logo, BLOOMSBURY and the
Diana logo are trademarks of Bloomsbury Publishing Plc**

First published in hardback, 2016
Paperback edition, 2018

British Library Cataloguing-in-Publication Data
A catalogue record for this book is available from the British Library.

ISBN: PB: 978-1-50992-114-0
HB: 978-1-84946-734-6

Library of Congress Cataloging-in-Publication Data

Names : Palmer, Ellie, editor. | Cornford, Tom, editor. | Guinchard, Audrey, editor. |
Marique, Yseult, editor.

Title: Access to justice : beyond the policies and politics of austerity /
edited by Ellie Palmer, Tom Cornford, Audrey Guinchard, and Yseult Marique.

Other titles : Beyond the policies and politics of austerity

Description: Oxford ; Portland, OR : Hart Publishing, 2016. | Includes bibliographical
references and index.

Identifiers : LCCN 2015039088 | ISBN 9781849467346 (hardback : alk. paper)

Subjects: LCSH: Legal aid—Great Britain. | Legal assistance to the poor—Great Britain. |
Legal aid—Great Britain—Finance. | Legal assistance to the poor—Great Britain—Finance.

Classification: LCC KD512.A927 2016 | DDC 362.5/8—dc23 LC record available
at http://lccn.loc.gov/2015039088

Typeset by Compuscript Ltd, Shannon

To find out more about our authors and books visit www.hartpublishing.co.uk. Here you will find extracts, author
information, details of forthcoming events and the option to sign up for our newsletters.

This book is dedicated to Ellie's grandsons, Jacob, Callum and Arturo; Sally Weatherill, Oliver Cornford and William Cornford; Audrey's husband Stuart; and Yseult's parents Etienne and Anne-Marie Marique.

FOREWORD

THE RT HON SIR STEPHEN SEDLEY

2015 was the year in which Britain celebrated the eight-hundredth anniversary of Magna Carta, with its ringing promise that the Crown would neither sell nor delay nor deny justice to anyone. It was also a year in which an austerity programme initiated by a Labour government and developed by a Conservative–Liberal Democrat coalition began to bite so deeply into the accessibility of justice as to call into question whether Magna Carta any longer meant anything.

Running parallel to the steady erosion, at least in England and Wales, of what we had come, perhaps complacently, to regard as an entrenched human right, the seminar series on which this book is based looked carefully and realistically at both sides of the issue: the shrinking availability of public funds and the practical possibilities of doing more with less. The volume seeks in particular to distinguish between those inroads into access to justice which are unacceptable on any principled view and those which are either unavoidable or at least negotiable. Wherever possible it does so, in contrast sometimes to central government, from an ascertained evidence base. Even if some of the alternative ways of delivering services which the latter part of the book considers, and perhaps other ways of delivering justice too, have been prompted by the swing of the fiscal and political wrecking-ball, something positive may emerge.

The political Achilles' heel of legal services has arguably been legal aid. The 1949 Act which brought it into being eschewed a national legal service in favour of publicly bank rolling the private legal profession. The Treasury disliked it from the start: all it could ever see was an annual haemorrhage of public money; the return on it—public justice—didn't show up on the state's accounts. The exploitation of legal aid by parts of the private profession made it ripe for reform; but the result has been a series of amputations which are now leaving major sectors of the population without access to legal advice or representation. The Treasury, meanwhile, has woken up to the fact that access to justice can be not merely self-financing, but a source of profit: increasingly unaffordable court fees are now set at a level which pays for the entire court system with money over.

It is easy but unproductive to watch in despair as justice becomes an item on a profit and loss account and the privilege of the prosperous. But austerity is still a political reality, and justice is still the cement of a civilised society. The ecumenical participation in the seminars from which these chapters are drawn—policymakers, judges, practitioners, academics, advisers—gives the book a sobriety and an authority which political argument may lack. Is it too much to hope that the Secretary of State for Justice, who as Lord Chancellor bears constitutional responsibility for the undertaking given at Runnymede, will read it?

Stephen Sedley
Oxford

ACKNOWLEDGEMENTS

This edited collection is born of a series of seminars comprising a dedicated team of academics and practitioners from both sides of the Scottish border: advisers, distinguished speakers, including senior members of the judiciary and a core group of expert discussants who so generously gave of their time to ensuring the continuing success of the *Access to Justice* seminars beyond the life of the series. We wish to extend our gratitude to everyone who participated, for their unstinting commitment to our project.

We would also like to express a particular debt of gratitude to Sir Nicholas Blake, then President of the Upper Tribunal Immigration and Asylum Chamber, Shona Simon President of Employment Tribunals Scotland and the dedicated members of our strategic planning committee—Mike Adler, Nony Ardill, Varda Bondy, Tom Cornford, Mavis Maclean, Martin Partington, Alan Paterson, Maurice Sunkin, Carol Storer, David Williams and Nick Wikeley—whose diverse experiences and accomplishments in the academic, judicial, practitioner and administrative spheres have contributed greatly to the breadth, profundity and creative energy of this volume.

It is also notable that a number of contributors to this volume have paid tribute to influential seminar papers by Alan Patterson, Richard Susskind and Roger Smith, whose ideas continue to shape past and present debates about the impact of legal aid rationing and technological innovation on the accessibility of justice and the future of professional legal services, including the provision of legal education in the United Kingdom. We would also wish to pay tribute here to seminal evidence- based papers by Stephen Cobb QC, Professor Graham Cookson of the University of Surrey, Guy Mansfield QC, Colin McKay, then Deputy Director in the Justice Directorate Scotland, Assistant Professor Nell Munro of the University of Nottingham, James Sandbach and Sarah Veale CBE (Head of the Equality and Human Rights Department at the TUC) whose authoritative contributions for a variety of reasons, including the passage of time, have not appeared in this volume.

Furthermore, despite the passage of time we would also like to acknowledge our debt to the most stalwart members of the core discussion group: Nony Ardill, Varda Bondy, Audrey Guinchard, Anna Hardiman-McCartney, Steve Hynes, Morag McDermont, Tom Mullen, Paul Yates, Yseult Marique, Richard Miller and James Sandbach, whose diverse legal, socio-political and socio-legal backgrounds were key to the quality of the informed discussions on which we have built.

And finally, we would wish to thank our dedicated graduate student reporters, Joanne Easton, Stephen Sondem and Laura Wrixon, whose enthusiasm and commitment to the ideals of access to justice were not only evident in their participation at the seminars, but shine through the excellent recording of the speaker papers which they so generously found time to produce for our dedicated website.

Turning then to the present, I would like to acknowledge my gratitude to Tom, Audrey and Yseult for their perseverance and hard work, our expert contributors for their patient good humour, and to Richard Hart for insisting, that, despite the passage of time, this timely and important collection of academic and practitioner speaker papers should not be allowed to escape the light of day.

Ellie Palmer
25 September 2015

CONTENTS

Foreword vii

Acknowledgements ix

List of Contributors xiii

Introduction 1
Tom Cornford, Audrey Guinchard, Yseult Marique and Ellie Palmer

Part I: Access to Justice: Theoretical, Legal and Policy Background

1. Access to Justice: The View from the Law Society 13
   Andrew Caplen

2. The Meaning of Access to Justice 27
   Tom Cornford

3. Principles of Access: Comparing Health and Legal Services 41
   Albert Weale

4. Europe to the Rescue? EU Law, the ECHR and Legal Aid 53
   Steve Peers

Part II: Pressure Points on the Justice System

5. Access to Justice in Administrative Law
   and Administrative Justice 69
   Tom Mullen

6. Immigration and Access to Justice: A Critical Analysis of
   Recent Restrictions 105
   Robert Thomas

7. The Impact of Austerity and Structural Reforms on the
   Accessibility of Tribunal Justice 135
   Stewart Wright

8. Thirteen Years of Advice Delivery in Islington: A Case Study 143
   Lorna Reid

9. Complexity, Housing and Access to Justice 157
   Andrew Brookes and Caroline Hunter

10. Access to Justice in the Employment Tribunal: Private
    Disputes or Public Concerns?..175
    Nicole Busby and Morag McDermont

11. Renegotiating Family Justice...197
    Mavis Maclean CBE

12. Access to Justice for Young People: Beyond the
    Policies and Politics of Austerity..211
    James Kenrick and Ellie Palmer

Part III: Alternative Approaches to Funding Legal Services

13. A Revolution in 'Lawyering'? Implications for
    Welfare Law of Alternative Business Structures............................237
    Frank H Stephen

14. CourtNav and Pro Bono in an Age of Austerity 249
    Paul Yates

15. The French Approach to Access to Justice...................................259
    Audrey Guinchard and Simon Wesley

16. How Scotland has Approached the Challenge of Austerity 287
    Sarah O'Neill

Index 303

LIST OF CONTRIBUTORS

Andrew Brookes is Deputy District Judge and Head of Housing and Property Dispute Resolution at Anthony Gold Solicitors. Andrew spent six years as chair of the Housing Law Practitioners' Association and is ranked as a leading individual in the field of social housing in *Chambers 2015*. He is currently on the editorial board of the *Journal of Housing Law* and regularly writes and lectures on housing law. Andrew's clients include tenants and other private individuals, residents' associations, social landlords, private landlords and commercial organisations. He also has wide ranging experience of judicial review cases of all kinds. His reported cases cover such matters as the scope of a local authority's duty towards intentionally homeless persons, decisions in the Lands Tribunal relating to residential service charges, the enforcement of a mortgage over commercial property and a successful judicial review of a local authority's decision to increase parking charges.

Nicole Busby is Professor of Labour Law at the Strathclyde Law School. Her research focuses on the effect of legal interventions on individuals' working lives and she is particularly interested in exploring the wider socio-economic environment in which the labour market operates, including the impact of state regulation. Her current work relates to the relationship between paid work and unpaid care, the constitutionalisation of labour rights (with particular reference to the EU constitution post-Lisbon) and claimants' experiences of the UK's Employment Tribunal system. She is the author of *A Right to Care? Unpaid Care Work in EU Employment Law* (Oxford University Press, 2011), co-author (with Grace James) of *A History of Regulating Working Families: Strategies and Stereotypes, Strains and Solutions* (Hart Publishing, forthcoming 2016), co-editor (with Grace James) of *Families, Care-giving and Paid Work: Challenging Labour Law in the 21st Century* (Edward Elgar, 2011) and (with Douglas Brodie and Rebecca Zahn) *The Future Regulation of Work* (Palgrave Macmillan, 2016).

Andrew Caplen is the immediate Past President of the Law Society of England and Wales. During his year as President he took the question of 'Access to Justice' as his major theme. In September 2014 he launched, alongside the Lord Chief Justice, the Law Society's 'Access to Justice' campaign and in June 2015 assisted in the launch at Chancery Lane of Oxfam's 'Lawyers against Poverty' initiative. Andrew has both written and spoken widely on these issues. In 2015 he co-authored *Speaking Up—Defending and Delivering Access to Justice Today* (published by Theos). He also presented the annual Beckly Lecture at the 2015 Methodist Conference.

Andrew Caplen's involvement with Legal Aid and Access to Justice issues has continued throughout his legal career. He was a Duty Solicitor for many years and has been involved in a number of pro bono initiatives. He was also Chair of the Law Society's Access to Justice Committee from 2008 to 2012 and one of the co-authors of the Society's 'Access to Justice Review'. Andrew is a Consultant with Heppenstalls Solicitors Limited of Lymington and New Milton.

Tom Cornford is a senior lecturer in the School of Law, University of Essex where he teaches public law, tort law and various courses in legal and political theory. He is the author of writings on administrative law and the tort liability of public authorities, notably *Towards a Public Law of Tort* (Ashgate, 2008).

Audrey Guinchard established the LLB English and French Laws with Master 1/Maîtrise at the University of Essex and co-directed it for 12 years. Her current research focuses on cybercrime and how new technologies affect criminal law and human rights. Since April 2013, she has been the co-investigator responsible for the legal aspects of a project funded by the EPSRC on the 'Digital prosumer—Establishing a "Futures Market" for Digital Personhood Data'. The project notably reflects on the issues of privacy, data protection and commercialisation of personal data. Her interest in human rights and access to justice stems from her own research in criminal law and on the concept of legal certainty and predictability at common law, as well as from her teaching of French law, which covers the French justice system, its concept of law and access to law and justice.

Caroline Hunter is a Professor at York Law School, University of York. She is currently Head of the Law School. After working in practice as a barrister at the start of her career, she has since developed an academic profile combining teaching, research, training and legal practice, focusing in particular on the interaction of housing law, policy and practice. She has led a number of socio-legal projects on housing law, relating in particular to possession proceedings, anti-social behaviour and homelessness and has published widely on these subjects. She is deputy general editor of the *Journal of Housing Law* and is currently co-authoring a book with Professor Helen Carr (University of Kent) provisionally entitled: *Governing the Homeless: Law, Governance and Plurality at the Margins* (Palgrave Macmillan, forthcoming). She sits as a part-time fee paid judge of the First-tier Tribunal (Property Chamber).

James Kenrick is an expert on young people's legal advice needs. He works at Youth Access, the national membership organisation for youth advice and counselling services, where he is responsible for developing the quality and quantity of youth advice services. He has authored numerous reports and articles, including 'The Advice Needs of Young People—The Evidence (2009), 'Young People's Access To Advice—The Evidence' (2009) and 'The Outcomes And Impact Of Youth Advice—The Evidence' (2011). More recently, he has worked to integrate legal advice services with health, housing and social care services. James is also co-Chair of Just Rights, the campaign for fair access to advice, advocacy and legal representation for children and young people, and a trustee of the Advice Services Alliance. Before joining Youth Access, James worked for 10 years as an advice worker in Law Centres and independent advice agencies.

Mavis Maclean CBE is a Senior Research Fellow of St Hilda's College Oxford and a Founding Director of the Oxford Centre for Family Law and Policy (OXFLAP) at the Department of Social Policy and Intervention, Oxford. She was a panel member of the Bristol Royal Infirmary Inquiry, and Academic Adviser at the Ministry of Justice for many years. Recent books include 'Family Justice: The Work of Family Judges in Uncertain Times with John Eekelaar (Hart, 2014) and *Delivering Family Justice in the 21st Century* edited with John Eekelaar and Benoit Bastard, (Onati International Series, Hart, 2015).

Yseult Marique is a Senior Lecturer at the University of Essex. Her comparative research in the area of European administrative law is concerned with administrative justice and the regulation of public contracts in Europe. Her recent research has focused on the interplay between administrative law, contract law and regulation, in shaping how public money is spent and controlled in the modern European 'economic constitution'. This growing body of comparative work raises important questions about the distinctiveness of the UK's legal framework of economic governance, which have gained heightened significance in the context of continuing austerity. Yseult's research has been widely published in English, French, Belgian and international journals; she has published chapters in edited collections and reports for public and commercial bodies in the UK and other European jurisdictions. Her monograph *Public-Private Partnerships and the Law: Regulation, Institutions and Community* (Cheltenham, Edward Elgar, foreword by Professor John S Bell) was published in 2014. Yseult holds a law degree from the Université libre de Bruxelles (ULB), and a D Phil from the University of Cambridge (with a PhD by equivalence from the ULB). She holds a postgraduate degree in notariaat from the Vrije Universiteit Brussels (VUB).

Morag McDermont is Professor of Socio-Legal Studies at the University of Bristol Law School, and Principal Investigator for two research programmes: 'New Sites of Legal Consciousness: A Case Study of UK Advice Agencies' which examines the role played by advice agencies in a rapidly changing legal landscape (funded by the European research Council, see www.bristol.ac.uk/law/research/centres-projects-themes/aanslc/cab-project/) and 'Productive Margins: Regulating for Engagement', a collaborative programme with community organisations to co-produce research about ways in which regulatory systems can be re-designed to promote engaged decision-making in politics, policy and the arts (funded by the ESRC, see www.productivemargins.ac.uk). Her research has been shaped by 15 years' working in local government and voluntary sector housing organisations. She has published two books: *Regulating Social Housing: Governing Decline* (Glasshouse, 2006) with Dave Cowan; and *Governing, Independence and Expertise: the Business of Housing Associations* (Hart, 2010), a study of the historical role played by the National Housing Federation in the governance of social housing.

Tom Mullen is Professor of Law at the University of Glasgow. His research interests include constitutional law, administrative law, legal process and housing law, and he has written widely on these subjects. He has a particular interest in administrative justice and is currently writing a book, *Administrative Justice and Citizens Grievances* (forthcoming) in the UK. He has advised both parliamentary and executive government bodies, including the House of Commons Select Committee on Scottish Affairs, the Scottish Government, the Scottish Committee of the Administrative Justice and Tribunals Council (on tribunal reform in Scotland), and was a member of the Administrative Justice Steering Group (2008–09) which wrote the key report, 'Administrative Justice in Scotland—The Way Forward'. He is currently a member of the Scottish Tribunals and Administrative Justice Advisory Committee. Recent publications include: 'Protective Expenses Orders and Public Interest Litigation' 36 (2015), *Edinburgh Law Review* 19 'A Holistic Approach to Administrative Justice?' in M Adler (ed), *Administrative Justice in Context* (Hart, 2010), and '*Entick v Carrington* in Scots Law' in Adam Tomkins and Paul Scott (eds), Entick v Carrington: *250 years of the Rule of Law?* (Hart, 2015).

Sarah O'Neill is a non-practising solicitor, with experience in the private, public and voluntary sectors. She is currently an independent consultant specialising in legal and consumer policy, and has many years' experience of working on access to justice issues. She was Director of Policy and Solicitor at Consumer Focus Scotland from 2008–12. Prior to that, she was Legal Officer at the Scottish Consumer Council for 10 years. She has represented the consumer interest on numerous expert groups on justice issues, such as the policy group established by Lord Gill to advise on his civil courts review and the reference group for Sheriff Principal Taylor's review of expenses and funding of civil litigation. She was a member of the Sheriff Court Rules Council from 2005–11. Sarah is a chairperson member of the Homeowner Housing Panel and Private Rented Housing Panel. She is currently a member of the Scottish Tribunals and Administrative Justice Advisory Committee, and of a Redress Expert Panel established by the Scottish Government to advise the Consumer and Competition Policy for Scotland Working Group. She is also a member of the Scottish Mediation Network's board of trustees.

Ellie Palmer is Emeritus Professor in the School of Law and Human Rights Centre at the University of Essex where she began her distinguished academic career as a commercial lawyer. However, for the past 15 years and more, her research interests have been in the areas of public law and human rights, especially socio-economic rights. She has particular research interests in the development of judicial and extra-judicial mechanisms of accountability for the fair distribution of centrally allocated health and welfare resources; and in the use of international standards to protect socially marginalised vulnerable adults and children living in poverty.

She has written extensively on both. Since 2009, when her leading monograph *Judicial Review Socio-economic Rights and the Human Rights Act* (Hart, 2007) was reprinted in paperback, the theme of austerity has brought new dimensions to her constitutional and administrative law teaching and research. She is currently contributing to a number of national and international research projects concerning the socio-economic implications of austerity on the lives of vulnerable individuals and groups, especially in mainland Europe. She is also working on her latest monograph, *Welfare Human Rights and States Protection,* based on research-led undergraduate and post-graduate teaching, which she introduced at Essex in the wake of the economic downturn.

Steve Peers is a Professor of EU Law and Human Rights Law at the Law School, University of Essex. His books include: *EU Justice and Home Affairs Law* 4th edn (Oxford, Oxford University Press, forthcoming 2016); *Brexit: The Legal Framework for Withdrawal from the EU or Renegotiation of EU Membereship* (Hart, forthcoming 2016); *EU Immigration and Asylum Law: Text and Commentary* 2nd edn, 3 volumes (Martinus Nijhoff, 2012–15) with Elspeth Gould and Jonathan Tomkin; *European Union Law* (Oxford University Press, 2014) edited with Catherine Barnard; *The EU Charter of Fundamental Rights: A Commentary* (Hart, 2014) edited with Tamara Hervey, Jeff Kenner and Angela Ward; and *The EU Citizenship Directive* with Elspeth Gould and Jonathan Tomkin (Oxford University Press, 2014). He is also the author of over 50 articles on various aspects of EU law, in particular relating to human rights, justice and home affairs, data protection, EU/UK relations, constitutional law, free movement of EU citizens and external relations. He has also worked as a consultant, contributor or adviser to a number of bodies and organisations, including as an expert for the EU Fundamental Rights Agency, a consultant to the European Commission, the European Parliament, the Foreign and Commonwealth Office, the Irish Attorney-General and the Council of Europe, as a contributor to the work of human rights NGOs, and as an expert appearing before House of Commons and House of Lords Select Committees.

Lorna Reid worked as a specialist welfare benefits caseworker in Islington, London, for 20 years. In that time she developed a network of holistic advice projects aimed at reaching those most in need who often were unable to access mainstream services and worked closely with statutory and third sector providers to maximise impact. Lorna has extensive experience of representing appellants in the First-tier and Upper Tribunals and delivers training to other advisers on how to prepare for and advocate in the Social Entitlement Tribunal. She currently manages a welfare rights team at Camden Council and is a principal legal officer at the Free Representation Unit.

Frank H Stephen is Emeritus Professor of Regulation in the School of Law at the University of Manchester where he was Professor of Regulation from 2005–14. He was previously a Professor in Economics at the University of Strathclyde. In 2010 he was President of the International Society for New Institutional Economics

(ISNIE). Frank has researched and written widely on the regulation of the legal professions. His work has been funded by ESRC, Office of Fair Trading, Leverhulme Trust, Scottish Executive, Law Society of Scotland, Faculty of Advocates and Swiss Ministry of Economics. He was a Special Adviser to the Joint Committee of the House of Lords and the Commons which considered the Draft Legal Services Bill in 2006 and the Scottish Parliaments Justice Committee when it considered the Legal Services (Scotland) Bill 2010. In 2013 Frank published a monograph *Lawyers, Markets and Regulation* (Edward Elgar, 2013) which examined UK policy on the regulation of the legal professions and examined the implications of the Legal Services Act 2007.

Robert Thomas is a Professor of Public Law at the School of Law, University of Manchester. His principal research interests are: public and administrative law; immigration and asylum law; and empirical legal research. He has published the following books: *Administrative Justice and Asylum Appeals* (Hart, 2011), which was the First Prize winner of the Society of Legal Scholars Peter Birks Prize for Outstanding Legal Scholarship, 2011; and has co-authored with Professor Mark Elliott the leading textbook *Public Law* 2nd edn (Oxford University Press, 2014).

Albert Weale is Emeritus Professor of Political Theory and Public Policy at University College London. Prior to taking up his post at UCL, he was Professor of Government and co-editor of the *British Journal of Political Science* at the University of Essex. Before that he was Professor of Politics at the University of East Anglia (1985–92), Lecturer in Politics (1976–85) and Assistant Director of the Institute for Research in the Social Sciences (1982–85) at the University of York, and Sir James Knott Fellow at the University of Newcastle upon Tyne. He graduated in Theology from Clare College Cambridge in 1971 and was awarded a D Phil in Social and Political Sciences at the University of Cambridge in 1977. His research and publications have been concentrated on issues of political theory and public policy, especially the theory of justice and the theory of democracy, health policy and comparative environmental policy. His principal publications include *Equality and Social Policy* (Routledge and Kegan Paul, 1978), *Political Theory and Social Policy* (Macmillan, 1983), *The New Politics of Pollution* (Manchester University Press, 1992), *Democracy* (Macmillan, 1999 and 2007 rev), *Democratic Citizenship and the European Union* (Manchester University Press, 2005), *Democratic Justice and the Social Contract* (Oxford University Press, 2013) and, with Shaun Heap, Martin Hollis, Bruce Lyons and Robert Sugden, *The Theory of Choice* (Blackwell, 1992) and with Geoffrey Pridham, Michelle Cini, Dimitrios Konstadakopulos, Martin Porter and Brendan Flynn, *Environmental Governance in Europe* (Oxford University Press, 2000) as well as a number of edited books, journal paper and chapters.

Simon Wesley has lived and worked in France since 1980. He is a former Solicitor (England & Wales), now practising as an Avocat à la Cour at the Lyon Bar. Simon is also an assistant Professor of Law at the University of Lyon 3 Law Faculty, where he teaches English law at the Institute of Comparative Law and the Institute of Law, Economics and Business Affairs. He practises as a consultant with a French business law firm. Before qualifying as a Solicitor, Simon obtained a degree in Social Sciences with Law at the University of Kent at Canterbury.

Stewart Wright was called to the Bar in 1993. He was appointed as a Legally Qualified Panel Member of the Appeal Tribunals in 2002 and became a Judge of the First-tier Tribunal, Social Entitlement Chamber in 2008. Before coming to the Bar he worked in a law centre for 7 years in the late 1980s and early 1990s. He was then at the Bar from 1993 to 1999. From 1999 to 2007 he was the Child Poverty Action Group's legal officer. This job meant he was responsible for running CPAG's test case strategy and in that role important social security cases. In October 2012 he was appointed Judge of the Upper Tribunal (Administrative Appeals Chamber).

Paul Yates runs Freshfields' London pro bono practice. Freshfields acts for a wide range of pro bono clients, from some of the world's largest international NGOs to individual victims of human trafficking. Paul appears as an advocate at the asylum support tribunal, and is vice-chair of the Asylum Support Appeals Project (ASAP). He also acts for victims of human trafficking in civil enforcement proceedings, and is closely involved in developing the firm's third-party intervention practice. Paul was previously seconded to the legal team of human rights group Liberty.

Introduction

TOM CORNFORD, AUDREY GUINCHARD,
YSEULT MARIQUE AND ELLIE PALMER

The millennium began with ambitious proposals by the New Labour Government to transform the justice system; driven, as in the case of other publicly funded services, by the goals of efficiency, and underpinned by market principles introduced for the commissioning of legal services. However, throughout the following decade there were growing concerns among legal professions, pressure groups and charities about the level of unmet need for *appropriate* services, especially for socially disadvantaged individuals and groups. Moreover, since 2011, the 'absolutist' approach to austerity that marked the tenure of the Coalition Government has done little to allay these concerns. Introduced at the same time as a complex opaque and contested reconfiguration of the welfare system, sweeping reforms of legal aid under the Legal Aid, Sentencing and Punishment of Offenders Act 2012 (LASPO), have coincided with increased pressures on courts, tribunals and advice agencies, leaving many vulnerable individuals without access to the kind of help that they need.

Furthermore, at a time of unprecedented need for protective public interest challenges and independent oversight of government decision-making in relation to the fair distribution and regulation of basic public services, shortly before the end of its tenure, the Coalition Government placed punitive restrictions on a court's powers to limit costs liabilities for organisations wishing to bring challenges; requiring them to order 'interveners' (NGOs and charities) to pay for any work done by another party, arising from their involvement in the case.[1]

A number of the chapters in this collection have focused directly on the implications of the Coalition legal aid reforms and other austerity measures for vulnerable individuals in need. Others have focused more broadly on theoretical issues of privatisation and government approaches to public services funding, investigating the need for a distinctive approach to state financing of *legal services* in the unwritten constitution of the United Kingdom. Thus, whether focusing on abstract notions of justice as fairness, or the exigencies of a safe system to deliver it, the chapters in this collection are universally concerned with fundamental questions about 'access to justice', a concept which, in contemporary legal and

---

[1] The Criminal Justice and Courts Act 2015, s 86.

socio-legal discourses, and in human rights and democratic political theory has acquired the status of a fundamental constitutional right.

As noted above, this collection of chapters builds on the investigations of a series of ESRC funded seminars, *Access to Justice in an Age of Austerity: Time for Proportionate Responses* (2011–13)[2] which brought together a core group of up to 40 discussants—senior civil servants from the Ministry of Justice and the Scottish Justice Department, members of the judiciary, representatives from the legal professions, Citizens Advice, law centres, members of consultative bodies, NGOs, academics and research students—to reflect on and discuss reforms of the past decade, proposals for 'proportionate' responses in the current crisis, and to identify future research directions and questions.

However, since our proposal had been written and our grant awarded shortly before the appointment of the Coalition Government, it became necessary to make some changes of substance and focus, especially to the later 2012–13 seminars. Thus, as well as investigating 'proportionate' responses to the reform of legal services and the funding of the justice system more generally, the focus of seminars 3, 4 and 5 shifted to a more practical examination of the proposed legal aid cuts and other austerity measures introduced by the Coalition Government. Moreover, participants had the opportunity to discuss and suggest practical solutions to very real cuts in budget and services that had taken place, or were shortly to be implemented under LASPO. Throughout the seminars, we adopted the broadest definition of what is entailed in the concept of access to justice. It was also understood that emphasis would be placed on solutions as well as problems created by cuts; and where possible, proposals for reform would be based on rigorous evidence-based research.

Of course, we had no illusions about the likely severity of the cuts, or their impact on both providers and recipients of legal services. For some time expenditure on legal aid has been recognised as unsustainable. It was also clear that under New Labour, policies of outsourcing, cost cutting, and a culture of blame in relation to providers of legal services would have continued. However, there was nothing to predict the scale of the legal aid cuts introduced by the Coalition Government in the LASPO Act, or the arbitrariness of blanket institutional measures adopted in the name of austerity, including self-representation in court; restriction to telephone advice—even for the most vulnerable groups in society; limited court office opening hours and ad hoc relocation of courts across England and Wales. Nor were stakeholders prepared for the Coalition's refusal to engage with economic evidence-based research that might point to different conclusions, or their indifference to concerns that many of the proposed cost-cutting measures would impact most severely on the vulnerable in society. One of the most fiercely fought political campaigns, highlighting the potential dangers of leaving

---

[2] See: www.essex.ac.uk/atj/.

vulnerable 18- to 25-year-olds 'out of scope' at the last hurdle made little impression on the Bill's promulgators.[3]

Over the two years of the seminars, discussion frequently returned to legal aid and the LASPO Act—its institutional and societal implications—especially for the most vulnerable members of society. However, by continuing to focus on our broader research agenda (systemic funding issues and pressure points on the justice system, including family, housing, immigration, employment and administrative tribunals and mental health) we had the benefit of speaker papers that were not only diverse in subject matter, but also unique in providing experiential commentary, evidence-based research, suggestions of solutions and useful comparators with other devolved nations (most notably Scotland and France).

Those in practice were able to offer insights into work which has improved community engagement, demonstrating the value of combined services. Lorna Reid (Islington Law Centre) presented the experience of several decade-long projects provided in partnership with Islington local authority services; highlighting their success in removing experiential barriers to the justice system for some the most vulnerable members of the community. James Kenrick (Youth Access) provided first-hand evidence of the importance of early intervention, in terms of advice for young people and the present lack of appropriate services for this vulnerable group.

At the same time, academics, judges and practitioners were able to share solid evidence-based research which often challenged the Government's justifications and contradicted their aims. Stephen Cobb QC, formerly Chairman of the Family Law Bar Association and recently appointed to the High Court bench, demonstrated the additional costs likely to arise due to extra burdens on the family law system which would outweigh any savings made by LASPO cuts. Nigel Balmer and Marisol Smith (both of the Legal Services Research Centre) presented a paper entitled 'Just a Phone Call Away: Is Telephone Advice Enough?' which suggested that, all things considered, the move to telephone advice would not benefit all users and the substantive benefits would be significantly lower than when receiving face-to-face advice.

Evidence-based presentations of this kind afforded a unique opportunity for the seminars to consider different models for improvement of services across the board. Furthermore, the engagement of policymakers and professionals on both sides of the Scottish border (CAB and Scottish Legal Aid Board)[4] as well as academics, judges and practitioners from both jurisdictions, contributed to fully informed debate. Practical solutions were discussed without overlooking the realities of problems arising in different institutional contexts, or in demographically disadvantaged localities with unwieldy numbers of vulnerable clients, most likely

---

[3] See: www.guardian.co.uk/law/2012/apr/23/lords-block-legal-aid-again.

[4] At the time of the seminars Colin McKay was Deputy Director in the Justice Directorate of the Scottish Government. His responsibilities included government policy on courts, access to justice, EU justice liaison and the Government's relationship with the judiciary and the legal profession. Colin Lancaster was Director of Policy and Development, Scottish Legal Aid Board.

to present with multiple problems that put them and their families at greatest risk. Several papers and discussions focused on the need for better initial decision-making, suggesting that appropriately trained decision-makers, in command of relevant evidence (supported by advice-givers and caseworkers) could effectively relieve the growing burdens on many courts and tribunals. Moreover, it was suggested that the currently high success rates in appellate courts and tribunals may be indicative of systemic failures to resolve basic problems much earlier in the decision-making process.

In a number of seminars, Scottish speakers provided important insights into alternative approaches, notably in relation to reducing the legal aid budget, and to avoiding duplication in work of appellate courts and administrative tribunals. However, Scottish presentations did not merely offer *theoretical* alternatives to LASPO. These expert presentations, of approaches already in place in Scotland (and subject to monitoring), satisfied one of the central objectives of the series: to highlight the importance of rigorous evidence-based research as a *sine qua non* for constitutionally appropriate reforms of the justice system. Colin McKay began by explaining how, since devolution, the Scottish system of legal aid had diverged from the English: the Scottish system had remained predominantly a judicaire one and had managed to retain the existing scope of legal aid without increasing per capita spending. It had done this by an integrated approach which involved pursuing structural efficiencies. With greater budgetary constraints, the pressure on the system was increasing, however.[5]

Nowhere more clearly was the contrast between the Scottish and Westminster approaches to fiscally responsible legal aid spending demonstrated than in Graham Cookson's paper, 'Analysing the economic justifications for the reforms to social welfare and family law legal aid'[6] which drew on the findings of his study commissioned by the Law Society of England and Wales: *Unintended Consequences: the Cost of the Government Legal Aid Reforms.*[7] Thus, challenging the Government's unscientific approach to the reduction of the UK budget deficit, the aim of his research had been to identify the potential impact of the reform to legal aid scope on the public purse; focusing in particular on the areas of law where the proposed cuts to legal aid were required to generate the largest savings: family law, social welfare law and clinical negligence.

It had been made clear that as part of the Coalition's fiscal plan to reduce the UK deficit, the Ministry of Justice was expected to save £2 billion per annum from its budget in the year 2014–15; a target to be achieved by substantial reforms to the legal aid system, estimated to deliver savings of £450 million per annum; and this was to be achieved by the crudest of strategies: to remove significant categories

---

[5] C McKay, 'The Scottish Government Response to Austerity', paper for ESRC Access to Justice Seminar Series, Seminar 2, *Revaluing a Market Based Approach to Legal Services* (14 July 2011) 2.

[6] A version of Cookson's seminar paper was later published in the *Journal of Social Welfare and Family Law*. See G Cookson, 'Analysing the Economic Justification for the Reforms to Social Welfare and Family Law Legal Aid' (2013) 35(1) *Journal of Social Welfare and Family Law* 21.

[7] See: www.lawsociety.org.uk/policy-campaigns/research-trends/research-publications/unintended-consequence-of-legal-aid-reforms/.

of law from the scope of legal aid. Moreover, since £941 million (approximately a quarter of legal aid expenditure) was for civil and family cases, the most significant savings were required to be made in those areas. It was axiomatic, however, that if the Coalition reforms were to make any meaningful contribution to reducing the fiscal deficit, the required savings needed to be weighed against the potential knock-on or consequential costs to the public purse.

Nonetheless, as reported by the Justice Select Committee and acknowledged by the Ministry of Justice, the magnitude of these knock-on effects had simply not been estimated. Indeed, the Government's *own* impact assessment had indicated that the reforms could generate significant knock-on costs, including 'reduced social cohesion, increased criminality, reduced business and economic efficiency, increased resource costs to other and increased transfer payments from other Departments'. Thus, relying on data from the Civil and Social Justice Survey combined with data from the Legal Services Commission and other publically available data, Professor Cookson's research had not only generated a crucial debate around the proportionality of the Coalition proposals in designated areas (family justice, welfare and clinical negligence) it had also laid the foundations for further in-depth research to establish the true economic magnitude of the predicted areas of costs. As explained in his seminar paper, Cookson's analysis had demonstrated that knock-on costs could be in the region of £139 million per annum, realising a net saving of significantly less than half (42 per cent) of the Government's prediction within the targeted areas.

Shortly before the LASPO Act came into force, Lord Neuberger had publicly voiced his concerns over the legal aid cuts, stating that he feared court costs would rise and that those facing legal challenges would begin to feel that the Government was not giving them access to justice, taking matters into their own hands.[8] Thus, from the beginning of the Coalition tenure, the seminars provided an important space for multidimensional and sustained dialogue with experts on access to justice issues, across academic and practitioner boundaries. Indeed, it soon became clear that growing concerns about the likely societal impact of the legal aid cuts, and the Government's indifference to rational argument and constructive policy debate, would not be allowed to undermine the commitment of stakeholders to seeking innovative and client-centred solutions, within systems already showing signs of chaos.

The seminars were organised around three interlocking themes which have been replicated in the three parts of this book.[9] The first was the nature of 'access

---

[8] See: http://bbc.co.uk/news/uk-21665319.

[9] The essays in the book are either updated versions of papers given at the seminars or, in some cases, newly solicited contributions. With two exceptions, they were submitted between November 2014 and July 2015. Each chapter states the law as it stood at the date of its completion. The date of completion of those chapters whose content is date-sensitive is as follows: Caplen—May 2015; Peers— June 2015; Mullen—May 2015; Thomas—December 2014; Reid—February 2015; Wright—May 2012; Brookes and Hunter—December 2014; Busby and McDermott—September 2014; Maclean— December 2014; Kenrick and Palmer—April 2015; Stephen—November 2014; Yates—July 2015; Wesley and Guinchard—July 2015; O'Neill—February 2015.

to justice' as an ideal and the question of what is necessary, in general terms, to achieve it. The second was the concrete reality of access to justice in England and Wales today, particularly in light of the changes wrought by the LASPO Act. Here the focus was on the parts of the law that impact most directly on the lives of ordinary citizens (and non-citizens in the case of immigrants), especially the poorest who stand to suffer most as the result of the Government's cuts to legal aid. Many of the contributions on this theme drew on empirical research. The third theme focused on methods for improving access to justice, including new economic models of service delivery and the increased use of technology.

Part I

The first part of the book, 'Access to Justice: Theoretical, Legal and Policy Background' begins with a contribution from Andrew Caplen, President of the Law Society. This provides a succinct and critical overview of the current state of access to justice in this country. It thus affords a useful rehearsal of the themes that are taken up in the rest of the book.

The following two chapters take a more theoretical turn. In his chapter, Tom Cornford considers the different meanings that have been assigned to the expression 'access to justice' and concludes that the core meaning is the requirement that each citizen be equally able to protect her legal rights. A corollary of this is that there is equality in the provision of legal services. In other words, wealth or social position should confer no advantage in legal matters and only the importance of the interests at stake should determine the level of legal assistance given. One way of ensuring this would be to provide a legal equivalent to the National Health Service, a state-funded system that furnished advice and representation in legal matters to every citizen on the basis of need rather than ability to pay. This notion that legal services could be treated in the same way as medical ones is taken up in his chapter by Albert Weale, who carefully plots the similarities and differences between the two types of service. In the case of health care, he concludes there is no reason in principle why citizens should not pay for services, the strongest arguments for state provision being based on market failure rather than on a right to equal health care services. In the case of legal services, by contrast, the right to equal provision is inherent in the notion of justice.

In the last chapter of the first section, Steve Peers puts UK concerns about access to justice in a wider context by setting out European Convention and EU law on the subject. An understanding of European Convention law in particular is useful in understanding the Coalition Government's reforms considered in the next part as they impose an important restraint on the Government's ability to reduce access to justice.

Part II

The second part of the book, 'Pressure Points on the Justice System', begins with a contribution from Tom Mullen in which he surveys the whole landscape of administrative justice and explains how the Government's reforms have altered it. He describes, inter alia, the abandonment of the movement (exemplified in the adoption of the uniform tribunal structure) towards a holistic approach to the area; the Government's attempts to weaken judicial review; the removal of rights of appeal in immigration matters; the introduction of administrative obstacles to appeal in social security matters; and the effects of cuts in legal aid.

Robert Thomas describes the severe restrictions on access to justice that the Government has imposed in the field of immigration both by reducing the categories of immigration cases for which legal aid is provided and by removing, in most cases, the right to appeal. While these restrictions will lead, Thomas argues, to many cases of injustice they may not reduce litigation as much as the Government hopes. The inability to appeal may increase the incidence of judicial review and the courts have found, in the *Gudanaviciene*[10] and *Public Law Project*[11] cases, certain of the limitations on legal aid to be unlawful.

In their chapters, Stewart Wright, at the time of writing his chapter a Judge of the Social Entitlement of the First-tier Tribunal,[12] and Lorna Reid, a welfare benefits caseworker, address from their different perspectives, the problems of access to justice in the field of social security law. Wright describes the challenges faced by the Social Entitlement chamber, and Reid a number of innovative schemes for providing advice to benefit applicants in the London Borough of Islington. A lesson of Reid's chapter is one that recurs throughout Part II: that advice given early to those in need is key to avoiding disputes and appeals later on.

In their chapter on housing and access to justice, Andrew Brookes and Caroline Hunter emphasise the complexity of housing issues—the way in which they can give rise to multiple forms of proceeding in different courts and tribunals—and their tendency to form part of larger clusters of problems: those suffering difficulties with housing are often afflicted by a variety of other difficulties including difficulties with finance generally, with welfare benefits and with mental health. As in other areas, money can be saved and much trouble avoided by the giving of good advice. In one sense, housing has been less hard hit than other areas of the law, because more housing matters remain within the scope of legal aid. But a

[10] *Gudanaviciene v Director of Legal Aid Casework* [2014] EWCA Civ 1622; [2014] EWHC Admin 1840.
[11] *R (Public Law Project) v Secretary of State for Justice* [2014] EWHC Admin 2365.
[12] He has since been elevated to the Upper Tribunal, Tax and Chancery Chamber.

striking finding of Brookes and Hunter's chapter is that the availability of housing advice has fallen drastically since 2010 not because there is no legal aid for housing matters, but because the cuts in legal aid have wiped out many providers of legal advice. The chapter ends with a number of positive suggestions the boldest of which is for a more interventionist court, on the model of some US criminal courts, which seeks proactively to deal with the clusters of problems suffered by litigants.

Nicole Busby and Morag McDermont situate the Government's exclusion of employment matters from the scope of legal aid and introduction of fees for using the Employment Tribunal in a wider context: that of the change during the last four decades from a conception of the employment relationship as a collective matter (labour law) to one according to which it concerns dealings between private individuals (employment law). The authors find the assumption underpinning the Government's reforms—that much litigation against employers is vexatious—to be unsupported and that the reforms are bringing about an unjustifiable tipping of the balance of power in favour of employers and against employees. The chapter ends by suggesting a radical reform—the creation of a more inquisitorial form of tribunal—and by making more modest proposals aimed at assisting litigants in person and ensuring the enforcement of awards.

In her chapter, Mavis Maclean judges the Government's changes to legal aid in family matters in the light of the set of elements identified by Lady Hale as necessary for equal access to justice: a legal framework; access to remedies for wrongs; and lawyers to facilitate the process. Maclean questions the Government's emphasis on mediation as a substitute for legal assistance and, drawing on empirical work, throws doubt on the assumed dichotomy between rigid, legalistic lawyers and flexible, responsive mediators. Family lawyers, she argues, are often flexible and responsive and their legal expertise is required to ensure the formation and enforcement of public legal norms.

In the final chapter in Part II, James Kenrick and Ellie Palmer examine access to justice for an often neglected group: young adults in the age range 16 to 25.

The chapter canvases familiar themes—the clustering of problems, the importance of timely intervention and the ill effects of LASPO—as well questioning the assumption that disadvantaged young people are easily capable of finding answers to their legal problems online. It ends with a proposal for a service specifically targeted at young people's legal needs.

A number of themes are common to the chapters in Part II: the clustering of legal problems of various types and the need for holistic and targeted approaches to dealing with them; the need to deal with poor initial decision-making and the absence of initiatives on the part of the Government to address this problem; the dichotomy between the private settlement of disagreements, often favouring stronger parties, on the one hand and the application of fair and democratically created public legal norms on the other and the Government's tipping of the scales in favour of the former; the need for more hands-on and inquisitorial courts and tribunals; the devastating nature of many of the cuts made to legal aid and the way in which they have severely reduced the number of providers of legal assistance; the likely persistence of legal challenges to decisions of public authorities in spite (and sometimes because of) the cuts and restrictions; the lack of adequate justification for much of the Government's programme of reform; and the disturbing phenomenon of the Government's general indifference to evidence.

Part III

The chapters in the third section, 'Alternative Approaches to Funding Legal Services' strike a more optimistic note by either suggesting ways in which access to justice could be improved within the constraints of the current framework or, in the case of the last two chapters, describing the approach taken in other jurisdictions.

Frank Stephen's chapter discusses the effects of an earlier piece of legislation than LASPO, the Legal Services Act 2007. This Act permits legal services to be provided by businesses—referred to in the Act as Alternative Business Structures (ABSs)—as well as by lawyers practising as sole practitioners or in partnerships. The consequences of this for the provision of legal services in welfare matters have often been taken to be deleterious. Stephen argues, however, that ABSs may do a better job of providing such services than traditional legally aided solicitors firms because of economies of scale and greater specialisation.

Paul Yates describes CourtNav, an important initiative set up by the Pro Bono Unit at the solicitors firm Freshfields Bruckhaus Deringer and the Royal Courts of Justice Advice Bureau. The purpose is to provide an online programme to enable litigants in person (of whom there are an increasing number) to fill out court forms without the presence of a legal adviser. Yates' chapter also contains interesting reflections on the relationship between the giving of pro bono legal assistance and the provision of state funded legal aid. In the English courts and in the jurisprudence of the European Court of Human Rights, the availability of charitable or pro bono help is often given as a reason for withholding legal aid. The charitably inclined lawyer must thus take care that in giving help she does not deprive its recipient of the possibility of more reliable publicly funded support. 'A system more corrosive of the natural impulse to help a fellow human being', Yates observes, 'is hard to imagine'.

Audrey Guinchard and Simon Wesley describe the approach taken to access to justice in France. An in-depth empirical study would be required to determine whether the French do a better job than we do in ensuring access to legal services for all. However, the chapter certainly suggests a deeper ideological commitment to the ideal of access for all than exists in this country. Despite recurring difficulties in funding and a significantly lower budget for legal aid than in the UK, France considers all legal matters worthy of legal aid and offers either total or partial legal aid to all those in need.

Last, Sarah O'Neill's chapter describes the strategy adopted by the Scottish Executive for maintaining access to justice in the face of financial stringency. It is a very different strategy from the English one. Where the Westminster government has simply removed many matters from the scope of legal aid while restricting eligibility to the poorest, the Scottish Government has kept all matters in scope for most of the population. It has done this by demanding contributions from the users of legal aid, proportionate to their ability to pay; by creating specialised law centres dealing with the kinds of legal problem not adequately dealt with by solicitors in private practice; by targeting services at those most in need; and by a variety of measures reducing the cost and incidence of litigation. The Scottish approach provides an illuminating example of what can be done where there is a genuine will to preserve access to justice as well as to save money.

Part I

Access to Justice: Theoretical, Legal and Policy Background

1

Access to Justice: The View from the Law Society

ANDREW CAPLEN

General election campaigns in the United Kingdom are generally fought on the battleground of the economy, the National Health Service and education, education, education. Questions of justice rarely come to the fore, although 'Law and Order' may find its way into political manifestos—for example, that a party was intending to be 'tough on crime, tough on the causes of crime'. But matters relating to the administration of our justice system, such as investment in and the efficiency of our courts and tribunals, rarely make the headlines. They are simply not regarded as being 'vote winners'.

The 2015 poll was no exception. Even though two clearly detrimental changes to our system of justice were 'pushed through' in the last days of the old Parliament which, apart from the legal press, were barely mentioned, let alone criticised:

1. The Government made an incredible hike in the cost of court fees for many mid-ranking civil actions of up to 622% (that is in some circumstances 40 times higher than in New York State).
2. The introduction of the Criminal Courts' Charge imposing a non-means tested penalty for those convicted of criminal offences. For example, in 'either way' matters (that is those that can be heard in either the magistrates' court or the Crown Court) heard by magistrates, a 'guilty plea' will mean a mandatory £180 charge irrespective of the financial circumstances of the defendant, without the ability for the Court to consider any mitigating factors. For conviction after a 'not guilty' plea this rises to £900.

'Access to Justice' did not 'hit the mark' either. The changes, cutbacks in legal aid that had been brought in by the outgoing government were barely mentioned. The major political parties 'steered well clear'.

However, a government's prime responsibility is surely to provide for the proper administration of justice within its boundaries and that includes providing adequate and affordable access to that system. This includes both the areas of civil and criminal law, the first regulating conduct between parties, the latter relating to the duty of the state to keep order, to 'keep the peace' within its realm.

The area of criminal law is clearly of importance so far as the provision of access to justice is concerned. The state will generally be the prosecuting authority. Without adequate resources being made available for an individual to defend himself, the balance of the scales of justice are weighted against the individual and towards the state. Access to justice in respect of civil law is also of vital importance. These cases frequently involve complex, life-changing issues, particularly when they are concerned with matters such as homelessness, refugee status, employment and children.

There is no doubt that recent changes have impacted on the provision of access to justice to some of the most disadvantaged members of our society. The intention of this chapter is to consider some of the problems that have arisen—primarily in relation to cuts in legal aid—and then to conclude by asking whether there is hope for the future.

How have We Got to where We Are?

The first real attempt to bring the legal aid budget under control occurred in the early 1990s when Lord Mackay of Clashfern was Lord Chancellor. Expenditure had been increasing over a number of years. Reasons for this included the effect of the Police and Criminal Evidence Act 1984 which had created a statutory Duty Solicitor scheme, giving for the first time those arrested the right for a lawyer to be present at their police station interview. There had also been an increasing public awareness of legal rights and obligations which understandably had resulted in citizens increasingly wanting to take the benefit of those rights and to enforce those duties. The legal aid budget was, however, essentially demand-driven rather than means-limited and the Government was concerned.

Pressure built in earnest with the election of the Labour Party to government in 1997. David Blunkett referred to the 'fat cats of legal aid', ignoring the fact that many legal aid lawyers earned incomes of little over £20,000 per year. Then Jack Straw, when Justice Secretary, continually stated that our legal aid system was 'the most expensive in the world', a mantra repeated by the Coalition Government when it came into office at the 2010 General Election.

The latter comment was particularly unfortunate. First, it was not actually true—recent research puts England and Wales further down such a list. Second, this attempt at a comparison is very much comparing 'apples with pears'. We have a common law adversarial system where a higher proportion of the cost is expended on lawyers, whereas in a civil law investigatory system more is 'loaded' onto the judicial function. Further, even if we are/were spending a higher proportion than other countries, could it be that there are problems within our social fabric that result in the need for such advice and assistance? Would it not be much more appropriate to focus attention there?

It was clear that whoever came into power in 2010 would look again at the legal aid budget either by cutting the fees paid to those lawyers providing such services (it should be mentioned that this was even though they had not received an increase in either actual or real terms for nearly 20 years) or by reducing the scope of matters covered by the scheme. The 'driving force' was the need for austerity, although there was clearly also a measure of ideology involved. And the result— The Legal Aid, Sentencing and Punishment of Offenders Act 2012 (LASPO), which came into force on 1 April 2013.

This Act removed a number of matters from scope:

1. Legal aid for clinical negligence cases is now only available where a child has suffered neurological injury, resulting in them being severely disabled during pregnancy, childbirth or the eight-week postnatal period.
2. Legal aid is now no longer available in the area of employment unless the matter involves a breach of the Equality Act 2010 or it arises in relation to the exploitation of an individual who is a victim of human trafficking.
3. Legal aid remains available for public law family cases (eg, in care proceedings). However, it is generally only available for private family law cases (such as contact or divorce) if there is evidence of domestic violence or child abuse or in child abduction cases.
4. Housing law cases are now beyond scope unless there is a serious disrepair or homelessness, possession proceedings or for antisocial behaviour cases in the county court.
5. Debt cases are excluded unless there is an immediate risk to the debtor's home.
6. Most immigration work is no longer covered by legal aid—except for persons in immigration detention or where torture is involved or in respect of claims arising under the Refugee Convention.
7. Education cases are only covered in respect of Special Educational Needs.
8. Welfare benefit cases are also excluded except for appeals to the Upper Tribunal or higher courts.

The Consequences

There have been a number of clear consequences as a result of the cuts and changes brought in by LASPO. The first relates to those who had provided such services previously, the lawyers operating primarily as small high street solicitors' practices or as self-employed junior barristers. Their business models had been created on a throughput of legal aid work at a particular price. These changes have severely challenged their ability to survive as sustainable businesses and with the closure of their practices the expertise of individuals advising in these areas is undoubtedly being lost.

Primarily, however, the effect has been on the potential recipients of such legal advice and assistance—the clients, the individuals, those involved in often difficult legal circumstances. If a matter is no longer covered by the scheme or, even if it still is but an individual no longer meets the income or capital thresholds due to the reduction in those financial parameters, then there are just four options: to somehow obtain the money to instruct a lawyer privately; to hope that a lawyer will be prepared to provide some measure of help on a pro bono basis; to represent themselves as a litigant in person; or to just walk away.

According to the National Audit Office's recent report, approximately 300,000 matters were funded by legal aid in the first 12 months after LASPO came into force. This is significantly less than the 665,000 matters that the Legal Aid Agency would have expected to fund if the 'reforms' had not gone ahead. This demonstrates that the cuts have had a significant direct impact. These figures do not however show the indirect impact on the individuals denied access to professional help.

It is useful to consider the issue of litigants in person. For example, figures issued by Cafcass for disputes involving children show that prior to LASPO coming into force 22 per cent of cases commenced with both parties being represented by lawyers. After the cuts, that figure has shrunk to just 4 per cent.

Conducting your own argument in court is not, of course, prohibited. It is, however, generally seen as being beneficial to both the courts and litigants for all parties to be legally represented.

There are five main reasons for this:

1. A litigator or advocate, whether a solicitor or barrister, is legally trained. Both the substantive law and court procedures can often be complex. When litigants act in person, hearings frequently take longer because judges need to spend time explaining procedural issues to the unrepresented parties.

2. It helps keep in check high emotions, something which is particularly likely to come to the fore in family cases. In such proceedings it can often be difficult to separate strong feelings from what is appropriate or acceptable from a legal perspective.

3. Because litigants in person can risk the quality of the hearing, for example, sometimes it can be difficult to appreciate exactly what evidence and legal points are relevant and which are not. Irrelevant issues may be raised and important ones missed, thus risking unfairness to the final outcome.

4. Litigants in person are much more likely to submit incomplete documentation or fail to follow the required procedural steps. They will often have to rely on the judge to an extent that could raise concerns as to the appearance of bias.

5. Finally, cases are more likely to proceed to a fully contested final hearing because there is no advice available from qualified lawyers as to what is a reasonable basis upon which to settle the matter.

The potential difficulties were highlighted in the recent family law case of *Q v Q*. Here the father was a convicted sex offender who was seeking contact with his child. Experts were instructed to advise the court as to whether he posed a risk to that child. However, because he was ineligible for legal aid, no funding was available for those experts to attend court to give evidence, resulting in the case grinding to a complete halt.

An additional difficulty was that the father did not speak very good English. Again, in the absence of legal aid, there was no money available for the translation of court documents into his own language.

The President of the Family Division (Sir James Munby) said:

> The absence of public funding for those too impoverished to pay for their own representation potentially creates at least three major problems: first, the denial of legal advice and assistance in drafting documents; second. and most obvious, the denial of professional advocacy in the courtroom; third, the denial of the ability to bring to court a professional witness whose fees for attending are beyond the ability of the litigant to pay.

The situation with regard to those who just 'walk away' is even more disturbing. Legal aid *is* still available for victims of domestic violence. It is clearly right that it should be as those unfortunate enough to be caught up in violent relationships need the protection that the law provides, including, for example, the ability to obtain non-molestation injunctions in order to protect them from further abuse.

However, LASPO changed the initial requirements that needed to be fulfilled before someone can receive public funding to resolve disputes over finances or arrangements for children. Individuals must now provide 'prescribed evidence' indicating that they have suffered domestic violence within two years prior to an application for legal aid being submitted. The stringent nature of these requirements has caused considerable difficulties. Many victims simply do not have the documentary evidence, particularly if there has been psychological rather than physical abuse.

As an aside, a disturbing aspect that has arisen has been the need at times for GPs to provide medical report letters, a specific type of 'prescribed evidence' under the regulations. Anecdotally, some GPs are seeking to charge up to £80 for these letters even though the person suffering such abuse would almost certainly be on income support levels. No funding has been provided to GPs by the Government for this.

Research carried out in 2014 by Rights for Women, Women's Aid and Welsh Women's Aid has concluded that these new evidential burdens are having a considerable adverse effect. Over half of the respondents—women who had suffered or were suffering as a result of an abusive partner—simply did not have the evidence required to obtain legal aid, often for very good reasons. Victims are frequently too isolated or too frightened to speak out at the time. Further, as mentioned above, if the abuse is psychological then it can be much more difficult to prove.

Further, the research showed that up to 60 per cent of the women who could not obtain legal aid because of these increased burdens just 'walked away', meaning that they did not have the benefit of the remedies that the law was designed to provide.

On 10 September 2014 the *Guardian* newspaper reported on these difficulties under the headline: 'Women will die—it's not too dramatic to say that'. The article has a point.[1]

The Attitude of Government

Governments do, of course, have many conflicting priorities. National security has to be balanced against individual freedoms, welfare programmes with the need for fiscal stability. The latter has been the principal argument used to justify the cuts to legal aid. As has frequently been reported, the 2008 financial crisis has caused the need for stringent austerity measures in many countries, the UK included.

Governments do, however, make political choices and thus decisions have been made to ring-fence the budgets of some departments, for example, Health and Education. Justice—even though one of the fundamental responsibilities of the state—has not been protected, meaning that potential areas for savings have had to be identified and then, once located, implemented; hence the sustained pressure on the legal aid budget.

It is clear that successive Lord Chancellors have looked carefully at their obligations under the European Convention on Human Rights (ECHR). Defendants in criminal cases must generally be assisted which is why the focus here has been to reduce rates of payment and to reduce the number of firms providing defence services, so that economies of scale can allow for further fee reductions. This is why matters have been taken out of scope in civil law matters—the requirements on governments to provide public funding for such cases under the ECHR are much more limited.

However, legal aid was a fundamental part of the post-Second World War welfare reforms. The wider reforms stemmed from the Beveridge Report which sought to consider how to improve the state's existing national schemes of social insurance, ie, to provide safety nets designed to ensure that everyone had access to the same rights of citizenship.

In the 1948 House of Commons debate on the Legal Aid and Advice Bill, the then Attorney General, Sir Hartley Shawcross, opened by saying: 'This is a bill which will open the doors of the courts freely to all persons who may wish to avail themselves of British justice, without regard to the question of wealth or their ability to pay'. In other words, the UK Government had accepted that its responsibility was not just as a lawmaker, but also the enabler of putting those laws into practice, a noble aspiration.

---

[1] See: www.theguardian.com/society/2014/sep/10/women-die-legal-aid-rules-domestic-violence-victims.

Further, writing in the *Solicitors Journal*, John Halford and Mike Schwarz said:

Legal Aid is not a welfare benefit; it is an equalising measure. Its aim is to ensure that everyone subject to UK jurisdiction can enjoy their rights in a meaningful way through accessing legal advice when it would otherwise be unaffordable and representation funded to the extent necessary to ensure that the merits of any court case will determine the outcome, rather than the relative wealth or power of the opposing powers.[2]

Fast forwarding to today. It is clear that the high ideals of the Attlee Government have disappeared into the mists of time. The Parliamentary Justice Select Committee report on the changes/cuts (published in February 2015) is evidence of this. Their report is rightly damning. It states that the outgoing government's policy on civil legal aid had failed to meet three of its four original objectives: it had failed to discourage unnecessary litigation at the public expense; it had failed to show that the changes were better value for money to the taxpayer; and, most important of all, it had failed to target legal aid at those who needed it most. The only one of its objectives that had succeeded was to reduce the civil legal aid spend; the rest all failed. Sir Alan Beith, Chair of the Justice Select Committee said:

Many of the problems which we have identified could have been avoided with better research, a better evidence base to work from, and better public information about the reforms. It is vitally important that the Ministry of Justice work to remedy this from now on, so that a review of the policy can be undertaken.

Alternative Means of Providing Access to Justice?

It is clear that there is no political will to refinance the legal aid budget. The 30 per cent plus cuts in expenditure over the course of the last three years are unlikely to see any substantial measure of restoration. At best there may be a review of discrete issues such as the evidential requirements in respect of domestic violence or a small amount of funding being targeted at social welfare law.

The underlying issues behind the need for this type of public funding will not, however, simply disappear into the ether. Matrimonial disputes will still occur, children will still need to be taken into care, refugees will continue to arrive at our shores and wish to apply for asylum, families will still be made homeless. It may even be that some behaviours will be accentuated as a result of these cuts. For example, residential landlords might be tempted to act more unscrupulously if there is less chance that they will be 'subject to check' as a result of court action.

Are there, however, in the absence of our government taking responsibility, alternative methods of providing the access to justice that will still be so vitally necessary?

---

[2] John Halford and Mike Schwarz, 'Legal aid cuts: more detail, more devils' *Solicitors Journal* (6 September 2013).

Practical Solutions

Alternative Ways of Working for Lawyers

The costs of running a regulated legal practice are high. Commercial rents and business rates, staff and administration expenses, professional indemnity insurance premiums and regulatory requirements all contribute to a high cost base that has to be funded by a certain level of fee income. But are there things that solicitors can do to provide their services in a slightly cheaper format?

One suggestion has been the 'unbundling of legal services'. Solicitors have traditionally worked on a retainer basis with fees calculated in accordance with an agreed hourly rate, meaning that the cost to the client will depend upon the amount of time that his/her solicitor spends in relation to the matter. Further, a solicitor would normally have been instructed at the outset of the matter and, subject to the payment of fees, continued acting until its ultimate conclusion.

'Unbundling' is where a solicitor provides legal services for an agreed section of a case at a fixed fee. So, for example, the solicitor may be instructed just to advise at the outset of a matrimonial matter or upon the split of financial assets or to arrange for representation at court for a substantive hearing.

This process is being increasingly utilised. There are regulatory issues that a solicitor will need to consider carefully (the Law Society has issued a Practice Note with some guidance to assist its members) but there has been an increasing measure of 'take-up' by litigants, primarily those from middle income backgrounds (ie, not those who would have been entitled to legal aid anyway).

There have also been suggestions of various forms of technological solutions. These can and do work—an increase in digital working, for example. Further, there has also been an increase in the number of video hearings held within the criminal justice process.

Once again, this could be a partial solution that has the potential to provide access to justice primarily for one group of citizens more than another. If used by individuals acting as remote litigants in person, they will require a certain amount of computer literacy. However, many of those who qualify on an income/capital basis for legal aid are likely to still require face-to-face assistance from a lawyer.

Alternative Ways of Providing Legal Services

Pro bono legal advice is where a lawyer provides his/her services free of charge. It is not a new phenomenon, having probably existed for as long as advocates have been used to expound someone else's cause. Its existence is rarely trumpeted though—and understandably so. Those who give of their time on a voluntary basis generally do so for altruistic reasons rather than because they crave publicity.

There is a strong feeling within the legal profession that successive governments have heralded the call for the legal profession to do more and more pro bono work in order to 'make up the gap' as they further and further reduce the availability of legal aid. In other words, the idea is that services that were once paid for should now be provided free of charge.

This is without doubt a novel way of running a justice system—but it is clear that politicians do think this way. A suggestion has been made more than once that the high-earning City and London-based international law firms should either provide a substantial measure of pro bono services themselves or fund others to do so. This would be eminently unfair. A requirement that one profession should work for free without an obligation on all others to do so would be inequitable. Surely the idea of the 'Big Society' was not to require a few to donate their time but not others? Further, if those who did not perform such work had to contribute financially to others who did, would that not be a form of 'stealth tax'—one that only applied to lawyers?

In any event, much of the legal profession does engage in pro bono work via either LawWorks, the Bar Pro Bono unit, assisting at a local Citizens Advice Bureau or law centre or distinct schemes set up by individual firms. In fact, current estimates indicate that 65 per cent of solicitors were engaged in pro bono legal work last year. Only perhaps the Church can claim such a high number of members engaged in working free of charge.

Pro bono legal work should be celebrated, but it should not be made compulsory. It can provide many individuals with the ability to have their cases heard in even the highest courts in the land. It is, however, far from being a substitute for a properly funded system of legal aid.

One practical difficulty is the skill set required to assist matters that were once within the scope of the legal aid scheme. The legal sector has increasingly segmented over the course of the last 30 years or so. The expertise to advise individuals with housing cases, matrimonial affairs, asylum applications etc is primarily within the high street solicitors' domain and not that of the major City law firms (which concentrate on large-scale commercial issues).

Organisations such as LawWorks are encouraging City lawyers to consider 'secondary areas of specialisations' so that they can assist, but this can never take the place of those local firms often providing advice to very local people. However, as the financial constraints 'hit', these local firms and their business models become less and less sustainable and increasing numbers are having to either close or change specialisations, with the result that previously held expertise is diminishing and could eventually disappear.

Another solution that has been mooted is to encourage and allow unqualified legal providers to offer more and more services to the public. An example is the group of advisers known as 'MacKenzie friends', ie, where an individual, although not a lawyer and thus without normal rights of audience before the court, is allowed to assist and speak on behalf of a litigant in person. MacKenzie seems to have an increasing number of 'friends' nowadays though, some of whom are charging handsomely for the benefit of their 'friendship'!

There are a number of difficulties with this type of legal services provider:

1. They are unqualified. Most lawyers have undergone a four-year period (at least) of academic study followed by either a training contract (if a solicitor) or pupillage (if a barrister).
2. They are unregulated, whereas solicitors are regulated by the Solicitors Regulation Authority and barristers by the Bar Standards Board. This means that they will not have the high on-costs of a regulated practice and will potentially be able to offer their services at a cheaper rate. It also means, however, that the level of protection available to their customers—the consumers of legal services—will be just about non-existent.
3. There will almost certainly be no procedures in place in the event of a complaint as the Office of Legal Complaints remit only covers regulated legal services providers, ie, lawyers.
4. They will not be 'officers of the court' with that overriding duty to the court beyond that to their clients.
5. They are unlikely to have sufficient professional indemnity insurance. Even though they may have insurance cover *at the time* that the services were provided, this will often be insufficient. Professional indemnity insurance works on the basis that the operative date for insurance purposes is the date of the claim (essentially when the mistake 'came to light') and not the date that the mistake was made. It is for this reason that a solicitor is required to maintain run-off insurance cover for a period of six years after he/she ceases to practise.
6. There is unlikely to be a compensation fund to protect a customer in the event of dishonesty or fraud by the provider of such services (unlike solicitors who jointly contribute towards their compensation fund).

The Legal Services Board's Consumer Panel has recently published its '2020 Vision' document which contemplates, inter alia, more unregulated legal services providers entering the legal services market, offering services at a lower cost and thus increasing the number of individuals who can access our justice system. It would almost certainly succeed in this aspiration, but at what cost?

So, What is the Solution?

Affordable, attainable access to justice is a fundamental human right. It is an intrinsic part of the rule of law because without it the rule of law is worthless—what merit is there in granting rights or imposing obligations if those rights cannot be exercised or those obligations enforced?

The year 2015 has seen the 800th anniversary of the sealing of the Magna Carta. Clause 40 states that 'to no one will we sell, deny, or delay right or justice' and yet by salami-slicing—if not decimating—the civil legal aid system this has surely been done.

So, where does the responsibility lie to rectify a clearly unsatisfactory situation? It is probably threefold: on the legal profession; on the general public; on the government.

On the Legal Profession

We have discussed some ways in which lawyers could assist in making their services more accessible, including at lower prices, for example, unbundling, fixed costings, and the greater use of technology. It is also appropriate that the pro bono work undertaken by so many solicitors and barristers should be both celebrated and further commitment encouraged. In this respect the attitude of both government and the public would undoubtedly assist. An expectation or an attempt at conscience pricking is less helpful than one based on constructive encouragement.

The Law Society of England and Wales has been involved in thought-leadership in this area for some years. For example, in 2010 it published its 'Access to Justice Review', setting out numerous suggestions for the future of access to justice, including ways in which costs could be saved within the legal process. Further, in May 2015 the Law Society published its 'Affordable Legal Services Review', building on the work that it has been doing in this area.

On the General Public

There needs to be a sea change in public attitudes when it comes to issues of justice. The reason that David Blunkett was able to talk about 'fat cats' was because it played into the mindset of the 'man in the street'.

As mentioned at the outset, election campaigns are almost always primarily concerned with the economy, health and education. This is undoubtedly because it is those areas that concern the voting public. Could it be that this is because such issues affect us personally, whereas those relating to justice are never—or very rarely—likely to do so? When it comes to the question of access to justice, are we like the priest and the Levite in the Good Samaritan story, passing by on the other side of the road?

There is an argument that says that 'you never miss what you have never had'. Could this explain the public apathy when it comes to issues of justice? That we have never experienced a system of injustice so that is not where our concerns lie.

The most enduring and important legacy of the Magna Carta celebrations in 2015 would surely be an open, proper and fully informed debate as to the growing deficiencies in the access to justice that we provide to some of our most vulnerable and disadvantaged citizens.

Paul Oestreicher said: 'A society's maturity and humanity will be measured by the degree of dignity it affords to the disaffected and the powerless'.[3]

On the Government

Bluntly, whatever the financial situation, whatever its ideology, whether it likes it or not the provision of access to justice is ultimately the responsibility of government. To repeat an earlier comment, security and justice are its fundamental duties. Although it would not be a popular view, these are of more importance than the provision of either state-funded health or education services.

The importance of justice as a priority can perhaps be seen most clearly when looking at the failure of legal systems abroad. Poverty is caused by a number of factors, many of which are difficult to overcome, but often the ability to escape from a state of poverty can be hampered by factors that have more to do with a breakdown in law and order: in essence, the absence of a working system of the rule of law.

An example: in northern Uganda, widows returning to their villages following the defeat of the Lord's Resistance Army have found their land has been seized by others preventing them from having the means to either feed their families or earn a living. Charities such as BMS World Mission are providing legal help to enable the recovery of that land.

The link between a properly functioning rule of law, access to justice and the ability to escape poverty is being increasingly recognised. The Department for International Development (DFID), for example, make grant funding available for organisations involved in rule of law projects in the developing world. Further, Oxfam and the Law Society of England and Wales launched a new initiative entitled 'Lawyers against Poverty' in June 2015. This is an initiative designed to raise awareness of these issues, building on the new 2015 Millennium Goals, which focus on the rule of law.

A South American saying: 'Once we gave people fish, then we gave them the rods and the nets so that they could catch their own fish. Now we have realised that the problem is that they are not being allowed to fish'.

The importance of access to justice cannot be underestimated. It is a fundamental corollary of 'the rule of law' because without access to justice the rule of law can be nothing more than just a concept, an ideal. If access to justice is absent, legal rights cannot be exercised and legal obligations cannot be enforced. Nor can public or private bodies be challenged through the courts, or individuals brought to account. Access to justice is essential for a humane, just and civilised society.[4]

---

[3] Paul Oestreicher, 'Thirty years of Human Rights' (The British Churches' Advisory Forum on Human Rights, 1980).

[4] Andrew Caplen and David McIlroy, '"Speaking Up"—Defending and Delivering Access to Justice Today' (*Theos*, 2 March 2015).

A quote from US Supreme Court Judge Brennan, 1956:

Nothing rankles more in the human heart than a brooding sense of injustice. Illness we can put up with, but injustice makes us want to pull things down. When only the rich can enjoy the law, as a doubtful luxury, and the poor, who need it most, cannot have it because its expense puts it beyond their reach, the threat to the existence of free democracy is not imaginary but very real, because democracy's very life depends upon making the machinery of justice so effective that every citizen shall believe in the benefit of impartiality and fairness.

Some Final Words

We are at a crossroads, perhaps at that proverbial 'last chance saloon', waiting to see which way this so important debate will progress. It is a place where these issues cannot afford to remain in abeyance for long. The continued risk of inefficient courts and demoralised judges 'clogged up' with litigants in person is a real one. As is that more and more individuals will just walk away from our system of justice, perhaps even taking matters into their own hands. As is the risk of growing instances of injustices.

Waiting for others to 'grasp the nettle', 'to take the lead', is not an option. Yes, there is a responsibility on the legal profession. Yes, there is a pressing need for the public to be as concerned about injustices in our own jurisdiction as they may be in totalitarian states or in the developing world. And, yes, of course, the prime responsibility is on our government to rethink its policies in this area.

The way that we do justice in the United Kingdom urgently requires a 'whole system review'—a full and wide-ranging consultation as to the sort of justice system and access to that justice that we should provide in twenty-first century Britain.

This is a responsibility that falls to each of us.

2

The Meaning of Access to Justice

TOM CORNFORD

Introduction

In the third of his recent Hamlyn lectures, Professor Paterson addresses the question of what the expression 'access to justice' means as follows:

> 'Access to Justice' as a phrase can be traced back to the nineteenth century, but as a concept it is a comparative newcomer to the political firmament, coming into frequent use only in the 1970s. Since then there has been no holding it. Hundreds of books, articles and reports have included it in their title, not to mention a swathe of initiatives from lawyer associations, politicians, governments, charities and NGOs around the world. As the redoubtable Roger Smith noted in 2010, 'In general … the phrase "access to justice" has a well-accepted, rather vague meaning and denotes something which is clearly—like the rule of law—a good thing and impossible to argue you are against. The strength and weakness of the phrase is in its nebulousness'. In short, access to justice is like 'community' in being a feel-good concept—one that everyone can sign up with uncritical examination.[1]

While there is considerable truth in this characterisation, a nebulous phrase is not the best starting point when attempting to advance an ideal capable of serving as a guide to action and I want to suggest that the phrase connotes a core idea that is worth differentiating from the other notions that have attached themselves to it.[2] Doing so, I will argue, has a number of advantages. It enables us to imagine the practical steps that would be necessary to the ideal's attainment; to work out the relationship between it and other goods and the extent to which the attainment of the one might entail the sacrifice of the others; and to consider whether the ideal is really attainable at all and, if not, what this tells us about our society.

---

[1] A Paterson, *Lawyers and the Public Good: Democracy in Action?* (The Hamlyn Lectures) (Cambridge, Cambridge University Press, 2011) 60.

[2] One could put the matter in another way by saying that 'access to justice' is an essentially contested concept or, as Ronald Dworkin has it, an 'interpretive concept'. An interpretive concept is something assumed to be desirable but whose exact nature is in dispute, the proponents of different interpretations being activated by competing moral, aesthetic or political outlooks.

Tom Cornford

The True Meaning of Access to Justice

We may think of the expression 'access to justice' as having both a descriptive and a normative aspect. In its descriptive aspect it simply denotes the general subject of the extent to which citizens are able to gain access to the legal services necessary to protect and vindicate their legal rights. Understood in this way, the expression is neither controversial nor its meaning nebulous although, as I shall argue below, some writers on access to justice sometimes extend the meaning so as to make it encompass justice in a more general sense. In its normative aspect, by contrast, it stands for an ideal and it is here that clarity is often lacking.

What is normatively central, I suggest, is that every citizen should be equally able to protect her legal rights. We might call this the ideal of equal access. The ability to defend legal rights is vastly enhanced by, and may often be dependent on, the availability to the right-holder of professional assistance of one kind or another. Yet it is notorious that the ability to gain access to legal assistance is wildly unequal. We can all think of examples of cases in which one side is able to get its way because it has better lawyers than the other side or, indeed, because the other side has no lawyers at all.[3] This sort of inequality is what the ideal of equal access forbids.

The ideal's centrality derives in part from its intimate relationship with two of the main doctrines by means of which liberal democratic states legitimate themselves.

The first is the doctrine of the rule of law. As the Smith quotation above mentions, this is itself a contested notion and it exists in many versions. Some are of a narrow, procedural character[4] while others involve the ascription to citizens of a particular set of rights;[5] and some define the rule of law as incompatible with the possession by public authorities of administrative discretion (and hence with government intervention in economic matters)[6] while others treat the rule of law and administrative discretion as in principle reconcilable.[7] What all versions of

---

[3] Any lawyer or student of the law will have her own example of such a case. Striking illustrations of the effects of systemic disparities in access to legal assistance are to be found in accounts of US criminal law: see, eg, Stephen B Bright, 'Counsel for the Poor: The Death Sentence not for the Worst Crime but for the Worst Lawyer' (1993–94)103 *Yale Law Journal* 1835.

[4] See especially that advanced by Joseph Raz in 'The Rule of Law and its Virtue' (1977) 93 *Law Quarterly Review* 195.

[5] See, eg, R Dworkin, 'Political Judges and the Rule of Law' in R Dworkin, *A Matter of Principle* (Oxford, Clarendon Press, 1985); TRS Allan, *Constitutional Justice: A Liberal Theory of the Rule of Law* (Oxford, Oxford University Press, 2001). For a useful survey of different types of understanding of the rule of law see P Craig, 'Formal and Substantive Conceptions of the Rule of Law: An Analytical Framework' [1997] *Public Law* 467.

[6] eg, AV Dicey, *Introduction to the Study of the Law of the Constitution*, 10th edn (London, Macmillan, 1959); FA Hayek *The Constitution of Liberty* (London, Routledge, Kegan and Paul, 1960) Part II.

[7] eg, KC Davis, *Discretionary Justice: A Preliminary Inquiry* (Louisiana State University Press, 1969) and see the works referred to at nn 4 and 5 above.

the doctrine have in common, however, is the requirement that laws be applied in every case in accordance with their terms. In other words, if the law attaches a particular consequence to a person's possession of a particular characteristic X, then the consequence should follow where a person does in fact possess X. The consequence should not be more or less likely to follow as a result of a person's possession of some other, extraneous property Y. That one litigant has benefited from the best legal advice or has not so benefited is an extraneous property of the sort in question. It follows that the rule of law requires that access to such advantages must be equal so that the relative advantage or disadvantage of one citizen vis-a-vis another does not determine legal outcomes.[8]

The second doctrine is that of citizenship itself, in other words, the doctrine that all inhabitants of a country have a single legal status. Under the rule of law, each individual's case is worthy of equal consideration, whatever particular rights or entitlements are in consideration, and this in itself implies a basic uniformity of legal status. Countries with written constitutions typically recognise a more substantive notion of citizenship entailing the equal possession by each citizen of a set of fundamental rights. These rights must not be worth more or less to their possessors according to whether the possessors are more or less able to access the legal assistance needed to protect them. Access to assistance must be equal.

This notion of equal access to legal justice is quite explicit in many legal cultures. American commentators often point to the widespread use, in constitutional decisions and over courthouse doors, of the motto 'equal justice under law'.[9] Declarations to similar effect are to be found in the constitutional law of many systems.[10] Although no simple equivalent is to be found in English law, the same idea is surely implicit in English legal culture. Consider, for example, Dicey's second meaning of the rule of the law: 'that here every man, whatever be his rank or condition, is subject to the ordinary law of the realm and amenable to the jurisdiction of the ordinary tribunals'.[11] Dicey, of course, is especially concerned with the

---

[8] *cf* the words of the Legal Action Group: '[T]he ultimate policy aim must be that anyone with a legal problem has access to its just conclusion so that disputes are determined by the intrinsic merits of the arguments of either party, not by inequalities of wealth and power'. Legal Action Group, 'The Scope of Legal Services' in Legal Action Group, *A Strategy for Justice* (London, LAG, 1992) and reproduced in T Goriely and A Paterson, *A Reader on Resourcing Civil Justice* (Oxford, Oxford University Press, 1996). What equal access means, of course, raises questions of its own. I shall argue below that it means that judgments of entitlement to legal assistance should be based on need so that any two persons faced with legal problems of equivalent gravity should receive the same degree of legal assistance.

[9] See, eg, Deborah L Rhode, *Access to Justice* (Oxford, Oxford University Press, 2004) 3; David Luban, *Lawyers and Justice: An Ethical Study* (Princeton NJ, Princeton University Press, 1988).

[10] See, eg, s 3 of the Italian Constitution of 1948: 'All citizens … are equal before the law, without distinction of sex, race, language, religion, political opinion, or social and personal conditions'; German Basic Law Article 3(1): 'All persons shall be equal before the law'; Constitution of the Fifth French Republic Article 2: 'France … shall ensure the equality of all citizens before the law'; Constitution of the Republic of South Africa Article 9(1): 'Everyone is equal before the law and has the right to equal protection and benefit of the law'; Constitution of India Article 14: 'The State shall not deny to any person equality before the law or the equal protection of the laws within the territory of India'.

[11] Dicey (n 6) 193.

Tom Cornford

idea that public officials are subject to the same legal liabilities as ordinary citizens but it is implicit in his view that all ordinary citizens are subject to the same legal liabilities and enjoy the same legal rights as each other. (Note in this respect his reference three pages before, when contrasting the rule of law with its absence, to the story about Voltaire being unable to obtain legal redress against the duke who had him thrashed.)

I have said that citizenship and the rule of law entail equal access to legal assistance. Yet in any society characterised by inequalities of wealth and power a right can only be genuinely possessed equally if the state steps in to ensure that everyone has access—ideally, equal access—to legal assistance. The ideal of equal access thus entails a duty on the part of the state to guarantee to each citizen an equal capacity to protect her legal rights.

This need for government intervention is, incidentally, in tension with those versions of the rule of law that treat administrative discretion as anathema. It should not be thought on this account, however, that such versions of the rule of law do not entail a duty on the part of government to intervene. Just as much as the advocates of other versions of the rule of law, the proponents of the discretion-averse one, such as Dicey and Hayek, make central to their vision the idea that the law applies to everyone equally in accordance with its terms.[12] From this follows, for the reasons given above, the duty to ensure equal access to everyone. The result is a paradox but this does not seem to have bothered Dicey or Hayek, probably because they never thought through properly the implications of their insistence that all citizens be equal before the law.[13]

Other Interpretations of Access to Justice

If we turn now to other normative meanings that have been assigned to the expression 'access to justice', I suggest they are of two kinds. First, there are interpretations that align access to justice closely with social rights and second, there are pragmatic interpretations which involve abandoning or losing sight of the ideal of equal access to justice in favour of providing some or a bare minimum of legal assistance to poorer citizens. I deal with each in turn.

[12] Dicey's second meaning of the rule of law is discussed above. In *The Constitution of Liberty* (n 6) Hayek identifies equal application to all as the third requirement of true law (at 209) and finds the origin of the doctrine of the rule of law in 'isonomia' the ancient Greek principle of 'equality of laws to all manner of persons' or 'equal laws for the noble and the base' (at 164).

[13] The problem of the failure to accord equality before the law to the poor is mentioned by Hayek (n 6) in passing when discussing the acceptance of the rule of law in eighteenth century England: '[i]n other respects, progress was more slow, and it is probably true that, from the point of view of the poorest, the ideal of equality before the law long remained a somewhat doubtful fact' (at 172).

Access to Justice as a Social Right

[handwritten annotation: = In dissertation, discuss this and say why it's problematic. Also track legal aid history and say how it was never a welfare right but part of the rule of law]

The alignment of access to justice with social rights is well represented in two quotations. The first is from Cappelletti and Garth's classic multi-volume work on the subject:

> As the laissez-faire societies grew in size and complexity, the concept of human rights began to undergo a radical transformation. Since actions and relationships increasingly assumed a collective rather than an individual character, modern societies necessarily moved beyond the individualistic, laissez-faire view of rights reflected in eighteenth and nineteenth century bills of rights. The movement has been towards recognizing the social rights and duties of governments, communities, associations and individuals. These new human rights, exemplified by the Preamble of the French Constitution of 1946, are above all those necessary to make effective ie actually accessible to all, the rights proclaimed earlier. Among such rights typically affirmed in modern constitutions are the rights to work, to health, to material security, and to education. It has become commonplace to observe that affirmative action by the state is necessary to ensure the enjoyment by all of these basic social rights. It is therefore not surprising that the right of effective access to justice has gained particular attention as recent 'welfare state' reforms have increasingly sought to arm individuals with new substantive rights in their capacities as consumers, tenants, employees, and even citizens. Indeed, the right of effective access is increasingly being recognized as being of paramount importance among the new individual and social rights, since the possession of rights is meaningless without mechanisms for their effective vindication. Effective access to justice can thus be seen as the most basic requirement—the most basic 'human right'—of a modern, egalitarian legal system which purports to guarantee, and not merely proclaim, the legal rights of all.[14]

In the rest of the essay from which this quotation is drawn, the authors set out what they believe to be three phases in the development of access to justice. The first is the simple provision of legal aid. The second is the development of methods for the vindication of diffuse or group rights such as class and public interest actions. The third is what they call 'the new access to justice approach' and involves the whole repertoire of techniques by means of which the ability of the less well off to protect their legal rights can be improved and access to legal justice among all classes of person equalised. The techniques include: the creation of special tribunals to make adjudication cheaper, quicker and less encumbered by technicality; the substitution of arbitration and conciliation for adjudication; the sorting of legal tasks into the routine and the more difficult and the assignment of the easier tasks to paralegals; the use of group legal insurance plans; the use of new forms of technology; and the simplification of legislation.

The second quotation comes again from Roger Smith:

> A society with maximum access to justice is a society in which the exclusion from fair determination of rights and duties is not affected by the respective social, economic,

[14] M Cappelletti and B Garth (eds), *Access to Justice, Volume 1: A World Survey* (Milan/Alphen aan den rijn, A Giuffrè/A Sijthoff and Noordhoff, 1978–1979) 7.

political or other inequalities of the parties to any dispute. That requires an active battle against disadvantage. Testing for adequate access to justice means being able to select any potential inequality and being able to demonstrate that society has done its utmost to counteract its effect. Thus, we are not limited solely to the provision of representation for the unrepresented. We are concerned with the whole range of mechanisms to combat the disabling effects of sources of social exclusion such as racism, poverty, educational impoverishment and gender. The search is for ways of making constitutional rights real.[15]

As can be seen from the quotation from their book, Cappelletti and Garth align access to justice with social rights because their principal interest in it is as a means to the fulfilment of social rights. The normative meaning I have insisted on is nowhere rejected. In fact they endorse it while regarding it as 'utopian'. But it seems to them of secondary interest when set against the wider project of increasing substantive equality in society. Their approach is clearly informed by the general optimism that existed at the time they were writing about the possibility of reducing social inequality. They thus tend to elide the ideal of equal access to legal justice with the social rights towards whose attainment it is a means. Smith, by contrast, elides access to justice with social rights and with social justice generally because he sees possession of the latter as necessary to attainment of the former.

Are these authors right to elide access to justice with social rights in the ways that they do? In answering this question, the first thing to note is that, analytically speaking, access to justice is a civil not a social right. This can be seen more clearly if we consider TH Marshall's famous typology of types of citizenship right. In it, he distinguished between three parts of citizenship:

> I shall call these three parts, or elements, civil, political and social. The civil element is composed of the rights necessary for individual freedom—liberty of the person, freedom of speech, thought and faith, the right to own property and to conclude valid contracts, and the right to justice. The last is of a different order from the others, because it is the right to defend and assert all one's rights on terms of equality with others and by due process of law. This shows us that the institutions most directly associated with civil rights are the courts of justice. By the political element I mean the right to participate in the exercise of political power, as a member of a body invested with political authority or as an elector of the members of such a body. The corresponding institutions are parliament and councils of local government. By the social element I mean the whole range from the right to a modicum of economic welfare and security to the right to share to the full in the social heritage and to live the life of a civilized being according to the standards prevailing in the society. The institutions most closely connected with it are the educational system and the social services.[16]

On this account, the right of equal access to justice is a civil right. According to Marshall, taking England as his focus, civil rights were recognised in the eighteenth century, political rights in the course of the nineteenth and social rights in the twentieth. But as Marshall also recognised, little was done to ensure equal

---

[15] R Smith, *Justice: Redressing the Balance* (London, Legal Action Group, 1997) 9.
[16] TH Marshall, *Citizenship and Social Class and Other Essays* (Cambridge, Cambridge University Presss, 1950) 10.

access to justice until the passing of the Legal Advice and Assistance Act 1949 and this lack of interest in ensuring that most citizens could make use of their rights was the norm throughout the Western world prior to the twentieth century.

Historically, only one theoretical justification appears to have been advanced for this failure to equalise access. This was that civil rights were natural and negative rights. In other words, the rights were pre-social or pre-political and required of governments that they refrain from acting, not that they act positively so as to ensure that the rights were protected. The principle that one citizen's legal rights were as good as another's was sufficiently recognised, on this view, as long as the courts did not judge the weight of a right according to who it was attached to.

This type of justification for governmental passivity is now thoroughly discredited.[17] Even if we conceive of them as in some sense natural or universal, traditional civil rights such as the rights to life, bodily integrity or property require positive action on the part of government for their fulfilment just as much as do the more recently minted social rights. The belief in equal civil rights for all may thus be said originally to have rested on flawed foundations. And in consequence of this, it was only during the era of social rights that genuine attempts were made to ensure equal access to legal justice.[18]

But flawed origins do not invalidate a doctrine and it is striking that some left-wing critics of liberal legal ideology, while drawing attention to the gaps between theory and practice, have endorsed the central notion of the equality of legal rights without resting their approval on the claim that it is part of or conduces to substantive social equality.[19] It is striking also that while the rhetoric of the rule of law and of equal justice for all continue to be used as freely as ever—even and especially by those who do not believe in social rights—there appears to be no one prepared to offer a theoretical justification for the view that people's ability to defend their legal rights should be allowed to differ in accordance with their income.[20]

---

[17] See especially Henry Shue, *Basic Rights: Subsistence, Affluence and US Foreign Policy*, 2nd edn (Princeton NJ, Princeton University Press, 1996).

[18] As Marshall put it, speaking of the 'the barriers that separated civil rights from their remedies', 'the attitude of mind which inspired the efforts to remove ... these barriers grew out of a conception ... of equal social worth, not merely of equal natural rights' (Marshall (n 16) 40).

[19] The most famous such endorsement is to be found in EP Thompson's description of the rule of law as 'an unqualified human good' in the final chapter of *Whigs and Hunters* (London, Penguin Books, 1990) 266. Thompson's endorsement is not based on the assertion that equal protection for legal rights leads somehow to substantive equality. As he explains (at 264), the desirability of the rule of law lay (or lies) in the fact that while it may have been an instrument in the hands of the great property owners it also entailed protection for the holders of petty property rights. A similar and earlier defence of the rule of law, also drawing attention to the advantages of equal protection for unequal legal rights (ie, legal rights that entitled their holders to less) is to be found in Franz Neumann, *The Rule of Law: Political Theory and the Legal System in Modern Society* (Leamington Spa, Berg, 1986) chs 14 and 15, esp 256–57 and 282–83. By contrast, some other left-wing critics dismiss the rule of law just because it provides formal equality (by which is meant the kind whose value is recognised by Thompson and Neumann) and not substantive equality: see, eg, R Unger, *Knowledge and Politics* (New York, Free Press, 1975).

[20] Government claims that legal aid is too expensive do not rise to the level of reasoned justification, but reflect a mere refusal to address the question and are typically accompanied by claims that equally satisfactory legal assistance can be provided at lower cost: see, eg, Ministry of Justice, *Proposals for the Reform of Legal Aid in England and Wales* Consultation Paper CP12/10 (Cm 7967, 2010).

The nearest thing I have been able to find to a justification is in the work of the American judge and legal theorist Richard Posner. Posner suggests that the extent to which indigent criminal defendants are given assistance should be the subject of a kind of cost–benefit analysis.[21] It might be, he says, that the most desirable state of affairs was one in which indigent defendants had no more than barely competent counsel. This would be enough to ensure the acquittal of those who were clearly innocent but it would avoid the acquittal of those who were guilty, thereby avoiding the costs to society—in the form of harm to rights of property and personal security—that failure to prosecute criminals entails. The implicit consequence of this would be, of course, that a solvent white-collar criminal could expect his legal representatives to conduct the most thorough and ingenious defence, while the poor defendant could expect only a basic minimum. But in employing this kind of nakedly utilitarian reasoning, Posner is out on a limb. No one else appears to be prepared to offer similar justifications for the differential treatment of rich and poor defendants.

All this is to say that, while the attempt to achieve equal access to justice belongs to the era of social rights, the right of equal access to justice is a civil and not a social right. This has various implications for the kinds of view expressed by Cappelletti and Garth and by Smith. First, because access to justice is access to legal justice it is not to be confused with justice in a more general sense. There are other aspects of justice and other goods worth having and these may not be best attained by granting citizens legal rights. Justice in relation to, say, health or housing or social security may be best achieved by the exercise of administrative discretion. It may, moreover, be perfectly proper for a government to prioritise these other requirements of justice over access to legal justice. There may be a choice between, for example, better health and more perfect legal justice. If the state is to remain one governed by law, there must be a basic threshold below which expenditure on legal justice cannot fall but one can have more or less scrupulous adjudication and more or less delay in the legal system just as one can have more or less lavish health care. What is essential is that each citizen should be given the equal capacity to protect those interests that are made the subject of legal rights.

Second, the status of access to justice as a civil right gives it, or should in principle give it, a more secure position in our culture than social rights. The importance of civil rights is accepted across the political spectrum. The position of social rights, however strong the arguments made on their behalf, is less certain. Whether there should be specific legal rights to say, health care or housing remains a matter of dispute but no one can consistently deny that each citizen should be equally able to protect whatever legal rights she does have.

Third, the right of equal access to justice is more stringent than social rights are or need be. It is arguable that the need for social rights can be satisfied by providing citizens with the bare minimum necessary to survival or to a decent life; or the

---

[21] See R Posner, *The Problematics of Moral and Legal Theory* (Cambridge MA, Harvard University Press, 1999) 163–64.

bare minimum necessary to play a meaningful part in society.[22] The ideal of equal access demands, by contrast, that people's access to legal services is straightforwardly equal. The elision of access to justice with social rights and the idea that it is satisfied by providing a basic minimum tend to encourage the view that if there is a need for cuts in public spending, these can be achieved in part by reducing what is provided by way of legal aid to the poor. In a perfect system, there would be no difference in the degree of access to justice enjoyed by different sectors of society and a cut in spending would lead to an equal diminution in the extent to which each citizen's rights were protected. In our system, access to legal services is grossly unequal, but the ideal of equal access demands nonetheless that the need to reduce public spending (if there is such a need) should not be allowed to increase the gulf between rich and poor in access to legal services.

The Pragmatic Interpretation of Access to Justice

The second kind of 'other meaning' given to access to justice is the pragmatic one.

This involves the effective abandonment of the ideal of *equal* access as utopian or impossible of attainment. Understandably, many writers on access to justice are concerned with the question of what can be done for the poor given existing constraints on government spending and given, more generally, the unequal distribution of wealth and power in our society. They are less interested in thinking about how access could be made equal in the teeth of such inequalities or in how society would have to be changed in order to achieve equal access.[23] The aim is to ensure that every citizen has access to something rather than nothing in the way of legal services and, in litigation, that the weaker party has a sporting chance rather than perfect equality with her stronger adversary. This is the approach of a number of government reports and political parties' programmes which emphasise the need to reduce costs. One might say also that it is the approach of the European Court of Human Rights. Despite having developed the concept of 'equality of arms', the Court has never insisted on genuine equality between litigants.[24] To do so would require it to go beyond its policy of keeping all the states within its jurisdiction up to the standard of the more enlightened and to find fault even with the latter.

There is, however, nothing in the writings of proponents of the pragmatic approach to gainsay the assertion that the central legitimating doctrines of our law require that there be equal access to justice and not just a bare minimum or a sporting chance for the less well off. Such writers' proposals are simply the product of a pragmatic accommodation with circumstances rather than an attempt to

---

[22] For a good recent survey of the arguments for social rights which tends to support this view see Jeff King, *Judging Social Rights* (Cambridge, Cambridge University Press, 2012) ch 2.

[23] See, eg, Paterson (n 1) 71; Paterson and Goriely (n 8) 4–5.

[24] See especially *Steel and Morris v UK* 2005-II; 41 EHRR 403 and more generally DJ Harris et al, *Harris, O'Boyle & Warbrick Law of the European Convention on Human Rights*, 3rd edn (Oxford, Oxford University Press, 2014) 398–400 and 413.

determine what is right in principle. They offer no arguments to show that poorer citizens should be entitled to less in the way of legal services than their better off compatriots.

Attaining Access to Justice

How could True Access to Justice be Achieved?

To sum up the argument so far, the ideal of equal access is the core normative meaning of 'access to justice'. It is more demanding than the simple requirement that the less well off be given some opportunity to defend their legal rights and is a distinctively legal ideal, not to be confused with justice in the wider sense. As others have occasionally observed,[25] true fulfilment of this ideal of equal access requires restriction of the access of advantaged persons to legal services as well as its extension to the disadvantaged. If it were possible to achieve this, how might it be done in practice?

In the UK we are accustomed, on the one hand, to the idea that a public authority should fulfil a social right—the right to health—by providing all citizens with the subject of the right on the basis of need. On the other hand, we accept a state of affairs in which the state provides the subject of the right to legal assistance only in very limited circumstances and only to the very poorest. And yet, as I have argued above, the political ideas most widely accepted in our culture support a stronger case for equal access to justice than they do for equal access to health care. What is required therefore is something like a National Health Service for access to justice, with the important difference that, whereas it remains possible to pay for private health care, it ought to be impossible to obtain legal services outside the scheme of state assistance.

To do this, the whole business of giving legal advice and assistance, including the work of the private legal profession would have to be socialised. A first step would be to socialise the Bar, turning it into a salaried public service. Potential litigants would be entitled to its services free of charge. But since its budget would not be unlimited, the socialised Bar would have to include or be accompanied by a mechanism for deciding which among the possible cases presented to it were worth litigating. This would involve judgement both as to the importance to the individual litigant of the interest at stake and as to the strength of the public interest in having the matter litigated.[26]

---

[25] eg, Rhode (n 9) 6.

[26] One would also have to find a solution to the problem of what should happen when the grant of legal services is wrongly denied. To permit a right of legal challenge to decisions as to the grant of legal service would in itself require access to legal services, and this could lead to an infinite regress. There would have therefore to be some form of independent appeal whose results were final.

The solicitors' profession could also be socialised by setting up a comprehensive network of centres, again operated by salaried staff, that provided legal advice and other services currently provided by solicitors firms, such as mediation, conveyancing, the writing of wills, notarisation of documents, etc. Initial advice could be provided free of charge. Other services could also be provided free at the point of use, or for a fixed reasonable charge. Membership of the legal profession could be confined to those working for the salaried public service so that the various functions which it is the exclusive privilege of lawyers to perform could only be obtained via that route.

Of course, in any system which allows inequalities of wealth and in which there are large private as well as public organisations, it would be extremely difficult to eliminate the advantage that rich individuals and large private organisations enjoy in gaining access to legal assistance. A comprehensive and well-funded legal advice service of the sort suggested would wipe out small solicitors firms and mean that people on low and middle incomes would all rely on the service rather as they rely on the NHS in matters of health. But the rich could always employ people with legal training at a high salary to provide most of the services they require from the legal profession, even if those persons were no longer entitled to describe themselves as lawyers. On the other hand, a rule could be made that representation in courts and tribunals could only be by members of the salaried public services. This would go a long way towards eliminating the advantage that the rich enjoy in litigation, if not elsewhere.

The chief advantage of such a scheme would be that it might bring us close to a state of affairs in which there was genuinely equal protection of rights. As a corollary of this, it would bring a number of other benefits.

First, where the amount spent on legal services had to be reduced, it would be reduced for all: in a system in which the provision of certain sorts of legal service depended on the decisions of a socialised profession, austerity would mean a reduction in the amount spent on commercial litigation as well as on services which assisted the less well off.

Second, a socialised legal profession, while providing services to the poor which were of comparable quality to those provided to the better off, might—like the NHS—enjoy the support of the better off if they felt they were getting more at a lower price than they would be able to get privately.

Third, the result would be a legal profession which, rather than opposing innovation, would have a vested interest in pursuing all those developments that might provide a better service to more people at lower cost, including simplification of the law itself.[27]

---

[27] For a study emphasising the historical obstructiveness of the legal profession see B Abel-Smith and R Stevens, *Lawyers and the Courts: A Sociological Study of the English Legal System 1760–1965* (London, Heinemann, 1967).

Fourth, assuming that judges continued to be drawn from the ranks of practising lawyers, it would mean a judiciary accustomed to look at the public interest from the perspective of the public generally rather than from the perspective of the large private clients who most of the senior sitting judiciary have acted for during their careers at the Bar.[28]

Putting to one side for the moment the objection that the socialisation of the legal profession is highly unlikely in practice to occur, there are also, of course, many other objections to be made. Some would see as a monstrous threat to liberty the suggestion that the legal profession, which likes to see itself as a bulwark against tyranny, could be the subject of state control. Yet the judiciary is supposedly at once the guardian of our liberties and a branch of the state, and it is generally accepted that it is, or can in principle be made, independent. Why should not the same be true of the wider legal profession? Like the judiciary, a socialised legal profession would be dependent on state funding. But where the rich as well as the poor relied on it to operate effectively, there would be strong pressure for it to be adequately funded.[29]

Another objection arises from a paradoxical feature of the scheme I have just imagined, namely that while advanced in the interests of access to justice, it might be said to undermine the traditional understanding of a legal right. In the traditional understanding, possession of a legal right entails an absolute entitlement to have the right vindicated in a court of law. The imagined scheme makes the ability to vindicate one's right dependent on the exercise of discretion by a public body. Again this might be represented as a monstrous attack on the rights of citizens. But one must remember that at present many people have no access to the legal services that would enable them to vindicate their legal rights, while others must rely on exactly the sort of discretionary judgements which the imagined scheme involves. In the interests of equalising access to justice, the imagined scheme makes such discretionary justice the precondition for the vindication of all rights rather than just those of the less well off.

Why Attainment of True Access to Justice is Unlikely

Socialisation of the legal profession will not happen because there is no political will to do it and, what is simply the reverse side of the same coin, political opposition to it would be too strong. Moreover, even without using political channels, it seems very likely that powerful private interests would find ways around the

---

[28] *cf* Kate Malleson, 'Rethinking the Merit Principle in Judicial Selection' (2006) 33 *Journal of Law and Society* 126, 138: '[T]he senior judiciary has traditionally been recruited from an extremely narrow group of commercial chambers in London'.

[29] In the scheme I have suggested, the middle classes (but not the rich and big business) would have an interest in the effectiveness of the public advice service, whereas everyone (including the rich and big business) would have an interest in the effectiveness of the socialised Bar.

restrictions on access to legal services that I considered above. I have spoken in this chapter about differences in access to legal services between rich and poor. One must add to this the fact that the most copious users of legal services are artificial as opposed to natural legal persons. They are at an advantage vis-a-vis natural ones not just because they are 'repeat players'[30] who litigate much more often, but because they only exist and can only act through law and therefore inevitably make constant use of legal advice. This is true of private artificial legal persons— companies—as much as of public bodies. The picture conveyed in Dicey's version of the rule of the law—a picture of a world of legal equals—is thus a nostalgic fantasy in a double sense. It is usually criticised for its blindness to the special powers that the executive possessed even in Dicey's own time and its denial of the existence of the special body of law necessary to control those powers. But it also overlooks the way in which the modern business corporation with its vast resources and its need for all its actions to be informed by legal advice is bound to be at a legal advantage over ordinary citizens.

Conclusion

Properly understood, access to justice entails a right of equal access to legal assistance for every citizen. We do not have access to justice properly understood, however, but something weaker. We have a state of affairs in which courts, public authorities and other citizens are obliged in principle to respect our rights regardless of our social status or wealth but in which the degree to which they do respect them is likely to vary in accordance with our wealth. As citizens, the most we can hope for is the *chance* of protecting our rights rather than the certainty that our rights will be accorded equal weight with those of richer or more powerful persons.

The economic structure of our society makes it unlikely that this state of affairs can ever be entirely altered. Yet the unlikelihood of fully realising the ideal of equal access should not deter us from treating it as an aspiration. There is no reason to accept the gross inequality in access to legal services which presently exists. Initiatives to make legal services available to citizens should be aimed at equalising access and not just at providing legal services where there would otherwise be none. Nor should the fact that we are in a period of supposed austerity undermine efforts at equalisation. Ways should be found to spread the burden of austerity, such as increasing the proportion of court costs borne by wealthy litigants and taxing large law firms. The supposed need for cuts in public spending should not become a pretext for further widening the gap which exists with respect to legal services between the rich and powerful, on the one hand, and ordinary citizens, on the other.

---

[30] As to which see M Galanter, 'Why the "Haves" Come Out Ahead: Speculations on the Limits of Legal Change' (1974) 9 *Law & Society Review* 95.

3

Principles of Access: Comparing Health and Legal Services

ALBERT WEALE

The collection of chapters in this volume is concerned with the problem of access to justice, both as a matter of right and as a matter of policy. Discussions of access to justice sometimes make a comparison with access to health services.[1] This is not surprising. Access to medical services by patients, free at the point of use, has been effectively achieved in virtually all high-income countries. So the example of medical services potentially offers a model, or at least some experience of, how securing access to professional legal services to those in need might be organised. For many in the UK debate the obvious reference point is the National Health Service, but financially unencumbered access to health care has been secured widely throughout the high-income world, to the point where one informed observer could speak about it being the 'international standard'.[2] Indeed, such access is increasingly a feature of health policy developments in middle and even in some low-income countries. Hence, there is now considerable experience about what such access means in differing circumstances and conditions, as well as what are the problems and trade-offs implicit in matters of institutional design.

Against this background, my purpose in this chapter is to consider what lessons might be learnt about the design of institutions securing access to justice given the experience of health care. The chapter begins with some points about the various rationales that can be offered for general access to health care together with some conceptual points about what such access means, drawing a parallel with access to legal services. The second section then looks at the similarities between access to health care and to legal services, whilst the third section examines the differences. The fourth section then draws out some principles of institutional design, highlighting some of the complications involved.

---

[1] R Susskind, *The End of Lawyers? Rethinking the Nature of Legal Services* (Oxford, Oxford University Press, 2008).

[2] J White, *Competing Solutions: American Health Care Proposals and International Experience* (Washington DC, The Brookings Institution, 1995).

Rationales and Concepts

As with access to justice, universal health care access has been advocated by reference to a number of different assumptions and principles. For some, the principal rationale is to be found in the idea of the human right to health and the social and economic conditions of its progressive realisation. For others, access to health care is to be thought of as a right of citizenship, an element in the expansion of such rights over time from civil and political rights to social and economic rights, in line with the work of Marshall.[3] Others again will see universal access in health care as a public good, providing a generalised sense of security for all in the face of the inevitable need for medical care given the ills to which flesh is heir. Yet others see a public concern with universal access as stemming from the various forms of market failure that are characteristic of a competitive health care market.

These differing considerations and rationales interact in complex ways in any coherent justification of publicly secured universal health care. In this chapter I have only space to assert, rather than demonstrate, that the market failure rationale has an indispensable role in any such justification. The basic argument runs as follows. Many socio-economic rights may be secured by providing individuals and households with an income that is adequate to purchase goods such as food, clothing and heating. However, in the case of health care, even if income were distributed fairly (however 'fairly' is defined), there would still be a need for public action to correct for market failure in the supply of medical care. In particular, asymmetries of information between providers and consumers, problems of insuring for pre-existing conditions in health insurance markets and the potentially catastrophic nature of health costs mean that the public regulation and organisation of health care is necessary if universal access is to be secured. To deal with these problems, what is necessary is the organisation of a collectively guaranteed scheme of pre-payment, which White has usefully termed 'social savings', to enable patients and consumers access at point of need without financial constraint.[4] Such social savings can take the form of tax-based finance, schemes of social insurance with mandatory contributions by individuals or some mixture of the two. So, even if health is regarded as a human right, we still need to invoke considerations of market failure if universal access is seen to require collective finance and organisation.[5]

So far I have used the term 'universal access', the term used generally, for example, by the World Health Organization in its various proposals to increase

---

[3] TH Marshall, *Citizenship and Social Class and Other Essays* (Cambridge, Cambridge University Press, 1950).

[4] White (n 2).

[5] For a discussion of this argument see: T Marmor, J Mashaw and P Harvey, *America's Misunderstood Welfare State: Persistent Myths, Enduring Realities* (New York, Basic Books, 1990); N Barr, *The Welfare State as Piggy Bank: Information, Risk, Uncertainty and the Role of the State* (Oxford, Oxford University Press, 2001).

population access to health services.[6] However, although useful as a general short-hand, it needs greater specification. It is analytically valuable to think of access as having three components. The first is the most obvious one, namely absence of financial barriers to access on the part of patients. The second concerns the range of services to which access is secured, and in particular the degree to which those services are comprehensive in scope. The third is the quality of the services that are supplied.

It is easy to see why these three elements need to be thought of together. Access to a very limited range of services or services of poor quality in effect ends up as being access to virtually no services at all. Policymakers may seek to meet budget targets by limiting the range of services that are covered or diluting the standard of service that is provided. Thus, in health care various services (eg, social care or dentistry) may be excluded from coverage, so diluting comprehensiveness. Alternatively, queues may be allowed to develop in order to ration access, so diluting quality. Thus, if universal access is to be meaningful, consideration needs to be paid to the scope of coverage and to the quality of service provided, alongside the removal of financial barriers. Given this, the principle of universal access is best rendered as the principle that the task of the public authorities is to secure access to high quality, comprehensive services without financial barriers to access.[7] Even this might not be the 'gold standard' if, for example, there are geographical barriers to access occasioned by the spatial concentration of services or class gradients in actual use occasioned by social deprivation. However, as a reference point, the principle that universal access means access to a comprehensive range of services at a high quality without financial barriers to access can be taken as a first approximation to what is required.

In the present context, this principle also has the advantage that it can be carried across to legal services. The significance of spelling out the dimensions of coverage and quality is tacitly recognised in public discussion about access to justice. Thus, much of the complaint about the 2010 reforms to legal aid was that they cut out any responsibility for legal coverage in matters of family law or medical negligence. These are concerns about decreasing the comprehensiveness of coverage. Similarly, concerns about the reforms that turned on their limiting access to legally qualified practitioners, substituting less well-qualified personnel, were criticisms based on the quality component of access. So, those concerned with 'access to justice' should explicitly consider all three dimensions of evaluation—financial barriers to access, comprehensiveness and quality—in their appraisal of changes to any system.

One important question when thinking of the comparison between health and legal services is whether there is any parallel in legal services to 'public health', that

---

[6] For an interesting discussion of this goal in relation to fairness, see World Health Organization, *Making Fair Choices on the Path to Universal Health Coverage* (Geneva, World Health Organization, 2014), available at: apps.who.int/iris/bitstream/10665/112671/1/9789241507158_eng.pdf?ua=1.

[7] A Weale, 'Rationing Health Care: A Logical Solution to an Inconsistent Triad' (editorial) (1998) 7129 *British Medical Journal* 410.

is to say to matters like sanitary and hygiene measures to protect against communicable diseases or environmental protection to guard against the health threats from pollution. It has been argued that there is a useful comparison,[8] and that 'access to justice' should really be conceived more broadly as access to those legal services that prevent individuals encountering legal difficulties in the conduct of their affairs, for example, in the drawing up of wills or the arrangements for testamentary disposition. Some legal institutions, like the Land Registry the establishment of which was resisted by the legal profession throughout the nineteenth century,[9] provide a collective good to replace more cumbersome search procedures and so reduce transaction costs. More generally, public interest regulation in matters of consumer protection and health and safety can be thought of as forms of 'preventive law', by analogy with 'preventive health', because they reduce the number of occasions on which individual claims under tort or contractual breach need to be brought by consumers against producers, and so conduce to a greater all round efficiency of the economy. (Such regulation also means that the virtuous producers who would voluntarily comply with high standards are not disadvantaged relative to others, but that is a different story.)

Despite these points of comparison between preventive health and preventive law, in the remainder of what follows, I shall concentrate on access to justice in the sense in which it involves some form of dispute adjudication, either in civil actions or in disputes between individuals and the public authorities. This is partly for analytical focus, but it is mainly because it can be argued that there is a close conceptual connection between justice and the resolution of conflict. Thus, in his Tanner lectures, Stuart Hampshire argued that justice *is* conflict, so that, instead of looking for principles to evaluate the institutions and outcomes of a just society, we should take conflict in human societies as the norm, and construct an account of justice in procedural terms. There is, he wrote,

> a short list of indispensable procedures and institutions that all involve the fair weighing and balancing of contrary arguments bearing on an unavoidable and disputable issue. They are all subject to the single prescription *audi alteram partem* ('hear the other side'). Herbert Hart drew my attention to the centrality of this phrase, defining the principle of adversary argument, when justice is to be done and seen to be done. In each case the fairness of the public procedure depends upon this very general prescription's being followed.[10]

If we take this view, then there is something distinctive in thinking about access to justice specifically in relation to disputes and their adjudication and, as I shall suggest in the third section of this chapter, this raises special issues in the contrast between health and legal services.

Against this general conceptual and analytical background, what similarities exist between access to health services on the one hand and legal services on the other?

---

[8] Susskind (n 1) ch 7.

[9] A Offer, *Property and Politics 1870–1914: Landownership, Law, Ideology and Urban Development in England* (Cambridge, Cambridge University Press, 1981).

[10] Stuart Hampshire, *Justice is Conflict* (Princeton NJ, Princeton University Press, 2000) 8–9.

The Similarities Between Health and Legal Services

The first and most obvious point of comparison between health and legal services is that the removal of financial barriers at point of need is central to the successful securing of access for all but the most wealthy. In the case of health, the logic of the collective financing of care is that of risk-sharing. Those not in need of health care at some particular point of time contribute through taxes or social insurance to schemes of payment that relieve individuals of financial barriers to access when services are needed. However, the logic of removing financial barriers to access does not of itself imply no payment at point of use at all. In health care, depending on the particular system, there are typically various forms of co-payment, ranging from charges for pharmaceutical prescriptions or spectacles, to payments to visit general practitioners or 'hotel charges' for hospital stays. The exact design and operation of such schemes of co-payment can absorb a lot of time and attention from policymakers and administrators and there are obvious dangers in making point of use payments so onerous that they function as a barrier to access. Hence the need in all schemes to find some way of adjusting payment to the means of those obliged to pay. However, removal of financial barriers to access, as a matter of principle, does not imply that there is no obligation on those receiving the service to make some payment at point of use. If we then carry this principle across to the case of legal services, it might be argued that ensuring that those services extended beyond the very rich, who will pay for themselves, and the very poor, who will receive some form of public provision, requires some contribution on a test of means from the vast majority in the middle income groups.

A different form of co-payment arises when the range of services supplied in relation to a set of procedures is limited in some ways. For example, in health care, physiotherapy services after an operation may be made a matter of private purchase rather than collective provision, or cycles of IVF treatment may be limited in number, requiring those who want more treatment to pay for themselves. Probably the closest equivalent in legal services is the case where the prosecuting authorities refuse to press criminal charges leaving victims the option of bringing civil proceedings in relation to the damages that the committing of the crime has inflicted.

The second principal point of comparison between the medical and the legal cases is that the benefit provided through any collective guarantee is typically access to professional services that are the product of certified training and assessment. In both cases, access is access to a range of professionals and skilled personnel. In medicine there are doctors, nurses, physiotherapist, dentists, opticians, pharmacists and so on. In law the range of professionals may be more limited, but providers of legal services will include not only fully qualified lawyers, but also paralegal staff, those with specialised qualifications in such practices as conveyancing and those supplying services through such bodies as Citizens Advice. In both the legal and medical cases even relatively low levels of professional qualification can be expensive in training terms, involving costs that will need to be recovered somehow.

A third point of comparison is that both legal and health services seek a 'remedy' for the person who is presenting to qualified personnel, but in neither case can a successful outcome be guaranteed. This is most obviously the case with health services, since the inevitability of death means that remedies will eventually run out. However, even without going to that extreme, there are untreatable conditions that mean that even the most skilled medical personnel will fail sometimes in treatment, and the speciality of palliative care exists precisely to make those situations the least painful as possible for the patient. Similarly, with legal services, there is no guarantee of success in cases of dispute. So, whether we are considering treatment in the medical case or advice and advocacy in the legal case, outcomes are uncertain. This does not mean that outcomes are irrelevant. Surgeons whose patients end up dead more than the average, for any type of given case-load, and barristers who continually lose their cases should at some point be precluded from continuing in the job. But even the best physician or advocate will from time to time fail in their endeavours. Hence, all that can be guaranteed is access rather than outcome.

A fourth point of possible comparison is more contentious. It can be argued that securing universal access to either health or legal services gives rise to the problem of 'rationing' in each case. Increasing access means increasing demand on the services available. In this case, one of two alternatives is possible. Either increased resources will have to be found to finance the demand, or a mismatch between supply and demand will occur which will need to be met by some form of rationing. Since there are limits to the extent to which collective finance can be expected to expand to ensure that need is translated into effective demand, at some point, it is argued, rationing will occur. This logic has been extensively analysed in relation to health services, where waiting times for elective surgery, restrictions on access to expensive medicines and the imposition of stringent criteria of access to certain forms of care, for example bariatric surgery, are usually seen as forms of rationing balancing supply and collectively financed demand.

Although the problem of health care rationing is often discussed and the inevitability of such rationing assumed, the extent to which the problem is a serious one is hard to establish and the relevant evidence complicated. For example, although waiting times for elective surgery are common in some systems of care, for example in the UK, they seem to be absent in some social insurance systems like in France and Germany.[11] Moreover, good medicine is not necessarily expensive medicine. That some systems make it hard for some patients to secure access to expensive

---

[11] Z Or et al, 'Are Health Problems Systemic? Politics of Access and Choice under Beveridge and Bismarck Systems' (2010) 5 *Health Economics, Policy, and Law* 269. But compare, on the Netherlands, J Figueras, R Saltman, R Busse and H Dubois, 'Patterns and Performance in Social Health Insurance Systems' in R Saltman, R Buss and J Figueras (eds), *Social Health Insurance Systems in Western Europe* (Maidenhead, Open University Press, 2004).

therapies that extend life for just a few days or weeks does not mean that those systems are practising poor medicine. Instead they may simply embody humane standards of care. No doubt, in some sense, the demands on health services are 'infinite'. We can all wish that more and more resources are pumped into research and development of life-extending and life-enhancing therapies. However, we should not assume that rationing is inevitable in the sense that patients are denied access to medical care consistent with what a well-functioning and humane system of care would prescribe for patients in need.

Nevertheless, despite these qualifications, both health and legal systems will face problems of priority setting, that is to say determining whether and to what extent particular procedures or processes will be covered by collective financial provision. For example, patients may be rightfully denied access to therapies that are known to be ineffective, even if they would wish for those therapies. The parallel in legal terms may be the 'vexatious litigant', who seeks the vindication of the courts without having a meritorious case. Of course, it is a matter of empirical enquiry what proportion of presenting cases fall into these categories. But beyond such cases, there may well be claims of need that are not met, because such claims are not regarded as sufficiently urgent needs to secure the relevant priority.

So, in summary, access to legal services has a number of similarities with access to health services. In both cases, the policy task is to remove financial barriers to access whilst maintaining access to as comprehensive a range of services as possible, whilst also maintaining quality. In both cases, it is access rather than outcome that can be secured, there being no guarantee of remedy in either case, where the access is the services of suitably qualified professionals. And, in both cases, those designing schemes of access will have to set priorities in provision and criteria of eligibility, the effect of which may be to exclude some cases that with more generous collective funding would receive service.

The Differences Between Health and Legal Services

If these are the similarities, what are the differences? One major difference is that the outcomes of legal disputes are inherently positional in a way that is not true of medical outcomes. In a legal dispute the paradigm case is that one side wins and the other loses. This logic holds even if a plaintiff only wins on some points of the claim and not others. Hampshire's invocation of the principle of *audi alteram partem* as a principle of justice rests upon this feature of legal dispute. For if one side wins and the other loses, then it would not be just to make a decision without hearing both sides.

By contrast, health outcomes are not positional in this sense. The curing of one patient does not mean of itself that another patient cannot be cured. Of course there are variations, sometimes significant variations, in the performance of clinicians. It is sensible to secure the best medical advice that one can. To the extent to which the best clinician can treat only some and not all in need, securing access to the best is to that extent positional. Although Aneurin Bevan said that the purpose of the NHS was 'to universalise the best', this is best understood as an undertaking to raise access to good quality services rather than a promise to be taken literally, because literally speaking such a promise cannot be delivered. However, the fact that access to professional staff is subject to variability in professional performance does not mean that health benefits are inherently positional. After all, legal practitioners also vary in their professional abilities, and so the chance of winning one's case will depend in part on the skills of the person who acts as advocate. The relevant difference between medical and legal practice is not in the fact of professional differences of skill, but in the character of the outcome to which professional practice leads.

The positional feature of law has specific implications for legal representation. Patients may self-medicate in various ways, but there are limits on the procedures that they are able to carry out on themselves, and even in an era of online medicine, their access to medicines and diagnostic tests is restricted. By contrast, those who cannot afford legal representation can act as litigants in person. However, given the inherent positionality of legal remedies, litigants in person will be at a disadvantage relative to trained advocates, unless the courts go out of their way to be sympathetic. Courts may allow, for example, forms that are inappropriately completed or that are not filed by strict deadlines, but they will have to hear the arguments that are put to them, and the legal standing and force of those arguments are something that only trained professionals will be able fully to appreciate. Indeed, one of the principal skills of any legal professional is an understanding of what types of arguments are likely to carry weight and what types are not. When it comes to defence in criminal trials, the importance of skilled representation is enhanced, since whereas one can refuse a medical procedure, one cannot refuse being tried in a criminal court.

Second, a remedy in law has a different character from a remedy in medicine. In medicine the remedy consists in the restored well-being and health of the patient. Although family may also benefit, the outcome is essentially individual in character. In law, by contrast, the legal remedy will ipso facto be a change in social relations brought about by the payment of compensation, the restitution of goods or property wrongly acquired, public apology or the re-establishment of reputation and standing in the community. A legal remedy may or may not be financial, but it always involves a change of social status. A legal remedy represents a reallocation of the burdens and the benefits of social cooperation. The difference between the two practices is illustrated in the difference in respect of confidentiality between medicine and law. Clinicians are in breach of their duty of confidentiality if they tell the world about the successful treatment of one of their patients. Legal judgments are published, because there is a social dimension to the result of a hearing or tribunal decision. Whether a bankrupt is discharged or undischarged is a matter of public interest, but so too are the results of planning appeal, employment tribunal decisions and, even in some cases, private civil actions.

A third difference relates to the extent to which individuals have at different times in their lives to resort to medicine or law. There may be some particularly fortunate or stoical individuals who do not need to see a medical practitioner. However, in all but the poorest societies virtually everyone will have been born in the presence of skilled birth attendants, and pretty well everyone will need to resort to a doctor from time to time. With the law, by contrast the case is different. Leaving aside those instances in which the law facilitates social and economic transactions—for example house purchase, the writing of contractual terms, adoption and so on—most people, if fortunate enough, will be able to lead their lives without resort to legal advice arising from a civil dispute or contest with the public authorities. Both health care and legal advice are 'option goods' in the phrase of economists, that is to say goods that may not be enjoyed at present, but where there is an interest on the part of potential consumers in having the good available when needed. However, the use of the option will be more frequent and more widespread in the case of health care than legal advice.

This difference in the frequency with which the need for medical advice and the need for legal advice arises probably accounts for the widespread development of the insurance market in the case of health care by contrast with legal services. Even before the 'collective insurance' provided by modern states, health insurance on an individual or mutual basis was widespread. Since medical needs are predictable in the general case, but unpredictable in their individual incidence, they are natural candidates for insurance. Legal needs in relation to disputes are not something that people predict which is why insurance for legal advice and representation typically arises for individuals as an incidental feature of other purchases or activities, for example, owning a house or driving a car. (One can argue that, given the frequency of divorce, compulsory insurance ought to be a feature of all marriage contracts, but for most people that would reverse the normal triumph of hope over experience, and so is unlikely to be popular.)

Moreover, the need for legal advice may be thought to be more dependent on the prudence and concern with which one conducts one's affairs than is true of medical matters. For anyone contemplating litigation there is always a decision to be made as to whether the case is worth bringing or not. Interestingly, in this context, the areas where there is some contention about the suitability of collective coverage in matters of health are ones where the disease is thought to be self-inflicted, such as smoking-related diseases, or where there is some public sentiment that treatment is not a suitable response to the condition, as with infertility where people say that there is no human right to have a child. Whatever one thinks about the cogency of these sentiments, they would suggest that in matters over which people have personal control or where there is a sentiment of 'grin and bear it', support for collective insurance against the financial risks of legal action will be lower.

The final difference is more difficult to assess in detail, and it relates to the supply side of legal advice rather than the demand side. Historically, medical associations in many jurisdictions resisted the development of collective health provision and finance, because they wished to preserve the autonomy of their professions.

Even today, GPs in the UK's National Health Service, one of the most centralised health care systems in the world, still have the legal status of private contractors, as do dentists. Moreover, consultants are able to practise privately. Whether making all medical professionals salaried employees of the state would distort medical practice to the disadvantage of patients is a hard matter to assess. However, to the extent to which there are such threats, they are likely to be more indirect than the threat that would arise from making all legal practitioners salaried employees. Since law is an instrument of political control, making the practice of law dependent on state finance will increase the capacity of the government to control politics.

To this claim there are likely to be two responses. The first is that judges are employed by the state, and this, as such, does not affect their independence. However, it is one thing to have judges employed by the state in the context in which there is an independent legal profession. It is another matter to have judges as employees in a context in which all lawyers are employees. When all legal practice requires practitioners to be state paid, patterns of recruitment, promotion and practice will alter. Moreover, if the proposal is to have some legal practitioners as state employees whilst allowing private practice at the same time, the adversarial and positional character of legal dispute is likely to create an incentive for skilled practitioners to set up in lucrative private practice. No doubt there will be variations depending on the particular branch of law in which one practises, just as these days plastic surgeons do more private work than gerontologists. But a change in access is likely to depend on making legal practice a state monopoly, in a way that does not apply to medicine.

Implications for Institutional Design

The particular combination of characteristics that makes it hard to determine principles for the institutional design of access to legal services emerges from the comparisons and contrasts with health services identified above. The removal of the financial barriers to access for health care have in effect 'decommodified' that care,[12] but decommodification is not an intrinsic feature of universal health care access. It emerges from the existence of market failure in the health insurance market, arising from asymmetries of information between professionals on the one hand and patients and third-party payers (the insurers) on the other. However, we can conduct the thought experiment in which such market imperfections are wished away. In that case, we would not need collective organisation and finance. Provided that the distribution of income was fair, and consumers were far-sighted enough, we could imagine a functioning insurance market in health care that would provide different individuals with the package of care that they preferred.

---

[12] G Esping-Andersen, *The Three Worlds of Welfare Capitalism* (Cambridge, Polity Press, 1990).

For example, we can imagine that some individuals would care greatly about being treated in private rooms whereas others would not mind being on a ward with other patients. It is hard to see in itself what is wrong with such an arrangement, and Dworkin uses just such a thought experiment to highlight the role of market imperfections in the case for collectively organised health care.[13]

In the case of law, however, the principle of decommodification seems to have a deeper foundation. The idea that justice is something to be bought or sold is contrary to the notion of justice itself. It may be argued that this would not be a problem, since, provided a fair distribution of income could be achieved, 'equality of arms' would be secured for both sides of a dispute. However, this is to ignore a central element in the notion of justice itself. Hearing both sides is a matter of being responsive to the merits of the arguments of both sides, independently of their ability to pay for representation. The administration of justice is a direct implication of a commitment to the principle of the rule of law itself. Of course legal services have to be paid for. But the state's obligation to ensure justice, under its duty to uphold the rule of law, does not arise as a contingent matter of market failure, but as an essential element in its own purpose and functioning.

This argument is augmented by the difficulties of arranging a functioning insurance market in legal cases beyond such matters as house ownership and driving, in which insurance is a mandated individual responsibility. Those taking out any insurance will be aware of the potential moral hazard induced in the behaviour of others occasioned by the removal of financial barriers to legal action, and few people will think that they have an interest in taking out insurance in the event of their being accused of a crime. So, even if the commodification of legal services were thought appropriate, there would be no underlying logic of insurability that could be enhanced and regulated. In short, both practice and principle rule out a collective insurance arrangement.

The practical implications of these conclusions are explored in other chapters in this volume. In particular, some look to Scotland's system with its strict control of fees and rigorous scrutiny of merits as a possible model. It certainly seems preferable to the English model in which bulk contracts for a limited number of suppliers face all the problems that are increasingly being identified in the 'contractual state'. In this chapter, however, my principal aim has been to show where the parallel with health services is, and is not, illuminating.

---

[13] R Dworkin, 'Justice and the High Cost of Health' in R Dworkin, *Sovereign Virtue* (Cambridge MA, Harvard University Press, 2000).

4

Europe to the Rescue? EU Law, the ECHR and Legal Aid

STEVE PEERS

Introduction

Some potentially radical changes in public policy are prevented, or at least constrained somewhat, by the twin protections provided by European Union (EU) law and the European Convention on Human Rights (ECHR). Is this true of cut backs of legal aid in civil and administrative cases?

Legal aid in EU countries takes two forms: support for the costs of a lawyer, and exemption from court fees.[1] Some states provide for only one of these types of support, and some provide both. There are also alternative means of assisting litigants, namely: legal expenses insurance, legal advice centres, pro bono work and self-help services.[2] Across the EU, there is a wide discrepancy in the amount of legal aid expenditure per person, with most Member States spending less than €5 per person and expenditure being cut in many countries.[3]

The ECHR

Although Article 6(3)(c) ECHR guarantees legal aid as regards criminal matters, there is no express provision on legal aid in civil or administrative proceedings. However, starting with the 1979 judgment in *Airey v Ireland*,[4] the European Court

---

[1] See Justice and EU Fundamental Rights Agency, *Access to Justice in Europe: An Overview of Challenges and Opportunities* (2010), available at: http://fra.europa.eu/sites/default/files/fra_uploads/1520-report-access-to-justice_EN.pdf, ch 4.

[2] ibid, 53.

[3] See the 2015 EU Justice Scoreboard, figure 39, available at: http://ec.europa.eu/justice/effective-justice/files/justice_scoreboard_2015_en.pdf, 32.

[4] *Airey v Ireland* (1979) 32 Eur Ct HR Ser A: [1979] 2 EHRR 305.

of Human Rights (ECtHR) stated that the general right to a fair trial in Article 6(1) ECHR could include an implied right to legal aid in civil cases too, if this is necessary to ensure effective access to justice. The facts of the case concerned judicial separation proceedings, and the Court considered that the alternative of presenting her case in person would not fully guarantee the applicant's right to a fair trial, due to the complex procedural and substantive law, the need for expert advice as regards evidence and other witnesses, and the emotional impact of the case.

The Court rejected the argument that a right to legal aid in civil proceedings brought the ECHR unduly into the field of social rights, and that Article 6(3)(c) ECHR implied a contrario that there was no right to legal aid in civil matters. The key point was that 'despite the absence of a similar clause for civil litigation', Article 6(1)

> may sometimes compel the State to provide for the assistance of a lawyer when such assistance proves indispensable for an effective access to court either because legal representation is rendered compulsory, as is done by the domestic law of certain Contracting States for various types of litigation, or by reason of the complexity of the procedure or of the case.

Subsequent case law made clear that there is no general right to legal aid in all civil proceedings. Rather, any limitation on the right of access to the courts (the implied right which legal aid facilitates) cannot undermine the very core of the right. Limitations of the right must pursue a legitimate aim, and must also be proportionate in light of the legitimate aim which they seek to satisfy. For instance, in *Tolstoy-Miloslavsky* the applicant, a defendant in a libel case, challenged an order for security for costs of over £100,000 that he would have to pay within 14 days in order to bring an appeal.[5] The ECtHR ruled that there was a 'legitimate aim' for the costs order (protecting the other party from shouldering his own costs if the applicant could not pay them in the event of an unsuccessful appeal). The merits test imposed upon the proceedings could also be 'said to have been imposed in the interests of a fair administration of justice'. The security for costs requirement did not impair 'the very essence' of the right of access to court, because there had already been an extensive first-instance hearing; the sum was a reasonable estimate of the costs involved; the applicant could not have raised the money in a longer period of time; the national court took the merits into account when considering a possible waiver of an order for security of costs; the applicant was more interested in determining liability than costs (he had refused a proposed settlement); and there was a full judicial assessment of the costs issue. Therefore there was no 'arbitrariness' in issuing the order for security of costs.

In the case of *Kreuz v Poland*,[6] the ECtHR reiterated that a requirement to provide security for costs was in principle a legitimate restriction on access to court. But in that case, the required security amounted to a year's average salary.

[5] *Tolstoy Miloslavsky v United Kingdom* App no 18139/91 (Judgment, 13 July 1995).
[6] *Kreuz v Poland* App no 28249/95 (Judgment, 19 June 2001).

Although the applicant was a businessman, the dispute was 'related only loosely, if at all, to a business activity as such'. Rather it was a claim for damages against a public authority. Also, the national courts only considered his *hypothetical* earning capacity, not the amount which he actually earned, did not supply any evidence to contradict his account of his earnings, and made assumptions which were not supported by any evidence. Moreover, national law allows for the exemption from court fees to be revoked if the applicant's financial situation improves. On the whole, then, there was an insufficient balance between the state interest in collecting court fees and the applicant's right to vindicate his claim in the courts, since the required fee was excessive and deterred him from going to court at all.

Another key judgment is *Steel and Morris v United Kingdom*.[7] In a case involving libel defendants, the ECtHR began by reiterating the basic case law on when legal aid was necessary in civil cases pursuant to Article 6 ECHR. This

> must be determined on the basis of the particular facts and circumstances of each case and will depend, inter alia, upon the importance of what is at stake for the applicant in the proceedings, the complexity of the relevant law and procedure and the applicant's capacity to represent him or herself effectively.

Restrictions are possible if they 'pursue a legitimate aim and are proportionate'. So conditions can be imposed on 'the grant of legal aid based, inter alia, on the financial situation of the litigant or his or her prospects of success in the proceedings'. The state is not obliged to grant legal aid 'to ensure total equality of arms between the assisted person and the opposing party, as long as each side is afforded a reasonable opportunity to present his or her case under conditions that do not place him or her at a substantial disadvantage vis-à-vis the adversary'.

Applying these criteria, first of all, this case was different from previous judgments like *Airey* because 'the proceedings … were not determinative of important family rights and relationships', and usually there is a distinction between a defamation action aiming to protect an individual's reputation from an application for judicial separation, 'which regulates the legal relationship between two individuals and may have serious consequences for any children of the family'. But here the applicants did not bring the proceedings, but 'acted as defendants to protect their right to freedom of expression, a right accorded considerable importance under the Convention', and the damages awarded against them were huge in comparison with their modest incomes. The case was also distinct from prior judgments ruling that the English law of defamation and civil procedure is not complex enough to require legal aid,[8] since those rulings concerned a single allegation while *Steel and Morris* concerned the longest trial in English history, with thousands of pages of evidence, over 100 witnesses, judgments running to over 1000 pages and numerous legal and procedural issues.

---

[7] *Steel and Morris v United Kingdom* App no 68416/01 (Judgment, 15 February 2005).
[8] See, inter alia, *McVicar v United Kingdom* App no 46311/99 (Judgment, 7 May 2002).

Compared with prior cases, in which the defamation actions were brought by professionals, the applicants would have met the means test for legal aid and benefited from some pro bono legal assistance and latitude extended by the courts. But the ECtHR ruled that this was not a 'substitute for competent and sustained representation by an experienced lawyer familiar with the case and with the law of libel', and the 'disparity' between their legal assistance and the plaintiff's (McDonald's Restaurants) 'was of such a degree that it could not have failed, in this exceptionally demanding case, to have given rise to unfairness'. Therefore there was a breach of Article 6.

As for the form of legal aid granted, states have discretion to provide different forms of legal aid for different types of litigation. For instance, it was acceptable for the UK to exclude defamation cases from legal aid support, since it had granted potential litigants of defamation cases the right to two hours of free pre-litigation legal advice, if they had insufficient means.[9]

As regards one type of plaintiff (profit-making companies), the ECtHR ruled that their exclusion from a national legal aid scheme was acceptable since the discrimination between them and non-profit-making organisations and natural persons had an objective and reasonable justification (the possibility to deduct the legal costs from the company's tax bill).[10]

EU Law

EU law provides for three separate (but partly overlapping) forms of human rights protection, in Article 6 of the Treaty on European Union (TEU). First, human rights are protected in the form set out in the EU Charter of Fundamental Rights, which has the 'same legal value' as the EU Treaties (Article 6(1) TEU). Second, the EU is obliged to sign up to the ECHR in its own name (Article 6(2) TEU). However, that process has been stymied by a very negative opinion from the Court of Justice of the European Union (CJEU) on the draft Treaty which aimed to ensure accession.[11] It may be difficult or impossible to agree an alternative version of this Treaty which secures accession in a way which is compatible with EU law in the CJEU's opinion. In the meantime, the ECHR does not bind the EU as such.[12] Finally, Article 6(3) TEU provides that human rights are also still protected as 'general principles' of EU law.

---

[9] See *A v United Kingdom* App no 35373/97 (Judgment, 17 December 2002).

[10] *VP Diffusion Sarl v France* App no 14565/04 (Decision, 26 August 2008). See also (Decision, 24 November 2009).

[11] Opinion 2/2013, ECLI:EU:C:2014:2454. For the text of the draft Treaty, see: www.coe.int/t/dghl/standardsetting/hrpolicy/accession/Meeting_reports/47_1(2013)008rev2_EN.pdf.

[12] Case C-571/10 *Kamberaj*, ECLI:EU:C:2012:233.

Unlike the ECHR, the EU Charter refers to legal aid outside the criminal law context. This forms part of Article 47 of the Charter, which first of all guarantees 'an effective remedy before a tribunal' to '[e]veryone whose rights and freedoms guaranteed by the law of the Union' have been 'violated', 'in accordance with the conditions laid down' in the rest of Article 47.

The second paragraph of Article 47 goes on to state that: 'Everyone is entitled to a fair and public hearing within a reasonable time by an independent and impartial tribunal previously established by law. Everyone shall have the possibility of being advised, defended and represented'.

Finally, the third paragraph states that: 'Legal aid shall be made available to those who lack sufficient resources in so far as such aid is necessary to ensure effective access to justice'.

The 'general provisions' in Title VII of the Charter are also relevant. Article 51 of the Charter sets out its scope of application:

> 1. The provisions of this Charter are addressed to the institutions and bodies of the Union with due regard for the principle of subsidiarity and to the Member States only when they are implementing Union law. They shall therefore respect the rights, observe the principles and promote the application thereof in accordance with their respective powers.

> 2. This Charter does not establish any new power or task for the Community or the Union, or modify powers and tasks defined by the Treaties.

Article 52 sets out a number of rules on the limitation and interpretation of Charter rights. There is a general limitations rule in Article 52(1):

> 1. Any limitation on the exercise of the rights and freedoms recognised by this Charter must be provided for by law and respect the essence of those rights and freedoms. Subject to the principle of proportionality, limitations may be made only if they are necessary and genuinely meet objectives of general interest recognised by the Union or the need to protect the rights and freedoms of others.

Also, Article 52(3) describes the relationship between the Charter and the ECHR:

> 3. In so far as this Charter contains rights which correspond to rights guaranteed by the Convention for the Protection of Human Rights and Fundamental Freedoms, the meaning and scope of those rights shall be the same as those laid down by the said Convention. This provision shall not prevent Union law providing more extensive protection.

Unlike the original ECHR, there are official explanations to the Charter. Article 6(1) TEU stresses the importance of both the general provisions and these explanations:

> The rights, freedoms and principles in the Charter shall be interpreted in accordance with the general provisions in Title VII of the Charter governing its interpretation and application and with due regard to the explanations referred to in the Charter, that set out the sources of those provisions.

What do the explanations say about the relevant provisions of the Charter? First, the first paragraph of Article 47 is 'based on' Article 13 ECHR (on the right to an effective remedy), except that 'in Union law the protection is more extensive since it guarantees the right to an effective remedy before a court'. Next, the second paragraph 'corresponds to' Article 6(1) ECHR. However, the explanations state that:

> In Union law, the right to a fair hearing is not confined to disputes relating to civil law rights and obligations. That is one of the consequences of the fact that the Union is a community based on the rule of law ... Nevertheless, in all respects other than their scope, the guarantees afforded by the ECHR apply in a similar way to the Union.

As for the third paragraph of Article 47, the explanations note that according to the case law of the ECtHR, 'provision should be made for legal aid where the absence of such aid would make it impossible to ensure an effective remedy' (referring to *Airey v Ireland*). The explanations also note that there is 'a system of legal assistance for cases before the Court of Justice of the European Union'.

The explanations to Article 52(3), on the links between the Charter and the ECHR, are also relevant. They state that '[t]he reference to the ECHR covers both the Convention and the Protocols to it', and that the 'meaning and scope' of the rights are 'determined not only by the text of those instruments, but also by the case-law of the European Court of Human Rights and by the Court of Justice of the European Union'. But the explanations are less clear about the meaning of the second sentence of Article 52(3), simply restating that it 'is designed to allow the Union to guarantee more extensive protection'. The only elaboration on this is that '[i]n any event, the level of protection afforded by the Charter may never be lower than that guaranteed by the ECHR'.

Also, the explanations indicate which provisions of the Charter should be regarded as 'corresponding' to the ECHR. This list states that 'Article 47(2) and (3) corresponds to Article 6(1) of the ECHR, but the limitation to the determination of civil rights and obligations or criminal charges does not apply as regards Union law and its implementation'. Furthermore, the explanations state that Article 52(3) is 'intended to ensure the necessary consistency between the Charter and the ECHR' and that the 'meaning and scope' includes 'authorised limitations':

> This means in particular that the legislator, in laying down limitations to those rights, must comply with the same standards as are fixed by the detailed limitation arrangements laid down in the ECHR, which are thus made applicable for the rights covered by this paragraph, without thereby adversely affecting the autonomy of Union law and of that of the Court of Justice of the European Union.

Case Law

The leading case on Article 47(3) of the Charter is *DEB*, which concerned a claim for legal aid by a legal person. In this case, the legal person requesting legal aid was a company without any income or assets, which was arguing that Germany was liable in damages for a breach of EU law due to defective implementation of

EU legislation establishing an internal market for energy. The company did not have enough money to meet a demand of security for costs, so could not qualify to receive legal aid.[13]

The CJEU referred to Article 52(3) of the Charter, in particular the correspondence between Charter rights and the ECHR, and the explanations referring to the case law of the ECtHR and the *Airey* judgment. The explanations do not specify whether legal aid 'must be granted to a legal person or of the nature of the costs covered by that aid'. So the CJEU interpreted the rule 'in its context, in the light of other provisions of EU law, the law of the Member States and the case-law of the European Court of Human Rights'.

Applying these rules, the word 'person' in the various language versions of Article 47 did not exclude legal persons, and the other rules in Title VI of the Charter could apply to both natural and legal persons. Since legal aid was not referred to in the 'social rights' provisions of Title IV of the Charter, this suggested that it was not a form of social assistance. National law did not set out a common principle which Member States shared as regards the grant of legal aid to legal persons, although many Member States made a 'distinction between profit-making and non-profit-making legal persons'.

Next, the CJEU took account of ECtHR case law, referring to the right of effective access to court, which is not absolute. It incorporated into EU law the ECtHR criteria relating to legal aid:

> the question whether the provision of legal aid is necessary for a fair hearing must be determined on the basis of the particular facts and circumstances of each case and will depend, inter alia, upon the importance of what is at stake for the applicant in the proceedings, the complexity of the relevant law and procedure and the applicant's capacity to represent himself effectively ... Account may be taken, however, of the financial situation of the litigant or his prospects of success in the proceedings ... the European Court of Human Rights has similarly examined all the circumstances in order to determine whether the limitations applied to the right of access to the courts had undermined the very core of that right, whether those limitations pursued a legitimate aim and whether there was a reasonable relationship of proportionality between the means employed and the legitimate aim sought to be achieved.

Furthermore, the CJEU took account of ECtHR case law ruling that a selection procedure for legal aid 'must operate in a non-arbitrary manner', including the *VP Diffusion* decision on the permissible distinction between profit-making companies and others, and the *CMVMC O'Limo v Spain* decision.

From this, the CJEU concluded that 'the grant of legal aid to legal persons is not in principle impossible, but must be assessed in the light of the applicable rules and the situation of the company concerned'. It was possible to consider

---

[13] Case C-279/09 *DEB* [2010] ECR I-13845. See J Engström, 'The Principle of Effective Judicial Protection after the Lisbon Treaty: Reflection in the Light of Case C-279/09 DEB' (2011) 4(2) *Review of European Administrative Law* 53.

the 'subject-matter of the litigation ... in particular its economic importance', as well as the form of the legal person, 'the financial capacity of its shareholders; the objects of the company; the manner in which it has been set up; and, more specifically, the relationship between the resources allocated to it and the intended activity'. It then left all of these factors to be weighed up by the national court.

Subsequently, the CJEU reiterated this judgment in its order in the case of *GREP*,[14] which concerned the order to enforce a judgment of a German court in Austria, pursuant to the EU legislation on the jurisdiction, recognition and enforcement of judgments in civil and commercial matters.[15] *GREP* was the subject of the enforcement order, but could not get legal aid because Austrian law denies it to legal persons in enforcement proceedings. The CJEU ruled that the case fell within the scope of EU law because it concerned the application of rules in an EU Regulation (this aspect had merely been assumed by the Court in *DEB*). It then simply repeated what it had ruled in that prior judgment.

EU Legislation

A number of EU legislative measures contain express provisions on legal aid, and so any disputes concerning these provisions would obviously fall within the scope of EU law, and therefore the Charter.[16]

In the area of immigration and asylum law, the EU's asylum procedures legislation sets out a right to free legal assistance following a negative decision on the asylum application.[17] But Member States may provide that legal aid is granted: only for procedures before a court or tribunal, not for any other 'onward appeals or reviews'; subject to a means test; for designated legal advisers only; or 'only if the appeal or review is likely to succeed', subject (in the latter case) to an obligation to 'ensure that legal assistance and/or representation ... is not arbitrarily restricted'.[18] They can also impose financial or time limits on legal aid, subject again to a ban on arbitrarily restricting access to legal assistance, or provide that legal aid cannot be more favourable than that of nationals in similar cases.[19] Finally, they can demand to be reimbursed if 'the applicant's financial situation has improved considerably'

---

[14] Case C-156/12 *GREP* (Order, 13 June 2012).

[15] Council Regulation (EC) 44/2001 of 22 December 2000 on jurisdiction and the recognition and enforcement of judgments in civil and commercial matters [2001] OJ L12/1.

[16] Furthermore, as noted in the explanations to the Charter, the CJEU has its own legal aid system. See Arts 115–18 of the Court's Rules of Procedure ([2012] OJ L265/1).

[17] Art 15(2), Council Directive 2005/85/EC of 1 December 2005 on minimum standards on procedures in Member States for granting and withdrawing refugee status [2005] OJ L326/13.

[18] ibid, Art 15(3).

[19] ibid, Art 15(5).

or if the applicant gave false information that was the basis of the decision to grant legal aid.[20]

The second version of the procedures Directive specifies that legal aid covers the preparation of documents and the participation in the hearing.[21] Member States have an option, but not an obligation, to extend a legal aid right to cover the original administrative procedure which considers the asylum application.[22] There is a slightly different version of the optional merits test (where the appeal is 'considered by a court or tribunal or other competent authority to have no tangible prospect of success'), which appears to tilt the balance of the test towards the asylum seeker. The Directive also provides that there must be a review before a court or tribunal of any decision to refuse legal aid on this ground (unless it was a court or tribunal that refused legal aid in the first place); and there is an extra requirement that the applicant's 'effective access to justice is not hindered'.[23] The other previous conditions continue to apply, with the additional possibility that Member States can refuse legal aid in the case of repeat applications.[24] It might be arguable that the general principles of EU law require legal aid to be available during the administrative procedure, despite the absence of such a right under the Directive, although an equivalent claim relating to irregular migration was unsuccessful (see discussion below).

For asylum seekers challenging their detention, the revised Directive on reception conditions for asylum seekers provides that where detention of an asylum seeker has been ordered by the administration, the asylum seeker has the right to 'free legal assistance and representation' in the context of a judicial review of the detention order. This must 'at least' include 'the preparation of the required procedural documents and participation in the hearing before the judicial authorities on behalf of the applicant'.[25] As with the procedures Directive, Member States may: impose a means test and/or require asylum seekers to use specially designated legal advisers;[26] provide for fee caps and time limits, as long as this does 'not arbitrarily restrict access to legal assistance and representation'; specify that asylum seekers do not have better treatment 'than the treatment generally accorded to their nationals in matters pertaining to legal assistance';[27] and demand to be reimbursed, under the same conditions.[28]

---

[20] ibid, Art 15(6).

[21] Art 20(1), Directive 2013/32/EU of the European Parliament and of the Council of 26 June 2013 on common procedures for granting and withdrawing international protection [2013] OJ L180/60. This Directive applies to applications made on or after 20 July 2015 (Arts 51(2) and 52).

[22] ibid, Art 20(2).

[23] ibid, Art 20(3).

[24] ibid, Art 21.

[25] Art 9(6), Directive 2013/33/EU of the European Parliament and of the Council of 26 June 2013 laying down standards for the reception of applicants for international protection [2013] OJ L180/96. The persons offering legal assistance must have sufficient qualifications, and they must be free of any conflict of interests. This Directive applies from 20 July 2015 (Art 31).

[26] ibid, Art 9(7).

[27] ibid, Art 9(8).

[28] ibid, Art 9(9).

The same Directive also contains rules on legal aid for challenging decisions to withdraw benefits, or which limit asylum seekers' residence or free movement. In those cases, Member States must provide for free legal aid on request 'in so far as such aid is necessary to ensure effective access to justice'. Again, this extends to the preparation of documents and participation in the hearing[29] and Member States can impose a means test or require the use of specified lawyers.[30] In this case, Member States can also provide for legal aid to be refused if a 'competent authority' thinks the review has 'no tangible prospect of success', provided that 'legal assistance and representation is not arbitrarily restricted and that the applicant's effective access to justice is not hindered'.[31] The same possibilities of imposing fee or time limits, national treatment regarding legal aid, or demanding reimbursement apply.[32] Compared with the first version of the reception conditions Directive,[33] the provisions on legal aid in detention cases are new,[34] and there had been no detailed provision for legal aid to challenge the decisions to cut benefits or limit free movement in the prior Directive.[35]

There are also rules on legal aid in the 'Dublin III' Regulation, which regulates the determination of which a Member State is responsible for an asylum seeker.[36] If asylum seekers challenge this determination, they have the right to legal aid if they cannot afford the costs. Member States may apply a comparison with nationals and refuse legal aid if there is 'no tangible prospect of success' (subject to a legal review of this decision before a court or tribunal), subject to the rule that 'legal assistance and representation is not arbitrarily restricted and that the applicant's effective access to justice is not hindered'. The right extends to 'at least the preparation of the required procedural documents and representation before a court or tribunal', and Member States can restrict it to specialist legal advisers. As for detention during the Dublin procedure, the Dublin III Regulation requires that the rules in the reception condition Directive (including the legal aid rules) apply.[37]

---

[29] ibid, Art 26(2), Directive 2013/33. Again, the persons offering legal assistance must have sufficient qualifications and no conflict of interests.

[30] ibid, Art 26(3), first paragraph.

[31] ibid, Art 26(3), second paragraph.

[32] ibid, Arts 26(4) and (5).

[33] Council Directive 2003/9/EC of 27 January 2003 laying down minimum standards for the reception of asylum seekers [2003] OJ L31/18.

[34] The first version of the Directive had little relevance to detention issues: See Case C-534/11 *Arslan*, ECLI:EU:C:2014:343.

[35] Art 21(2) of Directive 2003/9/EC only requires Member States to lay down rules on 'procedures for access to legal assistance in such cases' in their national law.

[36] Art 27(6), Council Regulation (EU) 604/2013 of 26 June 2013 establishing the criteria and mechanisms for determining the Member State responsible for examining an application for international protection lodged in one of the Member States by a third-country national or a stateless person [2013] OJ L180/31. There was no such provision in the prior Dublin II Regulation (Council Regulation (EC) 343/2003 [2003] OJ L50/1).

[37] Art 28(4), Dublin III Regulation, referring to Arts 9–11 of that Directive.

For irregular migrants who are not asylum seekers,[38] the EU's returns Directive provides for legal aid on the same conditions as the asylum procedures Directive, in order to challenge a return decision or an entry ban.[39] The CJEU has held that EU law does not extend to a right to legal aid at an earlier point, during the administrative process that led up to the return decision being adopted.[40] It has not yet ruled on whether EU law might require a right to legal aid in order to challenge detention.[41]

As for civil law, the main rules are set out in Directive 2003/8/EC,[42] which specifically concerns the right to legal aid in cross-border civil proceedings. This Directive applies to all civil and commercial matters,[43] excluding only customs, revenue, and administrative matters.[44] It applies only to cross-border matters, which are defined as cases where the party applying for legal aid is domiciled or habitually resident in a Member State other than the Member State where the court is sitting or where the decision is to be enforced,[45] at the time when the application was submitted.[46] ⇒ So not applicable to citizens of a state ?

Directive 2003/8/EC provides for a right to legal aid for pre-judicial assistance with a view to a settlement and legal assistance and representation in court, including the costs of proceedings. However, Member States can apply a means test, and they do not have to provide legal aid for specialist tribunals where the parties can make their case effectively in person.[47] The legal aid must be granted without discrimination as regards EU citizens and legally resident third-country nationals.[48] Member States can reject claims which appear to be manifestly unfounded.[49] Also, if pre-litigation advice is offered, further legal aid 'may be refused or cancelled' on the merits of the case, as long as 'access to justice is guaranteed'.[50] Member States must consider the importance of the case to the individual, but can also consider

---

[38] See the case law on the scope of the EU's Returns Directive: Case C-357/09 PPU *Kadzoev* [2009] ECR I-11189 and Case C-534/11 *Arslan*, ECLI:EU:C:2014:343.

[39] Art 13(4), Directive 2008/115/EC of 16 December 2008 on common standards and procedures in Member States for returning illegally staying third-country nationals [2008] OJ L348/98. The reference to the asylum procedures Directive refers, as from 20 July 2015, to the second version of that Directive: see Art 53 and Annex III, Directive 2013/32/EU.

[40] Case C-249/13 *Boudjlida*, ECLI:EU:C:2014:2431, paras 64 and 65.

[41] See Case C-383/13 PPU *G and R*, ECLI:EU:C:2013:533.

[42] Directive 2003/8/EC of 27 January 2003 to improve access to justice in cross-border disputes by establishing minimum common rules relating to legal aid for such disputes [2003] OJ L26/41. For the background, see the EU Commission's Green Paper on Legal aid in civil matters: 'The problems confronting the cross-border litigant' COM (2000) 51.

[43] Art 2, Directive 2003/8/EC. On the definition of this concept, see S Peers, *EU Justice and Home Affairs Law* Vol 2, 4th edn (Oxford, Oxford University Press, forthcoming) ch 8.

[44] Art 1(2), Directive 2003/8/EC.

[45] ibid, Art 2(1). The rules determining where a person is domiciled are set out in other EU civil law legislation (Art 2(2), Directive 2003/8/EC).

[46] Art 2(3), Directive 2003/8/EC.

[47] ibid, Arts 3 and 5.

[48] ibid, Art 4.

[49] ibid, Art 6(1).

[50] ibid, Art 6(2).

the nature of the case if it concerns reputational damage but there is no material or financial loss, or if the claim arises directly from the applicant's trade or
profession.[51]

The Directive allocates costs between Member States. The Member State where
the court is sitting must cover the direct costs related to the cross-border nature of
the dispute as regards interpretation, translation of certain documents, and travel
costs of the applicant if the physical presence of the people presenting the case
is a legal obligation and the court decides that those people cannot be heard by
other means.[52] But the Member State of the applicant's domicile or habitual residence must pay the costs of the local lawyer or other person entitled to give legal
advice, as well as the translation of the application.[53] There are also provisions
concerning: legal aid in relation to enforcement; appeals; extrajudicial procedures
or authentic instruments;[54] and the procedure for transmitting and processing
legal aid applications.[55]

The Commission has reported on the application of this Directive in practice.[56]
In its view, the Directive has been satisfactorily applied by Member States, although
there is limited awareness of it or use of it in practice, and there are divergences
between Member States on interpretation of some provisions, and a limited notion
of 'cross-border' cases.

There are more detailed rules on legal aid in the specific field of maintenance
obligations in cross-border situations.[57] The right to legal aid in such cases applies
also to enforcement, review and appeal procedures.[58] It covers a long list of measures: pre-litigation assistance; legal assistance and representation in court; exemption from costs and fees; the costs incurred by the opposing party if the litigant
loses and would be liable to pay them; interpretation; translation of documents;
and travel costs (under the same conditions as the legal aid Directive).[59] Legal aid
also applies to maintenance support for children, although for some such cases,
Member States can refuse legal aid if the case is considered 'manifestly unfounded'
on the merits.[60] In other cases, Member States can impose a means test or a
merits test.[61]

---

[51] ibid, Art 6(3).
[52] ibid, Art 7.
[53] ibid, Art 8.
[54] ibid, Arts 7–11.
[55] ibid, Arts 12–16.
[56] Report from the Commission to the European Parliament, the council and the European
economic and social committee on the application of Directive 2003/8/EC to improve access to justice
in cross border disputes by establishing minimum common rules relating to legal aid for such disputes,
COM (2012) 71.
[57] Chapter V (Arts 44–47) of Council Regulation (EC) 4/2009 of 18 December 2008 on jurisdiction, applicable law, recognition and enforcement of decisions and cooperation in matters relating to
maintenance obligations [2009] OJ L7/1.
[58] Art 44(1), Regulation 4/2009.
[59] ibid, Art 45.
[60] ibid, Art 46.
[61] ibid, Art 47.

The EU has sought to develop the area of e-justice, which could potentially help to address some of the concerns about the costs of access to legal systems. This has taken the form (inter alia) of the development of an online portal giving access to national justice systems, and facilitation of videoconferencing and remote translation and interpretation.[62] However, the Commission has not assessed in any detail whether these measures have in practice facilitated access to justice, or whether further measures could be taken to this end.

Conclusions

Airey v Ireland

The ECHR requires legal aid to be granted in sensitive family law proceedings, but outside that area the right to legal aid can only be claimed in particularly complex cases like *Steel and Morris*. A more advanced approach can be seen in EU law, which takes the ECtHR case law as a starting point but does not entirely rule out the possibility of extending it (to legal persons, for instance). It might be arguable that legal aid must be granted as regards other areas of particular relevance to EU law, such as the free movement of persons.

ie. alongside the ECHR

A more advanced approach can be seen in the form of EU legislation which contains specific rules on legal aid, although it should be noted that the UK has opted out of some of the legislation discussed here (the UK is covered by the Dublin Regulation, the first-phase asylum procedures and reception conditions Directives, and the civil law measures discussed above). There is no CJEU case law yet on these specific rules, but they have shown a clear evolution towards widening their scope of coverage, to include the important issue of the detention of asylum seekers, disputes relating to asylum seekers' benefits and the Dublin rules on allocation of asylum seekers. The rules are subject to a number of limitations that broadly reflect the ECtHR case law (means tests, merits tests, reimbursement) and it is arguable that even in the absence of express rules, the EU Charter requires legal aid to be granted to challenge the detention of irregular migrants other than asylum seekers and the general principles of EU law require legal aid to be granted as regards the administrative procedures determining an asylum application. In the area of civil law, the EU law rules are useful in ensuring that legal aid is granted in maintenance cases with a cross-border element as well as (in less detail) other civil law cases with a cross-border element where the interests of justice require the grant of legal aid.

---

[62] Commission Communication, 'Towards a European e-Justice Strategy' COM (2008) 329.

Part II

Pressure Points on the Justice System

5

Access to Justice in Administrative Law and Administrative Justice

TOM MULLEN

Introduction

This chapter discusses access to justice in the context of administrative law and administrative justice. The focus will be mainly on the United Kingdom and English law dimensions of administrative law and administrative justice, but some account will be taken of developments in other parts of the UK. The meanings of these two expressions overlap substantially but are not identical. Both expressions are generally considered to include within their scope both the substantive principles of administrative law and the different types of remedies—judicial and non-judicial—that citizens[1] may use to seek redress of grievances against the state, for example, courts, tribunals, inquiries, and complaints procedures including ombudsmen. The increasing use of the term 'administrative justice' in recent years has been associated with a strong emphasis on the importance of studying initial decision-making by public authorities,[2] as opposed to administrative law scholarship's traditional emphasis on remedies, and an increasing willingness to analyse the system of remedies as a whole.[3] The term administrative justice is also conventionally regarded as including, not only decisions affecting citizens' rights and interests, but also other aspects of how citizens are treated by public bodies. Administrative justice can, therefore, encompass the 'non-decisional' failings of public bodies such as delay, rudeness and insensitivity in their treatment of citizens.

---

[1] I use the term 'citizen' as convenient shorthand for all the categories of persons who have dealings with public bodies. No nationality limitation is intended.

[2] See, eg, M Adler (ed), *Administrative Justice in Context* (Oxford, Hart Publishing, 2010) particularly chapters by M Adler, R Kagan, S Halliday and C Scott, and M Hertogh.

[3] See, eg, the Final Report of the Administrative Justice Steering Group (AJSG), *Administrative Justice in Scotland—The Way Forward* (2009), available at: www.consumerfocus.org.uk/scotland/files/2010/10/Administrative-Justice-in-Scotland-The-Way-Forward-Full-Report.pdf and the publications of the Administrative Justice and Tribunals Council.

The emphasis of this chapter is mainly on remedies rather than on initial decision-making and also on citizens' grievances arising from decisions affecting their rights and interests rather than on grievances concerning 'non-decisional' failings. This fits better with the themes of this book. However, it is informed by the concerns of administrative justice scholarship and the latter term will be used because of its wider connotations. The expression 'access to justice' can be used to mean a variety of things. In this chapter, I assume that the idea access to justice concerns the availability of legal remedies to address wrongs. A person has access to justice when there are effective remedies available to that person to vindicate his or her legal rights and advance his or her legally recognised interests. On a narrow conception of access to justice, what matters is that the remedies exist and that the person is free as a matter of law to use them. However, a broader conception— which I consider is more appropriate—suggests that persons should in practice be able to use those remedies without undue difficulty. This brings in consideration of the cost of using remedies and other possible obstacles to using them effectively.

In the United Kingdom, the primary focus of discussions of access to justice has been on civil litigation between private parties and on the criminal process. Administrative law and administrative justice have not until recently figured as prominently but, given the importance of the rights and interests at stake and the large numbers of citizens affected by decisions taken by state bureaucracies, it too deserves substantial attention. Administrative justice could be subsumed within the other two categories on the assumption that issues of administrative law can be classified as either civil or criminal in nature. There are certainly substantial over-laps between administrative justice on the one hand, and civil and criminal litiga-tion on the other. Thus, in the field of administrative justice, citizens have legal rights against the state and the remedies for failure to respect those rights include litigation in the ordinary courts. However, there are two features of administrative justice which are different from civil and criminal justice which constitute good reasons for treating it as a distinct area of concern for purposes of access to justice analysis. First, administrative justice makes use of a wider range of remedies to resolve disputes between citizen and state than do civil or criminal justice in which dispute resolution is confined mainly to the ordinary courts. These include not only tribunals, but also non-judicial remedies such as ombudsmen, complaints procedures and various hybrids including public inquiry-based decision-making processes. Indeed, the extensive use of non-judicial remedies is largely a reaction to perceived weaknesses and limitations of the courts.

Second, it has been assumed that lawyers and legal aid are not necessary to do justice in those alternative fora and that citizens can use them effectively them-selves. Whether this is indeed the case has long been controversial. Questions that have been raised include whether the unrepresented citizen is at a disadvantage in tribunals, whether adequate advice and assistance is in fact available and, if so, how it should be funded. However, the assumption has been an important influence on policy both in relation to legal aid and in the choice of remedies for administrative schemes. It is necessary, therefore, to consider the question whether there is access to justice in the field of administrative justice in the light of these distinctive features.

This chapter addresses the general question of whether there is adequate access to justice in the field of administrative justice in the context of the developments of the last 15 years, particularly the period since 2010. That general question may be broken down into two further questions:

1. The extent to which there are actually remedies available to the citizen in the sense that there is a right to challenge in an independent forum administrative decisions which deny his or her rights or are adverse to his or her interests.
2. Whether the remedies that exist are truly accessible in the sense that citizens can use those remedies without undue difficulty.

I will consider both in the following pages but, before going further, it is appropriate to explain the nature of administrative decisions and the characteristics of administrative justice remedies.

The Nature of Administrative Decisions and the Characteristics of Administrative Justice Remedies

The Nature of Administrative Decisions

Many areas of public policy require public bodies to make individualised decisions, ie, decisions that affect identifiable individuals. There are two basic reasons why we would want those decisions to be good decisions. First, we want them to respect the rights and interests of the individuals affected by those decisions. Second, we want the policies legitimately adopted by elected and accountable governments to be properly implemented. In many areas of social policy, policies cannot be implemented without taking decisions affecting individuals. Most individualised administrative decisions are intended to be made according to authoritative standards, rather than in any other way, for example, by agreement between the decision-maker and the affected citizen or by random allocation.[4] These standards, therefore, are the criteria by reference to which public bodies and their officials should take decisions. Those standards for decision are often expressed in legislation or case law but also include less formal sources of guidance such as policy statements.

As the standards are often legal standards, we can invoke the rule of law—which requires that decisions made by government authorities affecting individuals

---

[4] See D Galligan, *Due Process and Fair Procedures: A Study of Administrative Procedures* (Oxford, Clarendon Press, 1996) 24–31 for an analysis of the different modes of decision-making.

should be made in accordance with the relevant laws—as a further reason for requiring decision-makers to follow them. The requirement of legality also implies that decisions should be correct on the facts as laws are made on the assumption that they will be applied to specific cases according to the actual factual circumstances. The basic requirements for a good administrative decision are, therefore, that it is based on a correct understanding of the law, and a correct view of the facts.

However, there is more to good decision-making in public administration than legality. In many contexts, the law gives decision-makers substantial discretion. That discretion ought to be exercised as well as it can be. Not only should the decision be lawful, it should be the best possible decision in the circumstances. By that I mean that the decision should in general advance the purposes of the administrative scheme in question, other generic objectives of public policy such as economy and efficiency, and important decision-making values such as consistency, transparency and respect for human rights. The third requirement of a good administrative decision is, therefore, that the decision reached is an appropriate exercise of any discretion that the decision-maker has. These are essentially substantive requirements to which we can add a requirement of procedural fairness in decision-making.

The Nature of Remedies for Bad Administrative Decisions

All of this has important implications for citizens' remedies, in particular, how broad the opportunity for citizens to challenge administrative decisions should be. If many administrative decisions have three elements—questions of law, questions of fact and questions of discretion—it follows that a person aggrieved by a decision may wish to challenge any or all of these elements, ie, to argue that the decision is defective because the decision-maker got the law wrong, because she or he got the facts wrong or because she or he exercised the discretion inappropriately. It seems clear that citizens should be able to challenge decisions based on errors of law or errors of fact. It is perhaps less clear that citizens should be able to challenge the discretionary element of the decision, what administrative lawyers would call the merits of the decision. This is because where the decision-maker has discretion there is room for disagreement as to what the 'correct' decision is; the appellate or review authority may be no better placed than the initial decision-maker to decide whether a decision is a good or bad, whether for reasons of relative competence or legitimacy, or for other reasons.

It can certainly be argued that full merits review is inappropriate and that citizens' remedies should be limited to challenging errors of law and errors of fact, and that they should be able to challenge the exercise of discretion only to the extent permitted by the established grounds for judicial review. However, there are strong arguments that can support the provision of an appeal or review on the merits against administrative decisions. They include that discretionary administrative decisions are often very important to the individuals affected (eg, a decision to deport a person from the UK on the grounds that his removal from the UK is conducive to the public good) and that effective implementation of policies, therefore, requires that officials make the right choices when exercising discretion. Unfortunately, there is not space to consider the arguments in detail in this chapter, but it is worth making the point that appeal or review on the merits is already well established in UK public administration. There is a right of appeal on the merits to an independent tribunal in many areas of public administration including all of the high volume decision-making systems (eg, social security, taxation, and immigration control). From a theoretical perspective it might seem that appeal or review on the merits is the 'gold standard' for citizens' remedies. The development of public policy suggests that it is also the default standard for remedies in UK public administration. Given that, I suggest that the onus should be on those who oppose allowing citizens to challenge decisions on the merits in any particular administrative context to justify that. In the rest of this chapter, I will, therefore, proceed on that assumption that the citizen should have the right to appeal against, or seek review of, an adverse decision on the merits.

The Characteristics of Administrative Justice Remedies

Before explaining the development of administrative remedies in the UK, it is helpful to compare the characteristics of the different types of citizens' remedy that have been used. I suggest that it is useful to consider five key characteristics when comparing remedies. One is, as noted above, the scope for challenging administrative decisions (fact, law or merits) which I will call the decision criteria. The others are whether the remedy is independent of the administration; whether decisions are binding; the methods used; and the degree of formality. The UK has developed five main types of remedy for citizens in dispute with public bodies each of which has a different mix of the five key characteristics.[5] Those types are:

— Adjudication in the ordinary courts
— Adjudication in tribunals
— public inquiries
— Internal complaints and review processes of public bodies
— Ombudsmen.

The development of public inquiry procedures was an important twentieth-century experiment in dispute resolution but, because their dispute resolution function has been largely confined to planning and other contexts affecting land use, public inquiries will not be discussed further in this chapter.[6]

---

[5] For a more detailed analysis along these lines, see T Mullen, 'A Holistic Approach to Administrative Justice?' in M Adler (ed), *Administrative Justice in Context* (Oxford, Hart Publishing, 2010).

[6] For a useful discussion of inquiries, see C Harlow and R Rawlings, *Law and Administration*, 3rd edn (Cambridge, Cambridge University Press, 2009) ch 13.

The characteristics of the other four remedies are summarised in Table 1 below.

Table 1: Key characteristics of redress mechanisms

	Independent	Decisions binding	Decision criteria	Method/ procedure	Formality
Courts	Yes	Yes	Legality	Adversarial Written and oral	High
Tribunals	Yes	Yes	Legality and merits	Adversarial/ inquisitorial Mainly oral	Variable, but tends to be low compared with courts
Internal complaints/ review	No	Yes	Legality, merits and maladministration	Inquisitorial Usually written	Low
Ombudsmen	Yes	No	Maladministration and injustice[7]	Inquisitorial Written	Low

To expand on the table, the ordinary courts have a high degree of independence from the administration, their decisions are binding, they make decisions according to the relevant law and the facts of the case, their methods are adversarial and their proceedings have traditionally exhibited a high degree of formality both in the sense that there are complex procedures to follow and in the sense that the tone of any hearings is formal (wigs, gowns, the style of courtrooms, legal language etc). Most tribunals share the first three characteristics with the difference that they frequently consider the merits of cases as well as questions of fact and law. Where they have tended to differ from the ordinary courts (there are significant exceptions) is in adopting a more inquisitorial approach and their proceedings have been less formal both in the sense that procedures are less complex than in the ordinary courts, and in the sense that the tone of hearings is less formal.

Ombudsmen share only one of the above characteristics with courts and tribunals, namely their independence from the administration. Their decisions are not binding, being merely recommendations to the body complained about. Their decision criteria are different from those used by courts and tribunals. The public sector ombudsmen may uphold a complaint where the complainant has sustained injustice in consequence of 'maladministration'. This formula does not permit a full-scale inquiry into the merits of decisions,[8] but provided both

---

[7] Some ombudsmen are also empowered to examine 'service failure'. See, eg, Scottish Public Services Ombudsman Act 2002, s 5.

[8] For discussion of the meaning of 'maladministration', see M Seneviratne, *Ombudsmen: Public Services and Administrative Justice*, 2nd edn (London, Butterworths, 2002) 115–18 and Parliamentary and

maladministration and injustice can be established, an ombudsman may uphold a complaint even though there has been no specific error of fact or law. Moreover, their remit goes beyond challenging decisions (which is all that courts and tribunals can do) and extends into to non-decisional failings in public administration such as rudeness, insensitivity and undue delay. Their methods are thoroughly inquisitorial and are backed by statutory power to compel witnesses and disclosure of documents. They may also be regarded as relatively informal both in the sense that procedures are not complex and that, as there are typically no hearings, information is gathered from complainants and witnesses by interview and correspondence.

Internal review and complaints procedures operated by public bodies are, by definition, not independent. Given that, it makes little sense to ask whether the decisions made are binding; suffice to say that public bodies are generally free to change decisions adverse to the citizens affected provided they do not act unlawfully in so doing. Methods are generally inquisitorial and procedures informal. Most are non-statutory but some are statutory.

In addition to the four main types of citizen's remedy, there are various hybrids (such as the former Independent Review Service for the Social Fund)[9] and other hard to classify arrangements. However, space does not permit discussion of these. Having explained the nature of citizens' remedies against the administration, in the next section I explain how this pattern of remedies developed.

The Development of Citizens' Remedies

Historical Development of Remedies

If we go back to the mid-nineteenth century, we find that there were two principal avenues for pursuing grievances against administrative bodies: the courts and elected representatives. Claims might be made in the courts for breach of private law rights or by way of judicial review although that remedy was in England and Wales limited to the High Court.[10] Individuals might also ask their MP to pursue a grievance against a government department. Since then, a variety of alternatives has developed.[11] The first to emerge was the public inquiry which grew out

---

Health Services Ombudsman, *Principles of Good Administration* (2009), available at: www.ombudsman. org.uk/__data/assets/pdf_file/0013/1039/0188-Principles-of-Good-Administration-bookletweb.pdf.

[9] The discretionary Social Fund was abolished with effect from April 2013.

[10] The supervisory jurisdiction was exercised by the Court of Session in Scotland and in Northern Ireland by its High Court.

[11] For a brief overview of the development of remedies in general, see *Administrative Justice in Scotland* (n 3) paras 3.1–3.21 and P Craig, *Administrative Law*, 7th edn (London, Sweet & Maxwell, 2012). On the development of tribunals, see R Wraith and P Hutchesson, *Administrative Tribunals*

of private Bill procedure in Parliament. Also, in the nineteenth century, the pre-
cursors of tribunals emerged.[12] The modern type of tribunal began to emerge
before the First World War and proliferated throughout the twentieth century.
From the 1960s onwards, a series of ombudsmen was created to deal with complaints against public bodies. More recently still, public bodies in general have
been strongly encouraged to have in-house complaints procedures covering all
their functions and in some cases there is a statutory requirement to operate complaints procedures. Also, in a number of contexts, public authorities were given a
statutory obligation to review their own decisions.[13]

One of the key drivers of the development of citizens' remedies since the
late nineteenth century has been a perception held by government policymakers that courts were not suitable for resolving the disputes that arose from modern schemes of public administration. They were thought to be slow, excessively
formal, disproportionately costly, and the judges lacking in relevant expertise and
unsympathetic to much regulatory and social welfare legislation and so likely
to interpret it contrary to its intent.[14] These concerns were echoed by the trade
unions when they were influential in the policy process and by the Labour Party.[15]
However, although the desire to bypass the courts was common to many policy
areas, the actual development of citizens' remedies was ad hoc and remedies were
created in piecemeal fashion. Thus, separate tribunals were created for each area
of public administration where an alternative to the courts was desired by policymakers. The main reason for this was that responsibility for tribunals rested with
the departments responsible for the relevant area of policy. There was no central
point within government for considering policy on tribunals generally, far less
administrative justice as a whole. Even after the Franks Committee laid down general principles,[16] tribunals continued to differ from one another in many respects.

This led to the criticism that what had developed was a complex and disorderly
landscape of administrative justice with several defects.[17] One was that different

---

(London, Allen & Unwin/Royal Institute of Public Administration, 1973). On public inquiries, see
R Wraith and P Lamb, *Public Inquiries as an Instrument of Government* (London, Allen & Unwin, 1971).
On ombudsmen, see Seneviratne (n 8) 40–44.

[12] C Stebbings, *Legal Foundations of Tribunals in Nineteenth Century England* (Cambridge,
Cambridge University Press, 2006).

[13] See, eg, s 202 of the Housing Act 1996 which gives an applicant for assistance under the homelessness legislation the right to request a review of any adverse decision by the relevant local authority.

[14] See, eg, *Administrative Justice in Scotland* (n 3) para 3.5; HW Arthur, *'Without the Law': Administrative Justice and Legal Pluralism in Nineteenth-Century England* (Toronto, University of Toronto
Press, 1985) 144–46; Wraith and Hutchesson (n 11) 33.

[15] C Harlow and R Rawlings, *Law and Administration*, 1st edn (London, Weidenfeld & Nicolson,
1984) 71–72.

[16] *Report of the Committee on Administrative Tribunals and Enquiries* (Cmnd 218, 1957).

[17] See, eg, C Harlow and R Rawlings, *Law and Administration*, 2nd edn (London, Butterworths,
1997); Department for Constitutional Affairs, *Transforming Public Services: Complaints Redress and
Tribunals* (Cm 6243, 2004). On tribunals specifically, see the Leggatt Report, *Tribunals for Users* (2001),
available at: webarchive.nationalarchives.gov.uk/+/; www.tribunals-review.org.uk/leggatthtm/leg-ov.
htm.

decisions were subject to different types of remedy, for example, some decisions were subject to appeals on the merits to a tribunal. Other decisions were only subject to judicial review. For some grievances, no judicial remedy was available but there was a right to complain to an ombudsman. There seemed to be no clear or good rationale for the choice of remedies in different areas. Another criticism was that even where analogous decisions were subject to remedies of the same general type, there were differences in important details of those remedies. Thus, there was no uniform model for tribunals; they differed in their composition, time limits for appealing and procedures. The 2004 White Paper, *Transforming Public Services: Complaints Redress and Tribunals* (2004)[18] summed up the development of citizens' remedies by saying that, 'Administrative justice can be described as a system but it was not created as a system and no coherent design or design principle has ever been applied systematically to it. It is a patchwork'.[19] In fact, a trend towards rationalisation of administrative justice remedies had already begun with the Leggatt inquiry. The recommendations of the Leggatt inquiry in its report, *Tribunals for Users* (2001) which sought to make the tribunal 'system' more coherent and user-friendly, were largely accepted by the Government and enacted by the Tribunals, Courts and Enforcement Act 2007 (TCEA). TCEA replaced many existing specialist tribunals with a unified tribunal structure comprised of a new First-tier Tribunal and a new (mainly appellate) Upper Tribunal. The restructuring affected predominantly tribunals whose jurisdiction covered the whole of the UK or Great Britain or England and Wales. It did not apply to devolved tribunals. However, the Scottish Government is implementing a similar reform with regard to devolved tribunals in Scotland,[20] and rationalisation of devolved tribunals in Northern Ireland is also proposed.[21]

Ombudsmen have also been rationalised. Devolution of government to Scotland, Wales and Northern Ireland provided an opportunity to rethink the existing structure. The Scottish Public Services Ombudsman (SPSO) was created in 2002 as a 'one-stop-shop' for complaints of maladministration in all devolved public services.[22] A similar approach was taken in Wales with the establishment of the Public Services Ombudsman for Wales in 2006[23] and in Northern Ireland with the Northern Ireland Ombudsman.[24] Those reforms left England as the only 'nation' in the UK without a rationalised ombudsman service. However, the Cabinet Office has recently published a consultation proposing a new single Public

---

[18] *Transforming Public Services: Complaints Redress and Tribunals* (Cm 6243, 2004).

[19] ibid, para 4.21.

[20] See Tribunals (Scotland) Act 2014.

[21] Department of Justice NI, *Future Administration and Structure of Tribunals in Northern Ireland—Consultative Document* (2013), available at: www.dojni.gov.uk/index/public-consultations/archive-consultations/tribunal-reform-in-northern-ireland-consultation.pdf.

[22] See the Scottish Public Services Ombudsman Act 2002.

[23] See the Public Services Ombudsman (Wales) Act 2005.

[24] The offices of the Northern Ireland Commissioner for Complaints and the Assembly Ombudsman for Northern Ireland operate as a single complaints service under this title.

Service Ombudsman to replace the Parliamentary Ombudsman,[25] the Health Service Commissioner, and the Local Government Ombudsman.[26]

The 2004 White Paper, mentioned above was infused with the rationalising spirit. It was the first government document to analyse the field of administrative justice as a whole, and envisaged a broad rethinking of administrative justice encompassing initial decision-making as well as appeals and complaints. The White Paper suggested that the Government wanted to develop a new approach labelled 'proportionate dispute resolution'. This meant adopting a strategy which,[27]

> turns on its head the Department's traditional emphasis first on courts, judges and court procedure, and second on legal aid to pay mainly for litigation lawyers. It starts instead with the real world problems people face. The aim is to develop a range of policies and services that, so far as possible, will help people to avoid problems and legal disputes in the first place; and where they cannot, provides tailored solutions to resolve the dispute as quickly and cost-effectively as possible. It can be summed up as 'Proportionate Dispute Resolution'.[28]

The menu of possible options for dispute resolution included adjudication, arbitration, conciliation, early neutral evaluation, mediation, negotiation and ombudsmen. Adjudication and ombudsmen were long-established processes for dispute resolution in the field of administrative justice, but the others were not. The broader vision is discussed further below.

Despite the growth of these alternatives, the courts remain significant administrative justice institutions because of the availability of judicial review and statutory rights of appeal. The courts in England and Wales had already had a major overview following the Woolf report in the 1990s, although judicial review reform was not a major issue in that review. However, procedures for judicial review in England and Wales were reformed in 2000 following the Bowman report.[29] More recently, Lord Gill led a review of the civil courts in Scotland, which included recommendations on judicial review, and many of its recommendations (including on judicial review) are being implemented by the Courts and Tribunals (Scotland) Act 2014.

Advice, Assistance and Representation

As noted above, much of the development in remedies that took place in the twentieth century was predicated on the assumption that disputes between citizen and

---

[25] Formally known as the Parliamentary Commissioner for Administration.

[26] Formally known as the Commission for Local Administration in England.

[27] Cm 6243, para 2.2. For discussion, See M Adler, 'Tribunal Reform: Proportionate Dispute Resolution and the Pursuit of Administrative Justice' (2006) 69 *Modern Law Review* 958.

[28] The 'department' referred to was the Department of Constitutional Affairs, previously the Lord Chancellor's Department and now the Ministry of Justice.

[29] Lord Chancellor's Department, *Review of the Crown Office List* (2000).

state were better dealt with by bodies other than the ordinary courts. The second important assumption affecting administrative justice remedies was that citizens who were in dispute with the state could reasonably be expected to use such 'alternative' remedies themselves rather than rely on lawyers or others to present their cases on their behalf. Alternative remedies were in general thought to provide do-it-yourself justice; lawyers were only needed in the courts. In the case of tribunals it was claimed that a combination of informality, freedom from technicality and the ability of the tribunal to take an inquisitorial approach meant that the unrepresented appellant should not be disadvantaged. That explained the fact that, although there were a few exceptions, legal aid was not available for representation at most tribunal hearings and, more generally, the absence of any coordinated programme of public funding for advice and representation for those in dispute with the state. The perception that it was possible to design user-friendly processes which citizens could use to present cases themselves was later applied to the courts as well when the small claims procedure was created for the county court in 1973.[30]

However giving advice, assistance and representation in many areas of administrative law was never a monopoly of lawyers. Trade unions played a significant role in providing representation at industrial tribunals and in tribunals dealing with certain social security benefits. Citizens Advice Bureaux have long been an important source of advice on social security benefits and in other areas. Local authorities developed advice services and in the 1980s local authority welfare rights services became a major source of advice and representation in social security appeal tribunals. A wide variety of third-sector organisations, often concentrating on specific client groups such as the homeless or disabled persons has over time provided advice, guidance and support and sometime also representation.

Having said that much legal advice and much representation is provided by non-lawyers, it is important to note that lawyers have been a substantial source of advice and representation in certain areas, for example, immigration control in which legal representation at tribunals has long been common. There has been significant public funding specifically for advice from lawyers on administrative law matters since legal advice and assistance was added to the legal aid scheme. Thereafter, the key distinction was that between legal advice and general legal help on the one hand, and on the other representation at oral hearings. Representation at hearings was typically funded in the ordinary courts but not in most tribunals. Although there were exceptions and the extent of these varied over time, it remained true that legal aid was widely available for representation at hearings in courts but not in tribunals, and this could be traced back to the assumption that citizens did not in general need representation at tribunals.

---

[30] Using powers conferred by the County Courts Act 1959, s 59. Analogous procedures were created in the sheriff court in Scotland and the county court in Northern Ireland.

The Leggatt review of tribunals provided an opportunity to reconsider this assumption but Leggatt reaffirmed the established view as did the 2004 White Paper which underpinned the TCEA tribunal reforms. So, into the twenty-first century, the governing assumption has remained that citizens are in general able to represent themselves in tribunals and in small claims in the county court and in various other non-court fora.[31]

The State of Administrative Justice
Before the 2010–15 Coalition

The 2010 General Election represented a significant watershed for administrative justice. Since 2010 the Government's attitude to administrative justice appears to have changed, and the majority of policy developments in administrative justice have decreased rather than improved access to justice. It is, therefore, worth summarising the position that had been arrived at immediately before the 2010 General Election, as regards the availability and use of citizens' remedies.[32]

A right of appeal to a court or to an independent tribunal on the merits was available in many areas of public administration including most of the high volume decision-making functions (eg, immigration control, social security). In some other cases, there was a right of appeal to a court or tribunal restricted to points of law. However, there remained a number of decision-making functions in respect of which there was no right of appeal to a court or tribunal, leaving judicial review as the only judicial remedy.

The great majority of functions could also be made the subject of a complaint to the body which made the decision. Complaints procedures generally allowed citizens to complain about non-decisional matters such as delay, rudeness, and insensitivity, but might also give the opportunity to question the correctness of a decision. Some complaints procedures routed complaints to an independent body or incorporated an independent element; most did not. Many complaints could also be addressed to an ombudsman, but the statutory ombudsmen generally required that lower-level complaints procedures be exhausted first.

The gaps in this system were that some decisions on important matters were not subject to an appeal on the merits to an independent judicial body, for example, community care decisions.[33] In other areas of public administration in

---

[31] Leggatt Report (n 17) para 4.21; *Transforming Public Services* (n 17) ch 10. Representation has been less of an issue in relation to ombudsmen.

[32] At the time of writing, the Coalition has been replaced by a majority Conservative government following the 2015 General Election.

[33] See also AJTC Scottish Committee, *Right to Appeal* (2012), available at: ajtc.justice.gov.uk/docs/decisons_with_no_apeal__web_final.pdf.

which there was an independent tribunal to hear appeals, certain decisions were not appealable (eg, immigration control). Similarly, some rights of appeal were restricted to a point of law (homelessness) whereas others extended to the merits (most tribunals).

Neither the possibility of judicial review nor of complaining to an ombudsman could be considered a satisfactory substitute for appeal or review on the merits. On an application for judicial review, the court can review only the legality of the decision and not its merits. Not only is the court excluded from considering the substantive merits, but also the scope for review of the facts is very limited.[34] These limitations are particularly important as the evidence from tribunal adjudication suggests that many successful appeals result from the introduction of new evidence, the tribunal taking a different view of the facts or the substantive merits from the original decision-maker rather than from identifying errors of law.[35] Moreover, judicial review, being confined to the High Court, is an expensive procedure and this would exclude many people who were neither poor enough to qualify for legal aid nor rich enough to contemplate financing a High Court action.

Complaint to an ombudsman is not equivalent to appeal or review on the merits for two reasons. The first is that ombudsmen's decisions are not binding. The second is that the scope for challenging decisions (ie, the need to prove maladministration causing injustice) is not entirely clear. The term 'maladministration' has never been precisely defined,[36] but it is clear that in practice ombudsmen exercise more restraint in second guessing initial decisions than do tribunals. There may have been good reasons for some of the remaining gaps in the system of remedies, and for the differences between different administrative programmes, but UK governments had never clearly articulated principles for the choice or design of grievance redress institutions.[37] Policy development had certainly become less ad hoc in the first decade of the twenty-first century, but 'ad-hocery' had not been banished. More fundamentally, successive governments had not fully pursued the logic of any model of administrative justice. In the twentieth century, the dominant aim was that of providing informal justice through a series of alternatives to the courts. This was meant to be do-it-yourself justice but we never reached the point where citizens could use remedies effectively themselves across the full spectrum of administrative law. The alternatives were certainly less formal and in some cases less expensive than the courts but they were not user-friendly

---

[34] *E v Secretary of State for the Home Department* [2004] EWCA Civ 49, [2004] QB 1044.

[35] See the Report by the President of the Social Entitlement Chamber of the First-tier Tribunal, *President's Report 2007/2008* (Tribunals Service, 2008), available at: www.judiciary.gov.uk/wp-content/uploads/JCO/Documents/Reports/president-appeal-tribunals-report-2008-09.pdf.

[36] Seneviratne (n 8) 40–44.

[37] V Bondy and A Le Sueur, *Designing Redress: A Study about Grievances against Public Bodies* (London, Public Law Project, 2012), available at: www.publiclawproject.org.uk/resources/123/designing-redress-a-study-about-grievances-against-public-bodies.

enough for citizens to do without advisers and advocates. Either the remedies had to be made even more user-friendly or there had to be a more systematic approach to advice and representation. Neither was forthcoming.

Administrative Justice: Coalition Policies and the Effect of Austerity

We can now consider the approach taken to administrative justice by the Coalition Government of 2010–15 including the effect of austerity policies. This section of the chapter identifies a number of areas in which access to justice has, or may have been, weakened since 2010. The main developments were: (1) the failure to pursue the holistic approach to administrative justice, including failure to attach any attention priority to 'right first time'; (2) the attempt to weaken judicial review; (3) important rights of appeal have been removed (in immigration cases); (4) a failure to address those areas in which there were not adequate remedies; (5) in areas where there had been satisfactory remedies, new obstacles to their use have been created (in particular mandatory reconsideration in social security); and (6) cuts in legal aid and a decline in the availability of advice, assistance and representation to citizens in dispute with the state. Whilst it is relatively straightforward to identify the adverse effects on access to justice of the changes to citizens' remedies, it is less easy in some cases to establish that those changes are the product of austerity, as opposed to changes the incoming government might have introduced even if economic circumstances had been more favourable.

The Holistic Vision of Administrative Justice

As described above, the 2004 White Paper promised a new approach to administrative justice. The only major reform delivered by the time of the change of government in 2010 was the restructuring of tribunals. Little progress was made on the rest of the agenda—experimenting with remedies, improving initial decision-making etc. The only other specific change was the creation of the Administrative Justice and Tribunals Council (AJTC) which replaced the Council on Tribunals. This meant that for the first time there was a body with responsibility for oversight of administrative justice as a whole. The Council did some good work but its influence on government was limited and it was abolished like many other public bodies by the Coalition Government under the Public Bodies Act 2011.[38] More generally, the Coalition Government between 2010 and 2015 showed little interest in the broader agenda of administrative justice reform set out in the 2004 White

---

[38] With effect from 19 August 2013. For analysis, see M Adler, 'The Rise and Fall of Administrative Justice: A Cautionary Tale' (2012) 8 *Socio-Legal Review* 28.

Paper. The Ministry of Justice did publish a strategy document in December 2012, but this has not had substantial consequences.[39]

The abolition of the AJTC, strongly criticised by the Public Administration Committee,[40] was a backward step, not only because it removed the only point in the system of government that considered administrative justice as a whole, but also because it removed an important source of independent scrutiny of administrative justice policy, confirming its status as the 'Cinderella' of the justice system.[41] It can be regarded as a consequence of austerity politics as, although the Government stated that its principal objective in cutting the number of quangos was to improve democratic accountability, it also emphasised the benefits of reducing public expenditure[42] and conceded that the decision to abolish the AJTC did not reflect adversely on the work that it had done.

Undermining Judicial Review

Judicial review is clearly not the most important citizens' remedy in terms of quantity; the number of judicial reviews in any year is dwarfed by the number of appeals taken to tribunals. Moreover, immigration control is the only area of public administration that generates a large number of judicial reviews every year. Nor is it clear how far it exercises a more diffuse positive effect on public administration by articulating standards of good administration and influencing decision-makers to adopt them. Much of the literature on the impact of judicial review is sceptical of the suggestion that it has much impact on routine decision-making in public administration.[43] However, it is an important part of the administrative justice system because, as an inherent jurisdiction of the court, it can provide a remedy where no other remedy is available, even if that remedy is limited to questions of legality.

Moreover, we must consider the quality as well as the quantity of judicial reviews. Most judicial reviews have no legal implications for anyone other than the parties. However, a significant minority are in effect challenges to policy. Judicial review

---

[39] Administrative Justice and Tribunals: A Strategic Work Programme 2013–16, available at: www.gov.uk/government/uploads/system/uploads/attachment_data/file/217315/admin-justice-tribs-strategic-work-programme.pdf.

[40] Public Administration Select Committee, *Future Oversight of Administrative Justice: The Proposed Abolition of The Administrative Justice and Tribunals Council*, Twenty First Report (HC 2010–12, 1621), available at: www.publications.parliament.uk/pa/cm201012/cmselect/cmpubadm/1621/1621.pdf.

[41] Written evidence submitted by the AJTC to the Public Administration Select Committee inquiry into Oversight of Administrative Justice, available at: www.parliament.uk/documents/commons-committees/public-administration/written-evidence-OAJ.pdf.

[42] HC Deb 14 October 2010, vol 516, col 506.

[43] See, eg, S Halliday, *Judicial Review and Compliance with Administrative Law* (Oxford, Hart Publishing, 2003) and the essays in M Hertogh and S Halliday (eds), *Judicial Review And Bureaucratic Impact: International and Interdisciplinary Perspectives* (Cambridge, Cambridge University Press, 2004).

has increasingly become a vehicle for challenging policy developments whose legality is unclear. Some of these cases are challenges to one-off policy decisions with no immediate implications for other decisions, for example, the attempt to review the decision by the Director of the Serious Fraud Office not to continue an investigation into corruption in arms sales to Saudi Arabia.[44] Such cases can be regarded as reinforcing the rule of law in the sense of ensuring that the executive governs lawfully. However, other cases have involved policies which govern large numbers of decisions and, therefore, had the potential to affect large numbers of people who were adversely affected by a policy which has been struck down. One recent example is provided by *R (Reilly) v Secretary of State for Work and Pensions*[45] in which applicants for Jobseeker's Allowance successfully challenged the existing approach to compulsory employment training for claimants which required them to undertake an unpaid work experience placement. Another is provided by *R (Alvi) v Secretary of State for the Home Department*[46] in which the Supreme Court effectively invalidated a policy of refusing entry clearances to enter the UK for employment unless the job the applicant was coming to appeared on the list of skilled occupations used by the Home Office on the basis that the list did not appear in the Immigration Rules presented to Parliament. Many others could have been cited.[47] It is important to note that, whereas some of these cases were test cases brought in the name of individuals with a direct interest (although often supported by interest groups), others were brought by public interest advocates with no personal stake in the outcome, an increasingly common phenomenon.

The extent to which the affected section of the public ultimately benefits will, of course, vary. Sometimes, there is no long-term gain, for example, where the executive reconsiders the matter following judicial review but is able to reinstate the original policy. However, this is clearly, in principle, a constitutionally important function for judicial review. We must, therefore be concerned if judicial review becomes less available to citizens both because individuals directly affected by decisions may not have access to a remedy and because challenges to unlawful policies which govern many decisions may become less likely or be delayed.

Judicial review came under sustained attack during the 2010–05 Coalition Government. This was not the first time government ministers had attempted to constrain judicial review. As Thomas reminds us in his chapter,[48] in 2003–04

---

[44] *Regina (Corner House Research) v Director of the Serious Fraud Office* [2008] UKHL 60, [2009] 1 AC 756. The application for judicial review succeeded in the High Court but failed in the House of Lords.

[45] *R (Reilly) v Secretary of State for Work and Pensions* [2013] UKSC 68, [2014] AC 453.

[46] *R (Alvi) v Secretary of State for the Home Department* [2012] UKSC 33, [2012] 1 WLR 2208.

[47] See, eg, decisions challenging aspects of the Housing Benefit Regulations abolishing the spare room subsidy (popularly known as the 'bedroom tax'): *R. (Cotton) v Secretary of State for Work and Pensions* [2014] EWHC 3437 (Admin); *R (A) v Secretary of State for Work and Pensions* [2015] EWHC 159 (Admin); *R (Hardy) v Sandwell MBC* [2015] EWHC 890 (Admin).

[48] R Thomas, 'Immigration and Access to Justice: A Critical Analysis of Recent Restrictions, chapter 6 in this volume.

David Blunkett, the Home Secretary reacted angrily to judicial reviews overturning Home Office decisions in asylum cases. This led the Government to try to insulate Home Office decision-making from review with an extraordinarily drafted ouster clause in the Asylum and Immigration (Treatment of Claimants, etc) Bill. However, the clause excited widespread opposition and was eventually withdrawn.[49] The key differences between the Coalition's attack on judicial review and earlier examples are that it was conducted across a much wider front and that it has led to significant changes in the judicial review process.

The Coalition Government's concerns were set out in two consultation papers, *Judicial Review: proposals for reform*[50] and *Judicial Review: proposals for further reform*[51] and in the Government's responses to the consultations.[52] The case for reform set out in these documents was that judicial review was being abused in some cases. There were too many weak cases lacking legal merit, and judicial review was being used as a delaying tactic in cases with no reasonable prospect of success. In some cases it was stifling innovation and frustrating reforms, including reforms aimed at stimulating growth and promoting economic recovery. Judicial review was being used inappropriately as a campaign tactic, ie, used merely to generate publicity or express opposition to the policies of the elected government. The Government also emphasised that some weak applications were funded by the taxpayer through the expense incurred by the defendant public authority, the cost of court resources and in some cases legal aid costs. These abuses of judicial review were causing congestion and delay in the courts, adding to the costs of public services and having an adverse impact on economic recovery and growth (ie, when delaying infrastructure proposals).[53] Despite an overwhelmingly negative response from consultees the Government pressed ahead with a number of reforms, some being achieved by secondary legislation and others by provisions of the Criminal Justice and Courts Act 2015 (the 2015 Act).

The reforms consulted on were:

—   Reducing the time limits for bringing a judicial review in planning and procurement cases and streamlining the process for handling challenges to planning decisions.

---

[49]   R Rawlings, 'Review, Revenge and Retreat' (2005) 68 *Modern Law Review* 378.

[50]   Ministry of Justice, *Judicial Review: proposals for reform* (Cm 8515, 2012), available at: consult.justice.gov.uk/digital-communications/judicial-review-reform/supporting_documents/judicialreviewreform.pdf.

[51]   Ministry of Justice, *Judicial Review: proposals for further reform* (Cm 8703, 2013), available at: www.gov.uk/government/uploads/system/uploads/attachment_data/file/264091/8703.pdf.

[52]   Ministry of Justice, *Reform of Judicial Review: the Government Response* (Cm 8611, 2013), available at: www.gov.uk/government/uploads/system/uploads/attachment_data/file/228535/8611.pdf; and Ministry of Justice, *Judicial Review: Proposals for Further Reform: the Government Response* (Cm 8811, 2014), available at: consult.justice.gov.uk/digital-communications/judicial-review/results/judicial-review---proposals-for-further-reform-government-response.pdf.

[53]   These criticisms are summarised in the forewords to the four command papers.

— Limiting the right of local authorities to challenge decisions on nationally significant infrastructure projects.
— Removing the right to an oral reconsideration of a refusal of permission where the case is assessed by a judge as totally without merit.
— Refusing a remedy where a successful judicial review would be highly likely not to bring any substantive benefit to the claimant (the 'no difference argument') and possibly refusing permission to seek judicial review on that basis.
— Revising the rules of standing in public interest cases.
— Considering alternatives to judicial review to enforce the Public Sector Equality Duty (PSED).
— Restricting legal aid payments to cases in which permission is granted and restricting legal aid for planning challenges.
— Changes to the costs rules (relating to wasted costs orders; protective costs orders; awarding costs against third-party interveners and non-parties; costs of oral permission hearings).
— Changing the rules for leapfrog appeals.
— Increasing fees.[54]

In the event the Government decided not to proceed with several of the proposals, including the proposals for a stricter test for standing and limiting the right of local authorities to challenge decisions on national infrastructure projects. It deferred the question of alternative remedies for enforcing the PSED for consideration, along with other issues relating to the PSED, by the Government Equalities Office.[55] However, it did implement most of the other recommendations and I will briefly review a selection of these.

Planning Cases Etc

The time limits for bringing a judicial review in planning and procurement cases were reduced from three months to six weeks and 30 days respectively.[56] A planning fast track using specialist planning judges was introduced in the Administrative Court on 1 July 2013 designed to identify planning cases as early as possible, to give them priority and ensure they progress swiftly through the system. A permission filter for challenges under the statutory review provisions analogous to that for judicial review was introduced.[57] These changes were designed to address the Government's concerns about adverse impact of judicial review on economic recovery and growth.

---

[54] This was the subject of a separate consultation: Ministry of Justice, *Court Fees: Proposals for reform* (Cm 8751, 2013).

[55] Cm 8811 (n 52).

[56] Changes made with effect from 1 July 2013 by amendment of the Civil Procedure Rules.

[57] ss 91 and 92 of the Criminal Justice and Courts Act, amending ss 288 and 289 of the Town and Country Planning Act 1990.

Weak Cases

Where a judge assesses a claim as totally without merit, the claimant no longer has the right to oral renewal of the application.[58]

Minor Procedural Defects

Two reforms were made to the process of judicial review to address this concern.[59] First, the court must refuse to grant relief on an application for judicial review if it appears to the court to be highly likely that the outcome for the applicant would not have been substantially different if the conduct complained of had not occurred. Second, the High Court must refuse to grant leave for judicial review if it appears highly likely that the outcome for the applicant would not have been substantially different if the conduct complained of had not occurred. It may consider this question of its own motion and must do so if the defendant asks it. However, in either case that requirement may be disregarded for reasons of exceptional public interest, but the court must so certify if it invokes the public interest exception.

Costs

There have been several changes to the costs regime in judicial review dealing. There are new requirements relating to disclosure of financial resources by applicants[60] and the court may award costs against persons who are not parties to proceedings on the basis that they are providing financial support for the purposes of the proceedings or are likely or able to do so.[61]

There are new restrictions on cost capping.[62] A costs capping order may be made only if leave to apply for judicial review has been granted, and the court may make a costs capping order only if satisfied that: (i) the proceedings are public interest proceedings; (ii) in the absence of the order, the applicant for judicial review would withdraw the application for judicial review or cease to participate in the proceedings; and (iii) it would be reasonable for the applicant for judicial review to do so. The section goes on to define 'public interest proceedings' and to state matters to which the court must have regard when deciding whether proceedings are public interest proceedings. These provisions are largely a restatement of the existing position but, worryingly, the Lord Chancellor may by regulations amend this section by adding, omitting or amending matters to which the court must

---

[58] Change made with effect from 1 July 2013 by amendment of the Civil Procedure Rules.
[59] Criminal Justice and Courts Act 2015, s 84.
[60] ibid, s 85.
[61] ibid, s 86.
[62] ibid, ss 88, 89.

have regard when determining whether proceedings are public interest proceedings. The Lord Chancellor may also make regulations excluding from this regime environmental cases which are covered by the Aarhus Convention and the EU Public Participation Directive.

The court may not order a party to pay the intervener's costs save in exceptional circumstances which are to be specified by rules of court. However, the court *must* order an intervener to pay a party's costs that the court considers have been incurred by the relevant party as a result of the intervener's involvement in that stage of the proceedings if any one of four conditions is met. These include that the intervener's evidence and representations, taken as a whole, have not been of significant assistance to the court, and that a significant part of the intervener's evidence and representations relates to matters that it is not necessary for the court to consider in order to resolve the issues that are the subject of that stage in the proceedings. The court does not have to make an order if there are exceptional circumstances. Again, the criteria will be specified by rules of court.

The Government has also implemented the proposal to introduce a principle that the costs of an oral permission hearing should usually be recoverable from an unsuccessful claimant.

Legal Aid

The Government decided to implement the proposal that providers should be paid for work done in relation to an application for permission to seek judicial review only if permission is actually granted by the court. However, the Legal Aid Agency was given discretion to pay providers in some cases concluded prior to a permission decision. This could be done where it considered it is reasonable to do so in the circumstances of the case, taking into account in particular: (i) the reason why the provider did not obtain a costs order or costs agreement in favour of the legally aided person; (ii) the extent to which, and the reason why, the legally aided person obtained the outcome sought in the proceedings; and (iii) the strength of the application for permission at the time it was filed, based on the law and on the facts which the provider knew or ought to have known at that time.[63]

Fees

The Government proposed various fee increases on the basis that the existing fees did not reflect the costs incurred in proceedings.[64] The various fee proposals are

---

[63] See the Civil Legal Aid (Remuneration) (Amendment) (No 3) Regulations 2014, SI 2014/607.

[64] Ministry of Justice, *Court Fees: Proposals for Reform Part One Consultation Response: Cost Recovery* (Cm 8845, 2014) paras 62–65.

being considered as part of the wider review of civil court fees that the Government has been undertaking.

Evaluation of Judicial Review Changes

The Government's attempts to reform the judicial review process have been highly controversial.[65] The first criticism is that the evidence base for its claim that abuse of judicial review is a substantial problem is slight. Neither the first nor the second consultation contained a serious analysis of the supposed problems, far less a convincing case that they were substantial enough to require reform of the process. The second consultation presented two case studies of unsuccessful applications for judicial review chosen to illustrate the adverse effect of judicial review on economic development and its abuse as a tactic in a political campaign, but there was nothing to indicate that these were in any way representative of judicial review applications generally. Some statistical data was presented, including the level of applications, growth over time, rates at which applications for leave are granted and oral hearings. However, there was little by way of analysis to accompany it and it was hard to see that it proved anything. The Public Law Project—with good reason—accused the Government of 'relying on anecdotal and impressionistic evidence' and employing 'misleading and inaccurate statistics'.[66] The analysis of withdrawn applications provides a good example of evidence-free speculation. The paper noted that over 40 per cent of all applications lodged in 2012 were withdrawn before consideration of permission by the court. It went on to say that, although the reasons for withdrawal are not recorded and there was some evidence to suggest that many of these cases may be settled on terms favourable to the claimant, 'The Government wants to be sure that there are not also cases where the respondent concedes simply because they are unwilling to face the delays and costs that a prolonged legal battle can involve'. Yet no evidence whatsoever is offered to support the suggestion that public authorities with arguable cases fail to fight them because of delay and costs. No convincing case was presented that there is a need to reform the judicial review process.

Nonetheless, significant changes have been made to judicial review, some of which are likely to impede access to justice. Thus, for example, the new requirement to consider when granting permission whether the outcome for the applicant would have been substantially different creates a risk that worthwhile cases will be

---

[65] See, eg, Public Law Project, *Response to the Judicial Review: Proposals for Further Reform Consultation*, available at: www.publiclawproject.org.uk/resources/147/public-law-project-response-to-judicial-review-proposals-for-further-reform-consultation. There was a very large number of responses. A summary of responses may be found at: consult.justice.gov.uk/digital-communications/judicial-review/results/judicial-review---proposals-for-further-reform-government-response---annex-a.pdf.

[66] Public Law Project (n 65) paras 7 and 10.

refused permission as the 'no difference' judgment may be somewhat speculative and when made at permission stage will not be based on full consideration of the issues. However, for that reason, judges may be reluctant to refuse permission on this basis. If that does happen, the reform will not have the effect that the Government hoped for.

The decision to drop the proposal to restrict standing must be welcomed, but it should not have been made in the first place. The second consultation amounted to an attempt to de-legitimise the public interest model of judicial review that has developed in recent years.[67] There was no recognition that the courts have developed this model because it performs the valuable constitutional function of ensuring the rule of law by facilitating challenges to executive decisions where challenges based purely on private interests would not be competent or would be unlikely to be brought.[68] Although public interest standing has not been restricted, the new rules permitting costs to be awarded against third-party interveners may deter some useful public interest interventions by making it less likely that protective costs orders will be obtained. This may reduce access to justice for vulnerable groups as public interest cases are often brought on their behalf. The Lord Chancellor's power to amend the 2015 Act by secondary legislation raises the possibility that the availability of cost protection may be reduced in future without adequate parliamentary scrutiny.

However, the most worrying changes are to legal aid; they create a risk that good cases will simply not proceed. The policy of not paying solicitors for work done in relation to an application for permission to seek judicial review unless permission is actually granted by the court creates a risk that they will not be paid for doing a substantial amount of work.[69]

Whilst the outcome of the reform process is not as bad as it could have been, certain proposals having been dropped, it would be wrong to assume that the threat to judicial review has been seen off; the new government may return to the theme that judicial review is being abused and propose further reforms.

Removal of Existing Rights of Appeal

The Coalition Government has drastically reduced rights of appeal to an independent tribunal over large areas of immigration control. Despite its importance, I will

---

[67] See, eg T Mullen, 'Protective Expenses Orders and Public Interest Litigation' (2015) 19 *Edinburgh Law Review* 36.

[68] See, eg, *AXA General Insurance Limited v HM Advocate* [2011] UKSC 46; and J Miles, 'Standing in a Multi-Layered Constitution' in N Bamforth and P Leyland, *Public Law in a Multi-Layered Constitution* (Oxford, Hart Publishing, 2003).

[69] Initially, the Government's changes allowed no discretion to make exceptions to this rule. In *R (Ben Hoare Bell Solicitors) v Lord Chancellor* [2015] EWHC 523 (Admin) the High Court upheld a challenge to the legality of this reform on the basis that the relevant regulation extended so far that it conflicted with and frustrated the purpose of the civil legal aid scheme enacted by Part 1 of LASPO.

deal with this issue briefly as it is discussed in more detail in Thomas' chapter.[70] Immigration appeals were first introduced in 1969.[71] Following the Nationality, Immigration and Asylum Act 2002, appeals lay against most of the important decisions concerning a person's immigration status, including refusal of leave to enter the UK, refusal of entry clearance and decisions to remove or deport. In general, it was also possible to appeal decisions relating to asylum claims although these were subject to a variety of complex rules. This remained true up until 2008 when the Labour Government began a process of restricting appeals which the Coalition Government continued. The process culminated in the Immigration Act 2014 which restricts appeals to the First-tier Tribunal to three situations. These are appeals against:

— Refusal of an asylum or humanitarian protection claim
— Refusal of a human rights claim
— Revocation of refugee or humanitarian protection status.

All of the other decisions made in the administration of immigration control are not subject to appeal. The effect of these provisions is that there will be no appeal, for example, against refusal of visa or entry clearance where the applicant seeks to enter the UK for employment, or as a visitor or against refusal of an application for settlement in the UK or an application by a spouse seeking to join a person already here unless there is a convention right, refugee or humanitarian protection argument to be made. Similarly, there will be no appeal against deportation or removal unless one of these arguments can be made. Restrictions of rights of appeal on this scale are dramatic and unprecedented.

All decisions not subject to appeal are subject to administrative review under the immigration rules.[72] The administrative review procedure was formerly restricted to refusal of applications under the points-based system and is now being extended across the board. Reviews are carried out by officials of the Home Office and so are not independent or a judicial remedy, and the evidence suggests that they are not likely to be an adequate substitute.[73] It is also important to note that, in other contexts in which there is a right of administrative review, it merely postpones access to an independent tribunal; it does not replace it.

The only judicial remedy available to most of those aggrieved by adverse immigration decisions will be an application for judicial review which continues to have the limitations described above.

Amendments to cure the invalidity were made by the Civil Legal Aid (Remuneration) (Amendment) Regulations 2015, SI 2015/898, by adding further exceptions to the general rule that legal aid providers are paid for work done before permission only if permission is actually granted by the court.

[70] Above (n 48).
[71] See the Immigration Appeals Act 1969.
[72] Immigration Rules, Appendix AR, available at: www.gov.uk/government/uploads/system/uploads/attachment_data/file/364777/Immigration_Rules_-_Appendix_AR.pdf.
[73] See R Thomas, above (n 48).

It is worth examining the arguments the Government used to support this change. As Thomas points out in his chapter, the main justification given by government has been that appeal rights are routinely abused by those who have no good case yet seek to prevent or delay their removal from the UK. This claim has not been substantiated. From time to time, the Government has pointed to specific cases which have caused it concern but no systematic analysis of the scale of 'abuse' has ever been presented. Such evidence as there is suggests the contrary, for example, the high rate of success on appeal.[74] If anything, this and other evidence suggests that the most striking defect of this administrative system is the poor quality of initial decision-making.[75] Even if there were evidence that a very large proportion of appeals were groundless, that would not by itself constitute justification for withdrawing appeal rights. The fact that some people abuse a right is hardly a sufficient argument for withdrawing it from all. Withdrawing appeal rights penalises those who have well-founded claims and therefore creates injustice. The argument that some people might abuse the right to an independent determination of a legal claim would not be accepted in any other context. Yet this elementary point has not been addressed by government.

The Government has also failed to explain why it has chosen to withdraw appeal rights rather than to pursue alternative solutions to the 'problem'. These might include improving the gathering of evidence to support the Home Office case and improving the presentation of appeals by the Home Office.

The fact that a convincing case has not been made for such a drastic reduction of appeal rights betrays the real reasons for the measure. Immigration is a politically sensitive matter and removing appeal rights provides a surer way of increasing the proportion of administrative decisions to refuse entry or to remove persons from the UK that are ultimately effective, precisely because those decisions cannot be challenged in an independent forum. It might be objected that aggrieved persons may still seek judicial review which is an independent forum, but given that judicial review is restricted to questions of legality and appeal on the merits will be excluded, it will be likely to correct fewer bad decisions than a right of appeal on the merits. So, although some of those who no longer have rights of appeal will seek judicial review, overall it is likely that far fewer decisions will successfully be challenged than before, thus achieving the Government's goal. So, in this context, political pragmatism has trumped elementary principles of justice.

---

[74] See AJTC, *Securing Fairness and Redress: Administrative Justice at Risk?* (2011), available at: http://ajtc.justice.gov.uk/docs/AJTC_at_risk_(10.11)_web.pdf.

[75] See, eg, National Audit Office, *Improving the Speed and Quality of Asylum Decisions* (HC 2003–04, 535); National Audit Office, *Management of Asylum Applications by the UK Border Agency* (HC 2008–09, 124); Home Affairs Committee, *The Work of the Immigration Directorates (April–September 2013)*, Fifteenth Report (HC 2013–14, 820).

The Failure to Address those Areas in which there were Not Adequate Remedies

As noted above, by 2010, although in many areas of public administration there was a right of appeal to an independent tribunal on the merits against administrative decisions, there remained some decisions in respect of which there was no such appeal. Little progress has been made in addressing this issue since 2010. Examples could be given from several areas, including housing law, but I will illustrate this point by reference to community care policy.

Community Care

Local authorities make a wide variety of decisions under community care legislation many of which may give rise to citizens' grievances. These decisions have been made under the National Assistance Act 1948, the Chronically Sick and Disabled Persons Act 1970, the National Health Service and Community Care Act 1990 and, most recently, the Care Act 2014. The system of community care is to undergo a major overhaul under the Care Act 2014. However, the types of decision made will continue to be broadly the same as before. They will include:

— Assessing a person's need for community care services
— Assessing the needs of carers
— Deciding which services are to be provided
— Deciding whether any services that are provided qualify as 'free personal care'
— Making financial assessments for those personal and nursing care services that have to be paid for. This last includes assessing any residential care contribution and, in relation to care at home, anything which is not 'free personal care'.

In this area remedies have actually been improved. Before the 2014 Act, there was no independent appeal against these decisions. Where it could plausibly be argued that a decision relating to assessment of need or the provision of services was unlawful, the person aggrieved could seek judicial review. The only statutory remedy was to make a complaint under the relevant regulations.[76] This will be replaced by a new grievance system under the 2014 Act. Section 72 of the Act permits the Secretary of State to make regulations providing for appeals against decisions taken by local authorities under Part 1 of the Act. Although the section is not yet in force, the Government has consulted on draft regulations. It proposes a three stage process: (i) early resolution stage; (ii) independent review; and (iii) local authority decision. During the first stage the local authority attempts to resolve the issue locally and early. At the second stage, the local authority appoints an

---

[76] The Local Authority Social Services and National Health Service Complaints (England) Regulations 2009, SI 2009/309.

independent reviewer to review the local authority's original decision and to make a recommendation. The Independent Reviewer is required to review the local authority's decision to ensure it was reasonable with reference to relevant regulations and guidance, the facts of the appeal and taking into account local policy. At the third stage, the local authority makes a decision considering the Independent Reviewer's recommendation. The Independent Reviewer's recommendation is not binding on the local authority so it may reaffirm the original decision.[77] If the decision after appeal remains adverse to the appellant, there is no further redress within the appeals system. Any person wishing to take a grievance further would have to seek judicial review or complain to the Local Government Ombudsman.

Whilst this represents an improvement on the previous system, it is not equivalent to the standard appeal to a tribunal found in many other areas of public administration. Whilst there is an independent element, the process as a whole is not independent because the final decision rests with the local authority. The decision criteria for the Independent Reviewer may also be narrower than the usual tribunal criteria as it is not clear that they extend to the merits of the decision appealed against. It seems clear that the reviewer could treat a decision as flawed for error of law or error of fact, but it is not clear whether the reviewer can substitute his or her own view of what a reasonable decision would be on the facts of the case, or whether his or her role is merely to consider whether the local authority decision falls within the range of reasonable responses. The latter is essentially the *Wednesbury* unreasonableness/irrationality standard used in judicial review. If the latter, more restrictive interpretation is adopted, then the Independent Reviewer's scope for classifying decisions as defective is less than that of the typical tribunal.

The obvious question is why some administrative decisions affecting rights or interests are subject to appeal on the merits in an independent forum yet others are not. It is clearly not a question of relative importance. The decisions described above are of vital importance to the persons concerned. One possible answer may be that the decisions concern the allocation of scarce resources and so the exercise of administrative discretion must take account not only of the circumstances of the applicant's case, but of the actual and potential demand on resources from other applicants to the service. However, this is not a wholly satisfactory explanation for the current pattern of citizens' remedies. For one thing, although it almost certainly has influenced government thinking on particular remedies, it has rarely been clearly articulated by government as the rationale for the design of remedies. Second, whilst the relative priority of an application for assistance out of scarce funds will often be a key consideration, it is not the only issue which goes to the merits, as opposed to the legality of a decision. Claims can be and are refused for reasons unrelated to scarcity or only loosely related to scarcity, for example,

---

[77] This bears a close resemblance to the system already operating in Scotland. See the Social Work (Scotland) Act 1968, s 5B and the Social Work (Representations Procedure) (Scotland) Order 1990, SSI 1990/2519. See also AJTC Scottish Committee, *Right to Appeal* (n 33).

disapproval of the applicant's conduct. Third, some disputes are mainly about the facts, and as we have seen these are commonly allocated to tribunals and the residual remedy judicial review is not particularly well suited to resolving disputes of fact. I am not trying to argue that it makes no difference whether a discretionary decision concerns the allocation of scarce resources. My point is that the fact that a decision involves allocation of scarce resources does not automatically preclude appeal or review on the merits and there may, therefore, be an argument for creating such rights where none currently exist.

Another possible rationale is that the decisions concerned are made by local authorities. Where individualised decisions are made by central departments, there is very frequently a right of appeal on the merits to a tribunal. By contrast, it is more common to find that there is no such right of appeal to a tribunal in the case of local authority decisions. The argument may be that decisions rest in part on local conditions of which the local authority is presumed to have knowledge. However, this is not necessarily a strong argument against review on the merits as it may be possible to incorporate local knowledge into a tribunal system through a regional structure. The objections to treating this as a convincing rationale for the current pattern of remedies are similar to those for the scarce resources rationale: it has rarely been clearly articulated and does not apply equally to all local authority services. A third argument is that local authorities are accountable to the public because councilors are elected and have a democratic mandate but this rationale would exclude some decisions which are currently subject to appeal.

Conclusions on Existence of Remedies

There is room for improvement as regards the availability of citizens' remedies in certain areas of social policy. There have been some limited improvements since 2010, notably in community care, but on a purely ad hoc basis. However, I would not argue that the lack of consistency in the availability of remedies against the administration and the nature of the remedies provided is a product of austerity politics. It is a consequence of the unsystematic approach to administrative justice that has prevailed over many decades. Having said that, times of austerity are not good times to be proposing new remedies which potentially add to the costs of government. So, the prospects for eliminating the anomalies that currently disadvantage citizens in some contexts are not good.

New Obstacles to Using Remedies

Immigration control provides an example of simply removing remedies. By contrast, in our largest administrative system, social security, what has happened is that new obstacles have been placed in the way of citizens using remedies which had long existed and had been generally operated in a fairly satisfactory manner.

In most years, appeals against social security benefits are the most numerous category of appeal to tribunals. Appeals relating to many categories of benefit have also had notably high success rates in recent years.[78] This is arguably the most important administrative appeal system. Yet the last two years has seen a dramatic drop in the number of appeals. In 2009–10 there were 339,213 appeals relating to social security and child support decisions (the vast majority relating to social security). By 2012–13 this had increased to 507,131. However, in the first quarter of 2014–15 (April to June 2014), the First-tier Tribunal received only 22,699 appeals relating to such decisions, a decrease of 86 per cent compared with the same period in 2013–14.[79] In the next quarter (July to September 2014) 24,969 appeals were received, a decrease of 81 per cent when compared with the same period in 2013–14.[80] Numbers rose in the quarter from October to December 2014 (the most recent quarter for which statistics are available) to 28,142 appeals but this was still a decrease of 65 per cent compared with the same period in 2013.[81] The decline is not, therefore, a purely short-term aberration.

What might explain this dramatic decline in the use of a well-established remedy? It would be implausible to suggest that there has been a swift and dramatic improvement in the quality of initial decision-making which has removed the incentive for most claimants to appeal, especially in the light of the well-documented deficiencies of decision-making in the Department for Work and Pensions (DWP) and the long-term failure of the DWP to improve matters.[82] There has been a long-term problem with the quality of initial decision-making and this has been reflected in very high volumes of appeals and very high success rates on appeal.[83] A more intuitively plausible explanation is that this is an effect of recent changes to the systems for decision-making and remedies in social security.

For many years, the position had been that a claimant dissatisfied with a decision could appeal it to a tribunal. The DWP would usually review the relevant decision

---

[78] See AJTC, *Securing Fairness and Redress* (n 74).

[79] Ministry of Justice, *Tribunals Statistics Quarterly: April to June 2013*, available at: www.gov.uk/government/uploads/system/uploads/attachment_data/file/239257/tribunal-stats-quarterly-april-june-2013.pdf and *Tribunal Statistics Quarterly: April to June 2014*, available at: www.gov.uk/government/statistics/tribunal-statistics-quarterly-april-to-june-2014.

[80] Ministry of Justice, *Tribunal and Gender Recognition Certificate Statistics Quarterly: July to September 2014*, available at: www.gov.uk/government/uploads/system/uploads/attachment_data/file/385759/tribunal-grc-statistics-quarterly-jul-sep-2014.pdf.

[81] Ministry of Justice, *Tribunal and Gender Recognition Certificate Statistics Quarterly: October to December 2014*, available at: www.gov.uk/government/statistics/tribunal-and-gender-recognition-statistics-quarterly-october-to-december-2014.

[82] See, eg, J Baldwin, N Wikely and R Young, *Judging Social Security* (Oxford, Clarendon Press, 1992); *President's Report 2007/2008* (Tribunals Service, 2008), Foreword, available at: www.appeals-service.gov.uk/Documents/SSCSA_PresRep07_08FINAL.pdf and numerous reports from parliamentary committees, including the Pensions Committee, First Special Report of Session 2009–10, *Decision Making and Appeals in the Benefits System* (HC 313), and Work and Pensions Committee, *Employment and Support Allowance and Work Capability Assessments*, First Report (HC 2014–15, 302).

[83] For analysis, see AJTC, *Securing Fairness and Redress* (n 74).

after receiving the appeal and this might result in the decision being revised before the appeal hearing. Section 102 of the Welfare Reform Act 2012 introduced mandatory review of decisions as the initial remedy for claimants aggrieved by decisions of the DWP.[84] Since October 2013 all benefit decisions must be reviewed by the DWP before an appeal can be lodged.[85] At the same time claimants have been required to lodge their appeals directly with HM Courts & Tribunals Service (HMCTS) ('direct lodgement'). Under the previous system, claimants had submitted their appeals to the DWP which then transmitted them to HMCTS.

The Government's stated reasons for introducing mandatory reconsideration were to resolve disputes as early as possible, reduce unnecessary demand on HMCTS by resolving more disputes internally, consider revising decisions where appropriate, provide a full explanation of decisions, and encourage claimants to identify and provide any additional evidence that may affect the decision, so that they receive a correct decision at the earliest opportunity.[86]

The reasons given for introducing direct lodgement of appeals were to align the appeals process for social security and child maintenance appeals with other major jurisdictions handled by HMCTS; to make sure that DWP was no longer involved in the administration of appeals, and could focus on its key role as a party to appeals; and to speed up and clarify the appeals process.[87] The DWP stated that the previous system whereby appeals were submitted to the DWP and then transferred to HMCTS could cause delay in arranging tribunals, and confusion for claimants who might not realise which organisation was responsible for an appeal at any given point.

It would require in-depth empirical research to be sure what are the reasons for the drop in the number of appeals. No such research has yet been completed but we have data from two recent surveys. The first is research carried out by Citizens Advice.[88] This was a small-scale study based on in-depth qualitative diaries and semi-structured qualitative interviews with 20 Citizens Advice Bureaux clients beginning in April 2014. The report makes the point that the process has become far more complex as a result of the changes:

> Prior to the introduction of mandatory reconsideration … For the claimant, the process was straightforward. If they disagreed with a decision, they could fill out an appeal form and would not need to engage with the process again until the date of their appeal hearing was confirmed. The introduction of mandatory reconsideration (as shown in figure 1) requires significant engagement with the process and steps two through to eight

---

[84] See also The Universal Credit, Personal Independence Payment, Jobseeker's Allowance and Employment and Support Allowance (Decisions and Appeals) Regulations 2013, SI 2013/381.

[85] ibid, Reg 7.

[86] Department for Work & Pensions, *Appeals Reform: An introduction* (August 2013), available at: www.gov.uk/government/uploads/system/uploads/attachment_data/file/236733/appeals-reform-introduction.pdf.

[87] ibid.

[88] Citizens Advice, *The cost of a second opinion* (July 2014), available at: www.citizensadvice.org.uk/global/migrated_documents/corporate/the-cost-of-a-second-opinion-report-july-2014final2.pdf.

now apply. Claimants must now contact the DWP to ask for a mandatory reconsideration, receive an explanation of the decision by telephone, clarify points of issue, identify if further evidence is needed and submit further evidence (if applicable). If the original decision is unchanged, and they wish to appeal, they must then submit an appeal form with the attached reconsideration notice attached directly to HMCTS.

To impose a more complex process with an additional stage creates a greater risk that claimants will not pursue appeals because of confusion or process fatigue. This is borne out by the findings of the research, which identifies cause for concern in three areas:

— Communications from DWP to claimants were inconsistent and information was unclear
— Claiming Jobseeker's Allowance was problematic for clients
— Claimants faced long delays before receiving a decision.

The CAB study was a very small-scale study but its findings are consistent with those of a much larger study carried out by the Low Commission. The Commission carried out a survey of 436 welfare rights advisers.[89] Respondents were asked how often in their experience the DWP got decisions right first time. Only 13 per cent of those who responded thought that decisions were mostly right first time. Of those who responded, 48 per cent thought that around 50 per cent of decisions were right first time, and 38 per cent thought they were rarely right first time. As for mandatory reconsideration, only 35 per cent of respondents thought that their clients were more likely to receive the right outcome without having to appeal as a consequence of mandatory reconsideration, and 65 per cent considered that their clients were *less likely* to receive the right outcome.

When asked to estimate the average waiting time for a decision following mandatory reconsideration, 2 per cent said two weeks, 51 per cent said 4–6 weeks and 47 per cent said eight weeks or more. Seventy per cent of advisers said that their clients' understanding of challenging a DWP decision was less clear than before. Advisers were also asked how they would describe the impact on the welfare of claimants during mandatory reconsideration. Only 4 per cent referred to satisfaction that a review was taking place, whereas 89 per cent referred to increased stress, 95 per cent to financial hardship and 49 per cent to being deterred from claiming other benefits.

These findings support each of the main findings of the CAB research and are also at odds with the Government's stated reasons for the reforms of the appeal system. Both reports suggest that there has been increased delay, poorer communication and considerable hardship for claimants. The Low Commission research also suggests that initial decisions are frequently inaccurate and that claimants are less likely than before to receive the right outcome without having to appeal.

---

[89] Low Commission on the Future of Legal Advice and Support, *Getting it Right in Social Welfare Law* (2014), available at: www.lowcommission.org.uk/dyn/1425469623929/Low-Commission-Report-Text-Proof-207050-.pdf.

Whilst we cannot be sure given the limited data, it seems more likely than not that well-founded grievances are not proceeding to appeal because of the introduction of mandatory reconsideration and the other changes to decision-making mentioned above. This is not because internal review by public bodies is inherently problematic, but because of the particular form that it has taken in social security administration. There are also concerns about mandatory reconsideration which go beyond its effect in obstructing access to appeal tribunals. There is no time limit on mandatory reconsideration which raises the possibility of justice being slower than under the previous system rather than quicker. Another change in policy is that no benefit is paid during the reconsideration stage which only serves to increase the injustice suffered from an adverse decision.[90]

Appeal rights have not been removed wholesale as they have in immigration control, but there is evidence that mandatory internal review and other changes to existing appeal systems are functioning as obstacles to effective access to the social security appeal systems. Confidence in access to justice has, therefore, been undermined in a key area of public administration which affects millions of people.

Declining Availability of Advice, Assistance and Representation

I have argued elsewhere that the UK has evolved two contrasting styles of adjudication: a formal, adversarial style and an informal, enabling style.[91] The former presupposes, and in fact requires, litigants to be represented by lawyers in order to participate in the legal process effectively. The latter is intended to permit citizens to use the legal process unrepresented. The former has been the traditional model of litigation in the ordinary courts. The latter has been the preferred approach in most tribunals and in simplified procedures introduced for the ordinary courts since the late 1960s such as small claims procedure in the county court.

As noted above, UK government policy has long proceeded on the assumption that citizens can effectively represent themselves in disputes with the state. This line was first taken in the case of appeals to tribunals, and although the Franks Committee thought that there were good arguments for extending legal aid to at least some tribunals,[92] this suggestion was not taken up except for the one or two particularly formal tribunals. The assumption was repeated, this time more emphatically, by the Leggatt review[93] and Leggatt's view was in turn endorsed by the 2004 White Paper. So, the general approach has consistently been that citizens

---

[90] Serious concern about the hardship experienced by claimants denied benefits has also been expressed in the context of sanctions for failing to observe job search requirements, which have been applied to an increasing proportion of claimants in recent years. See, eg, M Adler, 'Conditionality, Sanctions and the Weakness of Redress' in in EZ Brodkin and G Marston (eds), *Work and the Welfare State* (Copenhagen, Djøf Publishing, 2013).

[91] Mullen, 'A Holistic Approach to Administrative Justice?' (n 5).

[92] *Report of the Committee on Administrative Tribunals and Enquiries* (n 16) para 89.

[93] See, eg, Leggatt Report (n 17) para 4.21.

in dispute with the state do not in general need lawyers to operate their remedies against the administration effectively except where the remedy is litigation in the ordinary courts, for example, judicial review and statutory appeals. As a corollary, civil legal aid has not been available for funding representation at most tribunals. Where appeals lie to bodies which are neither courts nor conventional tribunals, for example, education appeal committees, the assumption that lawyers and legal aid are not necessary has also applied.

Whether citizens can effectively represent themselves when making use of rights of appeal to tribunals has been a contested question. Until a few years ago, the academic consensus was that representation was valuable, most importantly because it was likely to enhance the appellant's prospects of success. There was a substantial body of research which appeared to support this view.[94] More recent research by Adler deviates from the academic orthodoxy.[95] His study of five tribunals found much smaller 'representation premiums' than in earlier studies. However, it also found that success rates varied according to two factors: whether the applicant/appellant was represented, and whether the applicant/appellant had received pre-hearing advice. Those who had neither of these advantages were less likely to succeed in their appeal than those who had either representation or pre-hearing advice or both. Adler suggests two reasons for the difference between his results and those of earlier studies. First, that pre-hearing advice is important and helpful to applicants/appellants and this dimension may have been neglected in previous studies. Second, that the tribunals in question have, in the intervening years, become much better at implementing the enabling approach to adjudication.

There remains room for doubt as to whether representation (as opposed to pre-hearing advice) makes a marked difference to appellants' prospects of success. What we can say is that there is limited evidence to support the view that citizens can in general operate redress mechanisms effectively wholly without assistance; even the informal/enabling model requires, in order for it to work effectively, that citizens have access to advice or representation (although not necessarily from lawyers).

Accordingly, we may conclude that it is not reasonable to make policy on the assumption that citizens can operate the redress mechanisms that take the form of adjudication entirely unaided. They need help and if we are serious about access to justice that help ought to be provided. That help should take a variety of forms according to circumstances. In some contexts, it will require public funding for legal representation; in others, it will be sufficiently effective to provide funds for lay representation. In some contexts, pre-hearing advice should be sufficient. The only context in which it can reasonably be expected that citizens can operate

---

[94] See, eg, H Genn and Y Genn, *The Effectiveness of Representation at Tribunals: Report to the Lord Chancellor* (London, Lord Chancellor's Department, 1989); L Dickens, *Dismissed: A Study of Unfair Dismissal and the Industrial Tribunal System* (Oxford, Blackwell, 1985); Baldwin, Wikely and Young (n 82); and R Sainsbury, *Survey and Report into the Working of Medical Appeal Tribunals* (London, The Stationery Office, 1992).

[95] M Adler, 'Tribunals Ain't What They Used to Be' *Adjust Newsletter* (March 2009), available at: ajtc. justice.gov.uk/adjust/articles/AdlerTribunalsUsedToBe.pdf.

redress mechanisms unaided is when they are truly inquisitorial as in the case of the statutory ombudsmen. Conversely, where the remedy is in the courts they will usually need a lawyer.

There are two problems with current arrangements. First, research has suggested that in at least some tribunal contexts representation may enhance the prospects of success,[96] yet legal aid is not available or is available only on a restricted basis and availability of non-lawyer representation is patchy. The other is that following the Legal Aid, Sentencing and Punishment of Offenders Act 2012 (LASPO), legal aid availability in England and Wales has been further restricted.[97]

LASPO cut backs most obviously affect court-based remedies, ie, judicial review and those appeals against administrative decisions heard by the courts. The restrictions on legal aid for judicial review brought in under LASPO have been described above. The availability of legal aid to challenge decisions in other fora, for example, tribunals, has always been more limited. In most tribunals, full civil legal aid has never been available. However, it would be a mistake to think that no help was provided under the legal aid scheme in those areas in which the principal remedy is appeal to a tribunal and restrictions in legal aid have had an effect here as well. Immigration control had been an area in which there was substantial provision for legal aid but, as Thomas' chapter explains, LASPO has severely restricted legal aid in immigration cases.[98] There was substantial provision of legal help under legal aid contracts by way of advice and representation at tribunals. This was typically provided by specialist welfare benefits advisers rather than by lawyers. Representation was not directly funded but the funding of advice facilitated the provision of representation. However, LASPO removed welfare benefits from the scope of the legal aid scheme[99] and this appears to have led to a reduction in the availability of advice. In the Low Commission survey, advisers were asked what had been the impact of the legal aid reforms on their ability to support clients through the appeals process: 62 per cent reported a negative or substantial impact and 28 per cent limited or no impact.

Whilst it is difficult to quantify, it is likely that LASPO has had a significantly adverse effect on the availability of legal help not only on immigration appeals and welfare benefits, but also in other areas of administrative law. To that effect, we must add the broader effect of public sector funding cuts. In recent decades, much advice has been provided by the voluntary sector. Much of this is supported by public funds and much of that is channelled through local authorities. We know that thus far local authorities have borne the brunt of public spending cuts,[100]

---

[96] See sources at n 80 above.

[97] The legal aid reforms do not extend to Scotland or Northern Ireland where eligibility is substantially different.

[98] Above (n 48).

[99] Ministry of Justice, *Proposals for the Reform of Legal Aid in England and Wales* (Cm 7967, 2010).

[100] A Hastings, N Bailey, G Bramley, M Gannon and D Watkins, findings: *The Cost of the Cuts: their impact on local government and poorer communities* (York, Joseph Rowntree Foundation, 2015), available at: www.jrf.org.uk/sites/files/jrf/CostofCuts-Full.pdf.

so although it would be extremely difficult to quantify the effects, it is likely that advice services provided by the voluntary sector have suffered.[101] Taking these two effects together, it is likely that less advice and help is now available than before LASPO in a number of areas in which the principal means of challenging and administrative decision is an appeal to a tribunal.

The Future of Access to Justice within Administrative Justice

Policies pursued since 2010 have reduced access to justice within the field of administrative justice by removing remedies altogether (eg, immigration control); placing restrictive conditions on the granting of remedies (legal aid); cutting the availability of legal aid for advice and representation; cutting other public funding streams which have been used to support advice to individuals in dispute with public bodies (eg, support for the voluntary sector); increasing the financial dis-incentives to using existing remedies (costs rules in judicial review); and creat-ing administrative obstacles to using remedies (social security). The attempt to develop a holistic vision of administrative justice and to reshape the system in the light of that vision has been abandoned.

Instead, administrative justice policy has been shaped by the political consid-erations of particular policy areas. Established principles of administrative jus-tice have been sacrificed to the political imperatives of restricting immigration and cutting expenditure on social security benefits. More generally, the value of citizens being able to enforce their rights against the state, for which they need advice and sometimes representation, has been heavily discounted.

The manner in which new policies have been developed and presented since 2010 suggests a government which is not seriously committed to administrative justice.

A new single party government (Conservative) has just taken office at the time of writing. Although there is no particular reason to expect a change of approach, here is what I suggest it ought to do to secure access to justice in the sense that remedies for administrative injustice actually exist and citizens can use those remedies effectively. First, it ought to stop promoting the notion that existing rem-edies are being abused by individuals with weak cases and pressure groups with a political agenda. Second, it ought to restore the appeal rights it has taken away in immigration control. Third, it ought to reconsider some of the reforms it has made to the judicial review process. Fourth, it needs to undertake a thorough review of the recent changes to social security appeals to understand why the number of

---

[101] Ch 6 of Hastings et al (ibid), describes the general impact of spending cuts on the voluntary sector.

appeals has dropped so dramatically and what role those changes have played, reversing them if they are, as suggested here, operating as obstacles to access to justice. Fifth, it needs to develop a comprehensive strategy for ensuring access to justice in the field of administrative justice that encompasses not just provision of legal aid, but the whole network of funding streams and other policies that directly affect advice, support and representation for citizens. Sixth, it needs to reinstate the holistic approach to administrative justice that the 2004 White Paper promised so that it can consider initial decision-making alongside remedies,[102] what is the best possible mix of citizens' remedies and the implications of choice of remedies for advice, support and representation.

---

[102] The single most important thing the Government should do to enhance administrative justice is to improve the quality of initial decision-making in certain key public services.

6

Immigration and Access to Justice: A Critical Analysis of Recent Restrictions

ROBERT THOMAS[*]

Consider this. Shabana, from Pakistan, has been visiting her family in the UK and wants to stay with them. She thinks that she might qualify, but doesn't know for certain. The rules are complex. The Home Office refuses her application, but the reasons are unclear. Having paid the application fee, Shabana can't now afford any legal advice. Until recently, people could go to a tribunal, but you can't do that any more. Shabana has heard that you can lodge human rights appeals, except the Government does not like those. Someone suggests that Shabana applies for judicial review—you can get legal help if the court thinks you have a good case (but how can you persuade the court you have a good case if you can't get any legal assistance beforehand)? Shabana has a choice: does she reluctantly accept the decision or can she find a way to challenge it?

Against the background of Shabana's story, this chapter analyses restrictions upon access to immigration justice and their impact during the tenure of the Coalition Government. It is generally recognised that access to justice has been severely limited, but it is suggested here that immigration may have sustained some of the severest restrictions. Some people adversely affected by government decisions will find a way to challenge decisions that drastically affect their lives but, overall, the ability to access immigration justice has been significantly reduced. Furthermore, while the Coalition Government's policy of restricting access to immigration justice has been presented in the context of financial cost cutting, it is argued that the policy has largely been driven by the political and ideological forces informing the Government's wider deterrent immigration agenda.

The Coalition Government has proceeded by way of a four-pronged assault upon access to immigration justice comprising: (i) severely limiting legal aid; (ii) abolishing most immigration appeal rights and narrowing the grounds of appeal;

[*] I would like to thank Tom Mullen and Ellie Palmer for their comments. The usual disclaimer applies.

(iii) cutting legal aid in judicial review cases; and (iv) seeking to introduce the residence test, a near-blanket exclusion from legal aid for anyone not lawfully resident in the UK. Thus, stringent immigration policies have gone hand-in-hand with the restriction of opportunities to challenge adverse decisions; in some cases significantly limiting, and in others wholly undermining, access to immigration justice.

However, the Government has not succeeded on all fronts. The courts have mounted a rearguard action. Refusing to ignore the principle of equal protection before the law between citizens and non-citizens, the courts have prevented the Government from restricting access to justice for immigrants solely because of their status as non-citizens. Moreover, as we shall see, specific measures, such as the partial withdrawal of appeal rights, may in practice prove to be counterproductive.

Access to Justice and Immigration

The importance of access to justice, the practical ability of individuals to vindicate their legal rights, has been long recognised. 'If the plaintiff has a right', Holt CJ once noted, 'he must of necessity have a means to vindicate and maintain it, and a remedy … it is a vain thing to imagine a right without a remedy; for want of right and want of remedy are reciprocal'.[1] Developing this theme, Cranston has more recently extrapolated four justifications for recognising the importance of this multifaceted concept: to ensure equality before the law; to enforce legal rights effectively; to respond to unmet legal need; and to reduce social exclusion.[2]

Access to justice has many aspects. People should be treated fairly according to the law—if not, then they should be able to enforce their legal rights through appropriate redress, such as a court or tribunal, without encountering unnecessary obstacles. Since few people are competent in the law, professional legal assistance is often required. This is costly and has often been funded through publicly funded legal aid. As Bingham has stated, 'denial of legal protection to the poor litigant who cannot afford to pay is one enemy of the Rule of Law'.[3] In the mid-twentieth century, the expansion of legal aid was seen as one aspect of a wider public service owed by the state to its citizens.[4] Yet, the legal aid budget has been one focus for governments seeking to reduce public spending.

What is the situation when the people concerned are not the state's own citizens, but citizens from elsewhere who wish to enter the state under its immigration rules and procedures? The relevant overarching constitutional principle is that everyone is subject to the law and entitled to its protection irrespective of their nationality, immigration status, or residence. According to Lord Scarman, 'every

---

[1] *Ashby v White* [1702] 2 Ld Raym 938, 956.
[2] R Cranston, *How Law Works* (Oxford, Oxford University Press, 2006).
[3] T Bingham, *The Rule of Law* (London, Penguin, 2010) 88.
[4] Legal Aid and Advice Act 1949.

person within the jurisdiction enjoys the equal protection of our laws. There is no distinction between British nationals and others. He who is subject to English law is entitled to its protection'.[5] It is important to consider the degree to which the legal system fulfils this ideal—especially during a period of austerity and restrictive immigration policies.

Access to immigration justice is important for various reasons. Immigration law and its administration is a form of social control that affects some of the most fundamental aspects of an individual's life, such as: where in the world she can live; her family life, whether she can be detained, and whether an asylum claimant is at risk of persecution or torture. The immigrant must, of necessity, interact with a large bureaucracy for a decision and concerns have been perennially raised about the poor quality of many decisions.[6] The Home Office is regularly criticised for being disorganised, inefficient and incompetent. One strand of criticism is that caseworkers are poorly trained. Another is that the department habitually piles on the pressure to process decisions quickly at the expense of quality, a trend accelerated with budget cuts. A third strand is that the department's internal culture is often characterised by a culture of disbelief: caseworkers are predisposed toward refusing applications.[7]

Immigration law is a large and complex area of law. For the last 20 years or so, immigration has provided the bulk of all judicial review claims. Immigration has accounted for a high proportion of onward appeals to the higher courts, in particular, the Court of Appeal. The immigration tribunal is the second largest tribunal jurisdiction. Immigration law is also a fast-moving area, largely driven by changes in government policy, and sits at the intersection of national, EU and human rights law. It is a troubled and unstable area of law and practice characterised by bureaucratic failure, frequent legislative change, legal complexity, toxic politics, and a high volume of legal challenges.

Despite the importance of access to immigration justice, there are exceptionally strong countervailing forces at work. Fiscal retrenchment and austerity are supplemented by political and ideological forces particular to immigration.[8] Few, if any, other policy areas are as toxic, produce such heat, rather than light, and regularly attract high profile media attention, which in turn drives political action. The Government would argue that, during hard times, increased public anxiety justifies the need for a hostile environment for illegal immigrants and to cut out 'abuse'. Alternative explanations point to electoral politics and prejudice. Either

---

[5] *Khawaja v Secretary of State for the Home Department* [1984] 1 AC 74, 111 (Lord Scarman).

[6] See Amnesty International/Still Human Still Here, *A Question of Credibility: Why So Many Initial Asylum Decisions are Overturned on Appeal in the UK* (2013), available at: stillhumanstillhere.files.wordpress.com/2013/04/a-question-of-credibility-finall.pdf; Independent Chief Inspector of Borders and Immigration (ICIBI), *Entry Clearance Decision-Making* (2011), available at: icinspector.independent.gov.uk/wp-content/uploads/2011/02/Entry-Clearance-Decision-Making_A-Global-Review.pdf.

[7] House of Commons Home Affairs Committee, *Asylum* (HC 2013–14, 71) [12]–[13].

[8] On the general technique of understanding public law with reference to ideology, see P McAuslan, 'Administrative Law, Collective Consumption and Judicial Policy' (1983) 46 *Modern Law Review* 1.

way, immigration law has become more draconian: family reunion rules have been significantly toughened up, through a minimum income requirement;[9] the right to family and private life has been confined;[10] and the ability of illegal immigrants to access various services, both public (health care) and private (rented accommodation) has been limited.[11]

There is a further twist: the baneful politics of legal challenges against immigration decisions. Home Secretaries are subject to a higher number of legal challenges than their counterparts and are particularly prone to intemperate outbursts against the judiciary.[12] Ministers have sometimes lampooned appellants and blamed human rights laws, and the judges applying them, for politically unwelcome decisions (for instance, Theresa May's claim in 2011 that a cat prevented the deportation of an illegal immigrant).[13] Concerns about the quality of initial decisions and access to justice are far from ministerial minds. Instead, ministers have blamed immigrants for abusing and exploiting the system. More generally, there has been an ongoing political–legal conflict waged by ministers against immigrants, their representatives and the judiciary.

Learning from the Past?

Since 2010, Coalition ministers have sought to limit access to immigration justice. Such restrictions are nothing new, but part of the ordinary routine of immigration law. Reducing legal aid, appeal rights and judicial review have been common themes over the last 20 years. The question for ministers has been how to achieve their ends and which tactics to employ.

Broadly speaking, ministers have two ways to accomplish their objectives. The first is to introduce a single 'big bang' reform, that is, to propose a major wide-ranging reform in one go and to seek to drive it through against vested interests. For instance, between 2003 and 2004, the Labour Home Secretary, David Blunkett, mounted a full-scale attack on the use of judicial review by immigrants and asylum claimants by seeking to oust judicial review of immigration decisions. The risk with such a direct and major attempt at change is that it provokes intense

---

[9] Statement of Changes in Immigration Rules (HC 2012, 194), challenged unsuccessfully in *R (MM (Lebanon)) v Secretary of State for the Home Department* [2014] EWCA Civ 985.

[10] Immigration Act 2014, s 19.

[11] ibid, part III.

[12] 'Theresa May Criticises Judges For "Ignoring" Deportation Law' *BBC News* (17 February 2013), available at: www.bbc.co.uk/news/uk-21489072; 'Britain's Top Judge Attacks Theresa May's Criticism of Judiciary' *The Telegraph* (4 March 2013), available at: www.telegraph.co.uk/news/uknews/law-and-order/9908528/Britains-top-judge-attacks-Theresa-Mays-criticism-of-judiciary.html.

[13] 'Tory Conference Cat-fight: Clarke and May Clash Over Human Rights Act Story' *The Guardian* (4 October 2011), available at: www.theguardian.com/politics/2011/oct/04/theresa-may-clashes-judges-cat.

disagreement and arguments over matters of principle. Blunkett's ouster clause was opposed because it would place executive decision-making beyond judicial scrutiny.[14] This provoked an adverse reaction in the legal community and a governmental retreat.[15] It also prompted the Law Lords to warn that the doctrine of parliamentary sovereignty might need to be curtailed if there was a future threat to the rule of law.[16]

A second, and perhaps more astute ministerial policy, is to eschew a single bold reform for a number of smaller reforms. Each individual reform may provoke objections, but not as many as a single large-scale reform. Such a tactic may divide and weaken the opposition who are left fighting on multiple fronts over a longer period of time. It might also avoid or downplay the grand issues of principle accompanying a single big reform, but the collective impact may be just as effective. Following Blunkett's ouster clause, outright abolition of judicial review was off-limits or at least fraught with acute constitutional difficulties, but there are other ways to restrict immigration justice. If Coalition ministers have learnt from their predecessors, then we might find them chipping away piece-by-piece to restrict access to justice.

There have been other developments in the political-constitutional background—not least the role of the Lord Chancellor. Formerly, Lord Chancellors were senior lawyers gently reminding ministerial colleagues of the importance of judicial independence and the rule of law,[17] but now they are career politicians with different agendas.[18] The acute concern is highlighted by recent proposals on judicial review which have exposed the inherent conflict in the combined roles of Lord Chancellor and Secretary of State.[19] Two hardline enforcers, Home Secretary Theresa May and Lord Chancellor Chris Grayling, have been at the helm—both hostile to legal challenges and the European Convention on Human Rights.

---

[14] See papers collected in [2004] 9 *Judicial Review* 95–121.

[15] R Rawlings, 'Review, Revenge and Retreat' (2005) 68 *Modern Law Review* 378.

[16] In *Jackson v Her Majesty's Attorney General* [2005] UKHL 56, [102] Lord Steyn noted that if Parliament were to assert an extravagant power by removing judicial review, then the courts 'may have to consider whether this is a constitutional fundamental which even a sovereign Parliament ... cannot abolish'. See also T Mullen, 'Reflections on *Jackson v Attorney-General*: Questioning Sovereignty' (2007) 27 *Legal Studies* 1.

[17] In 2003, Lord Irvine had resigned as Lord Chancellor following his opposition to the proposed reforms under what later became the Constitutional Reform Act 2005. During the ouster clause battle of 2003/04, as Home Secretary David Blunkett capitulated when the recently-resigned Lord Irvine threatened to speak against the ouster clause during in the Lords. See 'Compromise Offer Over Asylum Row' *BBC News* (15 March 2004), available at: news.bbc.co.uk/1/hi/uk_politics/3511536.stm.

[18] Appointed in 2012, Chris Grayling MP is the first non-lawyer career politician to hold the position in modern times. Lord Lester has noted that 'the present Lord Chancellor is in a class of his own, because he is entirely miscast as Lord Chancellor. He would be perfectly cast in "House of Cards". He would be an ideal person in that sort of role because he is a very intelligent, extremely charming, very effective politician. However, ... I do not think he understands the rule of law' (HL Deb 7 May 2014, vol 752, col 1543).

[19] Joint Committee on Human Rights (JCHR), *The Implications for Access to Justice of the Government's Proposals to Reform Judicial Review* (2013–14, HL 174, HC 868) 23.

Mr Grayling has emphasised the need to 'deny foreigners legal aid'[20] whereas for Mrs May cutting abuse of immigration appeals by withdrawing such appeals has gone hand-in-hand with creating a hostile environment for immigrants.[21] Internal legal restraint within government has diminished thereby increasing the importance of judicial control.

The Legal System for Challenging Immigration Decisions

To assess the impact of the restrictions upon immigration justice, it is necessary to set out some of the background of the legal system for challenging immigration decisions. In 1967, the Wilson Committee concluded that it was 'fundamentally wrong and inconsistent with the rule of law that power to take decisions affecting a man's whole future should be vested in officers of the executive, from whose findings there is no appeal'.[22] The immigration appeals system was subsequently established.[23] The essential components were: a fact-based appeal determined by an adjudicator and a right of appeal to the Immigration Appeal Tribunal (IAT). The system was, by modern standards, fairly primitive: adjudicators were Home Office appointees and mostly former colonial officers.

During the 1970s and 1980s, appeals largely concerned matters such as family reunion from the Indian sub-continent and visitor appeals.[24] From the late 1980s, things started to change. The Government became concerned at the increasing number of appeals. Asylum claimants started to arrive and, without a specific appeal right, sought judicial review.[25] In 1993, visitor appeals were abolished and asylum appeals were introduced.[26] Asylum claims certified as manifestly unfounded attracted limited appeal rights.[27] In 1999, human rights and family visitor appeals were introduced.[28] Yet, the asylum system was creaking: the Home

---

[20] 'Why Should You Pay the Legal Bill of People Who Have Never Even Been to Britain? Deny Foreigners Legal Aid, Says Justice Minister Chris Grayling' *Daily Mail* (21 April 2014), available at: www.dailymail.co.uk/news/article-2609205/Why-pay-legal-bill-people-never-Britain-Deny-foreigners-legal-aid-says-Grayling.html.

[21] HC Deb 22 October 2013, vol 569, col 158 (Theresa May MP).

[22] *Report of the Committee on Immigration Appeals* (Cmnd 3387, 1967) [84].

[23] Immigration Act 1971.

[24] R Moore and T Wallace, *Slamming the Door: The Administration of Immigration Control* (London, Martin Robertson, 1975) 77–107; S Juss, *Discretion and Deviation in the Administration of Immigration Control* (London, Sweet & Maxwell, 1997).

[25] C Randall, 'An Asylum Policy for the UK' in S Spencer (ed), *Strangers and Citizens: A Positive Approach to Migrants and Refugees* (London, Rivers Oram Press, 1994).

[26] Asylum and Immigration Appeals Act 1993.

[27] Asylum and Immigration Act 1996.

[28] Immigration and Asylum Act 1999, ss 60(5)(a) and 65.

Office became overwhelmed with applications and backlogs developed—still a current issue in 2014.[29] Unsuccessful appellants often sought judicial review after the tribunal process. Legislation in 2002 sought to simplify appeal processes.[30]

By this time, the tribunal comprised some 700 immigration judges located at 10 main hearing centres with the IAT based in London.[31] By 2003–04, with immigration becoming a politically important topic, the Government had had enough. The single-tier Asylum and Immigration Tribunal (AIT) was introduced with limited onward appeal rights.[32] The initial plan had been to exclude judicial review but, in the event, a quick paper-based statutory review procedure was introduced.[33] In the meantime, wider tribunal reform was proceeding apace with the establishment of the First-tier and Upper Tribunals.[34]

In practice, the single-tier AIT did not function as well as expected. Both the Administrative Court and the Court of Appeal became overwhelmed. Delays increased. Judicial resources were being stretched to the limit. The system had, though, matured. The President was a High Court judge; and all immigration judges were legally qualified; and the tribunal had developed its own system of precedent.[35] The Home Office meanwhile, faced with backlogs, was in its normal crisis management mode.[36]

Putting institutional changes aside, thorny problems remained.[37] The tribunal was criticised for affording the Home Office preferential treatment.[38] The quality of interpretation was criticised.[39] Expert witnesses complained of being ignored by the tribunal.[40] Immigration judges were criticised for not carefully assessing

---

[29] Home Affairs Committee, *The Work of the Immigration Directorates (October–December 2013)* (HC 2013–14, 237) [49].

[30] Nationality, Immigration and Asylum Act 2002. See R Thomas, 'Asylum Appeals Overhauled Again' [2003] *Public Law* 260.

[31] D Pearl, 'Immigration and Asylum Appeals and Administrative Justice' in M Harris and M Partington (eds), *Administrative Justice in the 21st Century* (Oxford, Hart Publishing, 1999).

[32] Asylum and Immigration (Treatment of Claimants, etc) Act 2004. See R Thomas, 'Evaluating Tribunal Adjudication: Administrative Justice and Asylum Appeals' (2005) 25 *Legal Studies* 462.

[33] R Thomas, 'After the Ouster: Review and Reconsideration in a Single Tier Tribunal' [2006] *Public Law* 674.

[34] A Leggatt, *Tribunals for Users: One System, One Service. The Report of the Review of Tribunals by Sir Andrew Leggatt* (London, 2001); Department for Constitutional Affairs, *Transforming Public Services: Complaints Redress and Tribunals* (Cm 6243, 2004); Tribunals, Courts and Enforcement Act 2007.

[35] R Thomas, 'Consistency in Asylum Adjudication: Country Guidance and the Asylum Process in the United Kingdom' (2008) 20 *International Journal of Refugee Law* 48.

[36] C Painter, 'A Government Department in Meltdown: Crisis at the Home Office' (2008) 28 *Public Money & Management* 275.

[37] For a view from a former immigration judge, see G Care, 'The Judiciary, the State and the Refugee: The Evolution of Judicial Protection in Asylum—A UK Perspective' (2005) 28 *Fordham International Law Journal* 1421.

[38] M Quayum and M Chatwin, 'A Fair-handed Approach?' (2003) 153 *New Law Journal* 533.

[39] R Rycroft, 'Communicative Barriers in the Asylum Account' in P Shah (ed), *The Challenge of Asylum to Legal Systems* (London, Cavendish Publishing, 2005).

[40] D Rhys Jones and S Verity Smith, 'Medical Evidence in Asylum and Human Rights Appeals' (2004) 16 *International Journal of Refugee Law* 381; A Good, *Anthropology and Expertise in the Asylum Courts* (London, Routledge-Cavendish, 2007).

appellants' credibility.[41] Home Office presenting officers did not regularly attend hearings.[42] Tribunal decisions were often inconsistent and criticised by the higher courts.[43] Judges expressed concerns about maintaining judicial impartiality.[44] More recently, the detained fast-track asylum process has been found to carry 'an unacceptably high risk of unfairness' because of insufficient time for lawyers to advise clients.[45] Another issue is the complex edifice of appeals and the interaction with judicial review. Immigration appeals are very technical; 'an impenetrable jungle of intertwined statutory provisions and judicial decisions'.[46] Some decisions can be appealed; others cannot. Overstayers cannot appeal if the Home Office does not, as often occurs, simultaneously issue removal directions—thereby leaving the applicant in limbo.[47] Some decisions can be certified so that they only attract an appeal from outside the UK (non-suspensive appeals), but such certificates can be judicially reviewed.

In 2010, the jurisdiction was transferred into the First-tier and Upper Tribunals to give the advantages of expert adjudication in a specialist field, speed up the throughput of cases for determination, and maintain the essential features of independent judicial scrutiny of contentious cases (see Figure 1).[48] Three interlocking features sought to contain litigation within the tribunal system. First, the transfer of most immigration judicial reviews from the Administrative Court to the Upper Tribunal (Immigration and Asylum Chamber) (UTIAC) would reduce delays in the Administrative Court by allowing specialist UTIAC judges to hear such cases.[49] Second, the second-tier appeal criteria reserve to the higher courts only cases of real importance.[50] Third, judicial review of the UTIAC was similarly confined in *Cart*.[51] What had been originally established as an informal and simple

[41] R Thomas, 'Assessing the Credibility of Asylum Claims: EU and UK Approaches Examined' (2006) 8 *European Journal of Migration and Law* 79.

[42] C Hastings, A Ralph and I Johnston, 'Asylum Seekers Win Right to Stay Because of "Shambolic" Immigration Hearings' *The Telegraph* (18 April 2009).

[43] In *Koller v Secretary of State for the Home Department* [2001] EWCA Civ 1267, [26] Brooke LJ noted that some tribunal decisions were of 'uncertain quality', a view Brooke LJ revised in *R (Iran) v Secretary of State for the Home Department* [2005] EWCA Civ 982, [92]–[93].

[44] S Sedley, 'Asylum: Can the Judiciary Maintain its Independence?' (International Association of Refugee Law Judges World Conference, Wellington, New Zealand, April 2002).

[45] *Detention Action v Secretary of State for the Home Department* [2014] EWHC Admin 2245.

[46] *Sapkota v Secretary of State for the Home Department* [2011] EWCA Civ 1320, [127] (Jackson LJ).

[47] *Mirza v Secretary of State for the Home Department* [2011] EWCA Civ 159; *R (Daley-Murdock) v Secretary of State for the Home Department* [2011] EWCA Civ 161.

[48] Tribunals, Courts and Enforcement Act 2007. The formal titles are the First-tier Tribunal (Immigration and Asylum Chamber)—FTTIAC—and the Upper Tribunal (Immigration and Asylum Chamber)—UTIAC.

[49] In 2009, 'fresh claim' judicial reviews—those challenging the Home Office's refusal to consider the presentation of new material by someone refused asylum as a fresh asylum claim—were transferred: Borders, Citizenship and Immigration Act 2009, s 53. In 2013, most other immigration judicial reviews were transferred: Crime and Courts Act 2013, s 22.

[50] These criteria require that appeals from the UT to the Court of Appeal must raise an important point of principle or practice or contain some other compelling reason to be heard (Tribunals, Courts and Enforcement Act 2007, s 13(6)). See also *PR (Sri Lanka) v Secretary of State for the Home Department* [2012] 1 WLR 73.

[51] *R (Cart) v Upper Tribunal* [2011] UKSC 28. See also M Elliott and R Thomas, 'Tribunal Justice, Cart, and Proportionate Dispute Resolution' (2012) 71 *Cambridge Law Journal* 297.

system of redress had transformed into a highly legalised system with the tribunal increasingly taking on the type of work previously reserved for the higher courts.

Despite the upheavals, the immigration jurisdiction in 2010 seemed relatively secure. More generally, the period of 2004 to 2010 may, in retrospect, be the high-water mark for administrative justice.[52] The Labour Government's 2004 White Paper signalled a direct focus upon administrative justice and most tribunals were subsequently brought together into a unified system.[53] However, by 2011, the political backdrop had changed entirely with the Coalition's austerity policies. There were warnings that administrative justice was at risk.

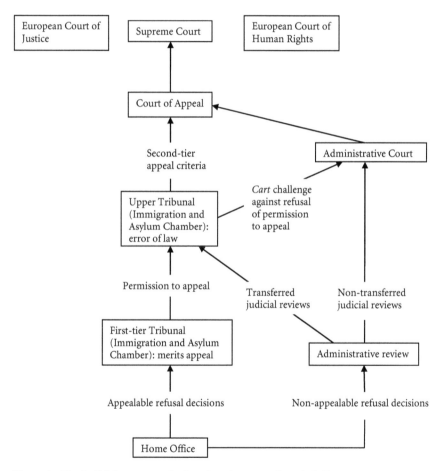

Figure 1: The judicial structure for immigration appeals and challenges

[52] M Adler, 'The Rise and Fall of Administrative Justice: A Cautionary Tale' (2012) 8 *Socio-Legal Review* 28.

[53] *Transforming Public Services* (n 34); Tribunals, Courts and Enforcement Act 2007.

Immigration Legal Aid

The Coalition Government's first line of attack was upon legal aid. The Legal Aid, Sentencing and Punishment of Offenders Act 2012 (LASPO) marked both a complete overhaul of the legal aid system and a radical reduction in eligibility. This section examines how the LASPO changes will impact upon individuals, how unrepresented appellants fare before the tribunal, and the exceptional funding scheme.

LASPO

In the pre-LASPO world, means-tested, merit-tested and fixed-fee legal aid was available for advice, assistance and representation for a variety of immigration issues, such as: citizenship; asylum; leave to enter or remain in the UK for visits, study or employment; and deportation. Given the concerns about the quality of immigration advice and unscrupulous advisers giving claimants incompetent advice, immigration services are regulated: no one may provide immigration advice unless appropriately qualified or regulated.[54] Often criticised by ministers, many committed immigration lawyers did a decent job under difficult circumstances for little financial reward and themselves criticised the Home Office's incompetence.[55] Despite the availability of legal aid, there were acute problems. The administration of legal aid by the Legal Services Commission had created difficulties for immigration advisers, especially in terms of cash flow. Two reputable providers—Refugee and Migrant Justice, and the Immigration Advisory Service—both folded in 2010–11. Advice deserts—areas of the country without lawyers to give advice—emerged. Fixed fees rewarded representatives who spent less time on a case.[56] Such concerns remain and have been accentuated.

The purpose of the legal aid reforms that resulted in LASPO[57] was to target legal aid where it was most needed.[58] For practitioners, LASPO represented 'an

---

[54] Lord Chancellor's Advisory Committee on Legal Education and Conduct, *Improving the Quality of Immigration Advice and Representation* (London, 1998); Immigration and Asylum Act 1999, part V (as amended). See also: http://oisc.homeoffice.gov.uk/.

[55] H MacIntrye, 'Imposed Dependency: Client Perspectives of Legal Representation in Asylum Claims' (2009) 23 *Journal of Immigration, Asylum, and Nationality Law* 181; D James and E Killick, 'Ethical Dilemmas? UK Immigration, Legal Aid Funding Reform and Caseworkers' (2010) 26 *Anthropology Today* 13.

[56] J Gibbs and D Hughes-Roberts, *Justice at Risk: Quality and Value for Money in Asylum Legal Aid* (London, Runnymede, 2012).

[57] Ministry of Justice (MoJ), *Proposals for the Reform of Legal Aid in England and Wales* (Cm 7967, 2010).

[58] MoJ, *Reform of Legal Aid in England and Wales: The Government Response* (Cm 8072, 2011) 3 and 8.

enormous assault on the availability of publicly funded legal services'.[59] Immigration cases would be almost entirely out of the scope of legal aid—for initial advice and representation before the tribunal and the higher courts. According to the Government, immigration cases did not require legal assistance given the accessibility of tribunals, the free availability of interpreters, the relative absence of points of law in first-tier appeals, and the provision of guidance from the Home Office.[60] The upshot was a radical reduction in immigration legal aid. Some cases remain within scope: asylum,[61] immigration detention,[62] national security cases,[63] victims of trafficking,[64] and immigration cases involving domestic violence.[65] But all other cases—family migration, deportation and removal, refugee family reunion, cases under Article 8 ECHR, and unaccompanied migrant children—no longer attract legal aid.

Reducing legal aid for those unable to pay for legal assistance creates obvious problems. People cannot access advice. They are denied professional advocacy before a court or tribunal. They are also unable to prepare their own cases adequately by, for instance, instructing an expert. The cuts were vigorously opposed on the following grounds:[66] the importance of immigration cases; the difficulties that often vulnerable individuals unfamiliar with the English language would experience in navigating complex immigration rules;[67] the inequality of arms between individuals and the Home Office; the Home Office's notorious conduct as a litigant;[68] and the challenges facing unrepresented individuals before an adversarial tribunal. Given that an unregulated person cannot provide immigration

---

[59] N Armstrong, 'LASPO, Immigration and *Maaouia v United Kingdom*' (2013) 18 *Judicial Review* 177.

[60] MoJ, *Proposals for the Reform of Legal Aid* (n 57) 133.

[61] LASPO Act 2012, Schedule 1, part 1, para 30(1).

[62] ibid, para 25(1).

[63] ibid, para 24(1).

[64] ibid, para 32(1).

[65] ibid, para 28(1).

[66] See, eg, Immigration Law Practitioners' Association (ILPA), *Response to the Ministry of Justice Consultation: Proposals for the Reform of Legal Aid in England and Wales* (2011); Immigration Advisory Service, *Response to the Ministry of Justice proposals for the Reform of Legal Aid* (2011).

[67] The complexity of immigration law has been highlighted by the courts. In *AA (Nigeria) v Secretary of State for the Home Department* [2010] EWCA Civ 773, [88] Longmore LJ noted that he was 'left perplexed and concerned how any individual whom the Immigration Rules affect can discover what the policy of the Secretary of State actually is at any particular time if it necessitates a trawl through Hansard or formal Home Office correspondence as well as through the comparatively complex Rules themselves. It seems that it is only with expensive legal assistance, funded by the taxpayer, that justice can be done'.

[68] See, eg, *AW v Entry Clearance Officer, Islamabad (Duties of Immigration Judge) Pakistan* [2008] UKAIT 00072, [4]: 'It is indeed within the knowledge of every member of this Tribunal that Entry Clearance Officers typically treat judicial directions, and regulations made by Parliament, with utter disdain'; *R (Jasbir Singh) v Secretary of State for the Home Department* [2013] EWHC 2873 (Admin), [7] and [12]: 'In each of the claims before the court now, the Secretary of State has simply failed to file a response to the claim with anything like promptness ... It is now common for a high proportion of asylum and immigration [judicial review] claims that are assigned to a judge for consideration of permission on paper not to have any acknowledgement of service or summary grounds issued by the Home Office'.

advice or representation, it was contradictory to suppose that individuals could self-represent. Concerns were raised that cutting legal aid would increase costs elsewhere; unrepresented appellants mean longer hearings.[69] Alternatives were advocated, such as better initial decision-making.[70] Non-alternatives were also identified: ADR is precluded by the Home Office's unwillingness to compromise.

A notable feature of LASPO was the almost total lack of parliamentary opposition. Campaigning against the measure mostly came from outside pressure groups. During LASPO's passage through Parliament, the withdrawal of immigration legal aid was barely mentioned in the Commons—perhaps because none of the political parties considered there was any political capital to be gained from the issue. An amendment to retain immigration within scope was defeated in the Lords.[71] The force of the political steam-roller was too great. From 2013, legal aid has been withdrawn for all immigration appeals other than asylum, immigration detention, domestic violence, trafficking, and national security cases.

The Impact of the Legal Aid Cuts

Predictably enough, the cuts have wrought pronounced effects.[72] The number of immigration legal help matter starts reduced from 52,710 in 2012/13 to 28,038 in 2013/14.[73] Poor initial decisions-making continues, but legal challenges no longer depend on the merits of a case, but upon the resources of those affected. Many practitioners have taken on more pro bono work. Yet, this is an unsustainable option that generates an acute ethical dilemma for practitioners between helping those in need and staying in business. Practitioners have been turning away some cases, such as complex refugee family reunion cases and abandoning areas, such as asylum, which remain within scope. Some practices have folded.[74] Immigrants who cannot access advice may be at risk of exploitation from unscrupulous advisers or employers. Others, including detainees, the mentally ill, the sick and those caring for small children are in no position to find the money. According to one practitioner, once word of the cuts got around, individuals started to withdraw:

> While a significant proportion of this client group have managed to scrape together (over time) sufficient funds to pay privately for some help, an equally significant proportion have simply disappeared. Yes, they still ring and ask for an appointment, but when

---

[69] Justice Committee, *Government's Proposed Reform of Legal Aid* (HC 2010–12, 681) [143].

[70] The Law Society, *Access to Justice Review* (2010) 20–21; Justice Committee, *Government's Proposed Reform of Legal Aid* (n 69) [60]; Administrative Justice and Tribunals Council, *Right First Time* (2011).

[71] HL Deb 12 March 2012, vol 736, cols 69–84.

[72] ILPA, *Written Evidence to the House of Commons Justice Committee Inquiry into the Impact of Changes to Civil Legal Aid Under the Legal Aid, Sentencing and Punishment of Offenders Act 2012* (2014), available at: http://data.parliament.uk/writtenevidence/committeeevidence.svc/evidencedocument/justice-committee/impact-of-changes-to-civil-legal-aid-under-laspo/written/8928.pdf.

[73] MoJ, *Legal Aid Statistics in England and Wales 2013–14* (2014) 49.

[74] 'Leading Civil Rights Lawyers Tooks Chambers Closes, Blaming Legal Aid Cuts' *The Independent* (23 September 2013), available at: www.independent.co.uk/news/uk/home-news/leading-civil-rights-lawyers-tooks-chambers-closes-blaming-legal-aid-cuts-8835371.html.

informed about the changes to legal aid, they say they will need to 'think about it' and never call back. The concern is that these clients—already living under the radar because of their lack of status—simply disappear without a chance of obtaining even the most basic advice about their options. As time has gone on and word has got around, the phone calls from those requesting legal aid have eased off.[75]

The depressing risk is that many people cannot enforce their rights. Those unable to regularise their immigration status may end up in destitution. The cuts have coincided with other changes, such as complex and restrictive rules on family migration, which result in more individuals being unable to join, reunite, or remain with family members. While the importance of family bonds has been emphasised by the courts,[76] individuals have been left without the necessary assistance to navigate complex legal rules and evidential requirements—a sharp contrast with domestic public family law cases which still attract legal aid.[77]

One unforeseen consequence has been the reduction in requests for publicly funded work generally, even for cases left within the scope of legal aid partly because of confusion amongst referring agencies and clients. In other categories, cases seemingly eligible for legal aid may be caught out because the relevant exemption is too narrow. To illustrate: legal aid remains for detention cases, but is unavailable for claims resulting from abuse by a public authority of its position of powers, despite cases demonstrating the mistreatment of immigration detainees.[78] The suggestion that detainees use the internal prisons complaints system is unsatisfactory.[79] Another dysfunctional consequence is that some individuals may lodge expensive judicial review claims (which remain within scope) rather than seek cheaper initial advice.

An especially sensitive area concerns unaccompanied minors whose cases will often raise family life issues. Unaccompanied minors simply cannot navigate the legal issues or self-represent. Such children are predominantly under the care of social services from a local authority, which, given its duty under the Children Act 1989, is likely to fund any legal costs. Costs are, therefore, shifted from one part of public spending to another. There are also acute concerns about the quality of some representation. Presented with evidence that the impact of the changes would 'devastate access to justice'[80] and the changes had been 'sleepwalked into',[81]

---

[75] J Renshaw, 'Fig Leaves & Failings' (2014) *New Law Journal* (8 April 2014).

[76] *Huang v Secretary of State for the Home Department* [2007] 2 AC 167, 186.

[77] F Meyler and S Woodhouse, 'Changing the Immigration Rules and Withdrawing the "Currency" of Legal Aid: The Impact of LASPO 2012 on Migrants and their Families' (2013) 35 *Journal of Social Welfare and Family Law* 55, 64–67.

[78] LASPO Act 2012, Schedule 1, part 1, para 21(1); *R (S) v Secretary of State for the Home Department* [2011] EWHC Admin 2120 (detention passed the high threshold required for a violation of Article 3 and amounted to inhuman or degrading treatment).

[79] JCHR, *The Implications for Access to Justice of the Government's Proposals to Reform Legal Aid* (2013–14, HL 100, HC 766) [96]–[101].

[80] JCHR, *Human Rights of Unaccompanied Migrant Children and Young People in the UK* (2013–14, HL 9, HC 196) [227] (evidence from the Children's Commissioner for Wales).

[81] ibid, (evidence from Solihull Council).

the Joint Committee on Human Rights (JCHR) in 2014 recommended that the Government *immediately* assess the availability and quality of representation and pay particular attention to the impact of withdrawing legal aid from unaccompanied migrant children.[82] In response, the Government noted its commitment to a post-implementation review of LASPO in 2016.[83]

Beyond the denial of justice for individuals, wider and longer-term consequences can be envisaged. If specialist immigration providers vacate the field, then the loss of expertise will be difficult, if not impossible, to replace. The risk is that unscrupulous advisers might step in. The development of substantive law is also likely to be inhibited in two ways. First, the lack of representation makes it more difficult for the Upper Tribunal to issue guidance to promote consistency amongst first-tier judges.[84] Second, practitioners will be unable to continue test-case strategies to secure rulings from the higher courts that set a more flexible and moderate tone for lower-level judges. Buried deep within the field and approaching cases with its own preconceptions, the tribunal has often been criticised for its stringent approach on key issues, such as the application of the right to family and private life under Article 8 ECHR, which is frequently used as a ground to challenge removal. By contrast, the elevated altitude at which the higher courts operate and their generalist perspective enables them to compare across different fields of law.[85] It is difficult to envisage similar test cases being brought post-LASPO. Withdrawing legal aid undermines not just individual adjudication, but also the wider development of the law.

How Do Unrepresented Appellants Fare?

By tradition, habit, and policy context, the Immigration Tribunal's predisposition is highly adversarial. Its formal position is that appeals work best with representation. Without legal aid, some individuals may represent themselves. A general perception is that the number of litigants in person has increased post-LASPO. Pre-hearing advice helps by filtering out hopeless cases and preparing stronger ones. Its absence means more unmeritorious claims and, almost certainly, some meritorious cases never being brought.[86] The challenge for courts and tribunals

---

[82] ibid, [223]–[234].

[83] *Government Response to the First Report from the JCHR: Human Rights of Unaccompanied Migrant Children and Young People in the UK* (Cm 8778, 2014) 23.

[84] See *JC v Secretary of State for Work and Pensions* (ESA) (Employment and support allowance: Post 28.3.11. WCA activity 16: coping with social engagement) [2014] UKUT 352 (AAC), [63].

[85] S Legomsky, *Specialized Justice: Courts, Administrative Tribunals, and a Cross-National Theory of Specialization* (Oxford, Oxford University Press, 1990) 15–16.

[86] Judicial Executive Board, *Written Evidence to the House of Commons Justice Committee Inquiry into the Impact of Changes to Civil Legal Aid Under the Legal Aid, Sentencing and Punishment of Offenders Act 2012* (2014), available at: http://data.parliament.uk/writtenevidence/committeeevidence. svc/evidencedocument/justice-committee/impact-of-changes-to-civil-legal-aid-under-laspo/ written/9472.pdf.

is to handle the increasing number of litigants in person effectively.[87] A long-espoused benefit of tribunals is their accessibility and informality of approach combined with a more interventionist approach.[88] The Leggatt report recommended an 'enabling' approach: tribunals should support litigants, compensate for their lack of skills or knowledge, and give them confidence in their own abilities to participate in the process.[89] Early empirical research indicated that unrepresented appellants were at a distinct disadvantage whereas more recent research concluded that the negative consequences of being unrepresented have been mitigated by more tribunals providing more assistance; the active, interventionist, and enabling approach of tribunals has reduced the 'representation premium'.[90]

Immigration judges are expected to give every assistance to unrepresented appellants.[91] Yet, judicial enabling capabilities are erratic. Some judges can handle unrepresented appellants effectively[92] whereas others have been criticised for asking new questions and identifying new adverse issues not previously raised. It cannot be assumed that the tribunal's experience in handling unrepresented appellants or, where an appellant cannot speak English, the provision of an interpreter will enable justice to be done. From the appellant's perspective, the concerns are obvious: being a litigant in person is a daunting challenge for anyone, but even more so for immigrant appellants, 'one-shotters' unable to speak English and adversaries of the Home Office, a well-established 'repeat player'.[93]

Such unevenness reflects both the wider dilemma of how to handle litigants in person effectively[94] and the significant potential for injustice for immigration appellants. It also highlights a comparison with other tribunals. Social security tribunals view their enabling function as central to access to justice.[95] Even this approach has limits: a tribunal cannot marshal evidence, take statements, or

---

[87] See *The Judicial Working Group on Litigants in Person: Report* (2013), available at: www.judiciary. gov.uk/wp-content/uploads/JCO/Documents/Reports/lip_2013.pdf.

[88] R Thomas, 'From "Adversarial v Inquisitorial" to "Active, Enabling, and Investigative": Developments in UK Tribunals' in L Jacobs and S Baglay (eds), *The Nature of Inquisitorial Processes in Administrative Regimes: Global Perspectives* (Farnham, Ashgate Publishing, 2013). Practice varies considerably between different tribunals. Social security tribunals are the most interventionist.

[89] Leggatt (n 34) [7.5].

[90] H Genn and Y Genn, *The Effectiveness of Representation in Tribunals* (London, Lord Chancellor's Department, 1989); M Adler, *Can Tribunals Deliver Justice in the Absence of Representation?* (ESRC, 2008), available at: www.esrc.ac.uk/my-esrc/grants/RES-000-23-0853/outputs/ Read/3ff71277-3c05-435b-a5a5-ef50c451afcf.

[91] *MNM v Secretary of State for the Home Department (Surendran guidelines for Adjudicators) (Kenya)* [2000] UKIAT 00005, Annex: The *Surendran Guidelines* [6]; Immigration Appellate Authority, *Adjudicator Guidance Note No 5: Unrepresented Appellants* (2003), available at: www.justice.gov.uk/ downloads/tribunals/immigration-and-asylum/lower/GuideNoteNo5.pdf.

[92] R Thomas, *Administrative Justice and Asylum Appeals* (Oxford, Hart Publishing, 2011) 125–28.

[93] M Galanter, 'Why the "Haves" Come Out Ahead: Speculations on the Limits of Legal Change' (1974) 9 *Law & Society Review* 95.

[94] R Moorhead, 'The Passive Arbiter: Litigants in Person and the Challenge to Neutrality' (2007) 16 *Social & Legal Studies* 405; P Cane, *Administrative Tribunals and Adjudication* (Oxford, Hart Publishing, 2009) 238–39.

[95] See the chapters by L Reid and S Wright, in this volume.

instruct expert witnesses. By contrast, immigration judges, operating against an adversarial backdrop, have not formulated an interventionist approach that can fully compensate for the lack of representation. Removing legal aid in such circumstances is akin to disarming one of the protagonists in a gladiatorial battle in which the other already has the upper hand. More generally, it has been argued that the complexity of immigration law combined with the volume of work generated by the Home Office's organisational dysfunction may have rendered the tribunal's basic purpose—cheap, efficient and effective justice—almost unattainable.[96]

LASPO also removed legal aid for onward appeals. The difficulties here are equally, if not more, acute for litigants in person. Onward appeals are limited to error of law grounds (appeals to the Court of Appeal are limited by the second-tier appeal criteria). Few, if any, litigants in person possess the knowledge to deal with this. Much will depend upon the individual judge. Without a clear change of tribunal approach, from adversarial to inquisitorial, LASPO is undermining effective justice for individuals and efficient judicial administration.

Exceptional Case Funding

LASPO's safety net is the exceptional case funding (ECF) scheme. If the absence of legal aid would breach ECHR or EU law rights or generate any risk of such a breach, then exceptional funding should be provided.[97] ECF applications are considered by the Legal Aid Agency (LAA) under guidance issued by the Lord Chancellor.[98] The test is whether withholding legal aid would make the risk of a breach of rights so substantial that funding is appropriate.[99] The 'overarching question' is 'whether the withholding of legal aid would make the assertion of the claim practically impossible or lead to an obvious unfairness in proceedings'—a high threshold indeed.[100] Factors to be considered include: the importance of the issues at stake; factual, procedural and legal complexity; and an individual's ability to self-represent. The European Court of Human Rights has held that immigration cases fall outside the scope of the right to a fair trial (Article 6 ECHR).[101] The Lord Chancellor's view was that there was nothing in the Strasbourg case law that obliged the state to provide legal aid in immigration proceedings to meet the procedural requirements of Article 8 ECHR.[102]

---

[96] C Yeo, 'Appeals and the Immigration Bill' (*Free Movement Blog*, 31 October 2013), available at: www.freemovement.org.uk/immigration-appeals-judicial-review-immigration-bill/.

[97] LASPO Act 2012, s 10(3).

[98] ibid, ss 4(3) and 10(2).

[99] MoJ, *Lord Chancellor's Exceptional Funding Guidance (Non-Inquests)* (London, MoJ, 2013) [7], available at: www.justice.gov.uk/downloads/legal-aid/funding-code/chancellors-guide-exceptional-funding-non-inquests.pdf.

[100] ibid, [18] and [41].

[101] ibid, [59] with reference to *Maaouia v France* (2001) 33 EHRR 42; *Eskelinen v Finland* (2007) 45 EHRR 43. For the argument that immigration cases should fall within Article 6, see Armstrong (n 60).

[102] MoJ, *Lord Chancellor's Exceptional Funding Guidance* (n 99) [60].

Upheld by the Government as a means of providing legal aid for fundamental rights cases, ECF was seen by others as a fig leaf to hide the injustices of LASPO, yet its initial operation 'proved to be worse than that'.[103] During the scheme's first nine months, a total of 1,151 applications were received, of which only 35 were granted.[104] Of the 187 applications concerning immigration matters, only three were granted. Exceptional funding has been exceptionally difficult to access. Other complaints include: the complex and bureaucratic application process, which acts as a disincentive; the absence of an emergency procedure; the failure to exempt children and others without capacity; and poor LAA decisions. Refused applicants have included children, persons without capacity, and litigants granted permission to appeal by the Court of Appeal.[105] For the JCHR, the ECF was not working as intended and could not be relied upon.[106]

A fundamental issue for immigration cases is the eligibility of Article 8 ECHR cases for legal aid. One inconsistency is that LASPO retained legal aid in some human rights cases, such as asylum and immigration detention (Articles 3 and 5 ECHR respectively), but not for Article 8 claims. Given Home Office delays over many years, many individuals waiting for an initial decision have developed a family life and resist removal on Article 8 ECHR grounds. Article 8 ECHR case law is complex and extensive. Without legal aid, the options are limited: self-fund; proceed without representation; complain to an MP; or withdraw.

However, the blanket exclusion of Article 8 ECHR cases was declared unlawful in *Gudanaviciene*.[107] Collins J ruled that the ECF guidance was defective because it set too high a threshold and failed to recognise that Article 8 carries with it certain procedural requirements. The European Court of Human Rights has held that although Article 8 ECHR does not contain any explicit procedural requirements, the decision-making process concerning an individual's family and private life must be fair and afford due respect to the interests protected by Article 8 ECHR.[108] There must be access to a court. One aspect of this concerns an individual's ability to present all necessary evidence to make his case and to understand and engage with the process. Furthermore, Collins J noted that aspects of the immigration process—

---

[103] Renshaw (n 75).

[104] MoJ, *Ad hoc Statistical Release: Legal Aid Exceptional Case Funding Application and Determination Statistics: 1 April to 31 December 2013* (2014), available at: www.gov.uk/government/uploads/system/uploads/attachment_data/file/289183/exceptional-case-funding-statistics-apr-13-dec_13.pdf.

[105] In *Gudanaviciene v Director of Legal Aid Casework* [2014] EWHC Admin 1840, [121] Collins J was 'clearly of the view that if the Court of Appeal gives leave to appeal, it will (provided the case is one which can attract ECF) prima facie be a case in which legal aid should be granted'.

[106] JCHR, *The Implications for Access to Justice* (n 79) [141]–[144].

[107] *Gudanaviciene* (n 105). This ruling was upheld by the Court of Appeal: [2014] EWCA Civ 1622.

[108] *P C & S v UK* (2002) 35 EHRR 1075, 1107; *W v UK* (1988) 10 EHRR 29, 119; *AK & L v Croatia* (App no 37965/11) [63]; *R (SB) v Governors of Denbigh High School* [2007] 1 AC 807, [29]. Article 8 claims will also affect the rights of other family members, particularly children, as recognised by *ZH (Tanzania) v Secretary of State for the Home Department* [2011] UKSC 4 and Borders, Citizenship and Immigration Act 2009, s 55 (the Secretary of State's duty to safeguard and promote the welfare of children in the United Kingdom when exercising immigration functions).

an adversarial tribunal process; the factual and legal complexity of appeals; the risk that vulnerable immigrants unable to speak English may be exploited by unscrupulous advisers—pointed toward the availability of legal aid. Consequently, the threshold for ECF eligibility—whether the refusal of legal aid would make the assertion of a right practically impossible or lead to obvious unfairness—was too high. If legal aid is needed to ensure that the Article 8 ECHR decision process is fair and effective, then it will have to be provided. For good measure, Collins J also held that, contrary to the Government's understanding, refugee family reunion cases were within the scope of legal aid under LASPO.[109]

Gudanaviciene represents clear judicial insistence upon the need for adequate and proper consideration of ECF claims in accordance with the procedural requirements of Article 8 ECHR. As Collins J noted, 'it is a fundamental principle that anyone in the UK is subject to its laws and is entitled to their protection. Thus there must be a fair and effective hearing available and the Guidance … produces unfairness'.[110] New guidance will have to lower the threshold. In the meantime, the appeals system has itself been reformed. It is this to which we now turn.

Limiting Appeals

The Coalition Government's second prong of attack against access to immigration justice was to significantly limit rights of appeal against Home Office decisions on individuals' immigration status.

Appeal Fees and Family Visitor Appeals

Access to tribunals may be 'just as important and fundamental as a right of access to the ordinary courts',[111] but, unlike judicial review, appeal rights can be confined and withdrawn with relative ease. The Government's initial step was to introduce appeal fees. Fees had previously operated and did not appear to discourage appeals.[112] A harbinger of things elsewhere, notably employment tribunals, fees were reintroduced in 2011.[113]

---

[109] *Gudanaviciene* (n 105) [104]–[109].

[110] *Gudanaviciene* (n 105) [124]. Alternatively, in a private family law case, *Q v Q* [2014] EWFC 31, Munby J held that there may be circumstances in which the court can properly direct that the cost of certain activities should be borne by HM Courts & Tribunals Service.

[111] *Saleem v Secretary of State for the Home Department* [2000] Imm AR 529, 544 (Hale LJ). See also *FP (Iran) v Secretary of State for the Home Department* [2007] EWCA Civ 13.

[112] V Gelsthorpe, R Thomas, D Howard and H Crawley, *Family Visitor Appeals: An Evaluation of the Decision to Appeal and Disparities in Success Rates by Appeal Type* (Home Office, 2003).

[113] MoJ, *Introducing Fee Charges for Appeals in the Immigration and Asylum Chambers of the First-tier Tribunal and the Upper Tribunal* Consultation Paper CP 10/10 (2011).

The next step was the piecemeal abolition of appeal rights by replacing them with administrative review. This had commenced under the Labour Government.[114] The Coalition Government prevented some in-country appeals from considering new evidence,[115] but its first major change was to abolish family visitor appeals. The volume of such appeals has been substantial. In 2010/11, 48,247 people refused a visa to visit their family in the UK appealed and 46 per cent succeeded.[116] One feature was that a significantly higher proportion of oral appeals were allowed compared with paper appeals; appeal procedures influence access to justice.[117] The Government argued that such appeals were disproportionately expensive and often used to submit new evidence that should have been presented earlier. The arguments were rebutted. New evidence is often adduced for valid reasons. Appeals enable refused applicants to clear their name. Decision-making at overseas posts is variable.[118] Nonetheless, family visitor appeals were withdrawn in 2013.[119]

Appeals and the Immigration Act 2014

The Coalition Government then sought a far more radical overhaul of appeals. In 2013, Theresa May, the Home Secretary, announced:

> We're going to cut the number of appeal rights. At the moment, the system is like a never-ending game of snakes and ladders, with almost 70,000 appeals heard every year. The winners are foreign criminals and immigration lawyers—while the losers are the victims of these crimes and the public. So we're going to cut the number of appeal rights from seventeen to four, and in doing so cut the total number of appeals by more than half.[120]

---

[114] Under the Immigration, Asylum and Nationality Act 2006 s 4(1) (brought into force 2008) appeal rights for those refused entry clearance under the points-based immigration system were replaced with administrative review. See also Home Office UKBA, *Report on Removal of Full Appeal Rights Against Refusal of Entry Clearance Decisions Under the Points-based System* (2011), available at: www.gov.uk/government/uploads/system/uploads/attachment_data/file/229027/9789999107563.pdf.

[115] UK Borders Act 2007, s 19 (brought into force 2011). This provision applies to in-country applications for leave to remain under the points-based immigration system.

[116] MoJ, *Tribunal Statistics Quarterly: January to March 2014* (2014), table 2.5, available at: www.gov.uk/government/publications/tribunal-statistics-quarterly-january-to-march-2014.

[117] Family visitor appeals were listed for an oral hearing of no more than an hour (Home Office presenting officers rarely attended to defend such appeals) or tribunal judges were given paper lists of 20 or so paper appeals per day. See R Thomas, 'Immigration Appeals for Family Visitors Refused Entry Clearance' [2004] *Public Law* 612, 631–39; H Genn and G Richardson, 'Tribunals in Transition: Resolution or Adjudication?' [2007] *Public Law* 116, 125–32.

[118] ICIBI, *Entry Clearance Decision-Making* (n 6).

[119] Crime and Courts Act 2013, s 52.

[120] Theresa May, speech at the Conservative Party conference, Manchester, September 2013, available at: http://conservativepartyconference.org.uk/Speeches/2013_Theresa_May.aspx.

Table 1: First-tier Tribunal (Immigration and Asylum) Appeals Determined, 2009/10 to 2013/14

	2009/10 Annual Total			2010/11 Annual Total			2011/12 Annual Total			2012/13 Annual Total			2013/14 Annual Total		
	Determined at hearing/ papers	Allowed %	Dismissed %	Determined at hearing/ papers	Allowed %	Dismissed %	Determined at hearing/ papers	Allowed %	Dismissed %	Determined at hearing/ papers	Allowed %	Dismissed %	Determined at hearing/ papers	Allowed %	Dismissed %
First-tier Tribunal (Immigration and Asylum Chamber)	**180,936**	**41**	**59**	**130,880**	**48**	**52**	**100,720**	**45**	**55**	**68,187**	**44**	**56**	**67,449**	**44**	**56**
Asylum	15,873	30	70	16,056	29	71	12,329	29	71	10,106	30	70	9,897	29	71
Managed Migration	32,158	52	48	40,609	56	44	28,626	51	49	21,669	49	51	28,719	49	51
Entry Clearance	71,779	36	64	25,009	51	49	23,090	51	49	12,815	50	50	14,278	48	52
Family Visit Visa	60,287	44	56	48,247	46	54	35,856	42	58	22,525	43	57	12,758	43	57
Deport and others	839	23	77	959	30	70	819	33	67	1,072	32	68	1,797	37	63

Source: Ministry of Justice, Tribunal Statistics Quarterly: January to March 2014 (2014), table 2.5

This was a disingenuous statement. The volume of appeals had more than halved from over 180,000 in 2009/10 to under 70,000 in 2013/14 (See table 1 above). Most appeals are not lodged by foreign criminals, but by individuals seeking entry clearance for work or family migration purposes or to extend their stay in the UK. In any event, even foreign criminals are entitled to challenge deportation decisions. Furthermore, in her readiness to castigate the reasonable usage of appeal rights as 'abuse',[121] May had overlooked the inconvenient fact that some 44 per cent of appeals are allowed (in 2010/11, 48 per cent were allowed)—amongst the highest rate of success across all tribunals.[122] Indeed, the Home Office had estimated that approximately 60 per cent of appeals succeed because of caseworking errors.[123] As one MP noted,

> [t]he Government's response to this high margin of error is not to seek to improve the quality of their decision making, but rather to reduce the opportunities for challenge. Instead of improving the bad administration and inefficiency at the heart of the Department, the Government are shifting the responsibility and attacking due process.[124]

The Government's other arguments were that the appeal system was unnecessarily complex and allowed individuals to exploit the system to delay their removal. Reform would reduce the case-load by 39,500 appeals each year, saving £219 million over 10 years.[125]

The JCHR argued that withdrawing appeals would undermine the common law right of access to a court or tribunal and the right to an effective remedy,[126] a move exacerbated by the proportion of successful appeals, the statutory duty to care for children subject to immigration control,[127] and legal aid and judicial review reforms.[128] The paradox was that, after years of seeking to reduce immigration judicial reviews by transferring them to the Upper Tribunal (Immigration and Asylum Chamber), the Government was now seeking to justify a significant reduction in appeal rights by reference to the continued availability of judicial review. As with legal aid cuts, the Government remained entirely unmoved.

The Immigration Act 2014 radically restructures appeal rights by limiting the range of appealable decisions. Under the 2014 Act, all previous appeal rights are

---

[121] HC Deb 22 October 2013, vol 569, col 158 (Theresa May MP).

[122] Comparable appeal success rates include social security appeals of which 40% are allowed: MoJ, *Tribunal Statistics Quarterly* (n 116) table 2.7.

[123] Home Office, *Impact Assessment of Reforming Immigration Appeal Rights* (2013) 7.

[124] HC Deb 22 October 2013, vol 569, col 199 (Barry Gardiner MP). See also HC Deb 22 October 2013, vol 569, col 189 (Fiona MacTaggart MP). Many MPs have an already high immigration case-load, but are not qualified immigration advisers. See Young Legal Aid Lawyers, *Nowhere Else to Turn: The Impact of Legal Aid Cuts on MPs' Ability to Help Their Constituents* (2012), available at: www.younglegalaidlawyers.org/sites/default/files/YLAL_Nowhere_else_to_turn.pdf

[125] Home Office, *Immigration Bill Factsheet: appeals (clauses 11–13)* (2013), available at: www.gov.uk/government/uploads/system/uploads/attachment_data/file/262789/Factsheet_05_-_Appeals.pdf.

[126] JCHR, *Legislative Scrutiny: Immigration Bill* (2013–14, HL 102, HC 935) [28]–[39] and (2013–14, HL 142, HC 1120) [85]–[93].

[127] Borders, Citizenship and Immigration Act 2009, s 55.

[128] JCHR, *Legislative Scrutiny* (n 126) [39].

replaced with a right of appeal against three types of decision only: (1) a refusal of an asylum or humanitarian protection claim; (2) a refusal of a human rights claim; and (3) a revocation of refugee status or humanitarian protection.[129] Ordinary appeal rights—for instance, against refusal to leave to remain in the UK or against refusal of settlement—are to be withdrawn, a massive restriction upon access to justice. In terms of the number of appeals, some 55,755 appellants who lodged appeals in 2013/14—82 per cent of all appellants—can no longer appeal. The 2014 Act also limits the grounds on which appeals can be lodged. Since the inception of the tribunal system,[130] appeals could be made on general public law grounds, that is, that the decision was 'not in accordance with the law (including immigration rules)'.[131] This ground of appeal has been withdrawn altogether.

The Government's comfort policy—to substitute appeals with administrative review[132]—provides little, if any, consolation. Such reviews are neither independent nor transparent, but merely involve a different caseworker taking another look at the papers (the Home Office marking its own homework). They significantly reduce participation and their robustness in practice has been inadequate.[133] Given the disparity in success rates—administrative review (21 per cent) and appeals (44 per cent)—is the former an effective remedy?[134] Without avenues for legal challenge, what is there to prevent the Home Office from taking whatever decisions it chooses? A report by the Chief Inspector on the independence and effectiveness of administrative review provides some transparency, but is no replacement for an independent appeal process.[135]

Another measure is targeted at the Government's principal bête noire: foreign criminals can now only appeal against deportation from outside the UK, unless this would create a real risk of serious irreversible harm.[136] The Government had been urged to go further by precluding foreign national prisoners from relying at all upon human rights grounds, but resisted on the ground that this would contravene the ECHR.[137] The measure, nevertheless, weakens appeal rights. Further, in

---

[129] Immigration Act 2014, s 15.

[130] Immigration Act 1971, s 19(1)(a)(i).

[131] Nationality, Immigration and Asylum Act 2002, ss 84(1)(a) and (e) and 86(3)(a).

[132] Home Office, *Immigration Bill—Statement of Intent: Administrative Review in Lieu of Appeals* (2013), available at: www.gov.uk/government/uploads/system/uploads/attachment_data/file/254851/SoI_Administrative_review.pdf.

[133] See, eg, Independent Chief Inspector of Borders and Immigration, *A Short-notice Inspection of Decision-making Quality in the Warsaw Visa Section* (2013), available at: http://icinspector.independent.gov.uk/wp-content/uploads/2013/12/An-Inspection-of-Decison-Making-Quality-in-the-Warsaw-Visa-Section.pdf (quality control conducted by Entry Clearance Managers (ECMs) in Warsaw was inadequate and fell well short of Home Office guidelines).

[134] These figures relate to administrative reviews completed from April to December 2013: HC Deb 7 May 2014, vol 580, col 225 (James Brokenshire MP, Minister for Security and Immigration). An issue for the future is whether Article 6 (the right to a fair trial) might have some bite in relation to administrative review.

[135] Immigration Act 2014, s 16.

[136] Nationality, Immigration and Asylum Act 2002, s 94B as inserted by the Immigration Act 2014, s 17(3).

[137] HC Deb 30 January 2014, vol 574, col 1062 (Theresa May MP, Home Secretary).

the ostensible pursuit of transparency for those appeals that remain, the tribunal is unable to consider a new matter, such as a human rights claim, 'unless the Secretary of State has given the Tribunal consent to do so'[138]—a clearly anomalous provision that undermines judicial independence.

The Immigration Act 2014 represents a significant hollowing-out of immigration appeals, for many years the UK's second largest tribunal system. Appeal rights subsequently added into the system—such as asylum appeals (introduced in 1993) and human rights appeals (introduced in 2000)—remain, but those appeals for which the system was originally created can now be jettisoned. The comparison with cognate jurisdictions is stark. Legal aid cuts have bitten elsewhere, but, in general, long-established appeal rights have not been abolished.[139] Mandatory reconsideration in social security has left appeals intact.[140] The Department for Work and Pensions has responded to concern about the number of allowed appeals by seeking to improve decision-making.[141] In immigration, things are very different: a higher appeal success rate has been castigated as 'abuse'; calls to improve decision-making have been largely unheeded;[142] and administrative review will replace, rather than supplement, appeal rights. Wider government policy on administrative justice is to provide proportionate remedies.[143] While parking appeals continue, immigration appeals have been abolished.

The End of Appeals?

The future may, though, be more complex than the Government has envisaged. One lesson from immigration litigation over the last 20 years is the symbiosis between appeals and judicial review: limiting the former increases recourse to the latter. Another lesson is that despite the obstacles placed in their path, people will find a way to challenge decisions that adversely affect their lives. Withdrawing appeals may transfer a sizeable amount of the First-tier Tribunal's case-load into the Upper Tribunal's judicial review in-tray. Of the 15,707 judicial review claims lodged in 2013, 13,210 (84 per cent) challenged immigration and asylum

[138] Nationality, Immigration and Asylum Act 2002, s 85(5) as inserted by the Immigration Act 2014, s 15(5).

[139] For instance, challenges against a child's exclusion from school have been weakened, but not altogether abolished: under the Education Act 2011 s 4, school exclusion appeals have been replaced with a review process which cannot order a child's reinstatement.

[140] Welfare Reform Act 2012, s 102.

[141] R Thomas, 'Administrative Justice, Better Decisions, and Organisational Learning' [2015] *Public Law* 111.

[142] The Independent Inspector has frequently recommended that the Home Office improve initial decision-making. See ICIBI, *An Inspection of Applications to Enter, Remain and Settle in the UK on the Basis of Marriage and Civil Partnerships* (2013) 43–45 and *An Inspection of Applications to Enter and Remain in the UK under the Tier 1 Investor and Entrepreneur Categories of the Points Based System* (2013) 37.

[143] MoJ, *Administrative Justice and Tribunals: A Strategic Work Programme 2012–16* (2012) 3.

decisions.[144] The Home Office itself had suggested that, once appeal rights are withdrawn, an additional 5,600 potential cases may seek judicial review.[145]

Substituting appeals with judicial review is, though, an odd and inefficient outcome. First, it prolongs the length of the decision-making process. Judicial review is not a fact-finding exercise. It is lengthy, costly, and successful challenges require decisions to be re-taken. Second, such judicial reviews will now be heard initially by the Upper Tribunal, which will cost more than appeals before the First-tier Tribunal—indeed, the reform simply removes fact-finding by the First-tier Tribunal while retaining the Upper Tribunal's error of law—but in many cases it is fact-finding that is essential.

Further, the removal of appeal rights may, over time, prove to be counterproductive. Indeed, the Immigration Act 2014 may prompt more judicial reviews *and* appeals. How so? Recall that previously an immigration decision could be appealed on the ground that it 'was not in accordance with the law (including immigration rules)'. At first glance, narrowing the grounds of appeal seems to place Home Office decisions above the law—except that both human rights appeals and judicial review remain. A twin-track approach may then emerge: appeals on human rights grounds and judicial review on public law grounds. A family migration appeal could generate both an appeal on human rights grounds (Article 8 ECHR) and judicial review on ordinary error of law grounds whereas previously there would only have been an appeal. Alternatively, Article 8 ECHR appeals may—despite the ostensible withdrawal of appeals on general public law grounds—involve the tribunal determining whether an infringement of family life was in accordance with the law. Case law requires tribunals to determine whether an alleged infringement of family life is in accordance with the law—this comes before any assessment of proportionality.[146] Limiting appeals may also produce satellite litigation to determine the important issue of which factual findings are binding (those of the tribunal in a human rights claim or those relied upon in judicial review proceedings). Non-suspensive appeals for foreign criminals will attract judicial review of the Home Office's certification that the appeal be heard from abroad because there is no real risk of serious irreversible harm.[147] There is also scope for judicial review challenges against administrative review.

Ironically, given the Government's concern about excessive legal challenges, the Immigration Act 2014 may inadvertently result in more challenges because of poor legislative design. As one commentator has noted, '[t]he twin bogeymen of judicial reviews and human rights claims will actually go forth and multiply: they

---

[144] MoJ, *Court Statistics Quarterly: January to March 2014* (2014) table 4.1 available at: www.gov.uk/government/statistics/court-statistics-quarterly-january-to-march-2014.

[145] Home Office, *Immigration Bill Factsheet* (n 125) 12–13 (this figure may be queried because it is drawn from the number of successful appeals, not the total number of appeals lodged).

[146] *R v Secretary of State for the Home Department, ex parte Razgar* [2004] 2 AC 368, 389. In *Razgar*, Lord Bingham listed five questions to be asked when removal is being resisted under Article 8.

[147] Existing decisions to certify certain decisions (ie, an asylum appellant comes from a designated safe country), which consequently generate limited appeal rights, can be challenged through judicial review.

will be the only avenues of redress for desperate people'.[148] Remedies will become more expensive and time-consuming for both the Government and individuals. Rather than resolving the issues, the 2014 Act may simply exacerbate the underlying problems.

Legal Aid Post-LASPO

LASPO was not the end of the legal aid reforms; a mere eight days after the Act came into force, the Government consulted on further restrictions.[149] The new Lord Chancellor's blunt headlines convey his general attitude: 'The judicial review system is not a promotional tool for countless Left-wing campaigners'; 'We must stop the legal aid abusers tarnishing Britain's justice system'.[150] Two measures in particular are important: removing legal aid for permission work in judicial review cases; and the residence test, the Government's third and fourth lines of attack.

Removing Legal Aid for Permission Work in Judicial Review Cases

The use of judicial review against immigration decisions has long frustrated the Home Office.[151] The essential concern is that judicial review is used as a tactical weapon to delay decision-making and the removal of those individuals who do not qualify to remain. At the same time, judicial review is there to impose legal control over the executive. There have been instances in which the Home Office has undertaken removals in the face of an injunction.[152] The courts have warned against hopeless judicial reviews[153] and protected the right of access to judicial review when the Home Office sought to remove people on less than 72 hours'

---

[148] Yeo (n 96).

[149] MoJ, *Transforming Legal Aid: Delivering a More Credible and Efficient System* Consultation Paper CP 14/2013 (2013).

[150] Chris Grayling, 'The Judicial Review System is Not a Promotional Tool for Countless Left-wing Campaigners' *Daily Mail* (6 September 2013), available at: www.dailymail.co.uk/news/article-2413135/CHRIS-GRAYLING-Judicial-review-promotional-tool-Left-wing-campaigners.html and 'We Must Stop the Legal Aid Abusers Tarnishing Britain's Justice System' *The Telegraph* (20 April 2014) available at: www.telegraph.co.uk/news/uknews/law-and-order/10777503/Chris-Grayling-We-must-stop-the-legal-aid-abusers-tarnishing-Britains-justice-system.html.

[151] R Thomas, 'The Impact of Judicial Review on Asylum' [2003] *Public Law* 479.

[152] 'Theresa May Rebuked Over Illegally Deported Asylum Seeker' *The Guardian* (30 April 2012), available at: www.theguardian.com/uk/2012/apr/30/theresa-may-deported-asylum-seeker.

[153] *R (Hamid) v Secretary of State for the Home Department* [2012] EWHC 3070 (Admin); 'Judge Warns Against "Hopeless" Applications to Halt Deportations' *The Guardian* (11 July 2013), available at: www.theguardian.com/law/2013/jul/11/judge-hopeless-application-halt-deportations. Between October 2012 and March 2014, 33% of the immigration and asylum judicial review that reached permission or oral renewal stage were classed as 'totally without merit', see MoJ, *Court Statistics Quarterly* (n 144) table 4.4.

notice.[154] Transferring immigration judicial reviews to the Upper Tribunal has been followed by a wider governmental project to restrict judicial review.[155] The Criminal Justice and Courts Bill 2014 contains much that will confine judicial review: the principle that permission for judicial review should not be granted where it is highly likely that the claim would not make any difference; restricting the availability of protective cost orders; and requiring interveners to pay more costs. LASPO did not generally affect legal aid for judicial review, but it did exclude legal aid from some types of immigration judicial review claims. These included repetitive judicial reviews raising the same issue as raised in a previous unsuccessful challenge less than a year previously, and judicial review claims challenging removal directions issued not more than a year after the decision to remove the individual from the UK or an appeal against that decision.[156]

In 2014, a wide-ranging restriction was introduced: legal aid would be available only for those judicial review cases granted permission to proceed except where the Lord Chancellor considers it reasonable to provide legal aid even though permission has not been granted.[157] The Government had argued that taxpayers should not pay for those weak judicial review cases refused permission to proceed, and that lawyers should bear the financial risk of the permission stage. However, not all judicial review claims refused permission are weak: 'Often the opposite is true. It is precisely because a claim has substantial merit that the public authority speedily addresses the grievance'.[158] The issue is exemplified by immigration judicial reviews. For many years, the Home Office has conceded many judicial review claims granted permission for pragmatic purposes because it recognises itself to be at fault. In some instances, the only way for an individual to receive any sort of communication from the Home Office has been to institute judicial review proceedings.[159] In summary, a fair amount of pre-litigation work occurs that never ends up in the law reports.[160] Much of this work is necessary for getting the Home Office to produce good decisions—yet, it will only be publicly funded if a judicial review claim is granted permission.

---

[154] *R (Medical Justice) v Secretary of State for the Home Department* [2011] EWCA Civ 1710.

[155] MoJ, *Judicial Review: proposals for reform* (Cm 8515, 2012); MoJ, *Judicial Review: Proposals for further reform* (Cm 8703, 2013); Criminal Justice and Courts Bill (2014–15).

[156] LASPO Act 2012, Schedule, 1 part 1, paras 19(5) and (6). The Act specifically provided that some immigration judicial reviews remained within the scope of legal aid, such as: judicial review of non-appealable asylum decisions; judicial review of claims certified as manifestly unfounded which only attract a non-suspensive appeal; and judicial review claims of removal directions where prescribed conditions, such as those concerning the period between the individual being given notice and the proposed time for removal, are met.

[157] The Civil Legal Aid (Remuneration) (Amendment) (No 3) Regulations, SI 2014/607 (brought into force April 2014) applies to all judicial review claims.

[158] HL Deb 7 May 2014, vol 753, col 1541 (Lord Pannick).

[159] ibid, col 1548 (Lord Carlile of Berriew).

[160] See generally V Bondy and M Sunkin, *The Dynamics of Judicial Review Litigation: The Resolution of Public Law Challenges Before Final Hearing* (2009), available at: www.publiclawproject.org.uk/data/resources/9/TheDynamicsofJudicialReviewLitigation.pdf.

A second concern is that the measure will make public law litigation more risky by exerting a 'chilling effect' on public law providers. Given that judicial review is an inherently risky form of litigation, this measure may well have a damaging effect on the right of individuals without means to secure advice and representation for the purposes of pursuing a judicial review. The likely substantial reduction in the number of providers willing to provide public law assistance will exert a detrimental effect on access to justice, legal protection and legal accountability of government.[161] The JCHR concluded that the measure's chilling effect would impact adversely on access to justice because meritorious judicial review cases would not be brought, a claim denied by the Government.[162]

The Residence Test

Having already restricted legal aid in immigration appeals, the Government's fourth line of attack was to cut legal aid for non-residents in all other forms of legal action. Under the residence test, only those individuals with a strong connection with the UK, a minimum of 12 months' lawful residence, would qualify for legal aid.[163] This meant that those people with a better than 50 per cent chance of success would be unable to vindicate their legal rights solely on the ground that they were not residents. According to the Government, '[w]e have made it absolutely clear that for the residence test it is important that they are *our people*—that they have some link to this country'.[164] Asylum claimants and refugees were exempt; there were also some case-based exemptions, such as, immigration detention. However, those without 12 months' residence would not qualify at all for civil legal aid for any form of legal action, such as children-related judicial reviews, special educational needs cases, and individuals who lack mental capacity and are protected persons, even though they had a better than 50 per cent chance of success.

The residence test would have rendered access to justice dependent not upon the merits of a case, but an individual's location in the world and discriminated against people. As one MP noted, '[t]he test fails consistently to recognise that recent migrants are no less likely to suffer wrongful treatment by public bodies than

---

[161] House of Lords Scrutiny of Secondary Legislation Committee, *Civil Legal Aid (Remuneration) (No 3) Regulations 2014* (2013–14, HL 157); JUSTICE, *Briefing note on the Civil Legal Aid (Remuneration)(Amendment) (No 3) Regulations* (2014), available at: www.justice.org.uk/data/files/resources/370/JUSTICE-Judicial-Review-Legal-Aid-Regulations-Briefing-March-2014.pdf; HL Deb 7 May 2014, vol 753, cols 1540–68.

[162] JCHR, *The Implications for Access to Justice* (n 19) [76].

[163] Draft Legal Aid, Sentencing and Punishment of Offenders Act 2012 (Amendment of Schedule 1) Order 2014.

[164] HC Deb 18 March 2014, vol 577, col 624 (Shailesh Vara MP, Parliamentary Under-Secretary of State) (emphasis added). The Government's argument that the residence test would save money was weakened by its inability to identify the costs to be saved.

others. Indeed, in many cases they are more vulnerable to such mistreatment'.[165] Individuals with meritorious cases to have been rendered ineligible for legal aid would have included: a slavery victim; a trafficking victim; a mother of an autistic child facing removal; a destitute victim of torture; a pregnant woman sleeping rough; and an amputee refused housing support. The JCHR warned that leaving migrant children without assistance or representation would contravene the United Nations Convention on the Rights of the Child.[166] Other concerns were that the test would deny justice in matters of especial gravity, breach assurances made during the passage of LASPO, and introduce a complex and impractical system of evidentiary requirements to demonstrate a connection with the UK. Linking legal aid entitlement to Home Office decisions about immigration status was 'a dangerous link to establish where fundamental rights are concerned'.[167] Further, the Government had been unable to state how much public money would be saved by the test.

Of crucial importance, the Government had introduced the residence test through secondary legislation, a method with certain political advantages, but also potential legal disadvantages for the Government. Getting the measure approved would present few difficulties because the Government could ensure that Parliamentarians with voting rights would not object, but the regulations could be legally challenged, which soon happened.[168] The Joint Committee on Statutory Instruments doubted the legality of the regulations as they made an unexpected use of the enabling power in LASPO.[169] For the JCHR, it was a basic constitutional requirement that legal aid should be available to make access to court possible in relation to important and legally complex disputes subject to means and merits tests and other proportionate limitations.[170] The Government was unrepentant. It did 'not consider that the proposed residence test would, if enacted, impede access to justice. Access to justice and access to taxpayer-funded legal aid are distinct concepts'.[171]

---

[165] House of Commons Fifth Delegated Legislation Committee, *Draft Legal Aid, Sentencing and Punishment of Offenders Act 2012 (Amendment of Schedule 1) Order 2014* (1 July 2014) col 15 (Sarah Teather MP).

[166] JCHR, *Legal Aid: Children and the Residence Test* (2014–15, HL 14, HC 234).

[167] ILPA, *Briefing on the Legal Aid, Sentencing and Punishment of Offenders Act 2012 (Amendment of Schedule 1) Order 2014 (the 'residence test')* (2014), available at: www.ilpa.org.uk/resources. php/29005/ilpa-briefing-to-the-house-of-commons-fifth-delegated-legislation-committee-for-its-consideration-of.

[168] See M Fordham, B Jaffey and R Mehta, 'The Legality of the Proposed Residence Test for Civil Legal Aid: Joint Opinion' (2013) 18 *Judicial Review* 219.

[169] Joint Committee on Statutory Instruments (JCSI), *First Report of Session 2014–15* (2014–15, HL 4, HC 332) [4.1]–[4.14].

[170] JCHR, *The Implications for Access to Justice* (n 79) 3.

[171] JCSI, *First Report of Session 2014–15* (n 169) 23. The Government relied upon *R (The Howard League for Penal Reform) v The Lord Chancellor* [2014] EWHC 709 (Admin) [47]: 'there is no corollary to the common law right of access to a court of a right to legal aid'. The European Court of Human Rights has ruled that, under Article 6 ECHR, the provision of legal aid is not required, except in exceptional cases: *Airey v Ireland* (1979–80) 2 EHRR 305; *Hooper v United Kingdom* [2005] 41 EHRR 1.

However, in *Public Law Project*[172] the High Court declared the residence test unlawful. The Court held that to introduce residence as a criterion of eligibility for legal aid went beyond the policy and object of the enabling statute. As the purpose of LASPO was to restrict legal aid to those cases judged to be of greatest need, it was impermissible to introduce a new criterion—residency—that had nothing to do with need. The residence test also resulted in discrimination that could not be justified by either the need to save public money or to maintain public confidence in the legal aid system. The residence test was unlawful because it contravened the overarching constitutional principle that everyone is entitled to equal protection of the law. Without primary legislation, the residence test could not proceed.

Conclusion

This chapter has surveyed restrictions to access to immigration justice under the Coalition Government. There is another side to the debate that cannot be over-looked, one rooted in the primacy of public policy and the capacity of an elected government to steer the country in accordance with its policy goals. Given the UK's fiscal deficit and competing demands on the public pursue, inherently dif-ficult decisions concerning the effective allocation of scarce resources are best left to politically accountable ministers. From this perspective, there is no reason why legal aid should be exempt from wider reductions in public spending. Looking to the longer term, ministers have been seeking to rebalance public finances. There are, however, weaknesses with this argument. Without access to justice, legal rights are rendered illusory; restricting access to justice is 'tantamount to repealing laws enacted by Parliament for the benefit of those affected'.[173] Cutting legal aid means that impoverished people are denied effective access to justice; it reinforces social inequality. Legal aid often saves money; cutting it increases the costs elsewhere in the system.[174] Further, some of the Government's measures, such as the residence test, were unaccompanied by any estimate of what amount of public money would be saved.

Furthermore, as this chapter has argued, the explanation for the Government's restrictions is not to be found solely in the need to reduce public spending, but in the ideological and political forces underpinning the Government's wider immi-gration agenda. The Government has gone further than in other areas of law by withdrawing appeal rights and seeking to introduce the residence test. Such meas-ures come on top of other problems: poor initial decision-making; bureaucratic incompetence and delay; and the tribunal's adversarial approach. Previously, legal remedies, such as tribunals, were introduced as a symbolic appearance of legality

---

[172] *R (Public Law Project) v Secretary of State for Justice* [2014] EWHC Admin 2365.

[173] S Cragg, 'Denial of Justice' (June 2014) *Legal Action* 3.

[174] eg, Brookes and Hunter, this volume.

to make oppressive policies more acceptable.[175] Since 2010, the Government has introduced tougher substantive policies *and* restricted legal remedies. Despite their inauspicious beginnings, immigration tribunals came to be a sufficiently independent and effective legal remedy—so much so that the Government was motivated to reduce access to them. Just as the economic slump and austerity have wrought a divisive toll upon already disadvantaged members of society,[176] so have restrictions on access to justice hit immigration harder than other areas of law.

The Government has been able to obstruct immigration justice because of the marginal political influence of migrants who have no direct representation or influence in the political process other than the lobbying of NGOs. Given the toxic politics involved, there are few mainstream politicians who would stand up for the rights and interests of migrants and their families. Yet, the Government has not achieved all of its plans. The intention of the 2014 Act is to reduce the number of appeals, but it may, because of poor legislative design, result in more legal challenges. The courts have provided something of a counterbalance to the Government by upholding the principle that everyone is entitled to the protection of the law and to vindicate their legal rights. *Gudanaviciene* and *Public Law Project* illustrate the Government's basic legal errors—overlooking the procedural requirements of Article 8 ECHR and introducing a discriminatory residence test that went beyond the policy and objects of the enabling statute. The Government, though, is undeterred.[177] Looking to the future, it is clearly the case that accessing immigration justice will become significantly more difficult and problematic than was previously the case. Many individuals are now altogether excluded from the justice system—especially those who are already marginalised, such as unaccompanied migrant children and overstayers. Some people will still find a way to challenge decisions, but only if they are first able to overcome the higher obstacles placed in their path. Access to immigration justice has been more restricted than in other areas and this has undermined the ability of the law to provide equal protection to all people.

---

[175] L Bridges, 'Legality and Immigration Control' (1975) 2 *British Journal of Law and Society* 221; T Prosser, 'Poverty, Ideology, and Legality: Supplementary Benefit Appeal Tribunals and their Predecessors' (1977) 4 *British Journal of Law and Society* 39.

[176] T Clark with A Heath, *Hard Times: The Divisive Toll of the Economic Slump* (New Haven CT, Yale University Press, 2014); M O'Hara, *Austerity Bites: A Journey to the Sharp End of Cuts in the UK* (Bristol, Policy Press, 2014).

[177] MoJ, *Government Response to the Joint Committee on Human Rights—Legal Aid: Children and the Residence Test* (Cm 8936, 2014)

7

The Impact of Austerity and Structural Reforms on the Accessibility of Tribunal Justice

STEWART WRIGHT

Introduction

There are many interesting, and at heart deeply political, questions raised by the title for this seminar.[1] For example: are benefits at a crossroads? Is the 'rights' model for benefit one the state remains in substance committed to? Are we 'all in this together? Does the social security system need reshaping and, if so, how should that be done? And how should advice services and legal aid be configured?

I am not, and should not, as a tribunal judge, address any of these. However, I have taken account of where we are now in terms of the delivery of benefits (based, it has to be said on a seeming political consensus), in framing how the social entitlement chamber may seek to aid access to justice.

There is also an issue about what is meant by the phrase *access to justice*. On a wider analysis of the substantive meaning of that phrase consideration may need to be given to justice in the wider sense—and thus issues such as the adequacy of benefit levels. I am not addressing that either.

This chapter is written from my perspective as a tribunal judge. What it seeks to address is how a citizen can *get to* an independent tribunal, the barriers that may be in his or her way, and how the tribunal can aid that person in accessing and achieving justice.

[1] The seminar at which the content of this chapter was first presented was entitled 'Benefits at the Crossroads: Delivering Justice in an Age of Austerity'.

Background: Personal

Having made the above disclaimers, it may help if I first give some personal background, as I hope that indicates that I may have an informed view about claimants accessing justice about their benefit entitlement.

Before coming to the Bar I worked in a law centre for seven years in the late 1980s and early 1990s. I was then at the Bar from 1993 to 1999.

From 1999 to 2007 I was the Child Poverty Action Group's legal officer. Doing that job I was responsible for running CPAG's test case strategy and under that important social security cases such as:

— *Hinchy v SSWP* [2005] UKHL 16 (on overpayments and 'disclosure').
— *Howker v SSWP* [2003] ICR 405 (misleading SSAC/Parliament).
— *RJM v SSWP* [2008] UKHL 63 (access of homeless person to Disability Benefit).
— *White and Runkee v UK* [2007] 2 FCR 178 (ECtHR) (rights of widowers to bereavement benefits).
— *Collins v SSWP* (C138/02) [2005] QB 145 (application of habitual residence test to workers moving within the EU).

I was a part-time social security judge from 2002 to 2011. I became a full-time judge from the end of 2011.

Background: Social Entitlement Tribunal

The social entitlement chamber of the First-tier Tribunal covers citizen/state disputes concerning social security benefits, tax credits, housing and council tax benefits, and asylum support; and party/party disputes about child support. These tribunal chambers were the culmination of the Leggatt review which found statutory force in the Tribunals, Courts and Enforcement Act 2007. The tribunal was previously called the Social Security Appeal Tribunal—with a similar scope to the above.

However, before 1984 the tribunal was split between the National Insurance Local Tribunal (dealing broadly with contributory benefit issues) and the Supplementary Benefit Appeal Tribunal (SBAT) (dealing with the means-tested, safety net benefits).[2] The latter tribunal had a purely lay membership—no lawyer—and advice was given by a clerk who was a DHSS employee. (An unsuccessful attempt

---

[2] Disputes about Housing Benefit and Council Tax Benefit had their final adjudication before local authority councillors from the local authority charged with administering the HB and CTB schemes, and this arrangement remained in place until 2 July 2001. It now seems unsurprising that the ECtHR in *Tsfayo v UK* [2006] ECHR 981, found this arrangement to breach Article 6 of the European Convention on Human Rights (ECHR).

was made to reintroduce this structure in 1996.) Also before 1984, the SBAT's decision could only be challenged by judicial review in the High Court and those courts were initially sceptical about the High Court having any but the most limited role—see Lord Denning (MR) in *R v The Preston SBAT ex parte Moore* (5 March 1975):

> It is plain that Parliament intended that the Supplementary Benefits Act should be administered with as little technicality as possible. It should not become the happy hunting ground for lawyers. The Courts should hesitate long before interfering by certiorari with the decisions of appeal tribunals. Otherwise the Courts would become engulfed with streams of cases … The Court should not enter into a meticulous discussion of the meaning of this or that word in the Act. They should leave the tribunals to interpret the Act in a broad reasonable way, according to the spirit and not the letter … The Courts should only interfere when the decision of the tribunal is unreasonable in the sense that no tribunal acquainted with the ordinary use of language could reasonably reach that decision.

It is difficult to imagine any court or tribunal adopting such an approach to the interpretation of a statutory phrase now.

Decisions of tribunals can be challenged, with permission, on a point of law to the Upper Tribunal and thereon to the Court of Appeal (and then the Supreme Court).

Important Access Features of the Social Entitlement Chamber

There is a no costs regime. Win or lose the appellant will not have to pay to come to the tribunal or the other side's costs, however abject his or her case may have been and regardless of how wastefully the appeal has been conducted. (The solution to these problems has to lie in good case management under the Tribunal Procedure Rules 2008—which include strike-out powers). It has consistently been recognised that to impose any cost provision on those who are often the poorest in society in order to access justice about their social security rights would constitute a real and unjustified fetter on their accessing justice.

Despite Lord Denning's view, and given the complexity of law to be applied, the tribunal is always chaired by a lawyer (now called a tribunal judge), who can sit with doctors, disability members and accountants. It is thus a specialist tribunal.

Perhaps the key to access is the tribunal's enabling or inquisitorial function. This has long been recognised: see, for example, Baroness Hale in *Kerr v Department for Social Development* [2004] UKHL 23 (paragraph 61):

> Ever since the decision of the Divisional Court in *R v Medical Appeal Tribunal (North Midland Region), Ex p Hubble* [1958] 2 QB 228, it has been accepted that the process of benefits adjudication is inquisitorial rather than adversarial. Diplock J as he then was said this of an industrial injury benefit claim at p 240:

'A claim by an insured person to benefit under the Act is not truly analogous to a lis inter partes. A claim to benefit is a claim to receive money out of the insurance funds … Any such claim requires investigation to determine whether any, and if so, what amount of benefit is payable out of the fund. In such an investigation, the minister or the insurance officer is not a party adverse to the claimant. If analogy be sought in the other branches of the law, it is to be found in an inquest rather than in an action'.

It is perhaps worth setting out here what Baroness Hale later said, in general, about tribunals, in *Gillies v Secretary of State for Work and Pensions* [2006] UKHL 2 (at paragraphs 36–37):

Tribunals were once regarded with the deepest of suspicion but they are now an essential part of our justice system. They are mostly there to secure justice between citizen and state in a wide variety of contexts, the most numerically important of which is entitlement to the financial benefits provided by the welfare state. Since the Report of the Donoughmore Committee on Ministers' Powers (Cmd 4060, 1932), it has been recognised that tribunals can have important advantages over courts of law. These are 'cheapness, accessibility, freedom from technicality, expedition and expert knowledge of their particular subject': see the Report of the Franks Committee on Administrative Tribunals and Enquiries (Cmnd 218, 1957, para 38). The Report of Sir Andrew Leggatt's Review of Tribunals, Tribunals for Users, One System, One Service (2001, paras 1.11 to 1.13) suggests three tests of whether tribunals rather than courts should decide cases. The first is participation: that users should be able to prepare and present their own cases effectively. The third is the need for expertise in the area of law involved: users should not have to explain to the tribunal what the law is. The second is the need for special expertise in the subject matter of the dispute:

Where the civil courts require expert opinion on the facts of the case, they generally rely on the evidence produced by the parties—increasingly jointly—or on a court-appointed assessor. Tribunals offer a different opportunity, by permitting decisions to be reached by a panel of people with a range of qualifications and expertise. … users clearly feel that the greater expertise makes for better decisions.

Expertise on the tribunal not only improves decision-making and reduces the need for outside expertise; it also thereby increases the accessibility and user-friendliness of the proceedings.

In my judgement, this aptly describes a number of the positives of the social entitlement chamber.

However, I consider that the enabling function is the unique selling point of the social entitlement chamber. The consequences of the enabling approach described in *Kerr* are far reaching and need some teasing out. They place the tribunal in a very different position from the courts generally and many other tribunals. So, for example, save for very rare examples, there are no rules of evidence. The claimant's mother's recollection of what a neighbour said to her about when her son had told the neighbour he had posted a letter is just as valid evidence as that of the claimant himself, though of course its provenance may mean it is to be accorded less weight. Second, because an appellant may be illiterate or otherwise not wholly competent to put forward his case, it is the duty of the tribunal to elicit the case from him by asking questions of him. This can extend to the tribunal seeking the person's medical records if the nature or history of his ill health is not clear. Or the tribunal might insist on a local authority producing further documents where it considers that those documents (unbeknown to the claimant) might assist his or her case.

The underpinning justification for all this is, as Baroness Hale explained at paragraph 41 of *Gillies*, that:

> Another relevant fact of tribunal life is that the benefits system exists to pay benefits to those who are entitled to them. As counsel put it to us in *Hinchy v Secretary of State for Work and Pensions* [2005] UKHL 16, [2005] 1 WLR 967, the system is there to ensure, so far as it can, that everyone receives what they are entitled to, neither more nor less.

Another important feature of this tribunal's enabling role has been its attempt to have the tribunal based at a venue that is local to the appellant and which is not, as far as is possible, associated with the formality of a court. This is an area which is under pressure due to the pressure to cut costs and use venues to their full capacity, a pressure that has increased since the Courts Service and the Tribunals Service merged. Although that merger may have many benefits, asking a nervous appellant to come to a magistrates' court to talk about their care needs is not one of them.

Progress

There has, in my opinion, been much in the way of progressing access to justice for benefit claimants since Lord Denning's views in *ex parte Moore* in 1975 (and the suggestion then that tribunals were meant to mainly be beyond challenge). The entitlement rules have been codified and the areas for discretion narrowed.[3] Further, the status of tribunals has been recognised as being equivalent to courts, the tribunals have become more specialist, and tribunals have been provided with procedural rules to enable them to case manage appeals.

Challenges/Barriers

However, despite these advances, the pressures on tribunals and the barriers to claimants exercising their rights of appeal are growing.

---

[3] Though the areas of discretion are growing. The discretionary social fund remains outside any appeal regime and decisions to recover overpayments of tax credits have always (ie, since 2002) been non-appealable. However under the Welfare Reform Act 2012 Council Tax Benefit is to be abolished and replaced with local, discretionary rebate schemes and the right of appeal against whether an overpayment of social security benefits is recoverable is removed.

Cuts in Advice Provision

Despite the enabling role described above, a key role advice centres play is in gathering evidence and, perhaps most importantly, getting the appellant to attend the hearing. It is difficult for the tribunal to exercise its enabling role if the appellant is not before them to ask questions or to get them to sign a medical consent form. Moreover, in the legally complicated cases good and specialist advice centres can help develop arguments that enable the law to be made clearer and work more effectively.

Benefit Changes

The recent changes from Incapacity Benefit to Employment and Support Allowance (ESA), and the poor level of medical adjudication, have led to the tribunal having to address far more (and a lot of the time unnecessary) appeals. As *Leggatt* said, tribunals should be there to deal with the difficult cases: the easy ones should be decided properly by good first-instance decision-makers. Successive administrations have failed to recognise this, and staff cuts would seem likely to only make matters worse. But too much time is taken up by the tribunals carrying out the first-tier fact-finding and adjudication that the first-tier agency is enjoined to carry out.

In the next couple of years, as well as the ESA changes, the ambition is to amalgamate most/all working age benefits into one benefit called Universal Credit. However, people will lose out from this change and experience tells us that the changeover will be far from smooth. So appeals will increase. Furthermore the abolition of the recoverable overpayment defence is bound to lead to many more appeals, at least initially. In addition Disability Living Allowance (DLA) is to go and be replaced by the Personal Independence Payment (PIP), and at the same time the lowest levels of DLA will not carry forward into PIP. That is bound to lead to many more appeals.

Increase in Appeals

Until a few years ago the social entitlement chamber would receive about 250,000 appeals a year. That made it by far the biggest jurisdiction in terms of receipts. Because of the above changes it is anticipated this receipts figure will have risen to 600,000 appeals by 2012/2013 and 700,000–750,000 appeals by 2013/2014— a three-fold increase. Despite taking on more judges, sitting on Saturdays, and using all facilities to the maximum (which may then involve asking an appellant to attend an appeal at a magistrates' court), this huge increase in appeals is bound to have an effect on when the appeals are heard.

Coupled with the above, at present the tribunal is having to deal with the poor and erratic (though perhaps now improving) performance of the company that provides interpreters to courts and tribunals. If an appeal has to be adjourned because the interpreter does not turn up, then that is a slot lost and the appeal then has to take up another, later slot. So this one mistake robs the tribunal of two, valuable appeal hearing slots.

Statutory Reconsideration

It is unclear whether this is a positive or a negative in terms of accessing justice. Under section 102 of the Welfare Reform Act 2012 *before* appealing a decision a claimant is compelled to first ask the Secretary of State to reconsider his decision. The positive aspect of this is that, *if done properly*, it should remove the easy appeals from the tribunal. However, as said above, there is nothing in past history to instil confidence that this will be done properly. Moreover, the deficit is that there is no time limit on carrying out a statutory reconsideration, and as this step has to be taken before any appeal can be made it prevents the tribunal from having any jurisdiction over the unreconsidered decision. If this becomes simply a tick box exercise, then all it will achieve is a lengthening of the time before an independent tribunal can consider the decision.[4]

Conclusions

If we ask the question with a view to the language of Article 6 of the ECHR, it seems plain that in terms of benefit claimants accessing tribunal justice within a reasonable period of time, the picture is likely to be considerably bleaker over the next few years. Quite how much bleaker is likely to depend on the 'perfect storm' of increasing appeals, reductions in benefits staff, and the loss of advice centres.

However, despite this, a remaining positive, I believe, is the enabling function of the tribunal once it has the appeal. Moreover, the Tribunal Procedure Rules do provide a mechanism for expediting the truly urgent appeals (though plainly there is a limit to this). So appellants should be encouraged to appeal, get what advice they can, and not forget about the appeal when they get the invite to the hearing a year later!

---

[4] On this issue, see further the section of the Mullen chapter in this volume under the heading 'New Obstacles to Using Remedies', pp 95–99.

8

Thirteen Years of Advice Delivery in Islington: A Case Study

LORNA REID

The biggest shake up of the welfare benefits system in the UK coincided with the Legal Aid, Sentencing and Punishment of Offenders Act 2012 (LASPO) which aimed to make savings in the legal aid bill by taking out of scope areas of legal advice including most aspects of social security law. There is no longer public funding for claimants to challenge a decision on their entitlement to welfare benefits apart from appeals to the Upper Tribunal of the Social Entitlement Chamber where a 'point of law' is concerned. First-tier Tribunal representation is not publicly funded. Recommendations in the 2004 White Paper on *Transforming Public Services: Complaints, Redress and Tribunals*,[1] accepted that 'some people will always need a lot of help, perhaps because of learning difficulties, physical difficulty or language problems', but aimed to increase the responsiveness of tribunals to enable an appellant to present their case without the need for a representative.

At the time, the White Paper recommendations flew in the face of the well-documented research in 1989 by Hazel Genn and Yvette Genn, *The Effect of Representation in Tribunals*[2] which found that the success of represented appellants at Social Security Tribunals was 18 per cent higher than those who had no representation. Research by Michael Adler in 2004, *Can Tribunals Deliver Justice in the Absence of Representation?*,[3] concluded that the increasingly inquisitorial, enabling and interventionist role of the First-tier Tribunal produced a surprisingly high success rate of 70 per cent for social security appeals and reduced the differential to 10 per cent for represented and unrepresented appellants.

Adler's research distinguished between those who had received pre-hearing advice and those who had not and found that those who had received pre-hearing advice did significantly better. It appeared that this advice contributed to the reduction in need for representation.

---

[1] Department for Constitutional Affairs, *Transforming Public Services: Complaints, Redress and Tribunals* (Cm 6243, 2004).

[2] H Genn and Y Genn, *The Effectiveness of Representation at Tribunals: Report to the Lord Chancellor* (London, Lord Chancellor's Department, 1989).

[3] Michael Adler, *Can Tribunals Deliver Justice in the Absence of Representation?* (ESRC, 2008), available at: www.esrc.ac.uk/my-esrc/grants/RES-000-23-0853/outputs/Read/3ff71277-3c05-435b-a5a5-ef50c451afcf.

Adler's findings supported the earlier view that it is access to legal advice and assistance that has the greatest impact on the outcome of a claimant's appeal against a negative decision on their entitlement to welfare benefits and tax credits. The role of representation is desirable and, in cases involving complex legislation, helpful and, at times, necessary, but it can be argued that it is the earlier legal intervention which secures justice for the social security claimant.

Without access to legal advice on new and increasingly complex social security legislation claimants are at risk of not ensuring their maximum entitlement. The purpose of welfare benefits is to enable those without an income or a low income or with specific needs to meet the expenses of daily living. There are minimum amounts prescribed according to circumstance. Receipt of less than the minimum amount allowable pushes the individual's income to below the official poverty line.[4]

Securing this minimum entitlement can start with making the correct application for the most appropriate benefit for an individual's needs and providing the relevant supporting information. It can also involve reviewing or appealing the decision on entitlement. This requires an understanding and application of statute and case law and an ability to follow the procedural rules of the Social Entitlement Tribunal.[5] Increasingly complex and restrictive rules of entitlement and rapidly developing case law call for specialist input to support vulnerable claimants.

Instead, the effect of LASPO has been to reduce the availability of specialist advice on social security matters. Since its introduction, 10 law centres in England have been forced to close[6] and, with each one, a reduction in access to advice and support on welfare rights has occurred.

Bucking this trend, Islington Law Centre in London has not only maintained its existing welfare rights services, but managed to increase its capacity and continue to offer representation at the Social Security and Child Support First-tier Tribunal for those claimants who require support.

Since 2008, Islington Law Centre has represented 900 claimants at the Social Security Tribunal across all areas of welfare benefits law with an 85 per cent success rate. Over £2.5 million in benefits entitlement has been secured for those claimants.

Central to this success for clients is early access to specialist welfare benefits advisers who have the expertise and experience to prepare both evidence and legal argument in support of the claims being made. Without this level of preparation, there is no doubt this success at the Social Security Tribunal would be markedly lower.

---

[4] *Monitoring Poverty and Social Exclusions 2011* (Joseph Rowntree Foundation).
[5] Tribunals, Courts and Enforcements Act 2007.
[6] Law Centres Federation.

Child Poverty: A National Epidemic?

The UK as a whole is marked by high levels of relative poverty compared with other advanced European nations. These high levels of poverty and income inequality are linked to a range of poorer outcomes for both parents and children.

The Child Poverty Act (2010) commits the Government to four targets to eradicate child poverty by 2020 and to minimise socio-economic disadvantage. The current national targets are that by 2020:

— Fewer than 10 per cent of children will be in relative poverty.
— Fewer than 5 per cent of children will be in households with absolute low income.
— Fewer than 5 per cent of children will experience material poverty.

The Act also requires the Government to produce a strategy every three years for reaching these goals. In April 2011, the Coalition Government published the national child poverty strategy—'New Approach to Child Poverty'. This strategy has five overarching principles: strengthening families; encouraging responsibility; promoting work; guaranteeing fairness; and providing support to the most vulnerable.

Welfare reform is central to both strategies and is a key government policy for tackling poverty. Early intervention is also a vital component. Frank Field's Independent Review of child poverty recommended an increased emphasis on providing high quality, integrated front line services, aimed at supporting parents and promoting the development of the poorest children.

Until recently, rates of child poverty were declining, but the economic downturn and the impact of welfare reforms have stalled this trend.

Data for 2011–12 indicated that 20 per cent (or 2.6 million) of children across the UK were living in households below 60 per cent median income, before housing costs (BHC) and 29 per cent (3.8 million) after housing costs (AHC).

Latest research from the Institute of Fiscal Studies estimates that, under current policies, over a million more children are expected to be in poverty in 2020 than in 2010.

The Local Experience

The rate of overall poverty in London is 28 per cent. Over half of those living in poverty (57 per cent)—adults and children—are living in households in work. Within the inner-London boroughs those figures are more acute.

Islington is a small, densely populated inner-London borough. It has a population of almost 200,000 and is a borough of stark contrasts with areas of affluence rubbing shoulders with areas of high deprivation. It is the eighth most deprived local authority in England, the fourth most deprived in London and has the second highest rate of child poverty in London: 45 per cent of its children live in poverty—17,000 children aged 0–19 years.[7]

Low-income households are spread across the borough and a significant proportion of residents rely on some form of benefits to make up their household income—26,000 adults claim benefits: 12 per cent of the local population.

Islington Council's Child Poverty Strategy reports that 21 per cent of children live in *severe poverty* where the household income is just 50 per cent of the national median.[8] Perhaps paradoxically, in the ward which borders the City of London, Bunhill, almost half of children living there (48 per cent) live in poverty.

Of all the children living in poverty in Islington, 86 per cent live in workless households.[9] Of all working households in Islington, 25 per cent claim Working Tax Credit to supplement their income as they are engaged in employment that does not pay enough to maintain a household without additional financial support.

These high levels of deprivation produce a picture of long-term benefit dependency, worklessness, high levels of chronic ill health and premature mortality.

The general employment rate and the proportion of Islington residents claiming out of work benefits are significantly worse than the national average—one in eight adult residents rely on welfare benefits to make up their household income.

Indicators of Poverty: Ill Health and Disability

Under previous local partnership arrangements between the local authority and the Department for Work & Pensions, a significant number of Islington residents suffering from ill health or disability successfully claimed Disability Living Allowance and other sickness benefits. This take-up campaign went some way to secure a more sustainable household income for those unable to undertake or sustain work.

The migration from Disability Living Allowance to Personal Independence Payment and the more strenuous statutory tests for Employment and Support Allowance are predicted to impact adversely on the 13,000 sick and disabled Islington residents who currently claim sickness benefits.

Children, again, will feel the impact of these reforms. One in five of households with child dependants have at least one adult with a long-term illness or disability and 16 per cent of Islington children live in households claiming Employment and Support Allowance or Incapacity Benefit because at least one adult in the household is unable to work due to ill health.

---

[7] Islington Council's Demographic Profile and Indicator of need, 2010.
[8] Child Poverty Strategy, Islington Council, 2013.
[9] ibid.

Of Islington children aged between 0 and 15 1,244 are disabled—approximately half of these children are in workless households.[10]

The Impact of Welfare Reform

Since 2011, 24 different measures have been implemented to reduce entitlement to welfare benefits, including limiting the annual increase in benefits to 1 per cent whilst the cost of living has increased by 5 per cent or 8 per cent if fuel costs are included.

These changes have had a huge impact on Islington's most vulnerable residents.

Coupled with the introduction of the 'bedroom tax' and the removal of crisis loans and the Community Care Grant from the Social Fund, the scale of the reforms has been estimated to reduce household income by an average of £1,800 per annum for over a third of residents reliant on any form of benefit support, including tax credits and Housing Benefit thus including those households in which at least one adult is engaged in employment.[11]

A report by the London Assembly found that food poverty is a growing crisis across London, evidenced by the increasing demand for food banks. Evidence from the Trussell Trust, which runs food banks across London, is that the numbers of people in Islington accessing support from food banks is rising: 415 people used Islington food banks from April to June 2013 compared with 58 in the same period in 2012.[12]

Securing the correct entitlement to social security benefits for these households is critical if they are not to fall deeper into poverty.

Putting a Price on Advice

For 13 years Islington Law Centre has been involved in forging local partnerships to build an integrated outreach model to make advice accessible to hard to reach communities and those most at risk of being unable to secure their full entitlement to social provision.

Currently two long-standing projects work in symmetry to maximise the reach of independent advice across the borough.

Whilst separately funded, each project provides a similar method of delivery and shares information and data which supports a more strategic approach to the delivery of advice and the development of social policy.

[10] ibid.
[11] ibid.
[12] Islington Council Child Poverty Strategy (draft consultation) 2013.

It is a relatively inexpensive model of advice delivery. Staffing costs are absorbed by the advice provider whilst the costs of overheads such as interview space are met by the funders and their partners.

By targeting recognisable cohorts such as those living in local authority housing or in areas of high deprivation, the projects concentrate resources on the greatest need whilst at the same time, cumulatively, providing universal access due to their geographical reach.

The development of this model of advice delivery came about through the forward thinking of the Legal Services Commission.

Islington Schools Advice Project

In 2002, the Legal Services Commission[13] through the Partnership Innovation Budget (PIB)[14] provided three years of funding for the Islington Schools Advice Project to establish a highly innovative way of delivering advice to the local community. The project was delivered jointly by Islington Law Centre and Islington People's Rights, organisations with a reputation for delivering specialist advice for over 40 years.

One of the aims of the project was to assess the effectiveness of bringing together specialists from the two agencies to jointly deliver advice on key legal areas rather than expecting clients to move between separate agencies.

The intention of the project was to provide holistic advice sessions to parents and carers at local schools. The project delivered both welfare benefits and housing advice, recognising that housing and benefit problems are often interlinked and that many families experience difficulties in both these areas. Islington People's Rights delivered the welfare benefits advice and Islington Law Centre delivered the housing advice. The coming together of two separate agencies to deliver a seamless service was a novel approach and involved the staff and their organisations in developing different and imaginative ways of working.

The aim was to take advice services to the heart of the community and to provide for previous unmet need. This was achieved by making links with local schools, working within education action zones[15] and other areas known to have high rates of poverty and social exclusion. At the outset of the project it was clear that it would be a challenging task, but that if successful there was potential to make a significant impact on the lives of local families.

---

[13] The Legal Services Commission (LSC) runs the legal aid scheme in England and Wales.

[14] The LSC's Partnership Innovation Budget was announced by the Lord Chancellor in December 2000 as a key element in developing the Community Legal Service.

[15] Education Action Zones (EAZ) are designed to address the issues of pockets within cities of acute educational problems. There are currently 117 Zones in existence nationally.

As the reputation of the project grew 19 schools took part, hosting regular advice sessions. The main point of contact in the schools was the home–school liaison workers who had direct contact and involvement with families experiencing difficulties. The staff members often spoke other languages in addition to English and were key to providing informal interpreting services, without which 35 per cent of clients seen would not have been able to fully access the service.

In the first 14 months of the project, 75 advice sessions were held which offered 900 face-to-face appointments. Of the clients accessing the service, 65 per cent had not accessed advice before. Of those accessing advice on welfare benefits, 26 per cent were in employment.

The impact of the project was long reaching. Of 30 concluded welfare benefits cases a total financial gain of £96,877 was secured. An analysis of a sample of 50 housing cases showed that the principal need for advice was on homelessness, disrepair, overcrowding and evictions and in 57 per cent of those cases suitable remedies were gained for families.

Significantly, one school reported a 12 per cent increase in attendance of children whose families had been advised by the project. This was largely attributed to the children no longer being taken out of school to interpret for their parents with the benefits agencies or local authority. However, anecdotally, the school also noted improved relationships with parents and an increase in engagement.

At the end of PIB funding, the local authority found a small reserve to allow the project to continue for a further 12 months. Meanwhile, the impact of the project caught the imagination of local providers, notably Homes for Islington which, in 2005, was the arm's length management organisation delivering housing services on behalf of Islington Council.[16] In 2012, control of council housing in Islington was reclaimed by Islington Council. In turn, the Independent Advice Project received continuation funding from Islington Council.

Independent Advice Project

The Independent Advice Project was piloted in partnership with the local authority, Islington Law Centre and Islington People's Rights in September 2005 in one ward. In April 2006, it was rolled out to cover all council tenants and leaseholders in Islington.

Again, the aim of the project was to provide access to free, independent specialist housing and welfare benefits advice for Islington residents. In April 2008, Islington Law Centre took on delivery of both housing and welfare benefits advice.

---

[16] 'Homes for Islington' is an arm's length management organisation (ALMO) which managed council housing stock in Islington from April 2004 to March 2012. It was owned by Islington Council and managed by a Board of Directors, made up of Islington tenants and leaseholders, council representatives and independent members.

Like its predecessor, the Islington Schools Advice Project, the Independent Advice Project aims to reach those for whom obtaining free, independent advice has proved difficult because of access problems, lack of knowledge of services, childcare, language difficulties or lack of capacity within other agencies to take on new cases.

The project addresses the prevention of homelessness and income maximisation. The emphasis is to work in partnership to help clients retain their tenancy.

Through the development of close working relationships between the voluntary and statutory services, Islington Law Centre is able to make use of a key procedure when advising clients. When an adviser identifies outstanding benefit issues which, when resolved, will increase the client's income thus making repayment of arrears more likely or which will be directly credited to the client's rent account, Islington Council agrees to a four-week hold on rent arrears recovery.

The hold in recovery action allows time for the matter to be resolved and strengthens the client's relationship with both the local authority and Islington Law Centre leading to greater cooperation.

In an assessment of the project carried out in 2011, it was found that one of the major outcomes of the project was that total rent arrears of council tenants was reduced by 53.7 per cent during the life of the project and that evictions for rent arrears were reduced by 59.3 per cent.

This is a significant and tangible indicator of the impact of advising tenants on how to manage rent arrears, avoid possession proceedings, avoid eviction, and repay rent arrears at affordable rates.

Three Advice Projects

In January 2012, Islington Law Centre launched the Three Advice Projects in areas identified as experiencing high levels of deprivation—Essex Road, Finsbury Park and South Islington. Building on previous experience the Three Advice Projects delivers advice sessions on debt as well as welfare benefits and housing. The project is funded jointly by Cripplegate Foundation[17] and Richard Cloudesley's Charity.[18]

The Three Advice Projects recognises the added value of partnership working. Local community centres, children's centres and other support services are involved in hosting the advice sessions, making referrals and supporting residents to access the project.

Where available, community groups hosting the advice sessions also provide local interpreters and valuable insight into the differing needs of their specific client groups.

[17] Cripplegate Foundation is an independent charity in Islington which makes grants in Islington and parts of the City of London for individuals and organisations.
[18] Richard Cloudesley's Charity is a charity endowed by the will of Richard Cloudesley on 13 January 1518, serving churches and medical needs in the Ancient Parish of Islington.

Crucially, clients are supported to seamlessly access advice on welfare benefits, housing and debt matters and benefit from the sharing of their information across all three areas of social welfare law within one organisation.

Getting it Right First Time

In 2009, Islington Law Centre received a small additional local authority grant for two years to increase its welfare benefits and debt advice to help Islington residents during the economic downturn. In a further example of successful partnership a form-filling clinic was set up and staffed by pro bono students at the BPP School of Law to assist welfare benefit claimants and debtors to make the correct applications. The aim was to get it right first time thus avoiding the cost and resources of challenging negative decisions.

The form-filling clinic was a relatively simple and inexpensive way of maximising advice resources. The funding covered the costs of a welfare benefits and debt supervisor to guide and supervise the form-filling clinic. The real added value for that funding came from the contribution of the BPP students as they were committed to seeing four clients at each clinic—more than could have been advised if relying solely on the law centre's own resources.[19]

Benefiting from Advice

In the last 13 years over 11,000 Islington residents have been advised through the advice projects and their client profile has remained fairly static: 75 per cent non-white British, 37 per cent classified as having a disability and 26 per cent in low-paid work. Overall, their vulnerability is striking.

The outcomes for these residents can easily be measured in pounds gained and a tenancy retained but less easy to measure is the impact they have on helping to stabilise households living in poverty.

One method of measuring this type of impact is to let those clients tell us themselves of their experience.

Mrs A, a single parent on Income Support, was being pursued by bailiffs for Council Tax arrears which arose as a result of an underpayment of Council Tax benefit. She said, 'I thought I would have a nervous breakdown. You helped me so much I don't know what I would have done'.

Mrs B told us, 'For years getting the right benefits was a nightmare. We first applied for Disability Living Allowance in 2003 but were told we didn't meet the

---

[19] Data on projects and client feedback collated by Islington Law Centre.

criteria. When we were finally awarded Disability Living Allowance in 2010 it was 101 per cent because of the Independent Advice Project. What the Independent Advice Project has done has been wonderful'.

Mr C was living with disrepair and, due to ill health, unable to manage his affairs, including applying for Housing Benefit to help him to pay his rent. He faced being evicted from his home. He said, 'Before I came to the appointment I was frightened and I didn't know what was going to happen. The adviser was brilliant and has worked it all out for me. I don't have any problems now. I find it easier to manage the rent and I am getting work done on my flat'.

Ms D was represented at a social security tribunal to secure an indefinite award of Disability Living Allowance. She said, 'It is a credit to the community and a front line service that must be protected at all costs. I received wonderful support from my caseworker'.

For Mr E it was the ease of making an appointment that was important. He said, 'You just book yourself, so that was really good. I did not have to go through any hassles or any problems before I could book my appointment'.

The Crossroads

With the withdrawal of legal help funding for welfare benefits advice, Islington Law Centre's Welfare Benefits Unit was wholly dependent on funding from Islington Council, Cripplegate Foundation and Richard Cloudesley's Charity.

At the same time, the Government announced cuts to local authority funding. In the four years from 2011/12 to 2014/15, Islington Council has had its central government grant cut by £120 million—a third of its budget. A further £17 million is to be cut in 2015/16.

In a bold move, Islington Council agreed to continue funding independent advice. But with this funding came a demand for a commitment to a programme that could grasp the nettle and mitigate the worst effects of the reforms for Islington residents.

With an eye on sustainability one requirement of the funding was that the law centre works with other agencies to enable seamless cross-referral of clients and legal matters and provide training for other smaller, and often bespoke, community groups to facilitate the cascading of information and improve those groups' capacity to provide advice to their particular client groups.

Another requirement was that the law centre facilitated the sharing of resources and information between statutory and third-sector provision to better inform the strategy to defend households against the worst impacts of benefit reform.

The law centre rose to the challenge. It has undertaken and delivered an ambitious programme of increasing the reach of specialist welfare benefits advice and tribunal representation, collaborative working with other organisations, and training and support for front line organisations.

The Local Response to Welfare Reform

Building on the commitment of continued funding from Islington Council, Cripplegate Foundation and Richard Cloudesley's Charity, Islington Law Centre made a successful bid for two-year funding from the Advice Service's Transition Fund[20] to facilitate working closely with other agencies to strengthen and increase their collective resources.

A training programme entitled Welfare Benefits First Aid was rolled out across the borough. It provided free training sessions for statutory, voluntary and third-sector organisations on how welfare reform was affecting residents, how that impact could be challenged, and how residents could be referred for advice. Over 50 local organisations took part.

The Islington Welfare Benefits Advisers' Forum was set up to bring together welfare benefits advisers working in a number of different settings: the local authority team, the Citizens Advice Bureau, those working within community language settings, with families of disabled children and homeless charities. It brought together a wide range of experience and expertise and provided a single voice for Islington residents in government consultations and in raising local concerns with Job Centre Plus around issues such as sanctions imposed on vulnerable claimants.

A guide to welfare reform was produced. This was a practical document. It outlined the changes to the rules of entitlement but, crucially, and in very simple terms, explained how residents could avoid the worst impacts of the reforms either by claiming passporting or exempting benefits, by challenging decisions, and by remaining in or taking up work. And each example was accompanied by a template letter for residents to complete to start initial claims.

Recognising that knowledge of entitlement is not enough, the form-filling clinic was re-established to assist with making initial claims. This time funding came from Islington Giving.[21] Again, staffed mainly by volunteers, the form-filling clinic has demonstrated how a little funding can go a long way within an environment of mutual support. Over 200 claimants have been assisted with making initial claims for benefits. Two-thirds of these claims were successful on application and have generated over £100,000 in additional income for residents who otherwise would have found it difficult to make a claim for appropriate benefits without help.

The core advice services continued and were able to absorb the additional demand generated by the roll out of welfare reform. Fulfilling its commitment to mitigate the worst effects of the reforms on residents, Islington Law Centre worked closely with other agencies, solicitors and barristers to develop successful

---

[20] The Big Lottery Fund (BIG) set up the Advice Services Transition Fund to enable local not-for-profit providers of advice services in England to continue to give vital help to people and communities.

[21] Islington Giving was set up in 2010 to encourage local people and business to donate to projects aimed at the relief of poverty and improving lives.

challenges to the bedroom tax[22] and won significant victories at the First-tier Tribunal for those looking after disabled adult dependants and on bedroom size and usage.

The Future

The local advice landscape remains precarious. Funding cuts meant that Disability Action Islington had to close its advice service which helped 1,000 residents per year. Islington Council's welfare rights home visiting team will cease from April 2015. The Advice Services Transition Fund ends in July 2015.

Amongst the advice sector there is a wider sense in which forward planning is difficult as a result of funding cuts, new legislation, changes in work practices such as zero hours contracts, and changing behaviours as people try to adjust to new pressures.

Whilst the network of advice provision in Islington makes its residents the envy of the rest of the country, there is still work to be done. Continued delays in medical assessments for residents awaiting the outcome of claims for sickness benefits, impending cuts to crisis support funding, and a reduction in discretionary housing payments all combine to trap households in unnecessary poverty.

The 2013 *Distant Neighbours* report by the New Economics Foundation (NEF) commissioned by Cripplegate Foundation highlighted the feeling of insecurity for low-income residents of the borough. It reported that those residents feel they have no control over their lives and fear destitution. It found that social isolation and mental ill health are worsening.

The Community Mental Health Profiles 2013 give an overview of mental health prevalence at a local, regional and national level.

Their data indicates that 13 per cent of adults in Islington have depression: higher than the national average of 12 per cent and much higher than the London average of 8 per cent. Islington also has the highest level of male suicides in London.

In *Distant Neighbours*, the NEF predicts that by 2020, Islington will be even more economically polarised and that by then a family will need to earn more than £90,000 a year to afford market rents in Islington. House buying will be out of reach for almost all but the very top earners. The NEF says this will leave Islington polarised, with very wealthy families at the top, a youthful and transient sector in the middle, and those on low incomes at the bottom living in social housing.

---

[22] The 'bedroom tax' (Reg B13, Housing Benefit Regulations 2006 (as amended)) came into force on 1 April 2013. It reduces Housing Benefit payments to those renting in the social sector by 14% if the claimant has one more bedroom than is necessary for the size of their family, or by 25% if there are two or more unnecessary bedrooms.

Social alienation and its attendant adverse impact on health, particularly mental health, will be a most likely consequence of living in such an economically polarised borough.

How to Respond

The challenge of defending Islington residents against deepening poverty is not going to be easy. The option of investing upstream to prevent poverty has so far proved to be cost effective. On average, from 2008 to 2014 for every £1 invested in the welfare rights advice service delivered by Islington Law Centre, £5 was gained for residents.

However, the growing demands and needs of Islington's poorest residents: housing, health, social care; employment; action against poverty, all threaten to outstrip the local authority's dwindling resources.

Collaboration and imagination across the statutory, voluntary and third sectors will necessarily play a big a part in building resilience and support amongst Islington's most vulnerable households.

The last 13 years has demonstrated that the borough has the capacity and commitment to meet the challenge. It has developed a model for delivering targeted advice to the communities where it is most needed and most effective, and is an example of how the delivery of justice has been able to continue in this age of austerity.

9

Complexity, Housing and Access to Justice

ANDREW BROOKES AND CAROLINE HUNTER

Introduction

The Arcades

— The Arcades is a block of 20 flats, originally built in the 1980s for student accommodation.
— It was subsequently sold to a property investor in 2003, who refurbished the flats and sold them on long leases.
— The block was built with insufficient expansion joints and this has led to cracking of the brickwork and penetrating damp. A number of flats have suffered insect infestation arising from the damp.
— A number of leaseholders some of whom are owner-occupiers and some of whom have bought leases in order to sub-let in the buy-to-let market are concerned about:
    — A number of flats which are empty and have subsequently been used for drug taking and raided by the police.
    — The failure of the freeholder to carry out any works to remedy the defect.
    — The level of service charges.

— Some of the subtenants have concerns about:
    — The state of their flats, including infestation, but also in some cases a failure to repair the heating system.
    — The repossession of flats where landlords have failed to pay their mortgage.

Mrs Slater

— Mrs Slater is an introductory tenant of a London borough.
— She has been a tenant for 12 months.
— She was previously an assured tenant of a housing association—but had to flee that tenancy because of domestic violence. She was rehoused by the Council as a homeless applicant.
— She is a single parent with two children—Darren aged 16 and Abi aged 9.
— Darren was convicted 9 months ago for breach of an ASBO, but as the breach was relatively minor given a community sentence. He moved out shortly after this to live with his grandparents and has not since been in any trouble.
— On the basis of that conviction the Council sought to terminate the introductory tenancy and two weeks ago obtained a possession order.
— Mrs Slater has been suffering from depression and did not obtain any advice in relation to those proceedings and did not take part in any stage of them.
— Because of the depression she has also recently lost her job. She has failed to complete the necessary forms to obtain Housing Benefit and is now in arrears of rent. While in work in order to make ends meet she is also took out a loan from a pay-day lender which she can no longer meet the payments on.
— The warrant for possession is due to be exercised tomorrow.
— She approached the Council, and had an interview with a housing adviser.
— The adviser told her that they could not do anything until the warrant was executed but that in any event she would be found intentionally homeless and would also be excluded from the Council waiting list.
— She says the Council has treated her with nothing but rudeness and contempt since the proceedings started.

Ms French

— Until seven months ago Ms French cohabited in a flat she and her partner had bought.
— They bought the property five years ago in joint names. Her partner provided the deposit of £3,000 from money his parents gave him and they took out a joint mortgage for the remainder of the purchase price.
— Since her partner moved out seven months ago he has made no payments towards the mortgage costs and she has struggled to meet them, but he has been insisting that the flat is sold to enable him to have his deposit money back.

— The partner's behaviour has become increasingly concerning and he recently came to the flat and threatened her.
— She is now in arrears of over £2,000 which is more than three months' worth of mortgage payments.
— The mortgage company obtained a possession order two weeks ago.

We have started this chapter with three fictional cases which seem relatively typical of the types of housing situations in which individuals find themselves and which lead to housing disputes. Ten years ago the Law Commission was asked to investigate how housing disputes were dealt with in England and Wales. The terms of reference for the Commission were as follows:

> To review the law and procedure relating to the resolution of housing disputes, and how in practice they serve landlords, tenants and other users, and to make such recommendations for reform as are necessary to secure a simple, effective and fair system.[1]

While these terms do not refer specifically to 'access to justice', it seems to us that this was exactly what was being considered. The Law Commission published its final report in 2008. That of course was just before current financial crisis took hold. The financial crisis was not only followed by a change of government, but also their proposals for and implementation of cuts to legal aid funding. Further the Jackson review of costs which was also completed after the Law Commission report has also had a major impact on the funding of housing cases.[2]

In this chapter we examine the prospects for access to justice for those involved in housing disputes in the light of this changed landscape. We start by outlining the reasons why housing law is such a complex and distinct area, making it difficult for easy self-help solutions to be advocated. We then consider the impact of the legal aid cuts and the Jackson review on housing cases, before turning to the three areas for change outlined by the Law Commission:

— Advice and assistance
— Non-formal dispute resolution
— Formal dispute resolution.

Given that none of the changes advocated by the Law Commission were taken up, and given also the cuts to legal aid and the impact of the Jackson review, it might be suggested that this is a bleak time for access to justice for those with housing problems. However, we conclude with some actual and potential reforms. What we want to argue is that we need to see the current situation of austerity as an opportunity for imagination. So rather than simply seeing the only way forward as

---

[1] Law Commission, *Housing: Proportionate Dispute Resolution* (Law Com No 309, 2008) para 1.6.
[2] Lord Justice Jackson, *Review of Civil Litigation Costs: Final Report* (London, TSO, 2009).

opposition to cuts in existing services, we should seek innovation and new working practices. To do this requires recognition of the distinct features of housing cases, and that successes have already occurred where the particularities of housing cases have been addressed.

What are the Distinct Features of Housing Cases?

There are five distinct elements worth considering about housing cases. The first relates to the complexity of the law and we will draw on our examples above to illustrate this. The second relates to the sheer volume of housing cases. These are both private landlords seeking to terminate assured shorthold tenancies and landlords and lenders seeking possession of homes due to rent or mortgage arrears. Third, we explore the lack of Alternative Dispute Remedies (ADR) such as mediation in housing cases as compared with other civil disputes. Fourth, the fact that housing disputes are frequently engendered through 'crisis' applications must be acknowledged. Finally, we must consider the characteristics of most of those who have housing problems and are likely to find themselves caught up in the civil justice system.

The Complexity of Housing Law

One of the issues identified by the Law Commission was the complexity of the notion of 'housing disputes'. They started on an attempt to classify them all, but concluded:

> In the end though we decided that there were so many different ways in which people lived their lives that, without a huge empirical investigation, no such list could ever be comprehensive. We were not convinced of the value of ourselves trying to produce such a list.[3]

It is worth reminding ourselves though of this complexity; not just of the nature of the dispute (how 'housing unhappiness' may arise from a complex interaction of facts), but also, once this is transformed into a dispute, the complexity of the potential legal responses to that dispute.

If we return to our typical cases set out at the beginning of this chapter, the first is focused on a particular property, while the second and third start from the point of view of the individual.

Thinking in terms of the property, as can be seen from just focusing on one block of flats, the fictional Arcades, there may be a complex range of problems affecting different owners and occupiers in different ways. If we then turn to an

---

[3] Law Commission, *Housing: Proportionate Dispute Resolution: An Issues Paper* (2006) para 1.22.

analysis of the potential legal claims, we see that these are many and with potentially different fora in which they might be brought.

So for the long-leaseholders:

— In relation to the drug-taking activities in the flats there is a potential claim in nuisance in the county court. It is not at all clear against whom it might be brought: the leaseholders of the neighbouring flats, their tenants or the freeholder.[4]

— In relation to the building defect, there may be a liability for failure to repair under the lease (but it will be subject to paying service charges for any repairs carried out). Any action to force the works to be carried out would take place in the county court.

— If and so far as any works are carried out the leaseholders may query the reasonableness of any service charges for the work in the First-tier Tribunal (Property Chamber).[5]

For the subtenants:

— There may be an actionable claim for disrepair under the Landlord and Tenant Act 1985, section 11 against their landlord which might be brought in the county court. The disrepair and infestation might also make the flats hazardous, such that if complaint is made to the relevant local authority they would have to take action under the Housing Act 2004.

— Whether the sub-tenants can resist any claims of possession by mortgages against their landlords will depend on their status as lawful and unlawful tenants.[6] Even if unlawful they may apply for delay in any repossession.[7]

What emerges by looking at the multiple owners and occupiers of a block of flats is the complexity of the law involved—there is a multiplicity of actions by a range of parties. There is no single forum where all these problems—many of which are interlinked through what may be seen as a downward spiral in terms of the management and maintenance of the building—can be resolved.

If we turn to Mrs Slater, again the first thing to note about this is the plethora of potential points for legal intervention:

— In terms of the termination of the introductory tenancy, she would have been given the opportunity to seek an internal review of the decision to terminate the introductory tenancy.[8]

---

[4] In general landlords are not responsible for the nuisance activities of their tenants: see, eg, *Hussain v Lancaster CC* (1998) 31 HLR 314. However, if the nuisance takes place in the common parts, then the freeholder might be liable: *Octavia Hill Housing Trust v Brumby* [2010] EWHC 1793 (QB).

[5] Under the Landlord and Tenant Act 1985, ss19 and 27A.

[6] ie, whether their immediate landlord had permission from the lender to let the flat. This will depend on the terms of the mortgage which are not likely to be disclosed to them.

[7] Mortgage Repossessions (Protection of Tenants etc) Act 2010.

[8] Housing Act 1996, s 128.

— In the possession action in the county court, although the court must grant possession if all the procedural steps have been followed, it is possible to raise public law and European Convention on Human Rights (Article 8) defences.[9]

— A judicial review challenge can in appropriate circumstances be made to the decision to issue the warrant for possession.

— In relation to any decisions about her homelessness or an application for an allocation of social housing she can seek an internal review.[10]

— From an internal review of the homelessness decision an appeal can be made on a point of law to the County Court.[11]

— There is no statutory appeal in relation to any allocation decision, but judicial review can be sought.

— Where the Council has treated Mrs Slater with rudeness and contempt, the appropriate course, after taking it up internally, is to complain to the Local Government Ombudsman.

So here again we see the complexity of housing problems, with potential early points of intervention, but in fact a failure, for understandable reasons, by a tenant to take any legal action. This leads to potential homelessness.

Finally, if we turn to Ms French we have here a case of an intertwining of property and family law. As she is unmarried her rights to the home and the extent of her share in it are primarily to be determined by principles of property law.[12] The threats from her partner, while potentially a matter of criminal law, could be dealt with through the provisions of the Family Law Act 1996 by excluding him from coming to the flat. While she may see the dispute with her former co-habitee as a matter of family business, the mortgage company will simply be exercising their rights, although she will have rights to seek suspension of the possession order under the Administration of Justice Act 1970, section 36.

There is a further point which may be made about the Mrs Slater and Ms French. Both illustrate a well-documented phenomenon of how for many people legal problems cluster.[13] Thus, housing and debt are often interrelated as are housing and family violence. Simply dealing with the immediate problem in both these cases—the threat of eviction—will not provide a long-term resolution.

---

[9] See *Hounslow LBC v Powell* [2011] UKSC 8; [2011] 2 AC 186. Although the bar for raising such defences is high, success is not impossible: see *Southend-on-Sea Borough Council v Armour* [2014] EWCA Civ 231.

[10] Housing Act 1996, ss 166A and 202.

[11] ibid, s 204.

[12] See, eg, *Jones v Kernott* [2011] UKSC 53. The ex-partner could seek sale through the Trusts of Land and Appointment of Trustees Act 1996, but given the possession order this might only be a dispute about any equity left from a sale by the mortgage company.

[13] See Hazel Genn, *Paths to Justice: What do People Think About Going to Law?* (Oxford, Hart Publishing, 1999); R Moorhead and M Robinson, *A Trouble Shared—Legal Problems Clusters in Solicitors' and Advice Agencies* (Department for Constitutional Affairs, 2006); A Buck, M Smith, J Sidaway and L Scanlan, *Piecing it Together: Exploring One-Stop Shop Legal Service Delivery in Community Legal Advice Centres* (Legal Services Commission, 2010).

While our three examples have not covered the whole range of potential housing cases, they do illustrate some of the reasons why the Law Commission found it impossible to come up with a comprehensive classification. They also illustrate why for those confronted with a housing problem understanding and using the law will not be easy or straightforward.

The Sheer Number of Court Hearings/Applications for Possession

Our second point about housing cases is a simple one and can be made briefly: housing makes up a large proportion of all civil cases. Between 2008 and 2013 possession cases alone have comprised between 12 and 15 per cent of all work (see Figure 1). This does not include other types of housing claims such as claims for housing disrepair, claims for unlawful eviction/harassment, claims regarding deposits, homelessness appeals etc, never mind those cases which go to the First-tier Tribunal (Property Chamber).

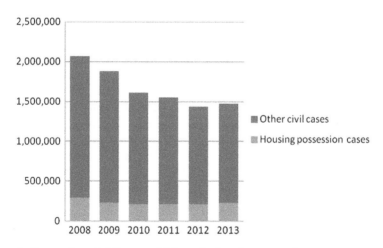

Figure 1: Proportion of civil cases which are for housing possession
Source: Judicial Statistics: www.gov.uk/government/statistics/court-statistics

Our point here is that housing is one of the key areas of 'business' for the civil justice system, where the state is involved in the day to day lives of many. While there has been a fall in the overall number of civil cases, the number of housing possession cases has remained broadly constant. While some types of claim, particularly mortgage possession actions, have declined in number recently, other types of possession claims have increased. One driver of the high number of claims is the expansion of the private rented sector.

The Lack of ADR/Mediation in Housing Cases

Although there has been some growth and/or experimentation with mediation in some areas of housing law,[14] in the bulk area, ie, possession claims, there has been no such move. This may be because for nearly 100 years, since the Increase of Rent and Mortgage Interest Act 1915, Parliament has given the civil courts the sole power to order possession of residential property.

However, both the pre-action protocols relating to possession of rented property and mortgaged property[15] for arrears call on the parties to negotiate prior to coming to court and there is no reason in principle why the matter should not be resolved through mediation. But this is subject to major provisos. The pre-action protocols do not apply to the private rented sector. Possession claims for assured shorthold tenancies in the private rented sector using a section 21 Notice[16] are not amenable to ADR/mediation. Given that many possession disputes are about payment of the rent or mortgage, there is little that can be done if the tenant or borrower simply does not have the resources to pay. Here the outcome is likely to be stark—loss of the home. This links to our point above about the clustering of problems: the housing issue cannot be resolved without the debt problem being addressed. That will usually not be a matter with which the landlord/lender is directly concerned and will involve other parties.

Further, in public law cases there is also often a binary divide. Either there is a duty towards a homeless person or not; either a property is hazardous and the authority must take action or not. Further, these are largely matters for the authority to decide in the first instance. However even here, with imagination, there may be space for negotiation and mediation around ways forward which fall outside the strict legal structures.

Nonetheless, the necessary consequence of this is that the march to ADR/mediation has, so far, had little impact or relevance for housing possession cases. The bulk of cases end up with proceedings being issued.

The Number of 'Crisis' Applications

As our examples of Mrs Slater and Ms French illustrate, it is often at a very late stage that those who are at risk of losing their home either seek help or seek to resist the loss of the home in person through the courts. It is often at the warrant for possession stage that the resistance begins.

---

[14] See, eg, L Webley, P Abrams and S Bacquet, 'Mediation through the Birmingham Court-based Scheme' (2006) 9 *Journal of Housing Law* 9.

[15] Discussed further below.

[16] Under the Housing Act 1988, s 21.

Warrants of possession are issued in their hundreds of thousands in the county court each year. Not all lead to repossession (see Figure 2). This is in part indicative of the fact that at this stage in proceedings borrowers and tenants will (finally) contact their lender or landlord.

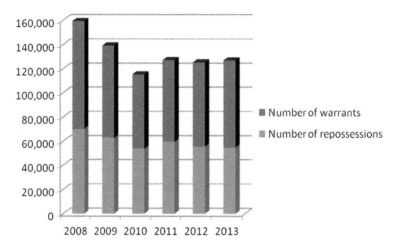

Figure 2: Total of warrants issued and evictions 2008–13
Source: Judicial Statistics: www.gov.uk/government/statistics/court-statistics

Where contact does not lead to agreement, tenants and borrowers very often apply to suspend warrants of possession to try to prevent evictions. These applications are commonly made at the very last minute, often the day before the warrant is due to be executed. It is a regular part of the diet of district judges to deal with these applications.

Of course it is not just housing cases which are the subject of urgent applications. In family cases, for example, domestic violence and Children Act applications also often take place at short notice. However, in terms of volume of applications it is clear that urgent housing applications are by far the most common. Coming to court at this late stage both provides limits to the legal points that may be made and inevitably means that any arrears have continued to escalate during the course of the proceedings, making settlement harder to achieve.

The Characteristics of those who Need Advice and Assistance in Housing Cases

As we have illustrated above, there is a wide range of housing problems and they are likely therefore to affect a range of different types of people. Nonetheless, given the type of problems which often cluster together with housing, it is unsurprising to find that there is evidence of ill health and in particular mental ill health.

Research for the Legal Services Commission into the work of Community Legal Advice Centres and Networks in 2010 found that,

> the clients that were observed had a range of health conditions including both physical and mental health needs. Pre-existing health problems could make it harder for advisors to manage sessions and to probe for clients' advice needs. Poor physical health made it more difficult for advisors to allow sessions to continue for as long as necessary because clients became tired as sessions continued. This was a particular issue for clients who had come to a session via a drop-in service and had already been waiting some time to be seen. However, it was working with clients with mental health problems that caused some of the greatest difficulties. At its very basic, there was an issue simply in the ability of such clients to take part in the advice process. As one advisor commented:
>
>> 'Yes, I've had several clients before where I've thought, I'm not sure you've got the capacity here to instruct me on this. And that is difficult, when you get clients like that, and you then have to write to the doctor and say, look, do you think they've got capacity? And the doctor doesn't really understand what you're asking. Very complex clients'.
>
> Beyond this, the mental health conditions of clients could make it awkward for advisors to probe and advisors of all types and specialisms singled out this group of clients as posing some of the greatest difficulties in the advice setting. Such clients were variously described as 'vulnerable' and 'unattentive'. In addition, many of these clients had memory problems which could be compounded by medication.[17]

The study did not just include those seeking advice on housing and related problems, and these types of problems are not just limited to housing disputes. However, other studies may indicate that mental health difficulties may be particularly prevalent for those with potential housing disputes. So, for example, in a study of families at risk of eviction for antisocial behaviour it was estimated by those working with the parents that 60 per cent of adults were depressed.[18] A study of homeless families going through the statutory homelessness route found that 52 per cent of all adult respondents had experience of anxiety, depression or other mental health problems.[19]

What are the Consequences of Legal Aid and Other Changes on Housing Cases?

The Impact of the Legal Aid Cuts

In February 2012[20] one of the authors of this chapter predicted that the cuts proposed in the Legal Aid, Sentencing and Punishment of Offenders Act 2012

---

[17] Buck, Smith, Sidaway and Scanlan (n 13) 105.

[18] J Nixon, C Hunter, S Myers, S Parr and D Sanderson, *Anti-Social Behaviour Intensive Family Support Projects: An evaluation of six pioneering projects* (ODPM, 2006).

[19] Nicholas Pleace, Suzanne Fitzpatrick, Sarah Johnsen, Deborah Quilgars and Diana Sanderson, *Statutory Homelessness in England: The experience of families and 16–17 year olds* (CLG, 2008).

[20] At the ESRC seminar which led to this collection.

(LASPO) would accelerate an already declining number of providers of housing advice. We make no excuse for returning to that and demonstrating the impact of LASPO and legal aid cuts more generally through looking at the supplier base.

The network of providers was always fragile and imperfect. The network consists of Not-for-Profit (NFP) agencies, particularly Citizens Advice bureaux and law centres. At least in most inner city areas, there are also private practice solicitors firms which specialise in legal aid housing work. Finally, there is a specialist Bar.

In some ways, housing was affected less than other areas by LASPO cuts to the scope of legal aid. Housing possession cases remained in scope, as did advice on unlawful eviction. However, advice on housing benefit issues, and all but the most serious disrepair, came out of scope.

Further, legal aid pay rates were subject to a 10 per cent cut. This 10 per cent cut was imposed on rates which had not actually increased since 1994. The reductions in those eligible for legal aid, particularly for debt and welfare benefits, tended to hit hardest those agencies like law centres which deliver much housing law advice. For both the NFP sector and private practice solicitors working on very tight margins, the 10 per cent reduction may make the difference between success and failure. Because of the implementation of the Jackson reforms (discussed below), it is far more difficult for housing specialists to plug the gap by doing more Conditional Fee Agreement (CFA) work.

Accordingly, the provider base has been hit hard since LASPO, resulting both from the cuts imposed by the Act combined with other changes. This is not exclusively a problem relating to housing advice. The nature and impact of the cuts has created a perfect storm for the supplier base of housing and other legal aid advisers.

The NFP agencies are suffering at best great uncertainty and at worse substantial cuts in their grant funding. Several law centres have already closed or face closure.[21] In March 2013, Shelter shut down nine of its advice centres.[22] One survey of legal aid funded civil practitioners found that 'almost one third of respondents (194 individuals) reported that they were at risk of redundancy as a result of the funding cuts. This translates to a potential loss of 1,479 years of experience from the sector'.[23] While not all of these were housing law practitioners a substantial proportion were and it is indicative of the mood of such practitioners across the country.

The impact can now be seen in more concrete numbers. By the end of 2013/14, the numbers of civil legal aid providers had nearly halved since 2007/08.

---

[21] Legal Action, 'Law Centre Closures' (*LAG News and Blog*, 12 February 2014), available at: www.legalactiongroupnews.org.uk/law-centre-closures/.

[22] Owen Bowcott, 'Legal aid cuts force closure of almost a third of Shelter offices' *The Guardian* (11 March 2013), available at: www.theguardian.com/law/2013/mar/11/legal-aid-cuts-shelter-offices?guni=Article:in%20body%20link.

[23] Natalie Byrom, *The State of the Sector: The impact of cuts to civil legal aid on practitioners and their clients* (Centre for Human Rights in Practice, University of Warwick, 2013) 5.

In 2012/13 there were 866 NFP legal aid providers. In 2013/14 there were just 95—a fall of almost 90 per cent.[24]

Finally, the Bar is now subject to fixed (prescribed) rates of pay for doing housing cases. Until now, the housing Bar has survived and even thrived. The nature of housing law, with the emphasis on court hearings, has helped the specialist housing Bar develop. In turn that has helped the development of case law which has created a virtuous circle where young barristers interested in social welfare law often gravitated towards housing as an interesting and varied area of law where they could make a reasonable living. The danger is that the imposition of prescribed rates, which inevitably will not rise in line with inflation, will cause the same demotivation and loss of experienced practitioners as has happened in other areas such as criminal law and family law.

As for the impact on those seeking housing law advice, in its starkest terms the cuts can be measured simply in persons who have not received advice. Legal Help is the starting point for most civil legal advice. Overall there was a reduction of 50 per cent in the number of number of cases receiving Legal Help between 2012/13 and 2013/14. Tracing a longer time frame for housing Legal Help matter starts, the figures are equally startling, as illustrated by Figure 3.

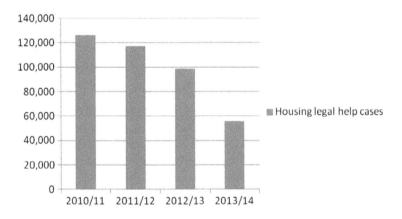

Figure 3: Housing legal help starts 2010/11 to 2013/14

Source: Judicial Statistics: www.gov.uk/government/statistics/court-statistics

The really incredible thing about these falls is that housing is one of the few areas where the majority of issues remain within the scope of legal aid. Unlike some other areas, for example, welfare benefits, the drop in numbers cannot be explained by the fact that the area of advice is now out of scope. It cannot be explained by

---

[24] Legal aid statistics in England & Wales, 2013–14. Also see Vicky Ling, 'Legal aid statistics 2013/14' 2014 (July/August) *Legal Action* 6.

a falling volume of claims, as the statistics for the number of possession claims started in court demonstrates. Rather, the fall is due to the collapse in the provider base as set out above.

There are other implications to these cuts. Some were pointed out by the Housing Law Practitioners Association (HLPA) and others when they were first proposed.[25] First, as discussed above, much work has been done on 'problem clustering'.[26] For example, when a person gets into debt that is likely to include rent or mortgage arrears. Those arrears are likely to lead to a possession claim. The Legal Service Commission (LSC)[27] decided at the end of the last decade to design its whole procurement strategy to try to tackle problem clustering. So, for example, the LSC did not let 'housing only' legal aid contracts, but instead let 'housing, debt and welfare benefits' contracts and 'family and housing' contracts.

LASPO represented a complete volte face in that it abolished legal aid for debt and welfare benefits altogether, leaving legal aid in place solely for housing possession claims. For the supplier base of advice providers, this meant that development strategies based on being able to supply a holistic service came to an abrupt end. For consumers of housing law services, the result was that they are now not be able to access crucial advice relating to debt and welfare benefits. The problem clusters, so long recognised, were completely ignored by LASPO.

Second, there is now a growing literature indicating that spending on housing legal aid saves the state money. Although, as Cookson and Mold have noted much of this evidence is of poor quality, they also note its results are consistent in demonstrating a positive effect of advice.[28] Thus, Citizens Advice has estimated that in respect of housing for every £1 spent on legal aid the state saves up to £2.34, a net saving of £1.34.[29] Shelter has estimated that each mortgage debt advice case provided by them costs the state £229 on average.[30]

Against this, the Government's own estimates suggest that the potential cost of providing help to struggling homeowners in each such case is £16,000. This sum is made up of the cost of paying Housing Benefit to rehouse in temporary accommodation or in the social rented sector those whose homes are repossessed. Evans

---

[25] See HLPA, *A response by the housing law practitioners' association to consultation paper cp 12/10: Proposals for the reform of legal aid in England and Wales* (February 2011), available at: www.hlpa.org.uk/cms/category/consultations/page/3/..

[26] Genn (n 13); Moorhead and Robinson (n 13); Buck, Smith, Sidaway and Scanlan (n 13).

[27] The predecessor of the current Legal Aid Agency.

[28] Graham Cookson and Freda Mold, *The business case for social welfare advice services. An evidence review: lay summary* (July/August 2014), available at: www.lowcommission.org.uk/dyn/1405934416347/LowCommissionPullout.pdf, 6.

[29] Citizens Advice, 'Towards a business case for legal aid' (Legal Services Research Centre, 8th international research conference, July 2010), available at: www.citizensadvice.org.uk/towards_a_business_case_for_legal_aid.pdf.

[30] Emma Ahmed, Catherine Davie, Nicola Hughes and Daniel Lindsay, *Results and recommendations: outcomes of advice for struggling homeowners* (Shelter, 2010), available at: http://england.shelter.org.uk/__data/assets/pdf_file/0005/275747/Outcomes_of_advice_for_struggling_homeowners.pdf, 8.

and McAteer estimate that the average cost of debt advice to tenants of social land-lords is £260, which produces a net saving to the social landlord of £239.[31]

Finally, there is the issue of the effect of the increase in numbers of litigants in person in housing cases. The impact of LASPO, combined with other changes such as the increase in the small claims limit, has increased the number of litigants in person. The complexity and technicality of housing possession claims, together with the fact that landlords are very often represented if not by lawyers, then by experienced officers, mean that the disadvantages faced by litigants in person are all the more clear in housing cases.

Research demonstrates that outcomes tend to be better for litigants who are represented.[32] Dealing with litigants in person can result in increased length of court hearings and demands on court staff. It seems likely that, because of the large number of court hearings in housing cases, the increase in the number of litigants in person will be keenly felt in the area of housing.

The Legal Aid, Sentencing and Punishment of Offenders Act Part 2: The 'Jackson' Reforms

At first sight, the impact of the Jackson reforms on housing cases is not obvi-ous. Part 2 of LASPO has nothing specific at all about housing cases. The reforms included provisions that:

— Successful claimants will no longer be able to recover success fees and after-the-event insurance from losing defendants.
— General damages will rise by 10 per cent.
— Success fees and insurance premiums will not be recoverable from the losing party.

The real target of the reforms was personal injury cases. The problem is that hous-ing cases became a casualty caught in the crossfire of the war between personal injury claimants and the insurance companies.

Conditional Fee Agreements (CFAs) in housing cases previously had a bad reputation. However, the regulation of claims management companies, combined with judicial intervention in limiting costs, has virtually stamped out bad practice such as door-stepping estates.

CFAs can be a useful tool in housing cases, particularly housing disrepair cases, but also other claims involving a money element such as unlawful eviction

---

[31] Gareth Evans and Mick McAteer, *Does debt advice pay? A business case for social landlords. Final report* (Financial Inclusion Centre, 2011), available at: www.hyde-housing.co.uk/client_files/library/special/Does_Debt%20Advice_Pay_A%20Business_Case_for_Social_Landlords_Final_Report.pdf, 8.

[32] Richard Moorhead and Mark Sefton, *Litigants in person: Unrepresented litigants in first instance proceedings* (Department for Constitutional Affairs, 2005); Caroline Hunter, Sarah Blandy, Dave Cowan, Judy Nixon, Emma Hitchings, Christina Pantazis and Sadie Parr, *The exercise of judicial discre-tion in rent arrears cases* (DCA Research Series 6/05, 2005).

claims. Anecdotally, many housing practitioners started using CFAs as legal aid was withdrawn from most housing disrepair cases. The reforms had the impact of removing the recoverability of success fees and after the event insurance (ATE) from housing cases. In personal injury cases this was ameliorated by introducing Qualified One Way Costs Shifting to protect claimants who are not successful in their claims having to pay the defendant's costs. This proposal was not implemented in housing cases. That means claimants in housing cases saw the worst of all worlds by having their access to justice reduced while still being exposed to adverse costs orders.

With local authorities in particular cutting back on housing repairs services as austerity bites, the need for social housing tenants to have access to legal redress is greater than ever. The consequence of the Jackson reforms is that housing cases, neglected and sidelined in the war raging over personal injury cases, are hardest hit.

County Court Counter Cuts

Our final point about the changing landscape relates to the impact of austerity cuts on the service offered by the courts themselves. One of the consequences of funding cuts generally within the Ministry of Justice has been both a reduction in the number of county courts[33] and a reduction in the counter service available at the remaining courts. Previously, an applicant who wished to apply to suspend a warrant of possession would be able to attend the court office at any time during normal court opening hours to submit their application. Now the opening of public counters at almost all county courts and family proceedings centres located within county courts are limited to a few hours a day. Moreover, most county courts now operate an appointment only system meaning an applicant has to telephone to even obtain an appointment. Even then, attention is only given to urgent applications, and work which is deemed to require a face-to-face service.

Hearings continue as normal, a telephone service continues to operate in normal working hours, and it is said that nobody who needs personal service will be turned away.

What impact has this had on housing cases? No research has been done. What happens to those many tenants/borrowers who come into court to make last minute applications to suspend warrants of possession? Although the court staff cannot of course give legal advice, they give practical help to court users all the time. They give out claim forms and application notice forms. They are an important source of information to 'signpost' court users to sources of advice, for example, to duty advice schemes at court and advice agencies. When tenants/borrowers stumble bewildered into court on the day of their possession hearing, it is to the court counter that they often go.

---

[33] Caroline Hunter, 'Cutting County Courts—What are the Implications?' (2010) 13 *Journal of Housing Law* 73.

These cuts are likely to have had a hidden but disproportionate impact on housing cases because of the large volume of court hearings and emergency applications we have described above. 'Access to justice' in this context is not an abstract concept but a very physical one.

So What can Work?

At this point we return to the analysis of the Law Commission. It pointed to three stages of the process through which an individual might navigate a housing dispute and made recommendations in relation to each of these.[34]

First, at the advice and assistance stage, 'triage plus' should be adopted as the basic organising principle for those providing advice and assistance with housing problems and disputes. In relation to this first, while there is much of interest in the Law Commission's proposals of how to prioritise and give advice through initial diagnosis and referral to appropriate agencies, the prognosis for housing advice and the collapse of advice providers set out above seems to make it unlikely that this will happen.

Second, other means of resolving disputes, outside formal adjudication, should be more actively encouraged and promoted. The introduction of pre-action protocols has, in our opinion, created some movement in relation to this. These provide a clear series of steps, for social landlords and lenders to follow, before they start court proceedings. The pre-action protocol for rent arrears applies to all social landlords and was introduced in 2006. While the figures for possession orders did reduce following the introduction of the rent arrears protocol, it is difficult to prove a direct causation. Nonetheless, there is some evidence that it did push landlords to reconsider their practices, and thus did contribute to that reduction and the maintenance of relatively low repossession levels[35] notwithstanding the financial crisis.[36]

The pre-action protocol for mortgage possession came into effect in late 2008, again before the financial crisis really bit. As with rent arrears, the drop in possession figures following the introduction of the pre-action protocol and their subsequent failure to increase[37] in the face of the economic crisis suggests that the

---

[34] Law Commission, *Housing: Proportionate Dispute Resolution* (n 1) para 1.23.

[35] There has been a gradual growth in rented possession orders since 2011: see Ministry of Justice, *Mortgage and landlord possession statistics quarterly April to June 2014* (Ministry of Justice, 7 August 2014), available at: www.gov.uk/government/uploads/system/uploads/attachment_data/file/341560/ mortgage-landlord-possession-statistics-April-June-2014.pdf, 9.

[36] Citizens Advice Bureaux, *Unfinished business: Housing associations' compliance with the rent arrears pre-action protocol and use of Ground 8* (CAB Evidence, May 2008); H Pawson, F Sosenko, D Cowan, J Croft, M Cole and C Hunter, *Rent Arrears Management Practices in the Housing Association Sector* (Tenants Services Authority, 2010).

[37] The number of mortgage possession orders continues to fall: Ministry of Justice, *Mortgage and landlord possession statistics quarterly April to June 2014* (Ministry of Justice, 7 August 2014), available at:

protocol had some impact, although there is some dispute as to how much it has actually changed the practices of lenders.[38] Whatever the direct causal evidence, we take the view that encouraging parties to exchange information and seek agreement before coming to court must be a positive development and one that is to be encouraged.

Third, the Law Commission suggested that there should be some rebalancing of the jurisdictions as between the courts and the First-tier and Upper Tribunals in the new Tribunals Service, combined with modernisation of procedural rules which affect the ability of the courts to act as efficiently as possible. There seems little prospect of the rebalancing happening. We do, however, want to focus our final remarks on this end stage of the process.

We have argued above that housing disputes are characterised by complex law, a large number of hearings, often at a late stage, with disputes that certainly have not thus far been considered amenable to mediation or other forms of ADR. In addition those whose home (or prospect of home) is in some way at risk are likely to be vulnerable in ways that may well affect their ability to engage in the legal process. This difficult combination means that the focus of any help will often need to be at the door of the court, picking up the last minute pieces. How then can this be achieved?

There is already some success in this regard with the use of 'duty adviser' schemes funded by the Legal Services Commission. These are schemes where an adviser is present at court on possession day to give advice to litigants in person who arrive unrepresented. Advisers give advice to defendants and can negotiate on their behalf with the landlord/lender's representatives. Advisers can also represent tenants/borrowers at the possession hearing. These schemes have the advantage of reaching those in need of advice exactly when they most need it.[39] Settlements reached out of court, and representation given in court, reduce the amount of court time required to hear the cases.

These sorts of initiatives work both in improving access to justice and protecting the public purse. They work because they recognise the peculiarities of housing law and housing cases and try to tackle those. In circumstances where the supplier base of advisers is much reduced, and with little chance of legal aid cuts being reversed, we suggest that it is these sorts of initiatives which should be pursued.

We suggested at the outset that rather than dwell on the negatives, this potential failure of access to justice for those in housing need should be approached with

---

www.gov.uk/government/uploads/system/uploads/attachment_data/file/341560/mortgage-landlord-possession-statistics-April-June-2014.pdf, 7.

[38] See AdviceUK, Citizens Advice, Money Advice Trust and Shelter, *Mortgage and Secured Loans Arrears: Adviser and Borrower Surveys* (April 2009), available at: www.citizensadvice.org.uk/mortgage_and_secured_loan_arrears_final_report.pdf; and Susan Bright and Lisa Whitehouse, *Information, Representation and Advice in Housing Cases* (April, 2014), available at: https://test-intranet.law.ox.ac.uk/ckfinder/userfiles/files/Housing_Possession_Report_April2014.pdf.

[39] See ibid, Bright and Whitehouse.

some imagination. In this regard we want to make a final suggestion of something that has not yet been tried, but which may become more necessary as judges are faced with more litigants in person with multiple problems. The suggestion comes out of our own experiences, including sitting as a judge of the First-tier Tribunal where it can be so frustrating knowing that you are not really dealing with the real problems which the litigant in person is facing. So we want to suggest a much more problem-solving role for the judge, and more broadly the court.

The problem-solving court is something of an import to these shores from the US criminal justice system. Drawing on the work of King,[40] Ward outlines the elements of a criminal jurisdiction problem-solving court thus:

> [J]udicial review and monitoring; addressing the interconnectivity between offending and other life circumstances; multi-disciplinary team working; consensual decision-making, and to this King adds empowering people who have offended to participate in their own rehabilitation.[41]

Problem-solving courts have not had great success in this country.[42] Nonetheless, we think that these principles could be translated to the civil area of housing. In the current climate the creation of a new 'housing court' covering all types of housing cases operating on these principles seems unlikely, but consider how much could be achieved if housing judges (in whatever fora):

— Were able to refer relevant parties not only for legal advice with a duty desk scheme, but also for health advice and counselling which would overcome some of the barriers to tackling their problems.

— Dealt with cases before them holistically—so that, for example, all debts were considered when seeking to consider how rent or mortgage arrears were to be paid.

— Could call before them local authority homeless departments so that they and the tenant/borrower could understand what the implications of eviction were in relation to any application as homelessness.

For many judges and indeed many others in the legal system this might well offend against the view of the judge as passive arbiter.[43] But maybe now in these straightened times is the opportunity to think radically about the role of the judge and to give him or her the necessary powers to actually resolve housing cases.

---

[40] MS King, 'Therapeutic Jurisprudence Initiatives in Australia and New Zealand and the Overseas Experience' (2011) 21(1) *Journal of Judicial Administration* 19.

[41] Jenni Ward, 'Are Problems-solving Courts the Way Forward for Justice?' *Howard League What is Justice?* Working Papers 2/2014 (Howard League for Penal Reform, 2014) 5.

[42] See Ward, ibid, and Ministry of Justice, *Response to the Proposal on the Future of North Liverpool Community Justice Centre* (Ministry of Justice, 2013).

[43] Richard Moorhead, 'The Passive Arbiter: Litigants in Person and the Challenge to Neutrality' (2007) 16 *Social & Legal Studies* 405.

10

Access to Justice in the Employment Tribunal: Private Disputes or Public Concerns?

NICOLE BUSBY AND MORAG McDERMONT*

Introduction

Brian's Story

Brian worked as a car valet for eight years. During this time he experienced verbal abuse and bullying from his manager. Matters came to a head when Brian attended a hospital appointment and his manager phoned him, swearing at him and demanding he return to work. Brian collapsed shortly afterwards and was advised by a nurse not to go back to work. Brian resigned from his job.

Brian did not belong to a trade union and could not afford to pay a solicitor for advice. Initially thinking there was nothing he could do, Brian was advised to go to his local Citizens Advice Bureau. As he was eligible for legal aid the CAB employment solicitor began to act on his behalf. She submitted an Employment Tribunal claim form (ET1) and meticulously prepared Brian's case for constructive dismissal for the hearing.

At the hearing Brian had to represent himself. He did not know which documents to hand over or how to arrange for the judge to read out his witness statement (as he was dyslexic). He could not understand many of the judge's questions, or provide a detailed account of the verbal abuse he experienced. The employer similarly represented himself. He also had difficulty following the tribunal protocols and took an aggressive approach throughout.

---

* The important role of the researchers on this project, Eleanor Kirk, Emily Rose and Adam Sales, is gratefully acknowledged. As a research team we collectively developed the methodology and worked through the analysis of the data. The pilot project was funded by the Society of Legal Scholars and the University of Bristol Law School. The follow-on research was funded by the European Research Council.

> *Brian won his case and was made a financial award. His ex-employer threatened Brian and his family in public. Brian eventually received his award, but only after instructing the services of a High Court enforcement officer under the Employment Tribunal Fast Track scheme.*

Brian's story will resonate with many who have been bullied or discriminated against at work or dismissed unfairly. However, Brian was lucky in a number of respects. First, although he had no representation at the Employment Tribunal (ET), his case had been prepared by the CAB solicitor who, at that time, was funded through legal aid to work on specified employment problems. As is discussed elsewhere in this book, the Coalition Government's cuts in legal aid have had a dramatic impact on access to justice, and if Brian had turned up at this CAB a year later it is highly unlikely that he would have had that level of support from someone who was legally qualified.

He was lucky in another respect: he did not have to pay any fees to get his case heard by an ET. The introduction, in July 2013, of fees to be paid by workers making claims, has dramatically altered the field of access to justice in employment disputes, initially reducing claims to the ET by 79 per cent.[1] However, even before the introduction of fees, those seeking justice faced many barriers. ETs do not always provide an 'easily accessible, speedy, informal and inexpensive' procedure for the settlement of disputes as intended by the Donovan Commission in its influential report.[2] The complex nature of contemporary employment law means that, without careful and expert preparation by a solicitor, cases such as Brian's are unlikely to succeed; many potential claimants, faced with having to 'go it alone', do not have the confidence to go to a tribunal.

In this chapter we explore the issues surrounding access to justice for workers against the backdrop of cuts to legal aid, the imposition of fees and other recent amendments to the already complex, restrictive and highly technical labour law framework.[3] The financial crisis and associated austerity measures have been cited by government as justification for these changes. We argue that their effect

---

[1] The overall number of claims between October and December 2013 was down 79% on the same period in 2012 according to the Ministry of Justice's statistics—see: www.gov.uk/government/publications/tribunal-statistics-quarterly-october-to-december-2013.

[2] *Report of the Royal Commission on Trade Unions and Employers' Associations 1965–1968*, known as the 'Donovan Commission' (Cmnd 3623, 1968) (London, HMSO) 157, para 578, which extended the jurisdiction of the (then) industrial tribunals to all employment disputes relating to the contract of employment or statutory employment claims.

[3] In this chapter, we use the term 'labour law' (rather than 'employment law') wherever possible as it has a wider scope which encompasses collective labour rights as well as those which arise out of the contract of employment and, thus, tend to be of an individual nature. Although the two terms are often used interchangeably, the distinction is important, particularly in light of what Keith Ewing has termed 'the democratic purpose of labour law', see K Ewing, 'Democratic Socialism and Labour Law' (1995) 24(2) *Industrial Law Journal* 103. Government policy and related documentation increasingly refer to 'employment law' which is symptomatic of the individualisation of the regulatory model as discussed in this chapter.

has been far more extensive and damaging than would be proportionate even in response to the deepest structural recession.[4] The net result is likely to be a further exacerbation of pre-existing inequalities of power between workers and employers which will be felt to such an extent that labour law is in severe danger of losing its democratic function.[5]

We begin by considering the operation of the labour market, the nature of employment relations and methods for resolving workplace disputes within the wider access to justice landscape, including the shifts in that landscape over the last 15 years or so. Using data from our research project, 'Citizens Advice Bureaux and Employment Disputes'[6] we are able to provide some salient examples of the impact of the current system on the experiences of a group of claimants to the ET. As some of these personal stories demonstrate, the denial of access to justice for those seeking redress against often powerful and unscrupulous employers can have devastating and long-lasting effects on the lives of individuals and their families. We argue that the current system does not provide a suitable and effective forum for resolving workplace disputes and that recent government reforms have exacerbated, rather than improved, pre-existing problems with the ET system, particularly for workers who experience unlawful treatment at work such as discrimination, unfair dismissal or non-payment of wages. We conclude by suggesting some alternative approaches by which employment disputes could be resolved or avoided while ensuring access to justice for both parties.

Surveying the Terrain

Since 2012, the policy and legal frameworks within which ETs operate have been dominated by some fundamental changes. These are having a profound effect on the ways in which viable claims are resolved (or not) due to their impact on the decision-making processes of and opportunities available to claimants. Such changes relate specifically to the Coalition's reform of the employment law framework, including the increase to the qualifying period for unfair dismissal claims from one year to two years,[7] the imposition of a fees regime[8] and the introduction

---

[4] See D Mangan, 'Employment Tribunal Reforms to Boost the Economy' (2013) 42(4) *Industrial Law Journal* 409 in which the author argues that, under recent 'austerity' reforms, employment rights have been delegated to second place—or worse—as tribunal procedure is commandeered as a tool for economic stimulation rather than a source of rights protection.

[5] Identified by Ewing (n 3) as 'importing public law principles—in the widest sense of that term—into the private relationship between employer and employee'.

[6] Funded by the European Research Council as part of a Starter Investigator Grant: 'New Sites of Legal Consciousness: a case study of UK advice agencies', Proposal no: 284152.

[7] The Unfair Dismissal and Statement of Reasons for Dismissal (Variation of Qualifying Period) Order 2012 came into force on 6 April 2012.

[8] The Employment Tribunals and the Employment Appeal Tribunal Fees Order 2013 came into force on 31 July 2013.

of the Acas early conciliation scheme.[9] The Coalition has rationalised these changes on the basis of a particular characterisation of the current system as being 'in crisis' and, thus, in need of reform and has articulated and promoted a specific diagnosis of what is going wrong and how to fix it. As explored below, the political rhetoric underpinning this diagnosis, which has been consistently advanced as a means of justifying recent reforms and of defending their impacts, asserts that ETs are a licence for employees to make unmerited or vexatious claims. We assert that this particular line of argument lacks any evidential basis and is ideologically grounded forming part of a wider ongoing strategy of deregulation of labour rights. The most obvious example of this is the imposition of fees.

The Impact of Fees on Workers' Access to Justice

On 29 July 2013 fees were introduced for those taking claims to an Employment Tribunal in the UK (except Northern Ireland). The fee structure for individual claims has two levels depending on the complexity of the claim. Straightforward claims for defined sums are classified as 'Level 1 Claims' and include such actions as unauthorised deductions from wages or redundancy payments. A fee of £160 is payable when the claim is lodged and a further £230 when the hearing begins. 'Level 2 Claims' involve more complex issues including unfair dismissal, discrimination and equal pay and attract a fee of £250 when the claim is lodged and a further £950. Cases which go on appeal to the Employment Appeal Tribunal (EAT) attract an initial fee of £400 and a hearing fee of £1200. There is also a fee structure for multiple claims which arise where two or more people bring proceedings arising out of the same facts, usually against a common employer: claims involving between two and 10 claimants are charged twice the applicable single fee; those involving between 11 and 200 claimants, four times the applicable single fee; and those with over 200 claimants, six times the applicable single fee. A waiver process, known as 'remission', by which individuals on low incomes are able to apply for a complete or partial exemption from fees was introduced alongside the fees regime.[10]

In the 2013 Survey of Employment Tribunal Applications, which was conducted prior to the introduction of fees, 49 per cent of the 2,000 claimants surveyed stated

---

[9] The Employment Tribunals (Early Conciliation: Exemptions and Rules of Procedure) Regulations 2014 came into force on 6 April 2014.

[10] See the Schedule to The Courts and Tribunals Fee Remissions Order 2013, SI 2013/2302. At the time of writing, the scheme has been amended twice since its introduction and the rate of successful applications has been considerably lower than expected. In its original impact assessment of tribunal fees the Ministry of Justice predicted that 31% of claimants would be eligible for fees, see: www.legislation.gov.uk/ukia/2013/1039/pdfs/ukia_20131039_en.pdf. However, according to information contained within a written answer in the House of Commons, only 24% of remission applications made between July and December 2013 were successful, representing only 5.5% of the overall number of claims for the period (HC Deb 12 May 2014, col 418W).

that a fee of £250 would have influenced their decision to go to the tribunal.[11] Official statistics for October–December 2013 record an overall drop of 79 per cent in the number of claims brought to the ET post-fees as compared with the same period predating their introduction.[12] This has been referred to as 'a victory for bad bosses' (TUC press release 29 July 2014), 'a major barrier to access to justice' (Law Society of Scotland press release 28 July 2014) and identified as being likely to deter individuals from making valid claims against employers (CAB press release 27 July 2014). In the face of such criticism of its flagship policy, the Government remained resolute, claiming that it was not right that 'hardworking taxpayers should pick up the bill for employment disputes in tribunals' and that 'It is reasonable to expect people to pay towards the £74m bill taxpayers' face for providing the service'.[13]

In the pre-fees environment a particular story dominated political discussions of the ET system. In this story there were 'too many' claims made by employees resulting in an overloaded tribunal system which was unable to manage its own case-load. Such claims were largely vexatious as workers sought financial gain through a 'compensation culture' against innocent employers unfairly targeted. Even where claims were ostensibly legitimate, they were viewed as being burdensome for business, acting as a disincentive for employers to hire staff in a time of austerity and economic downturn.[14]

Our research tells a very different story in which employers' power over workers predominates in a way which is completely at odds with the intentions underlying labour law's origins. Following publication of the first reliable evidence showing the impact of fees, the Government's stated rationale appears to have shifted: rather than being a response to too many vexatious claims, fees are now heralded as a means of recouping the financial burden for the taxpayer.[15] This can only

---

[11] See *Findings from the Survey of Employment Tribunal Applications* (Department for Business, Innovation & Skills, 2013), available at: www.gov.uk/government/uploads/system/uploads/attachment_data/file/316704/bis-14-708-survey-of-employment-tribunal-applications-2013.pdf, 38.

[12] See: www.gov.uk/government/publications/tribunal-statistics.

[13] Statement by Justice Minister Shailesh Vara, 28 July. This overlooks the fact that most claimants are also tax payers, or at least were at the time that the dispute with the employer arose, and are, thus, paying twice over.

[14] Addressing the Engineering Employers' Federation in November 2011, Business Secretary Vince Cable confirmed the Government's plans 'to radically reform employment relations' and spoke about 'a widespread feeling it is too easy to make unmerited claims' (see: www.gov.uk/government/speeches/reforming-employment-relations). When announcing the increase in the qualifying period for claiming unfair dismissal from one to two years, Chancellor George Osborne stated, 'We respect the right of those who spent their whole lives building up a business, not to see that achievement destroyed by a vexatious appeal to an employment tribunal. So we are now going to make it much less risky for businesses to hire people' (see: www.conservatives.com/News/Speeches/2011/10/Osborne_together_we_will_ride_out_the_storm.aspx).

[15] This was always evident in the background documents (see the Impact Assessment cited in n 10) but now took centre stage. In 2012, the MoJ estimated that £10 million would be recouped from ET fees which represented a dramatic reduction from the original 'cost recovery target' of 33% which would have produced annual fee income of £25 million. However, according to the HMCTS Annual Report and Accounts for 2012–13 (www.justice.gov.uk/downloads/publications/corporate-reports/hmcts/2014/hmcts-annual-report-2013-14.PDF, 85) the actual amount recouped following the dramatic reduction in claims was £5 million representing 6.7% of costs.

encourage speculation that, when faced with a 79 per cent drop in claims and a complete lack of evidence that such a dramatic reduction was the result of a fall in vexatious claims, ministers seized on an alternative justification.

Whatever the political rhetoric, fees are only one part of a much bigger picture. Even before the Coalition's preoccupation with reforming the ways in which employment disputes are dealt with, the ET system was the focus of political interest and the pre-Coalition picture was far from satisfactory. A pilot study conducted in the pre-fees era found that the process of taking a claim to an ET was experienced as overly legalistic, time-consuming and extremely stressful.[16] Those claimants who managed to navigate their way through the process to a full hearing found the court-like procedures baffling and alienating.[17] The reason for this has been convincingly explained as arising out of a process of 'institutional isomorphism' by which an organisation becomes similar to another which operates in the same field where both experience coercive pressures by the body controlling their resources, in this case government.[18] By this process the ETs have adopted the paradigm of the more established civil courts with the added influence of the normative effect of the common culture and key values of judges and legal representatives arising from their shared legal education and role socialisation. Furthermore, isomorphism has been identified as contributing to the ongoing juridification of employment relations,[19] which is largely the result of institutional pressures to conform including direct public policy interventions.

Such policy is part of an incremental but persistent movement away from collective dispute resolution by which trade unions and employers traditionally worked together through the process of collective bargaining to agree terms and conditions, dealing with disputes through negotiated settlements. In place of this process, employment relations have become increasingly individualised so that workers are deemed implicitly or expressly to have accepted pre-existing terms and conditions on the commencement of employment as part and parcel of a private contractual arrangement. Within this framework, disputes too are privatised with the expectation that the individual employee will deal retrospectively with any breach of contractual or statutory obligation by his or her employer on a one-by-one basis. This seismic shift away from collective bargaining and associated

---

[16] See M McDermont and N Busby, *Barriers to Justice in the Employment Tribunal System: Report of Pilot Research Project*, available at: www.bristol.ac.uk/law/research/centres-themes/aanslc/cab-project/publications/barrierstojustice.pdf; N Busby and M McDermont, 'Workers, Marginalised Voices and the Employment Tribunal System: Some Preliminary Findings' (2012) 41(2) *Industrial Law Journal* 166. See also J Aston et al, *The Experience of Claimants in Race Discrimination Employment Tribunal Cases* (DTI Employment Relations Research series no 55, 2006); M Peters et al, *Findings from the Survey of Claimants in Race Discrimination Employment Tribunal Cases* (DTI Employment Relations Research series no 54, 2006); and A Denvir et al, *The Experiences of Sexual Orientation and Religion or Belief Discrimination Employment Tribunal Claimants* (Ref: 02/07 Acas, 2007) 150.

[17] Busby and McDermont (n 16).

[18] S Corby and PL Latreille, 'Employment Tribunals and the Civil Courts: Isomorphism Exemplified' (2012) 41(4) *Industrial Law Journal* 387.

[19] ibid.

forms of industrial action, which generally encouraged a proactive approach to managing disputes *before* they escalated, has unsurprisingly led to a growth in the types of disputes which, if formalised, are likely to result in tribunal cases. Furthermore, in certain circumstances, the disintegration of collective power has meant that some workers now find themselves classified as self-employed or without any clear employment status and thus outside the scope of 'employment law' and the guaranteed protections that it, at least ostensibly, provides.

Of course not all of this change can be attributed to the Coalition Government's policy. Much of what we are now witnessing is the net result of various laws and policies enacted by previous UK governments over four decades in response to the effects of extraneous forces associated with globalisation of labour markets.[20] Neither is this phenomena unique to the UK with the governments of all developed economies engaged in the promotion of policy which is capable of maintaining flexibility (too often through deregulation) in order to remain competitive as new markets for goods and services open up in developing countries.[21] However, despite sharing a similar history and many common challenges with other jurisdictions, the Coalition Government elected to take a particular path in its reform of the ET and wider labour law system. This path has been endorsed and continued by the current Conservative Government which, shortly after coming to power in May 2015, introduced the Trade Union Bill which, among other things, proposes to raise the threshold required for legally constituted strike ballots and to enable employers to replace striking staff with agency workers. At the time of writing, the bill had passed its second reading in the House of Commons. If enacted, the bill will significantly restrict collective action by workers which is likely to result in the further individualisation of dispute resolution highlighted in this chapter on which we will now focus.

The ET System Under Review (2001 to 2015)

In 2001, the Labour Government instigated a consultation exercise on dispute resolution and tribunal reform. The resulting report entitled *Routes to Resolution: Improving Dispute Resolution in Britain*[22] set out the (then) government's vision for resolving disputes in the workplace based on three key principles: access to justice; fair and efficient tribunals; and a modern user-friendly public service. The rationale underlying the need for change was a perception that too many disputes were being referred to ETs without adequate efforts to resolve them in the workplace.

---

[20] See A Pollert, 'Britain and Individual Employment Rights: "Paper Tigers, Fierce in Appearance but Missing in Tooth and Claw"' (2007) 28(1) *Economic and Industrial Democracy* 110.

[21] See further B Hepple, *Labour Laws and Global Trade* (Oxford, Hart Publishing, 2005) and B Hepple (ed), *Social and Labour Rights in a Global Context: International and Comparative Perspectives* (Cambridge, Cambridge University Press, 2007).

[22] Department of Trade and Industry (2001).

Emphasis was, thus, placed on the early identification of grievances, encouraging employers and employees to discuss disputes and the promotion of alternative dispute resolution (ADR). In 2004, the framework provided by the Employment Act 2002,[23] accompanied by a revised Acas Code of Practice, was used to develop new three-step statutory disciplinary and grievance procedures with which employers and employees were required to comply before a claim to the ET could be made. Furthermore, the Regulations introduced fixed time periods for Acas conciliation in place of the previous arrangements under which Acas's statutory duty to conciliate had lasted up to the point at which all matters of liability and remedy had been determined by an ET. This was intended to encourage and facilitate the parties' engagement in conciliation at an early stage rather than, as had often been the case, shortly before a scheduled ET hearing.

In 2007, recognising the failure of the statutory procedure to reduce the number of ET claims, which had in fact risen in the intervening period, the Labour Government set up an independent review of the statutory procedure. The review, carried out by Michael Gibbons,[24] was intended to 'to identify options to simplify and improve aspects of employment dispute resolution and make the system work more effectively for employers and employees, *while preserving employment rights*' (our emphasis).[25] Gibbons' view of the system was that it was costly, overly complex and resulted in too many cases going to ETs and his self-stated aim was to provide recommendations which were 'genuinely deregulatory, and simplifying'.[26] Unsurprisingly, Gibbons' main recommendation was the repeal of the statutory grievance and disciplinary procedures[27] and the introduction of a revised Acas Code which is, once again, the main source of guidance. The emphasis on mediation and early conciliation within the Code is based on Gibbons' view that:

> Fundamentally, what is needed is a culture change, so that the parties to employment disputes think in terms of finding ways to achieve an early outcome that works for them, rather than in terms of fighting their case at a tribunal.[28]

This is a sentiment with which few would disagree but which undoubtedly needs to be underpinned by the principle of natural justice that requires that the right to a fair hearing is not unduly prevented where alternative methods of settlement have failed and that such a hearing should take place before an independent adjudicator—in this context a specialist employment judge. In addition, it is worth recalling that the Government's intention in commissioning the Gibbons Review was that employment rights should be preserved *alongside* a focus on ADR. With these points in mind, the actions of the Coalition Government will now be considered.

---

[23] The Employment Act 2002 (Dispute Resolution) Regulations 2004, which came into effect in October 2004.

[24] *Better Dispute Resolution: A Review of Employment Dispute Resolution in Great Britain* (Department of Trade and Industry, 2007), hereinafter 'the Gibbons Review'.

[25] The Gibbons Review (n 24) 7.

[26] ibid, 4.

[27] Accomplished by the Employment Act 2008 which came into force on 6 April 2009.

[28] The Gibbons Review (n 24) 38.

On coming to power in 2010, the Coalition Government launched itself into a frenzy of activity related to the reform, largely through deregulation, of the employment law framework. The Employment Law Review was instigated in 2010 and was aimed at reviewing laws for 'employers and employees, to ensure they maximise flexibility for both parties while protecting fairness and providing the competitive environment required for enterprise to thrive'.[29] This was supplemented in 2011 by a consultation entitled *Resolving Workplace Disputes*, the results of which were published in January 2011 and are the source of many of the recent reforms.[30] These reforms were further endorsed by recommendations made by venture capitalist Adrian Beecroft in his government commissioned review of employment law which, although prepared in October 2011, was not published in full until May 2012 amid much press coverage. Another important initiative influencing government policy and revealing its underlying rationale was the so-called 'Red Tape Challenge',[31] which ran until 2013, by which members of the public were encouraged to respond via a website to proposals to cut 'unnecessary' regulation. This approach was unmistakably based on a negative perception of regulation whereby there are simply too many laws in place which are overly bureaucratic and, thus, harmful to businesses and economic growth. Employment law was identified as a specific target for attention.

The Coalition's agenda surrounding labour market regulation and the resulting reform of employment law was rationalised on the grounds that it would encourage economic growth in the face of recession as part of a more general movement towards austerity. However, as the introduction of fees demonstrates, the policy's actual aim and impact have been to keep disputes away from the ET based on the assertion that too many claims are lodged which end in full hearings. Is this assertion correct? The number of cases has indeed increased dramatically since the 1970s but, as outlined above, the nature of industrial relations has completely changed over the intervening four decades as has the environment within which the employment relationship operates in large part due to changes in the law and in the predominant types and organisation of work.

In justifying its package of proposed reforms, the Government asserted that, 'Between 2008–09 and 2009–10, the number of claims rose by 56 per cent, from 151,000 to 236,100, a record number'[32] and that 'there were 218,100 claims in 2010/11, a 44 per cent increase on 2008/09'[33] In fact, the number of ET claims fell

---

[29] See Employment Law Review Annual Update 2012, available at: www.gov.uk/government/uploads/system/uploads/attachment_data/file/32146/12-p136-employment-law-review-2012.pdf, 5.

[30] Including the increase of the unfair dismissal qualifying period to two years, the ET fees regime and Acas early conciliation scheme.

[31] See: www.redtapechallenge.cabinetoffice.gov.uk/themehome/employment-related-law/.

[32] *Resolving Workplace Disputes: A Consultation* (Department for Business, Innovation & Skills, 2011), available at: www.gov.uk/government/uploads/system/uploads/attachment_data/file/31435/11-511-resolving-workplace-disputes-consultation.pdf, 15.

[33] Ministry of Justice, Press Release, 14 December 2011, available at: www.gov.uk/government/news/employment-tribunal-fees-to-benefit-business-and-taxpayers.

by 8 per cent in the (pre-fees) environment of 2010/11 compared with the previous year.[34] Furthermore, the headline figures cited by government, which include single claims (made by individual workers) and the total number of claimants covered by multiple claims, give a highly misleading impression of the actual workload of the ET system. Multiple claims, in which two or more workers claim against the same employer on the same or similar grounds, can (and often do) involve hundreds or even thousands of workers, yet result in a single hearing.

In addition to its creative accounting for ET statistics, the Coalition went on the offensive with senior ministers on both sides of the Coalition publicly declaring that the 'increasing' number of cases was due to a rise in 'unmerited' or 'vexatious' claims.[35] This overlooks the far more plausible explanation that the presence of a high number of cases in the system may indicate the recurrence of bad employment practices for which employers are (rightly) expected to bear the costs. There are, after all, financial penalties attached to unfairly dismissing an employee or discriminating against a worker because she is pregnant or on the grounds of his or her race, age or disability.[36] To categorise those claims which do not succeed as 'vexatious' goes against the tenets of natural justice and overlooks a range of reasons why cases might fail, some of which amount to barriers to access to justice in themselves. The expectation that all claims should be 'successful' in order to be meritorious clearly detracts from the purpose of the legal system in a democratic context. Furthermore, the argument that, what is after all a *right* to bring a claim to an ET imposes an unacceptable burden on business lacks any evidential basis as the vast majority of dismissal claims fail[37] and, even where they do succeed, the Government's own research has shown that claimants face insurmountable difficulties in enforcing remedies which all too often amount to relatively low rates of compensation.[38]

It could, thus, be argued that the Coalition's employment policy provided plenty of disincentives to raise claims with no investment made in actually resolving disputes. The only glimmer of hope in this respect is the Acas Early Conciliation (EC) scheme which makes it a legal requirement, in respect of all tribunal claims lodged on or after 6 May 2014, for a claimant to have made an Early Conciliation notification to Acas unless an exemption applies. Although registration

---

[34] Annual Tribunals Statistics, 1 April 2010 to 31 March 2011 (MoJ/HMCTS, 2011) 5.

[35] See, eg, the quotes from George Osborne and Vince Cable cited in n 14. Compare this with our own research findings in E Kirk, M McDermont and N Busby, 'Employment Tribunals: Debunking the Myths' (2015) (available at: www.bris.ac.uk/media-library/sites/policybristol/documents/employment_tribunal_claims.pdf).

[36] The Employment Rights Act 1996 prohibits unfair dismissal, and the Equality Act 2011 provides a range of protected characteristics on the grounds of which workers are protected from discrimination.

[37] J Hendy, 'The Forensic Lottery of Unfair Dismissal' in N Busby, M McDermont, E Rose and A Sales (eds), *Access to Justice in the Employment Tribunal: Surveying the Terrain* (Liverpool, Institute of Employment Rights, 2013).

[38] *Payment of Tribunal Awards: 2013 Study* (Department for Business, Innovation & Skills, 2013), available at: www.gov.uk/government/uploads/system/uploads/attachment_data/file/253558/bis-13-1270-enforcement-of-tribunal-awards.pdf.

with Acas is mandatory, participation in conciliation remains voluntary and either party can refuse to take part or withdraw from the process at any time. The scheme has received some positive feedback from employers and employees though so far there has been no independent evaluation.[39] However, the emphasis on this type of dispute resolution should be considered in light of the actual purpose of conciliation which is distinct from that of an ET hearing. Conciliation is a neutral process which is not concerned with the quality of the outcome or settlement, or with whether the settlement supports or undermines the social policy objectives behind the applicable legislation. The measure of success in conciliation, which is that both parties agree on the outcome, is not concerned with the reasonableness or fairness or justness of that agreement. There is, thus, an implicit but clear assumption that parties know their legal rights and understand the implications of the settlement. As Linda Dickens puts it:

> Arguably there is a conflict between the search for compromise, which is at the centre of conciliation and the pursuit of rights. Conciliation (and also mediation) may be viewed as treating an alleged injustice as equivalent to a disagreement between parties.[40]

The Coalition's desire to keep disputes out of the ET overlooks this important distinction and assumes that claimants, rather than being the victims of injustices, are merely involved in disagreements with their employers. The circumstances which are likely to lead to an ET hearing mean that it is more probable that the claimant will be seeking to assert his or her rights rather than looking to reach a compromise with the employer. Whether a claimant actually wants to go to the ET will often depend on whether he or she feels that the dispute in which they are involved can only be remedied by a full hearing before an impartial judge, illustrating that formalism is not always a bad thing. Early conciliation is unlikely to be a viable option in such cases.

The overall impact of the reforms under the Coalition Government—which looks set be continued and exacerbated by the current Conservative Government's Trade Union Bill (if enacted)—has been to contribute further to what Keith Ewing has identified as the loss of labour law's 'democratic function'.[41] This is the result of an incremental move away from the inclusion and acceptance of the collective notion of solidarity within the overall framework of laws and policies which regulate the labour market towards the individualisation of work and its governance. Writing in 1995, Ewing argued that labour (*not* employment) law could and should contribute to the recognition and achievement of social justice goals:

> First, it is about recognizing the fact that the private law relationship between employer and worker serves a public as well as a private function; and it is about importing public

---

[39] However, see Acas's evaluation of the first year of operation of the scheme at www.acas.org.uk/media/pdf/5/4/Evaluation-of-Acas-Early-Conciliation-2015.pdf.

[40] L Dickens, 'The Role of Conciliation in the Employment Tribunal System' in N Busby, M McDermont, E Rose and A Sales (eds), *Access to Justice in the Employment Tribunal: Surveying the Terrain* (Liverpool, Institute of Employment Rights, 2013).

[41] Ewing (n 3) 111.

law principles—in the widest sense of that term—into the private relationship between employer and employee. We may refer to the former as being the wider or social justice purpose of labour law; and to the latter as being the traditional or democratic purpose of labour law.[42]

Researching Workers' Experiences of Tribunals

It was against this backdrop that we identified a need to understand how workers encountered and experienced law in employment disputes, focusing attention on everyday encounters with law and on how workers with employment problems subjectively experience law. Our primary influence has been the *legal consciousness* scholarship.[43] This was developed as a methodology by socio-legal scholars in an attempt to move away from an understanding of law as primarily mediated through lawyers, courts and other court-like legal institutions, instead focusing on people's subjective experiences in everyday encounters with law. In looking at people's interaction with law and legality in their ordinary daily lives, it examines taken-for-granted assumptions about law and is as much interested in what people do *not* think about law as what they do think.[44] This is one reason why advice agencies can provide researchers with a window of insight. Their rationale is to help people in dealing with everyday instances of law in dealing with debt, loss of their home, workplace discrimination, exclusion from public spaces, or the multitude of sites where citizens are having to act as 'consumers' of services as well as goods. In these 'commonplace' settings, people's legal consciousness is constructed from a myriad of experiences, education and environments, as well as within encounters with legal institutions and actors—encounters that may not be recognised as 'legal' until the advice agency names them as such. Legal consciousness, then, is not reducible to what an individual thinks about law. It is not simply an understanding of legal capability that can be tested and measured, but a formation that varies across time and location, shaped by culture and experience.

We came to this research concerned about telling the stories of those unable to afford legal representation and who did not have access to trade union representation and so were most likely to find the system problematic—people like Brian.

---

[42] Ewing (n 3) 111.

[43] eg, P Ewick and S Silbey, *The Common Place of Law: Stories from Everyday Life* (Chicago IL, University of Chicago Press, 1998); D Cowan, 'Legal Consciousness: Some Observations' (2004) 67(2) *Modern Law Review* 928; S Silbey, 'After legal Consciousness' (2005) 1 *Annual Review of Law and Social Science* 323.

[44] LB Nielsen, 'Situating Legal Consciousness: Experiences and Attitudes of Ordinary Citizens about Law and Street Harassment' (2000) 34(4) *Law & Society Review* 1055.

In 2008, we conducted a pilot study for which we interviewed 10 clients who visited a CAB for an employment-related enquiry and who had submitted an ET1. This preliminary research provided us with insights into points of particular difficulty for unrepresented workers, including concerns around pre-hearing case management phone calls, the role of Acas conciliation (which for a number of our interviewees was fraught with difficulty), and a general lack of understanding of the ET system, as well as highlighting the importance of the role played by CAB advisers.[45] It suggested an urgent need for further research to explore how vulnerable workers can become genuine participants in processes aimed at resolving employment disputes.

We gained funding for a large-scale research project that would track CAB clients as 'cases' on the journeys they followed in their attempts to find resolutions to and justice in their employment disputes. The methodology was designed to bring to the fore the interactions between advice agency and client, worker and Acas negotiator, applicant and judge, as providing points at which to identify the 'social action' of law. Working with seven CABx in Scotland, England and Northern Ireland, we identified clients with potentially viable ET claims. We observed the initial interview between CAB adviser and client—a point at which the adviser frequently translates the client's problems into a legal dispute that can be taken through the legal process of the ET.[46] Following this initial contact, we recruited participants and then followed them through their journeys including (where appropriate) attending the ET hearing. We interviewed clients and kept in regular contact with them, in some cases (as with Brian) right to the point where they had experienced the violence of law through the actions of the bailiffs. In all, we have been in contact with more than 150 CAB clients with employment problems. Elsewhere we detail a range of findings from this research.[47]

As can be seen from the first section of this chapter, the landscape for resolving employment disputes changed dramatically during the course of our research, culminating in the introduction of fees. Our research methods enabled us to capture extremely rich and in-depth data about unrepresented claimants. It is this data, which we draw on below, that has led us to conclude that, regardless of the impact of fees, the ET system is in need of drastic overhaul. In the final section, we make some suggestions for reform, but before that we consider the ways in which CABx support clients with employment disputes and present a case study of one of these clients.

---

[45] McDermont and Busby (n 16); Busby and McDermont (n 16).

[46] M McDermont, 'Acts of Translation: UK Advice Agencies and the Creation of Matters-of-Public-Concern' (2013) 33(2) *Critical Social Policy* 218.

[47] Publications and reports are available from the project website: www.bristol.ac.uk/law/research/centres-themes/aanslc/cab-project/.

The Role of Citizens Advice Bureaux

In 1998, Abbott argued that Citizens Advice had become a new actor in UK industrial relations due to the decline of unions and the growth in small and non-unionised firms.[48] Employment-related queries have always been one of the principle categories of client queries for CABx (along with debt, benefits and housing).[49] Government research identified CABx as the most commonly cited external providers of advice to employees.[50] However, the resources that CABx can deploy and their expertise in the field of employment relations are geographically varied depending on funding, availability of pro bono lawyers and other factors.[51] As can be seen from Appendix, p196, the employment advice services provided by the bureaux in our study represent a range of approaches to providing client support. Two bureaux have in-house solicitors; several have workers who have developed an expertise in employment law over time; most can call on the support of solicitors with employment law expertise. Over the period of our research the bureaux in England had to change their approaches because of cuts in legal aid: for those who had received legal aid funding, services had to be restructured; for others, demand increased as other advice organisations and law centres closed or withdrew services. The three English bureaux in our study now all adopt a variant of the model developed by site E, that is, training up volunteers to have the skills and confidence to take on the less complex cases. As we explore elsewhere,[52] we found that, where a solicitor was involved he or she tended to run a case *for* the client, 'acting on their behalf'; the client often understood little about what was going on. Where a bureau believed the client had sufficient understanding of legal processes, and/or where there were insufficient bureau resources to provide more support, clients were expected to undertake a lot of the legal work themselves.

In the next section, we use the story of Rosa, a pseudonym for one of our research participants, to illustrate the issues faced by unrepresented workers attempting to access justice through the ET system.

---

[48] B Abbott, 'The Emergence of a New Industrial Relations Actor—the Role of the Citizens' Advice Bureaux?' (1998) 29(4) *Industrial Relations Journal* 257.

[49] For current statistics see: www.citizensadvice.org.uk/about-us/difference-we-make/advice-trends.

[50] 2008 research for the Department of Business, Enterprise & Regulatory Reform (BERR), quoted in R Dunstan and D Anderson, *Vulnerable Workers: Preliminary Findings from the Citizens Advice Client Research* (London, BERR, 2008) 3.

[51] On the varied quality of CAB support and advice, see A Pollert, 'The Lived Experiences of Isolation for Vulnerable Workers Facing Workplace Grievances in 21st Century Britain' (2010) 31 *Economic and Industrial Democracy* 62.

[52] A Sales and M McDermont, 'Justice in Employment Disputes? Early Results from a Study of the Role of Citizens Advice' (International Conference on Access to Justice and Legal Services, London, 2014), available at: www.bristol.ac.uk/law/research/centres-themes/aanslc/cab-project/publications/.

Rosa's Story

Rosa moved to London from southern Europe in search of work. Despite having a Master's degree, she worked as a cleaner, feeling that her English restricted her choice of work. After asking repeatedly for a written contract, she received four, one for each of her work locations. She was often paid late or less than she expected. Her single payslip did not state her hourly rate or hours worked but Rosa kept her own records. Eventually, Rosa could not afford the fares to work and resigned. She requested £430 of outstanding wages and was informed by her employer that she owed a similar amount for tax and an overpayment. Rosa was shocked and angry and, on the advice of a former colleague, went to her local CAB.

At her initial advice session with a pro bono solicitor, Rosa explained the issues and provided the documentary evidence she had collated. The solicitor informed her of the time frames for making an ET claim. He suggested that she fill in an ET1 form online. Rosa and the solicitor had difficulty understanding each other throughout the meeting. Having attempted to fill in the online form, Rosa went back to the CAB for help but was only offered minimal support—the bureau was under-resourced and over-stretched. Eventually she completed the form as best she could.

A date was set for a hearing, prior to which the employer named by Rosa on the ET1 (Employer A) disputed that he was Rosa's employer, claiming that she had worked for a subcontractor (Employer B). Rosa now worked as an au pair in Glasgow and her new employer (who happened to be a solicitor) assured her that the name of the company she had put on the ET1 was the same as that on the employment contract and the payslip. She helped Rosa to write to the ET explaining that she believed Employer A to be her employer and asking that she not be penalised if she had selected the wrong employer. This was accepted although Employer B never responded to the ET's correspondence.

Rosa felt uncomfortable about the prospect of attending the hearing. She was unrepresented and originally had no plans to be accompanied. She had deliberated about asking for a translator at the hearing, worried that she may not be able to say the 'magic words' to help her win her case. However, she decided not to ask for translation services on the grounds that such assistance would make her 'look stupid'.

Rosa travelled by bus from Scotland to London the day before the hearing, staying with her cousin who attended the tribunal with her. At the hearing, which took place before a judge sitting alone, Rosa was asked to explain her story, during which the judge asked a few questions and she was then asked to explain her documents: how they came about and their relevance. Employer A, who was also unrepresented, cross-examined Rosa, then provided his own evidence. When invited to question Employer A, Rosa simply shrugged her shoulders to which the judge replied, 'That's OK, you don't have to'. Employer A was asked to clarify a few points, including the contractual relationship with Employer B. The judge invited Rosa to view the page of the contract that they were referring to, which she did. When asked by the judge whether she wanted to comment, Rosa said that she didn't really know what she was looking at. Rosa became increasingly worried about time: she had booked a flight to her home country from Edinburgh. The hearing took longer than she expected and she was worried about missing the bus to Edinburgh. She could not afford to miss her bus or flight. When the judge asked her if she wanted to 'sum up', she said she had nothing to add, explaining that she had a bus to catch.

The judgment was given that same day: Employer B was held to be the employer and the claim against Employer A was dismissed. With respect to the unpaid wages, the judge noted that no counterevidence was provided by Employer A and that she accepted the claimant's evidence and version of events. When asked by the judge whether she understood the judgment, Rosa did not respond. The judge explained that a written judgment would be sent to all parties at which point Rosa asked the researcher to explain the outcome. She then indicated that this was 'OK' to the judge. Finally, the judge remarked that Rosa would probably need to go to a law centre for help to enforce the judgment. Outside the tribunal Rosa asked the researcher whether this meant that she would 'get my money'. The ET Service wrote to Rosa explaining how she should go about obtaining her award, a process that she initiated with the assistance of her new employer. Rosa was aware of the Fast Track scheme to help her recoup the award. However, by this stage she had left her job as an au pair and did not have anyone to help her with this. In addition, she did not want to risk the £60 fee to pay for this. Rosa decided not to pursue her award any further.

Is Rosa's Story Typical?

The data we have collected from over 130 CAB clients over a two-year period tells us that the problems Rosa encountered in trying to enforce a key term of the employment contract—payment for work carried out—are not untypical. Our findings[53] demonstrate that CAB clients often experience fear, not knowing what to expect, intimidation due to unfamiliar language and concepts, not being able to get their points across appropriately or articulately, and not being able to use the 'fancy' language of law. We have identified a number of points at which claimants experience particular difficulties.

— **The law relating to the employment problem**: the adviser will typi-
    cally inform the client of the (probable) law relating to their employment

[53] See: www.bristol.ac.uk/law/research/centres-themes/aanslc/cab-project/publications/interimreport.pdf.

problem. However, often the client does not fully understand legal terms such as 'unfair dismissal', or how they apply to their particular situation. In a sense law remains 'out there', relevant only in a very vague way to the participants. This may not matter when CAB advisers provide legal support to run the case. However, ignorance has consequences for clients where they deal with tribunal processes themselves. A lack of understanding at this point can limit clients' ability to fully engage with tribunal proceedings. This is only partly offset by employment judges' attempts to make employment courts less formal and 'legalistic'.

— **The process**: many participants were unaware of the standard path involved to implement their legal rights. They may engage in one aspect of the process with little or no knowledge of possible subsequent courses of action should their efforts fail to produce results. Not having a broader sense of the process contributes to participants' sense of a lack of control and feelings of isolation.

— **The potential timescales**: many participants felt that the process was defined by a sense of waiting—for the employer to act, to hear back from the CAB, for news from the Employment Tribunal Service. Participants begin to feel that their participation in the process is at the mercy of other institutions and individuals. Yet, in practice, the time periods involved are likely to be the norm for all claimants.

— **The roles of the various parties**: some participants were not sure what they were supposed to do during the process, or of the roles of a CAB adviser, of Acas or the ET. Having a better sense of who is doing what, as well as the expectations on themselves, would empower participants.

— **The potential costs**: a number of participants were fearful that they would be made to pay the employer's costs should they lose their claim. In some situations, intimidation tactics were applied by employers and their representatives. This put a small number of participants off pursuing their cases. Participants seldom had a prior sense of the psychological and emotional cost, particularly if a case went to a full hearing.

— **Attending the hearing**: almost all participants who faced the prospect of, or attended a hearing were apprehensive about it. Few had a good sense of the process involved or what would be expected of them. Many were intimidated by the unfamiliar language and concepts used in the tribunal and were concerned that they would not be able to communicate their points articulately. Our data indicate that ET judges generally attempt to ensure that participants have their say, but this does not necessarily allow them to do so as the whole experience is power infused and alien to them.

— **Enforcement**: it came as a surprise to some participants that they would not automatically receive the financial remedy awarded to them. The recoupment of awards proved problematic for many. Problems included not knowing how to go about this process, not having or wanting to risk the money involved, and the employer ceasing trading.

In the next section we make recommendations as to how some of these problems could be addressed. However, fundamentally we believe the ET system, in its present form, will continue to fail most unrepresented workers in providing access to justice. We therefore conclude by setting out a rights-based approach to reform.

The Future for Access to Justice in Employment Disputes

It is doubtful if ETs or their predecessors, industrial tribunals, ever met Donovan's ideal as places of 'easily accessible, speedy, informal and inexpensive' justice.[54] Our research findings, along with the experience of many of those currently working in the present system,[55] point to the need for a radical reappraisal of the whole system for providing justice in employment disputes. We would argue that such a reappraisal must start with a return to labour law's foundational principal that it should redress the imbalance of power inherent in most working relationships which is undoubtedly tipped in favour of the employer. In this final section we set out our ideas and proposals for the future of the employment disputes system that we believe should lead to a system more able to provide workers with access to justice.

Removing Complexity that Obscures Rights

An important first step would be to remove unnecessary complexity from employment law and return to a system of 'labour law'. This is not the Coalition's 'red-tape challenge', but rather a call to put workers' rights back at the centre of the system. Many procedural technicalities in effect obscure and write out many rights—paying a fee being only the most blatant technicality. The travesty of the Coalition's fees policy is that those employers who treat their workers badly now know that it is highly unlikely they will ever have to account for their actions to an independent third party because the affected worker will not be able to afford to take the dispute to an ET.

Establishing a simplified system for dealing with the less complex disputes, generally claims for unpaid wages or holiday pay, would be of benefit to many workers. These claims often amount to no more than £300. Some are dealt with by the small claims court but this is not necessarily the appropriate forum as, although the claims may be small, the specific circumstances may be complex and thus

---

[54] See n 2.

[55] See in particular barrister David Renton's visceral account, *Struck Out: Why Employment Tribunals Fail Workers and What Can be Done* (London, Pluto Press, 2012) and also Renton's and John Hendy QC's chapters in N Busby, M McDermont, E Rose and A Sales (eds), *Access to Justice in the Employment Tribunal: Surveying the Terrain* (Liverpool, Institute of Employment Rights, 2013).

require the attention of a specialist adjudicator. For example, it may be necessary to determine who the employer is (as in Rosa's case) before any claim can be settled. We would propose a regulatory mechanism similar to that which operates in the enforcement of minimum wage claims.[56] An adjudicator could consider case facts through simple written submissions, giving a decision and, where appropriate, an award. Complex cases that cannot be resolved this way could be referred to a formal hearing.

Recognising Rights Before an Independent Forum

Central to any system of workers' rights must be access to an independent forum for adjudication in cases which are not possible to resolve through internal dispute systems or by the simplified system outlined above. A key feature of our research has been the imbalance of power relations in the ET (real and perceived) between worker and employer. A return to the tripartite system of adjudication, which recognises the need to represent different interests in resolving disputes, would help to redress these imbalances. In engendering this approach, efforts should be made to make such hearings less *adversarial* and more *inquisitorial* by, among other things, removing dominant expert barristers (all too frequently pitted against the unrepresented claimant), and making room for a panel of experts to seek to understand the dispute and find a just resolution.

Even with a simplified system, many of the claimants in our research would find it very difficult to assert their rights without legal advice and representation which can be essential in ensuring that all parties are able to identify their rights and obligations and how best to articulate and apply them. To achieve this, those who are unable to pay for such assistance should be entitled to the services of a 'public advocate' provided and paid for by the state. In contemporary society the right to work, with the concomitant ability to earn a wage, is an essential element of individual freedom. A right to be legally represented in a process aimed at settling a dispute that has deprived a worker of his or her job is as fundamental as the right to legal representation when facing charges in a criminal court: in both cases, the claimant/accused is faced with a loss of liberty.

Enabling Unrepresented Clients to Assert their Rights

In addition to the wide-sweeping changes outlined above, which we recognise are extremely unlikely to find favour with policymakers in the current political climate, there are a number of other suggestions arising out of our research which could be implemented in the short-term.

---

[56] Note that it is HMRC which is responsible for raising court actions on behalf of workers in cases involving non-payment of the minimum wage.

Advice agencies and trade unions have an important role to play in the joint provision of information, advice, support and representation to workers. Unions have a wealth of experience of successfully supporting and representing workers. CAB training programmes, supported by the Citizens Advice Specialist Support Unit, 'webinars' and coursework, continue to provide volunteers with the skills and knowledge which enable them to support clients successfully. With the emphasis on early intervention before formal legal action, advisers interact with employers to mediate/negotiate on behalf of workers. However, because of the highly complex nature of employment law, all of the bureaux involved in our research emphasised that there was always a need for specialist legal support.

The Tribunal Service could support unrepresented claimants in a number of ways:

— Claimants should be provided with a broader understanding of the process as a whole including more information about how to prepare for a hearing and what to expect on the day, a better sense of the time frames involved at various stages and an understanding of why the process can take a long time. Clearer guidance on the roles of various actors would enable claimants to make use of the resources available to them in a more constructive and empowered way. Despite it having been submitted to rigorous 'plain English' tests, some of our participants found the written guidance offered by the ET Service unhelpful.

— The buildings and staff should be supportive of unrepresented claimants with the language and signage written in accessible English (with foreign language translations available), rather than 'legalese'. One participant was baffled by a sign in the tribunal waiting room which stated 'Do not forget your bundles'!

— It should be made clear at all stages that self-representation is encouraged and will be supported by ET staff. Judges should be aware of the additional pressures faced by unrepresented claimants. Rosa's lack of resources meant that she was constantly worried about whether she was going to miss her bus, leaving her unable to focus on the complexity of the proceedings.

Enforcement of Awards

A fundamental problem with the current system is the lack of an effective enforcement mechanism as demonstrated by our case studies. Many claimants are unaware that, even if a financial award is made in their favour, the ET cannot force the employer to pay up. Brian only got his award, having suffered an inordinate amount of stress, by paying for an enforcement action. The Government's own research[57] has found that less than half of all claimants given an award by the ET received full payment from their employer and 35 per cent received no payment

---

[57] Cited in n 38.

at all. In seems particularly unjust that, having suffered the expense and stress of a hearing, a worker whose claim has succeeded (against the odds) finds that he or she has to take further legal action to get any money owed. This situation is not new: Citizens Advice has been reporting on the non-payment of ET awards since 2004[58] and continued to argue in 2013 that the state should play a proactive role in enforcing ET awards.[59] HMRC already provides enforcement officers charged with recovering payment in respect of the minimum wage and tax debts. HMRC is likely to hold information on an employer's tax position which could assist in establishing viable assets, and unpaid ET awards could be added to the recovery of unpaid tax where appropriate.

Conclusion

As we have argued throughout this chapter, the failure of the ET system to provide access to justice for workers is undeniably linked with the individualisation of employment disputes which has been taking place for several decades. Part of the solution lies in looking for new models of collective action. Rather than being confined to the employment contract, the appropriate legal framework should be able to take account of the broader purpose of labour law: to redress the imbalance of power inherent in working relationships which undoubtedly favours employers in most cases. Within the current narrow construction of employment relations, workers' rights, once fundamental to the efficient exercise of the social contract, have become aligned with an agenda driven primarily by concerns of economic necessity so that they are seen as an extravagant luxury in times of boom which can be dispensed with in a 'time of austerity'. It is vital that we reconstitute labour law's democratic function by which individual disputes once again become matters of *public concern*.

---

[58] R Dunstan, *Empty Justice: The Non-Payment of Employment Tribunal Awards* (CAB, 2004).
[59] Citizens Advice, *The Cost of a Hollow Victory* (CAB, 2013) 9.

Appendix: Summary of participating bureaux employment advice delivery

Site	Location	% Ethnic minorities	% JSA claimants (% males)[60]	CAB employment service provided
A	London borough	46	4.5 (5.3)	— Generalist advice for less complex cases; CAB advisers with more specialist employment knowledge provide basic advice and undertake limited case work up to and at ET; clients with potential ongoing casework needs referred to local law centre — Pro bono solicitor offering one session per month
B	Town and surrounds, Scotland	<1	5.9 (8.3)	— Solicitor, acting for clients up to and at ET
C	Town and surrounds, Scotland	<1	5.7 (7.8)	— CAB adviser with specialist employment knowledge (including legal training), advice up to and occasionally at ET — Generalist advisers
D	Urban, England	9	4.5 (5.8)	— Employment solicitor will take on some discrimination cases, up to but not at ET — Generalist employment advice provided by volunteer team, supervised by employment solicitor, for less complex cases only
E	Urban, England	16	3.5 (4.5)	— CAB advisers with generalist/ specialist employment knowledge provide advice for less complex cases, undertaking casework, up to and sometimes at ET — Volunteer employment solicitor
F	Urban, Scotland	5	6.4 (9.2)	— CAB adviser with specialist employment knowledge (including legal training), advice up to and occasionally at ET
G	Urban/ rural, N Ireland	2	3.1 (3.7)	— CAB adviser with specialist employment knowledge, advice up to and occasionally at the industrial tribunal — Cases sometimes referred to local law centre

[60] Great Britain 3.3% (4.3%) males.

11

Renegotiating Family Justice

MAVIS MACLEAN CBE

Introduction

In the Henry Hodge Memorial Lecture of 2011 Lady Brenda Hale addressed the question of equal access to justice in the 'Big Society', a term being used at that time by the Conservative Party in the Coalition Government to describe a desirable alternative to the 'Big State'. She set out the three complementary and necessary elements required for such access: a just system of laws, carrying with them a set of appropriate remedies for wrongs, made workable by the contribution of the legal profession. In family law we are well equipped with the first of these: we have the Children Act 1989 with its clear and exemplary focus on the welfare of the child. As to the second item on the list, while family law is generally concerned with the future of those involved rather than the righting of past wrongs, there are a number of remedies for ensuring the best possible outcome for those engaged in family matters. And until recently we have been well supplied with legal services. Lawyers have traditionally been the first port of call for those needing help in reaching agreement about how to arrange their finances and care for their children after separation or divorce. Sadly, this is no longer the case for a number of reasons. The economic crisis has affected the demand for privately funded legal services, and government policy has set out to limit public funding for legal help with respect to family matters for those of limited resources. The argument put forward in the Legal Aid Consultation Paper of November 2010[1] was that

> there is a range of ... other cases which very often arise from a litigant's own decision about their personal life ... Where the issue is one which arises from the litigant's personal life, we are less likely to consider that these cases concern issues of the highest importance.

This principle led to the proposal to take all private law family disputes except those where the state has a direct interest, ie, domestic violence and public law

---

[1] Ministry of Justice, *Proposals for the Reform of Legal Aid in England and Wales* Consultation Paper CP 12/10 (Cm 7967, 2010).

work on child protection, out of the scope for public funding. The White Paper was followed by a draft Bill in 2011 which affirmed after consultation that government 'remained convinced that reform is necessary to avoid unnecessary litigation, reduce the cost of Legal Aid and deliver better overall value for money'.[2] The Legal Aid, Sentencing and Punishment of Offenders Act (LASPO) was passed in 2012 and came into effect the following year.

Access to lawyers for those without resources has a long history spanning many centuries in this jurisdiction. In the reign of Henry VII actions could be brought 'in forma pauperis' relieved from court fees and with lawyers acting pro bono. By 1942 in the view of EJ Cohn legal aid was considered to be 'a service which the modern state owes to its citizens as a matter of principle'.[3] 'The State is not responsible for the outbreak of epidemics, for old age or economic crises. But the State is responsible for the law'.[4] These words were cited only a year before the Coalition Government took office by Lord Bingham in his book *The Rule of Law*,[5] where he commented that 'few people are competent to conduct litigation without professional help: but solicitors and barristers, like plumbers and electricians, ordinarily charge a fee, and since litigation is labour intensive … the cost tends to be high'. Family matters, however, have always held a key position within the legal aid system since it was first established after the Second World War, as it was held that young people had hurried into marriage in these difficult times while serving their country and that if mistakes had been made then the country owed it to these young people to help them make a fresh start on family life.[6]

It is not surprising that governments concerned about rising public expenditure seek cheaper alternatives to these expensive professionals for dealing with family matters. Tribunals may appear to offer a solution for family cases, and have been considered here and in Australia, but when working well tend to become like courts as lawyers become more involved.[7] Arbitration is also attractive as an alternative to court but can be expensive as lawyers are drawn in both to represent clients and to act as arbitrators. The alternative solution most attractive to government as both cost-effective and good for the individuals concerned is to avoid having to call in a third party to make a decision by having the parties to a dispute reach their own solution through mediation. This looks particularly attractive in family matters where the purpose is to look ahead to how the parties can get on with their lives, rather than attributing blame and retribution for past wrongs, and

---

[2] Ministry of Justice, *Reform of Legal Aid in England and Wales: The Government Response* (Cm 8072, 2011).

[3] EJ Cohn, 'Legal Aid for the Poor: A Study of Comparative Law and Legal Reform' (1943) 59 *Law Quarterly Review* 250.

[4] ibid.

[5] T Bingham, *The Rule of Law* (London, Penguin, 2010) 87.

[6] M Maclean, 'Access to Justice in Post War Britain' in S Katz, J Eekelaar and M Maclean, *Cross Currents: Family Law and Policy in the United States and England* (Oxford, Oxford University Press, 2000).

[7] See H Genn and Y Genn, *The Effectiveness of Representation in Tribunals* (London, Lord Chancellor's Department, 1989).

to learn how to manage their affairs without further dispute. But this route too is not without difficulty, if the parties are unwilling to try it. Mediation cannot be forced. As Lord Dyson said,

> can it be right that parties who have exercised their right to go to court can be forced to sit down with the individual they believe to have wronged them to try to find a compromise which would probably leave them worse off than if they had had their day in court?[8]

Reluctance to engage in mediation is particularly difficult to manage where there is a question of power imbalance between the parties, as often appears to be the case in relationship breakdown family matters where a husband/partner may be better informed and more familiar with family finance, while a wife/partner may be more involved with the children.

In 2010, concerns about the cost and effectiveness of the family justice system in England and Wales began to be addressed by the Family Justice Review (FJR) chaired by David Norgrove which undertook a thorough and thoughtful review of the working of the family justice system in England and Wales, to consider and advise on the promotion of fair and informed settlement and agreement. This review was followed by the setting up of the Family Justice Modernisation programme to reform the administration of family justice, overseen by Lord Justice Ryder. Both of these pieces of work addressed the issue of costs, with the FJR advocating that the legal aid budget could be better spent if it were to be brought within an overall family justice service budget, and the modernisation programme advocating increased efficiencies and a greater focus on value for money in the system.[9] Sadly, both of these initiatives have been undermined by the changes to legal aid. The magnitude of the policy change is clear from the drafting of the 2012 Act which describes what is to be included within legal aid funding, not, as formerly, what is to be excluded. The 2012 Act, section 1, states only that 'The Lord Chancellor must secure that legal aid is made available in accordance with this part'. Under the previous legislation which it superseded (1999 Act, section 4) the Legal Services Commission was established to set up the Community Legal Service (CLS)

> for the purpose of promoting the availability to individuals of services of the descriptions specified in subsection 2, and in particular for securing (within the resources made available in accordance with this part) that individuals have access to services that effectively meet their needs.

The impact on access to justice of the change is considerable. Government appeared to take the view that the positive impact of the new policy of directing those approaching the courts to consider mediation which would be publicly funded for those who were financially eligible would mitigate the harsh impact of

---

[8] 'Mediation in the English legal order six years after Halsey' speech, October 2010, cited in Lady Hale 'Equal Access to Justice in the Big Society' (Sir Henry Hodge Memorial Lecture 2011) 20.

[9] Ministry of Justice, Department for Education and the Welsh Government, *Family Justice Review* (2011).

the changes, and that cases involving personal safety and other exceptional cases where basic human rights were threatened could be exempted. A particular cause for concern is the cases which, although technically private law matters, in fact share the characteristics of a public law case. In particular, there are highly conflicted parental contact and residence matters where there are welfare issues about possible abuse or neglect which will, as private law matters, fall outside the scope of public funding. Public law matters retain access to public funding, but the distinction between public and private law matters is not always clear-cut. And in the most recent Legal Aid Statistics for April to June 2014 although 125 applications for exceptional case funding (ECF) were made, only seven have been accepted for public funding, 95 refused, 20 rejected and three were withdrawn.[10] The main consideration in these decisions should be whether a fair trial can be conducted, rather than a detailed account of the family circumstances.[11]

It remains to be seen whether family mediation, for which legal aid remains available for those financially eligible, will fill the gap left by the absence of the lawyers, whether fewer matters will be brought forward for help with resolution in the legal setting (in the period April to June 2014 there were 29 per cent fewer cases than in the equivalent period in 2013)[12] or whether parties will represent themselves appearing as litigants in person (LiPs) with all the additional pressure on the courts that this may bring (the number of private law family cases where both parties were represented was 41 per cent lower in the period April to May 2014 than it had been for same period in 2014).[13] There is the additional concern that although these changes may appear to reduce the call on the public purse through the Lord Chancellors departmental budget, many family matters are associated in clusters with other issues such as housing, debt, unemployment and health. Failure to help through the courts may result in higher calls on other departmental budgets.[14]

It is hard to avoid the conclusion that governmental suspicion of the legal profession plays a part in the development of this policy, and in our view based on our previous research this suspicion rests on an outdated idea of what lawyers do in family cases.[15] When Philip Lewis examined assumptions about lawyers in policy statements in 2000[16] he identified the following: arm's length negotiation between lawyers reduces communication and increases tension and conflict; negotiating through lawyers is associated with getting the best deal at the other's expense; and lawyers interfere with agreements reached in mediation without their involvement. From the research Lewis reviewed, however, a different picture emerged,

---

[10] Ministry of Justice, *Legal Aid Statistics in England and Wales April to June 2014* (September 2014).

[11] J Burrows, 'State Funding for Family Proceedings' (November 2014) 44 *Family Law* 1602.

[12] Ministry of Justice, *Court Statistics Quarterly Bulletin*, September 2014; see (November 2014) *Family Law* 1507, available at: www.familylaw.co.uk.

[13] ibid.

[14] G Cookson, 'Analysing the Economic Justification for the Reforms to Social Welfare and Family Law Legal Aid' (2013) 35(1) *Journal of Social Welfare and Family Law* 21.

[15] J Eekelaar, M Maclean and S Beinart, *Family Lawyers: The Divorce Work of Solicitors* (Oxford, Hart Publishing, 2000); M Maclean and J Eekelaar, *Family Law Advocacy* (Oxford, Hart Publishing, 2009).

[16] Philip Lewis, *Assumptions about Lawyers in Policy Statements: a survey of relevant research* (London, Lord Chancellor's Department, 2000).

saying that 'private negotiation is far from desirable in all cases', and that 'lawyers at least sometimes are used not just to give advice or negotiate with the other party but to solve problems by dealing with third parties on the clients behalf'.

Lawyers and Mediators

Mediation often seems to be seen by policymakers as the alternative to lawyer involvement, but could more accurately be described as an alternative to litigation, or even adjudication. A more accurate but less ambitious description of mediation would be as one of a number of ways of supporting the negotiation between separating parties. This help with negotiation may be offered by a variety of professionals including both lawyers and mediators, and indeed lawyers working as mediators, and is widely used by parties in private law matters as they make arrangements about their finances and their children at the end of a marriage or a partnership. Lisa Webley in her meticulous analysis of the documents published concerned with the training and accreditation of family lawyers and family mediators shows how the assumptions that solicitors are adversarial and directive while mediators are facilitative and settlement oriented is an over simplification.[17] Both are settlement oriented. Increasing numbers of lawyers are training and working as mediators. The key difference between lawyers whether working as mediators or not and non-lawyer mediators is the part played by the legal framework. Lawyers work within it in a public setting, mediators work alongside it in a private setting. For the lawyers, there is a greater awareness of third parties, for example, any family lawyer while acting in the best interests of their client is expected to switch allegiance and act in the best interests of any child involved when necessary, just as a court would do under the Children Act 1989. A mediator, working in a private negotiation context, is required only to encourage the parties to consider the best interests of their children. The mediator works towards a private consensual agreement between the parties. The lawyer is required to work within a publicly accountable legal framework. As government moves from supporting publicly funded legal advice and representation to supporting mediation, the question arises: can we have family justice without family law? The answer may well be yes, but as no public record is made of mediation agreements, how can we tell?

Changes to Legal Aid

At the time of writing (November 2014) LASPO has been in effect for less than two years. Are there discernible effects on access to justice in family matters? Sadly, the evidence from court statistics is worrying. When the Act came into effect the

---

[17] Lisa Webley, *Adversarialism and Consensus* (New Orleans LA, Quid Pro Quo Books, 2010).

immediate impact was not the planned and expected increase in mediation, as the alternative to legal help, but a sharp decrease. The lawyers working on legal aid contracts had been responsible for a large proportion of referrals to mediation, at a time when the service was not widely known or appreciated in the general population. The parties of modest means who were no longer seeing lawyers after LASPO were thus unlikely to be aware of mediation as a possible alternative. In April to June 2013, before the cuts, 4,217 couples had attended publicly funded family mediation and information meetings. One year later, after the cuts, the figure had fallen to 2,544. The figure for new matter starts from the Ministry of Justice confirmed the overall picture, showing 3,781 cases in April June 2011, down to 2,623 in April June 2013. Government anxiety about having enough mediation capacity to cope with the change was quickly replaced by embarrassment at the downturn in demand for mediation and the difficulties experienced by mediation services which had prepared for an increased case-load and were now faced with falling demand and falling incomes. A Mediation Task Force was set up under the chairmanship of David Norgrove to examine how the Government might achieve its objectives. Their report published in the summer of 2014 was not optimistic, and in fact spoke of the need to recognise the contribution made by a variety of professionals including lawyers to the resolution of difficult family matters.

A number of mediation services have since closed, including long-established services in Bristol and Manchester. Government has tried to support the Family Mediation Council, the umbrella organisation for mediation services originally set up to facilitate contracting and working with the Legal Aid Commission, to develop data collection on service provision, numbers of mediators and mediations, training and accreditation and quality assurance, and to work towards a unified professional framework for practice.[18] But it remains difficult to ascertain clearly exactly how the services are working, and how far the service provides value for money. Traditionally mediation sought to establish national coverage, often using satellite premises, and often staffed by recently retired people from the caring professions who offered a limited number of sessions per week for minimal remuneration (£30 an hour is still a common level of remuneration) in various locations. Counting sessions, locations, or individual mediators has led to different and confusing impressions of the state of the services. The mediators have been angry with government for having encouraged them to think that they would become the first port of call for separating couples with substantial public funding, only to find that after investing in expansion that their workload had halved in the absence post-LASPO of referrals from the legal profession. There have been frequent calls for government to do more to explain and advertise the service to the public at large (though a recent MoJ survey of awareness of ADR and the

---

[18] See Stan Lestor, 'Dispute Resolution' Parts 1, 2 and 3 (September 2014) 44 *Family Law* 1338; (October 2014) 1472; (November 2014) 1610.

family justice system found a higher awareness of mediation than of the justice system).[19]

At the same time, the family solicitors doing private law work who had worked in the legal aid sector were badly hit by the sudden reduction in their case-load. A number of firms amalgamated or went out of business. Firms with a wider range of work focused on non-family work. But others took advantage of recent reductions in regulation to change their ways of working, developing their marketing skills, and beginning to offer free introductory sessions, packages for dealing with non-contested divorce and related children and financial matters, and for more complicated cases providing limited cost-effective services known as 'unbundling', ie, doing specific tasks for the client rather than taking on the entire case. Others began to train as mediators, and offer mediation services as part of their legal practice, together with other options such as advocacy, collaborative law, arbitration and forensic accountancy, even holistic non-adversarial family law and life coaching. The response of the legal profession was creative and proactive. A further development was that associated with the expansion of IT-based services. A number of websites now offer low cost effective help with mainly non-conflicted divorce, ranging from merely handling documents to maintaining links with legal firms and offering a graduated scheme of different levels of help at different prices. The Cooperative Society launched its Family Legal Services, with high quality documentation, clear pricing and value for money, and a full range of different levels of help with easy transferability between them. Wikivorce, a not-for-profit website offering high quality information, established a working partnership with a firm of solicitors which can support the website and also take on cases which become too difficult for IT to handle and need anything up to and including the 'full legal' service traditionally offered by family solicitors.[20]

If we return to Lady Hale's three elements in the process of securing access to justice:—a legal framework, access to remedies for wrongs, facilitated by lawyers—the key obstacle for those with family matters to manage and resolve centres around government's wish to reduce the cost of access to justice, and to do so by curtailing the role of family lawyers. The promotion of mediation as alternative dispute resolution has not, at least at the time of writing (November 2014) filled the gap. The concept remains difficult to explain. The term 'alternative' is confusing when it stands alone. We need to know what something is an alternative to. Is mediation an alternative to third-party advice or decision-making in the interest of self-development and autonomy? Or an alternative to costly demands from the legal profession on the public purse? It may well be that both elements are involved. The policy is pragmatic in the way it tries to limit public expenditure,

---

[19] Amy Summerfield and Laura Freeman, *Analytical Summary: Public Experiences of and Attitudes towards the Family Justice System* (Ministry of Justice, 2014).

[20] For a more detailed account see M Maclean and J Eekelaar, *Lawyers and Mediators: The Brave New World of Services for Separating Families* (Oxford, Hart Publishing, forthcoming).

but may also have an additional ideological element in the form of the neo-liberal belief in the intrinsic value of private ordering over public justice. Even with a good legal framework, remedies, and hard pressed but resourceful lawyers still working in the field, how does this additional focus on private ordering impact on access to justice in family matters? If decisions are made privately by individuals without any public sign of dispute, are consensual norms being upheld in a cohesive society or are the vulnerable at risk? Fair and informed outcomes may be the norm, but how can we know this? Do we value a common legal code, even if courts in this jurisdiction are not generally, as for example in France, the place where you go to argue for your divorce, but often the place where the decisions you and your partner have made are given public recognition and enforceability, and only in rare cases the place where a third party is asked to make decisions for you. Even though adjudication is rare, it provides a fair and informed legally supported benchmark for the decisions of the majority who can benefit from the judgment in making their own decisions. It is hard to imagine the rule of law without at least some contribution from the legal professions. In the face of cuts in public funding and the reduced resources available for private work, how are men and women making their journey through the changes associated with separation and divorce? What help do they seek and where do they find it? What contribution is being made by the legal profession and others? Will the development of DIY divorce through digital technology which enables the computer literate to carry out information searches and fill in forms online become more prominent?

If we wish to examine the case for continuing lawyer involvement in family matters, there are questions to be asked: what is the distinguishing characteristic of the lawyer's role in family work? What are the core tasks which can only or in part be carried out by lawyers? How might the role of the lawyer develop in the context of a more complex array of services for those coping with separation and divorce?

A brief exploratory study of the current divorce work of family solicitors[21] indicates that clients with adequate resources are continuing to use the full legal services traditionally provided by family lawyers, often helped to finance the process by the arrangements made by lawyers to seek loans and sometimes preceded by doing what they can to prepare online, sometimes using services from the additional menu of forensic accountancy, tax planning, mediation, arbitration, early neutral evaluation, collaborative law and even life coaching. Those who formerly met legal aid financial eligibility criteria may now find their way to the cost-effective packages offered by firms and by the new providers such as the CLS. The cost of failing to settle is becoming clearer. Those who before LASPO would have been able to use legal aid for legal help are now offered funding for mediation. Crisis work is being offered through a Resolution project funded by

---

[21] M Maclean, 'Delivering Family Justice: New Ways of Working for Lawyers in Divorce and Separation' in H Sommerlad, S Harris-Short, S Vaughan and R Young (eds), *The Futures of Legal Education and the Legal Profession* (Oxford, Hart Publishing, 2015).

the Department for Work & Pensions called 'Family Matters' which was initially expected to focus on mediation of disputes but now often involves crisis intervention for troubled clients on the margins of society. Those who find themselves in court are unlikely to be represented, though McKenzie Friends (able to accompany and quietly support a party in court but not speak for them) are increasing their activities which are now more often paid for.

Seeking Help

How do clients find their way towards professional help? What are they looking for? What is needed? Formal technical help? Counselling and behavioural therapy? Education in negotiation? Support in negotiation? Or partisan support in fighting battles on your behalf? Under the new post-LASPO and post-Children and Families Act regime, how do separating or divorcing couples make their way through the Family Justice system in achieving change in family status and the necessary financial and childcare arrangements?

Formal Civil Status: there is a distinction between private arrangements for separating cohabitants and the public process for change in civil status from married to divorce. For the married, forms must be sent to court and fees paid to achieve the change in legal civil status and arrangements for the children must be set down for potential scrutiny. For both groups, the state takes no further part in parenting arrangements except in the unlikely event of issues around neglect or abuse, and unless a parent seeks help in obtaining financial support for a child via the Child Maintenance Enforcement Commission.

Finance: it is perfectly possible for any couple to make financial arrangements privately either between themselves or with the help of family and friends, or with more formal advisers from the voluntary sector, such as a Citizens Advice Bureau, or a financial adviser or solicitor to help with understanding how property, especially the family home, is owned and might be transferred or sold and shared, how pension funds are dealt with, and how ongoing needs for financial support may flow particularly between former couples with dependent children. These arrangements may be consensual and private, but in some circumstances, particularly where a house is to be sold, or pension funds shared, the couple may wish to have the arrangement set out in a consent order of the court so that in the event of either party changing their mind there is some enforceability to the agreement. The help of a lawyer is usually required for drafting such an order to make sure that the parties have understood and agree with what is being asked for, and that the request is in a form which a court could accept and enforce. The importance of this work to the parties and to the court in order to avoid future litigation is recognised by the Legal Aid Authority: where the parties are financially eligible and have been in dispute and therefore referred to mediation, the cost of converting a Memorandum of Understanding into a court order is funded (up to a maximum of £300). If the Legal Aid Authority is willing to pay, the implication is that the work is definitely necessary and of value. Of divorcing couples, 40 per cent obtain a court order on finance on separation,[22] though only 10 per cent take part in a final hearing. Incidentally, this figure is close to the proportion of the population whose houses are owner-occupied. Where there is a house to be sold or ownership transferred, certainty is needed.

So far we have been looking at situations where there may be unhappiness and confusion, but not necessarily any dispute in the sense of a matter which the parties cannot resolve without formal intervention. Divorce and separation involve a great deal of information gathering, discussion and decision-making. Many of these activities may result in difficult negotiations and hard decision-making, but perhaps not all of these situations should be defined as 'disputes'. It is difficult to be precise about using the term in the continuum of where formal interventions occur in offering information, support, guidance, help with negotiation, and finally help with dispute resolution whether through mediation (facilitated two-party private discussion negotiation and agreement), lawyer-led negotiation (leading to agreement but involving active intervention by professionals within a legal framework which may or may not involve a court) or, more rarely, third-party decision-making in arbitration (private and non-enforceable) or adjudication (public and enforceable). We might ask whether all these procedures are taking place within the justice system. What is the role of the legal professions? Is access to justice only important for those in dispute or also for those who do not know what the law would say about their position and might benefit from doing so?

Perhaps the differences between legal help with decision-making, whether consensual or not, and the help of mediators in facilitating agreement is not as clear-cut as has been thought. From our ongoing small study of the Delivery of Family Justice in which we are observing the work of family solicitors, family solicitors who are also mediators, and non-lawyer mediators there are clearly more common elements than might be expected from the literature.

We started from a set of assumptions about the work of lawyers and mediators, and comment on these in the light of our observations about key aspects of their work in practice. For example:

1. Arm's length negotiation and direct dealing with parties and others

Re lawyers: the assumption is often made that negotiation is conducted at arm's length, and is therefore likely to give rise to conflict. But from observation we saw the lawyers able to be clear when talking to a client one-to-one, not worried about maintaining impartiality as a mediator must, and developing a warm relationship with their client while already having a good relationship with the solicitor for the other party. In addition, the lawyer can deal directly with third parties like banks or mortgage lenders.

---

[22] E Hitchings, J Miles and H Woodward, 'Assembling the Jigsaw Puzzle: Understanding Financial Settlement on Divorce' (March 2014) 44 *Family Law* 304.

Re mediators: the assumption is that mediators are able to deal directly with both parties and facilitate constructive conversation and increase mutual trust. But the mediators also have to work hard and skilfully to maintain impartiality and equality in dealings with both parties together, and may find it difficult to inspire confidence. The mediator is assumed to work only within the room, but as parties are likely to use email to raise questions or concerns it becomes more and more difficult to maintain this isolation without causing frustration.

2. Giving orders and facilitating proposals

Re lawyers: the assumption is that the lawyers tell clients what to do. In observation we saw lawyers ask for information, give advice, and then take instructions, giving the client informed choice about which path to take.

Re mediators: mediators are assumed to be facilitating a conversation, not working towards a preferred outcome. We observed some mediators who rarely respond directly to a party, but reframe questions, which can be irritating and upsetting for clients and foment hostility, as the client does not feel understood or supported.

Proposals: where do they come from? How are they selected and developed? What if a proposal lies outside the legal frame? The assumption is that the lawyer gives orders, seeking the best possible outcome for his individual client, and advises on a proposal which will sit within what a court would accept. In observations we saw them take instructions, putting the children first as required by the Children Act 1989, finding and supporting an outcome that is best for all in the long term, after considering new partnerships, relocation and other issues which might arise. Mediators are assumed to encourage, or elicit, proposals. They may give examples but not suggest outcomes, nor push for one over another even if one appears better for everyone. In observation, however, we saw that proposals were sometimes made by the mediator and were argued for, and were dismissed. If a proposal lay outside what a court would accept there were a variety of responses in practice ranging from non-intervention to telling the parties that this was the case if both agreed to hear this information.

3. Legal framework

Re lawyers: lawyers are assumed to always work within the law, though there is a significant difference between specialists and non-specialist family lawyers. In observation also they were aware of the legal framework and would give information and advice.

Re mediators: mediators are assumed to have some knowledge of the legal framework from their brief training. In observation, they were not always aware or did not raise legal concerns with clients.

These comments indicate what we expected (on the basis of the literature and professional documentation) to see and what we actually saw while sitting in with members of each group. We were particularly interested in the new group of solicitor mediators (not described in the section above) who in observation sessions were able to offer something from both worlds: not adversarially oriented legal advice but generous and relevant legal information, which would refer to what a court might think, would put children first even at the risk of unpicking an agreement, and enabled the drafting of a Memorandum of Understanding (MOU) which could become consent orders without difficulty. They were ready and able to form warm supportive relationship, and to look beyond immediate conflict to what might happen in the future.

Re Costs: mediation is assumed to be cheaper, but in our experience the costs of mediation and legal advice were not universally as dissimilar as we expected and were more variable (leaving aside Legal Aid Authority rates). Mediation can cost as much as £500 per hour for complex financial matters, or as little as £60 per hour when scale rates are used; they can also be free to the client on legal aid. Both parties pay, usually for a 90-minute session, plus VAT. A couple rarely attend more than five sessions and record-keeping is kept to a minimum among mediators coming from the counselling tradition. Mediation has traditionally avoided the kinds of costs which can increase rapidly as a result of ongoing interaction with the lawyer outside face-to-face meetings. These costs do not arise with a mediator who does not have contact with either party outside the mediation session for fear of losing impartiality, or a lawyer mediator who may engage more but may not charge for time outside the session. Lawyers are assumed to be expensive, and indeed can be. But Legal Packages for non-conflicted matters can cost only a few hundred pounds. A website may be free, while a big money case can incur legal costs of several million. A financial mediation can take from three to up to 10 sessions of 90 minutes with two paying clients. Prices vary in the private sector, but are often in the order of £120 per hour each; with VAT the total cost could range from just under £1,000 to over £4,000 and there would also be the cost of legal help with reaching a consent order and court fees. A solicitor mediator will usually charge at the same hourly rate for mediation or legal advice, sometimes by the session, sometimes per person. Mediation clients in financial matters will usually also require the help of a solicitor to check and draft a consent order and legal services also carry a wide range of costs. A high street lawyer in a low-income area may charge under £1,000 for divorce with financial arrangements, a central London specialist could charge up to £5,000 solely for a consent order, £15,000 for agreement after voluntary disclosure, or £30,000 for requiring judicial input in a Financial Dispute Resolution hearing. The Coop Legal Services charge £25 for their Divorce Pack, £99 for document checking and legal help online or over the phone. Wikivorce is free. Law firms have been taking care to define costs, and to reduce expense by having free intake sessions, making skilful use of IT, for example, for appointments and recording rather than using support staff, and unbundling to cut the costs of more complex cases. The picture is complex, moving and confusing for the potential client, and worrying for those thinking about access to justice.

In private law the numbers of cases coming to court are falling, while the proportion without representation increases. Mediation is not so far taking up the shortfall, though lawyer mediators may prove more popular as closer to a 'one stop shop'.

But even in public law, where pressure is on to reduce the duration of cases but legal aid remains available, the President of the Family Division felt compelled to set out his views on the failure of government in a public law children matter initiated by the state to make it possible for him to conduct a fair trial where two parents with learning difficulties in a care case were earning just above the financial eligibility level for legal aid, but were unable to pay for help and unable to present their position to the court. On 31 October 2014 Sir James Munby said:

> Thus far the State has simply washed its hands of the problem, leaving the solution to the problem which the State itself has created—for the State has brought the proceedings but declined all responsibility for ensuring that the parents are able to participate effectively in the proceedings it has brought—to the goodwill, the charity, of the legal profession.[23]

In this case where the parents stood to lose their children the solicitors had worked pro bono and even agreed to reimburse the Official Solicitor should a costs order be made against him, a risk which the Official Solicitor was not prepared to take.

This judgment came days after the Ministry of Justice had announced attempts to deal with the pressure points on the justice system in family cases by setting up pilot advice and support services in five areas on a six-month trial to support litigants in person. These services will be run by the Children and Family Courts Advice and Support Service, and are a welcome addition to the 'support' aspect of CAFCASS work. They will also provide training for mediators in how to recognise when a child may be close to the threshold for establishing neglect or abuse and should be referred to local authority social services. The initiative does not, however, provide much by way of a substitute for the publicly funded work of the legal profession ended by LASPO. It is curious that it is the much criticised lawyers who are taking the lead in helping families in difficulty through pro bono work and by developing new, accessible and cost effective ways of working in not only providing dispute resolution, court- based in the last resort, but also information, advice, help with third parties such as mortgage lenders, and support in planning for the best possible future for themselves and their children. We suggest that Lady Hale's tripod for access to justice needs all three legs: good laws, good remedies, and good lawyers.

---

[23] *In the Matter of D (A Child)* [2014] EWFC 39, [31].

12

Access to Justice for Young People: Beyond the Policies and Politics of Austerity

JAMES KENRICK AND ELLIE PALMER

Introduction

Children under 18, and young adults whose capacity is restricted because of learning disability or mental ill health, cannot be expected to navigate complex legal processes. In many cases they will require the assistance of a lawyer (rather than a parent, litigation friend or non-legal advocate) to effectively participate in proceedings which affect them. In those circumstances, legal advice, assistance and representation are necessary in order for them to exercise their rights effectively in a wide range of circumstances.[1]

Notwithstanding the general principle that the welfare of the child is paramount, consideration of the specific legal needs of children and young people within the civil justice system is often limited either to cases in which the child or young person is affected by someone else's dispute, as in many private family law cases, or to cases where the child or young person is the passive subject of a dispute brought on their behalf by their parents or carer, as in many education and clinical negligence cases.

This chapter focuses on the largely ignored group of young people (primarily aged between 16 and 25) who need legal advice in their own right in order to deal with their problems independently from the needs or support of parents or carers. It argues for a distinctive participative evidence-based approach to the design and delivery of legal services for children and young people, which would be both cost-effective and consistent with UK international obligations to give effect to socio-economic rights under the United Nations Convention on the Rights of the Child (UNCRC). In doing so, the chapter:

— Highlights the distinctive nature of young people's civil legal needs, advice-seeking behaviour and access to legal advice and representation, with a particular focus on social welfare law.

---

[1] Office of the Children's Commissioner, *Legal Aid changes since April 2013: Child Rights Impact Assessment* (London, OCC, 2014).

— Examines entrenched political, institutional and legal factors (especially the impact and implications of cuts to legal aid under the Legal Aid, Sentencing and Punishment of Offenders Act 2012(LASPO).[2]

— Presents the findings of a cumulative body of research that underscores the close relationship between civil justice problems and mental health issues for this vulnerable group, and their resistance (by comparison with other age groups) to the use of technology for accessing advice that they often urgently need.

— In conclusion, looking beyond the politics of austerity, it argues for a radical, albeit cost-effective, participative approach to the design and delivery of legal services for children and young people, consistent with UK obligations to give *meaningful* effect to their basic socio-economic rights under the UNCRC.

The chapter is in three main parts. The first part focuses on the distinctive and acute nature of young people's advice needs; their long-term marginalisation in the civil justice system; and the socio-economic implications of political and institutional failures to take account of their inherent vulnerabilities, particularly in the case of disadvantaged young people without adults on whom to depend. The second part focuses on the impact of LASPO on children and young people acting independently from parents or carers. The third part argues for the provision of dedicated interconnected cost-effective services—legal information, advice and representation—that take account of young people's clearly articulated perceptions of their unmet needs (see Appendix).

Young People's Needs for Advice and their Marginalisation in the Civil Justice System

The Determinants of Young People's Advice Needs

Four key interrelated psychological and social phenomena contribute to the acuity of young people's legal advice needs: (i) the changing nature of the adolescent transition; (ii) the association of adolescent patterns of cognitive behaviour with their neurological development; (iii) systemic patterns of social exclusion; and (iv) problem 'triggers' related to environmental disadvantage or key life events.

The Adolescent Transition

Paths to adulthood have become more complex in recent years and the achievement of full social and financial independence more protracted. For a growing

---

[2] Part 1 of the Legal Aid, Sentencing and Punishment of Offenders Act 2012 came into force on 1 April 2013.

number of young people, especially those who lack emotional and economic support from dependable adults, the transition from youth to adulthood is increasingly fraught with difficulties that can mark the beginning of long-term social and health-related problems. At particular risk are those young people who have experienced 'accelerated' or 'fast track' transitions; in cases where independence and responsibility have been thrust upon them at an early age, for example, through becoming a young parent, an early school leaver, an asylum seeker or a young carer.[3]

Cognitive Behaviour and Neurological Development

Advanced understandings of young people's cognitive and neurological development reinforce the importance of accepting the *distinctive* nature of their legal needs (in contrast to those of older adults).[4] Where, as in the United Kingdom, negative attitudes towards young people are prevalent, there is likely to be a corresponding lack of 'trust' and disassociation by young people from political and institutional structures.[5]

Social Exclusion

Moreover, statistical evidence supports the view that young people are disproportionately and increasingly prone to a range of social welfare problems—homelessness, unemployment, substance misuse, teenage pregnancy and mental health issues—which increase the risk of an unsuccessful adolescent transition and frequently give rise to the need for advice.[6] Without effective intervention, social exclusion in youth can continue long into adulthood and be passed down to the next generation.

Problem 'Triggers'

Young people's social welfare problems often begin with changes in life circumstances or significant life events: leaving home or care; leaving education; getting or losing a job; being the victim or perpetrator of crime; or arriving in the UK as a refugee or asylum seeker. Thus, many social welfare problems for which young people urgently need advice and support (such as housing or benefit claims) may

---

[3] See, eg, *Transitions: Young Adults with Complex Lives: A Social Exclusion Unit Final Report* (Social Exclusion Unit, 2005).

[4] See, eg, S-J Blakemore, 'The Developing Social Brain: Implications for Education' (2010) 65(6) *Neuron* 744.

[5] The UN Committee on the Rights of the Child has expressed concern at 'the general climate of intolerance and negative public attitudes towards children, especially adolescents' in the UK. UN Committee on the Rights of the Child, *Forty-ninth session: Consideration of reports submitted by states parties under article 44 of the Convention: Concluding Observations: United Kingdom of Great Britain and Northern Ireland* (Geneva, United Nations, 2008).

[6] J Kenrick, *The Advice Needs of Young People – The Evidence* (London, Youth Access, 2009).

arise directly from the actions or inaction of local or central government departments; problems which, if unresolved, may give rise to clusters of multiple serious problems.[7]

The Prevalence, Nature, Pattern and Severity of Legal Need

In the UK, since the beginning of the economic downturn, a range of factors including high youth unemployment, welfare reforms and cuts to youth services and advice services taken in the name of austerity have led to a sharp rise in advice need.[8] However, based on the fact that many advice agencies and solicitors see relatively few young people, it has traditionally been assumed that their legal needs are relatively low.

Yet, by the time of the 2008–10 recession, young people aged 16 to 25 were experiencing at least 2.3 million 'difficult to solve' civil justice problems each year in England and Wales.[9] Moreover, slightly more recent data, from the 2010 Civil and Social Justice Panel Survey, demonstrated that 34.2 per cent of this age group had experienced at least one civil justice problem, slightly above the figure of 32.8 per cent for the general population; and that amongst 22- to 24-year-olds, the figure was as high as 43 per cent.[10] It is also now known that their problems are likely to relate to housing (landlord and tenant), homelessness, employment, discrimination and involvement with the police; which means that they account for a disproportionate number of the entire cohort with problems in key areas of social welfare law (traditionally catered for by the not-for-profit advice sector).[11] We also know that the pattern of young people's legal advice needs change as they get older: whereas a 14 or 15-year-old client is most likely to experience a family or education problem, a 16 or 17-year-old is more likely to need help in relation to homelessness, and a 23 or 24-year-old is to have a problem with welfare benefits, debt or rented housing.[12]

It is also clear, however, that legal problems are not evenly distributed amongst the young population, and that they cluster around disadvantaged young people. Thus, as well as being vulnerable on account of their age, as many as 80 per cent of young people with civil legal problems fall into one or more additional categories of 'vulnerability' including lone parenthood, victims of crime, people with disabilities or mental health problems.[13] Furthermore, disadvantaged young adults are particularly prone to experiencing multiple and severe problems, which by their

---

[7] Kenrick, *The Advice Needs of Young People* (n 6).

[8] See, eg, Youth Access, *Picking up the Pieces* (London, Youth Access, 2013).

[9] Kenrick, *The Advice Needs of Young People* (n 6).

[10] P Pleasence, *Civil Legal Problems: Young People, Social Exclusion and Crime* (London, Youth Access/Law Centres Federation/JustRights, 2011) 1–2.

[11] Kenrick, *The Advice Needs of Young People* (n 6).

[12] ibid.

[13] Pleasence (n 10) 10.

nature are more likely to require specialist legal intervention in order to prevent situations escalating and spiralling out of control.[14] They are also significantly more likely than the population as a whole to worry about their legal problems and to report a causal relationship with stress-related illness, violence (aimed at them), loss of home, loss of confidence and general physical ill health.[15]

However, disadvantaged or not (whether classified by subject category, 'face-to-face' or remote services, or disproportionate impact that problems have on their lives) there is evidence that young people experience relatively severe legal problems which they are seldom equipped with the knowledge and skills—the 'legal capability'—to resolve without expert advice. Thus, although the law assumes an overnight transition to full legal capacity at the age of 18, cognitive behavioural research has shown that the teenage brain is still developing well into the twenties;[16] and that consistent with the psychological and socio-economic complexities of the protracted adolescent transition, young people's legal problems (in particular social welfare problems) rarely develop in isolation from practical, emotional and personal issues such as relationship breakdown, stress, depression, abuse, drugs and alcohol or education.[17] Thus, when added to their relative inexperience of 'the system' compared with older adults, it is not surprising, that young people without support feel overwhelmed when confronted with civil problems that impact so severely on their lives. Nor is it surprising that, when widely consulted, young people would articulate the need for legal services to be provided in a single venue catering specifically for their age group; lending weight to accumulative research findings that age-appropriate legal advice services should be provided in one place and closely integrated with other kinds of services that young people use[18] (see Appendix).

The Marginalisation of Young People in the Civil Justice System

Despite their relative inability to handle their problems alone, it is also clear that young people are significantly *less* likely than the general population to seek advice when they need it, and *more* likely to avoid, delay or retreat if not immediately successful;[19] or to fail in their efforts to get advice because it is simply unavailable. Data from the 2010 Civil and Social Justice Panel Survey shows that only 16 per cent of 16- to 17-year-olds with 'difficult to solve' civil justice problems managed

---

[14] Kenrick, *The Advice Needs of Young People* (n 6).

[15] NJ Balmer, T Tam and P Pleasence, *Young People and Civil Justice: Findings from the 2004 English and Welsh Civil and Social Justice Survey* (London, Youth Access, 2007).

[16] The National Institute for Mental Health has an ongoing project studying the teenage brain, available at: www.nimh.nih.gov/publicat/teenbrain.cfm.

[17] See, eg, NJ Balmer and P Pleasence, *The Legal Problems and Mental Health Needs of Youth Advice Service Users* (London, Youth Access, 2012); and Pleasence (n 10).

[18] J Kenrick, *Young People's Access to Advice—the evidence* (London, Youth Access, 2009).

[19] ibid.

to get advice from a formal source—half as many as 25- to 59-year-olds with broadly similar problems.[20] Only 7 per cent reached a recognised legal advice provider, such as a solicitor, law centre or Citizens Advice Bureau. Moreover, young people tend to be particularly unlikely to obtain advice when they have social welfare problems.[21]

Turning then to consider legal aid—through which only a small minority of young people's legal problems have historically been addressed—a clear pattern emerges. Before LASPO, official figures showed that 16- to 24-year-olds accounted for a mere 8 per cent of civil legal aid clients[22]—approximately half of the ratio that would have been expected had supply been measured against the proportion of civil legal problems known to be experienced by young people, even without factoring in their relative vulnerability.

Analysis of Civil and Social Justice Survey data in 2007 found that young people were more likely to experience housing problems than any other age group: around a quarter of all rented housing problems and a third of all homelessness problems were experienced by those under the age of 25.[23] Yet, although accounting for less than 15 per cent of all legal aid housing cases, there was evidence that a disproportionate amount of legal aid resources were being spent on the 25- to 49-year-old age group. Moreover, even when young people were given housing advice through legal aid, Legal Services Commission data showed that solicitors and advice agencies spent less time on young people's cases and achieved worse case outcomes for them.[24]

There are many factors, not least the low turnout at elections of young people in England and Wales,[25] to explain the indifference of successive governments to addressing their continuing marginalisation. However, perhaps most significantly, the long-standing structure of legal aid funding around subject categories such as family, housing or social security rather than client needs, has led to a preponderance of generic all-age/all-client services, which fail to cater adequately for groups who present with specific person-centred problems relating to their status, for example, as young people or immigrants. Less than half of 1 per cent of all private practice solicitors firms specifically target young people.[26]

---

[20] Pleasence (n 10) 13.

[21] Kenrick, *Young People's Access to Advice* (n 18).

[22] Ministry of Justice, *Reform of Legal Aid in England and Wales: Equality Impact Assessment* (2011). See Table 7, 131.

[23] J Kenrick, *Locked Out: The prevalence and impact of housing and homelessness problems amongst young people, and the impact of good advice* (London, Youth Access, 2007).

[24] ibid.

[25] Compare the participation of young people in the Scottish Referendum and in the General Election of May 2015.

[26] Analysis of 2006 Legal Advice Workforce Survey data—see Youth Access, *The Youth Advice Workforce: Now & In The Future* (London, Youth Access, 2009) for further details.

Thus, in 2006, the author of an internal report for Citizens Advice concluded that the generic homogeneous CAB model struggles to meet young people's specific legal needs, and is unable to provide specialist support on their related emotional, personal and health problems.[27] In turn, young people often cite 'mistrust of authority', 'concern that they will be judged or not treated seriously' or a general perception that 'services like the CAB are not for me', as explanations for their reticence. However, for many beleaguered agencies which already serve large numbers of disadvantaged adults, young people are no more deserving of support than any other group, and they see no reason to adapt to a less generic model.[28]

However, it would be wrong to suggest that 'mainstream' adult advice services are not capable of getting things right for young people. Law centres, such as Islington Law Centre[29] have had outstanding success in developing outreach and other targeted services for young people, whilst the only CAB in England and Wales developed just for young people, The Cabin in Stockton-on-Tees, had been dealing with over 10,000 enquiries a year from young people by the start of this decade. Not only does this highlight the advantages of a distinctive youth focused approach, it also shows that there is a disturbing level of unmet need in areas where young people who are less well served slip through the net.

The Significance of Mental Health

It has become clear that young people's legal needs are unlikely to be met, without understanding the strong correlations with their mental health and the resulting implications for service design. Examining data from the Civil and Social Justice Survey on 18- to 24-year-olds, Sefton found a close relationship between social welfare legal problems, mental health and youth. Social welfare problems were reported much more often by those who were experiencing mental health problems (44 per cent), than by those who were not (16 per cent). Homelessness problems were 15 times more common amongst those with mental health problems. Similarly, Sefton found that young people with social welfare problems were three times more likely to report mental health problems, compared with those not reporting social welfare problems (31 per cent versus 9 per cent). Again, a link with homelessness problems stood out: 62 per cent of those who reported homelessness also reported mental health problems.[30] (See Figure 1.)

---

[27] L Wintersteiger, *Citizens Advice Access Strategy: The advice and volunteering needs of young people* (London, Citizens Advice, 2007).

[28] Kenrick, *Young People's Access to Advice* (n 18).

[29] As to which, see Lorna Reid's chapter in this volume.

[30] M Sefton, *With Rights in Mind: Is there a role for social welfare law advice in improving young people's mental health? A review of evidence* (London, Youth Access, 2010).

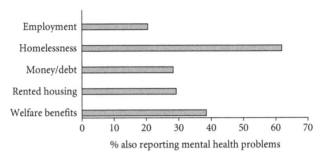

Figure 1: Percentage of 18- to 24-year-olds reporting social welfare problems who also reported mental health problems

(*Source:* LSRC, 2009) (*Source:* Sefton 2010)

Balmer et al examined the subject further, analysing data from the longitudinal 2010–12 Civil and Social Justice Panel Surveys for links between legal problems, mental health and disadvantage. Like Sefton, they found a very close association between young people's social welfare legal problems and mental illness. The association became particularly dramatic when two measures of disadvantage—NEET (Not in Education, Employment or Training) status and social isolation—were added to the analysis. As many as 49 per cent of young people who were socially isolated *and* NEET *and* reported a social welfare legal problem also had mental health problems—five times greater than the non-NEET, non-isolated, no legal problem group. The likelihood of mental health problems increased yet further where *multiple* legal issues were present. The study also found that young people's mental health deteriorated as new legal problems emerged.[31]

Balmer and Pleasence had earlier studied the clients of youth advice services, finding 'exceptionally high levels of mental illness'. Around two-thirds of young people attending youth advice services for advice on social welfare issues had scores on a standardised scale that met or exceeded common cut-off points for cases of mental illness and 17 per cent had scores indicating severe mental health problems (compared with 2.6 per cent of the general population). Nearly half of young clients reported that their health had suffered as a result of their social welfare problems, with 26 per cent visiting a doctor or counsellor as a result. However, after receiving advice, as many as 64 per cent of clients felt that this had resulted in improvements in stress levels; 34 per cent also reporting improvements in their general health (see Figure 2). Advice was calculated to be 'clearly cost-effective' on grounds of mental health improvements alone.[32]

---

[31] NJ Balmer, P Pleasence and A Hagell, *Health Inequality and Access to Justice: Young People, Mental Health and Legal Issues* (Youth Access, 2015).

[32] Balmer and Pleasence (n 17).

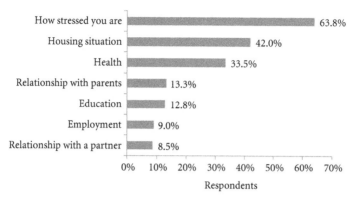

Figure 2: The extent to which clients felt advice had led to improvements in a range of areas

(*Source:* Balmer and Pleasence 2012)

Taken together, the studies establish that social welfare legal problems should be considered to be key 'social determinants'[33] of young people's mental health and that they are therefore key factors to be taken into account when designing appropriate support and advice mechanisms. Significant savings could be made by taking preventive measures to address young people's social welfare legal problems and mental health problems in a coordinated way, and by recognising the benefits of services that can provide social welfare legal advice alongside therapeutic interventions in accessible young person-friendly settings. The research also underscores the importance of service models that are accessible to disadvantaged young people up to the age of 25.

Challenging the Myth of the 'Tech-Savvy' Generation

Over the past decade, there has been a pan-European shift towards the use of technology for the provision of cost-effective and efficient public advice and consultation services (including legal services). Moreover, although in the United Kingdom there have been mounting concerns about the inaccessibility of internet advice services for vulnerable groups (including the elderly and disabled people) it has generally been assumed that young people would feel at home navigating online advice services. However, contrary to that presumption, there is a significant body of research to suggest that vulnerable young people may be as reticent in seeking online advice, as they have proved to be in generic adult 'face-to-face' advice contexts.

---

[33] The World Health Organization defines the social determinants of health as 'the socio-economic conditions that influence the health of individuals and communities'.

Thus, not only has it been demonstrated that remote media, including telephone *and* internet are unsuited to generating the level of 'trust' necessary to encourage young people to divulge their complex personal or social welfare problems,[34] the most extensive independent research on use of remote media by young people, conducted by Denvir and others, has shown that although young people report high levels of internet access, they report low levels of use for purposes of seeking legal information and advice.[35] Fulsome use of the internet for purposes of social networking and entertainment—the primary internet functions for young people—do not necessarily imply a generation of 'techno-savvy' online advice seekers who will suddenly jump to the head of the lengthening queues for advice.[36] Denvir's study also suggests that even when young people do use internet legal services, they have very low levels of success in finding what they need, both in absolute terms and by comparison with older age groups.

The problem has perhaps been exacerbated by the initial lack of targeted specialist youth friendly sites such as YouthNet'sTheSite, but even when such sites do exist they may not have the desired effect. Denvir later undertook an experiment in which 100 young people aged 18 to 24, were asked to solve a hypothetical legal problem online. She found that participants typically spent less than 10 minutes searching a range of search engines and that they had often failed to consider either the jurisdictional relevance of the resulting information or the reliability of selected websites. Thus, the availability of *increased information* about their legal rights was shown to have had little bearing on their capacity to tackle the problem by taking appropriate action. Indeed the vast majority of participants indicated that, due to their own lack of life experience, if confronted with a similar problem in their daily lives, they would need to rely on support from family, friends or an adviser to find the help they needed.[37] In sum, Denvir's research confirms that although the internet has an increasingly important information function, its utility should not be overestimated, particularly in the case of young people, whose relative lack of legal capability leaves them especially vulnerable to poor outcomes when left to self-help through the internet or by any other method: 'The idea that technology will compensate for any lack of capacity on the part of the user is appealing in its simplicity, but this simplicity ultimately underestimates the centrality of the user to the process'.[38] Increasingly, it seems that online services will be

---

[34] Kenrick, *Young People's Access to Advice* (n 18).

[35] C Denvir, N Balmer and P Pleasence, 'Surfing the web—Recreation or resource? Exploring how young people in the UK use the Internet as an advice portal for problems with a legal dimension' (Legal Services Research Centre/UCL) published in (2011) 23 *Interacting with Computers* 96, available at: www.sciencedirect.com/science/article/pii/S0953543810000949.

[36] J Kenrick, 'Online advice services and the myth of the tech-savvy generation: Can we please have an evidence-based approach to the design of services?' (LegalVoice, October 2013) available at: www.legalvoice.org.uk/2013/10/09/online-advice-services-and-the-myth-of-the-tech-savvy-generation.

[37] C Denvir, *What is the net worth? Young people, civil justice and the Internet*, Doctoral Thesis (PhD thesis, University College London, 2014)' available at:. http://discovery.ucl.ac.uk/ 1437397.

[38] C Denvir and NJ Balmer, 'Digitally (De)Faulted? How do young people use the Internet to acquire knowledge of their rights?' (University College London, 2014), available at www.lawforlife.org.uk/wp-content/uploads/Cat-Denvir-YP-article.pdf.

accessed via smartphones and that a large proportion of young people do indeed possess such devices. Ownership of technology is not of itself sufficient, however. Evidence suggests that successful access to and use of online legal information and advice may, like other methods of delivery, be influenced more significantly by skills and affluence than by age.

Denvir's earlier study found that only one out of 46 18- to 24-year-olds with GCSE grades D–G had tried the internet to get advice, whilst none of 16 respondents with trade apprenticeships and none of 69 respondents without academic qualifications had done so.[39] Moreover, disadvantaged young people who experienced legal problems of the greatest severity, were considerably less likely to have access to landline telephones and the internet than their better off peers. Indeed, studies have revealed a worrying lack of technological skills amongst unemployed young people[40] highlighting that for young people with the greatest need for support—for example those in housing need, new parents and new arrivals in the UK—face-to-face contact with people they know and trust remains the most important information source.[41]

Psychological barriers to accessing advice (the most powerful of which is trust) have been found to be highly significant in the case of young people.[42] Moreover, remote media, including telephone and internet, have been shown to be less effective than face-to-face support in building the level of trust necessary for young people to talk openly about distressing personal or social welfare problems. Arguably, as suggested by the success of CourtNav,[43] some of the present limitations of legal advice technology may be overcome by the development of more sophisticated tailored online advice and information services. As yet, however, there is little evidence to justify such a rapid large-scale 'channel shift' away from more traditional face-to-face services for young people in search of legal advice.

Legal Aid Cuts: The Effects of LASPO on Young People

The Legal Aid, Sentencing and Punishment of Offenders Act 2012 (LASPO) came into force in April 2013, vastly reducing entitlement to legal aid in many areas of civil law. Although campaigners were successful in gaining a few minor concessions during the passage through Parliament of the LASPO Bill, the reforms will continue to have a major impact on children and young people's access to justice.

---

[39] Denvir, Balmer and Pleasence (n 35)

[40] *The Prince's Trust Digital Literacy Survey 2013* (London, The Prince's Trust, 2013), available at: www.princes-trust.org.uk/pdf/DIGITAL_LITERACY_2013B.pdf.

[41] R Eynon and A Geniets, *On the Periphery? Understanding Low and Discontinued Internet Use Amongst Young People in Britain* (Oxford, Oxford Internet Institute, 2012).

[42] Kenrick, *Young People's Access to Advice* (n 18).

[43] As to which see Paul Yates' chapter in this volume.

Few adults, let alone children, are capable of navigating the legal system alone, yet the Act will leave thousands of children and young people without advice or representation.

Access to Legal Aid Following LASPO

During the passage of the LASPO Bill in 2011–12, the Government had been invited repeatedly to reassure MPs and peers that legal aid for children who needed it in their own right would be protected.[44] At that time, the Government's own official estimates suggested that changes to the scope of legal aid would lead to a reduction in volume of 75,000 cases involving children and young people as the recipients of legal aid in their own right; a figure which included 6,000 children aged under 18 and 69,000 young people aged 18 to 24.[45]

The main protections provided in the LASPO measures were directed at child parties in family litigation—no safeguards were provided for children and young people in the majority of other categories. However, despite this gap, ministers repeatedly stated that 95 per cent of children's cases were protected and insisted that 'of the remaining cases, many would potentially be eligible for exceptional funding'.[46]

Three years later, data on the actual usage of civil legal aid by children and young people—before and for the first year after implementation of LASPO—were provided by the Ministry of Justice in response to parliamentary questions[47] thereby enabling analysis of the early impact of LASPO on case volumes where a child or young person was the applicant. As indicated below, the data was broken down by broad legal aid category (Family, Immigration and Asylum, and Social Welfare Law) and by age (children aged 18 and under, and young adults aged 19 to 25).[48]

Social Welfare Law:

— Numbers of social welfare law cases involving children fell by 65 per cent between 2009/10 and 2013/14 to just 1,477. Figures fell 42 per cent in the first year after the implementation of LASPO (2013/14) alone—to a level that was already 30 per cent below even the reduced levels anticipated by the Ministry of Justice's modelling.

---

[44] See, eg Lord McNally responding to LASPO Bill Committee Stage debate: HL Deb 16 January 2012, vol 734, col 447.

[45] Data provided by Ministry of Justice on 10 October 2011 in response to Freedom of Information requests made by JustRights and The Children's Society, available at: justrights.org.uk/sites/default/files/Data_on_legal_aid_and_CYP%202011.pdf.

[46] See, eg, statement given to the BBC on 17 April 2012, available at: www.bbc.co.uk/news/education-17728128.

[47] Written parliamentary answers by Mike Penning MP on 5 February 2015 in response to Parliamentary Questions 22917 and 22918 asked by Andy Slaughter MP.

[48] For further details of the data, see *Justice For The Young: A Snapshot* (JustRights, 2015), available at: http://justrights.org.uk/sites/default/files/Justice%20for%20young%20a%20snapshot.pdf.

— Cases involving young adults had also fallen well below anticipated levels (to just 11,530 in 2013/14) and were 71 per cent down on their peak in 2010/11. Figures fell by 56 per cent in 2013/14 alone.

Immigration and Asylum Law:

— Numbers of immigration and asylum cases peaked in 2010/11 before LASPO changes and have fallen rapidly since—to well below post-LASPO anticipated levels.

— Children's cases fell by 68 per cent in just three years to 4,159—barely half of the Government's anticipated post-LASPO levels. There was a 21 per cent fall in 2013/14.

— Young adults' cases fell by 58 per cent in the same three-year period (to 11,812) and by 20 per cent in 2013/14.

Family Law:

— Cases involving children (which are of course protected) rose by 57 per cent between 2010/11 and 2013/14 to 36,703. Numbers continued to rise (by 21 per cent) in the first year of LASPO to a level that was 57 per cent above government predictions.

— By contrast, family cases involving young adults fell by 22 per cent in 2013/14—but remained over twice the post-LASPO level anticipated by the Government.

It is notable that due to the large increase in family cases, which *are* protected, *overall* the number of cases involving children under 18 increased by 11 per cent in the first year following LASPO, to 42,339 outweighing quite dramatic falls in immigration and asylum law and social welfare law. Meanwhile, the number of cases involving young adults aged 19 to 24 had fallen by 31 per cent overall, to 67,903 although, proportionately, reductions in the areas of immigration and asylum and social welfare law were far greater than this.

These are early findings and one would expect numbers to fall further once pre-LASPO cases have worked their way through the system and the full impact of wider cuts to early intervention advice services has been felt. It is also important to bear in mind that young people are likely to have been disproportionately affected by subsequent restrictions on legal aid for prison law matters and judicial reviews.[49]

Based on evidence of the vulnerability of young people with legal problems,[50] it is now known that the following groups are likely to have been disproportionately impacted by cuts to legal aid: homeless young people; sexually exploited children;

---

[49] See *Judicial Review proposals—the impact on children and young people* (JustRights, 2014), available at: http://justrights.org.uk/sites/default/files/Judicial%20Review%20-%20JustRights%20briefing%20Lords%20Oct%20%202014_1.pdf.

[50] Pleasence (n 10) sets out evidence from the Civil and Social Justice Panel Survey of the vulnerability of young people with legal problems.

young people with mental health problems and learning disabilities; children affected by care proceedings; children in care and care leavers; trafficked children and young people; and young refugees and asylum seekers.[51]

Exceptional Funding: The Safety Net is Not Working

During the passage of the LASPO Bill, ministers had repeatedly reassured MPs and peers from all parties that an expanding Exceptional Case Funding scheme would provide an adequate safety net for children and young people denied access to advice following implementation of the reforms. For example, Lord McNally, then Justice Minister with responsibility for legal aid, stated on 16 January 2012, 'where a child brings an action without a litigation friend, this will be an important factor in deciding whether they have the ability to present their case'.[52] Moreover, in February 2015—nearly two years after implementation of LASPO—legal aid ministers continued to insist that 'the age of the child or young person applicant is one factor which caseworkers will always consider'.[53] It soon became clear, however, that assurances about exceptional funding were not being operationalised in decisions taken by Legal Aid Agency administrators.

The Government's pre-LASPO estimates of the percentage of 'out of scope' cases likely to be readmitted under the Exceptional Case Funding scheme had been modest[54] but nonetheless implied that at least 847 children and 4,888 young adults would be granted exceptional funding each year. However, an independent analysis of the number of cases involving young people aged 18 to 24 who had the potential to be readmitted into the legal aid scheme, found that as many as 43,500 legal help and 5,300 legal representation cases might have grounds each year on the basis of the applicant's mental health needs alone.[55] Moreover, after the event, the Ministry of Justice's data[56] shows that only 50 children and 95 young adults applied for Exceptional Case Funding in a 12-month period from October 2013 to September 2014; and that of those 145 applications, a mere 12 (representing 8 per cent) were granted, including just three (6 per cent) of the applications from children aged 18 and under.

Thus, contrary to government assurances that the Exceptional Case Funding scheme would provide a robust safety net for the most vulnerable categories of

---

[51] *Legal Aid cuts: child protection implications* (JustRights, 2013), available at: http://justrights.org.uk/sites/default/files/Legal_Aid_-_Child_Protection_Implications_sept_2013_FINAL.pdf.

[52] HL Deb 16 January 2012, vol 734, col 447.

[53] Written parliamentary answer by Shailesh Vara MP on 10 February 2015 in response to Parliamentary Question 223066.

[54] The Ministry of Justice's 'Impact Assessment Annex A: Scope' (*Reform of Legal Aid in England and Wales: The Government Response* (London, TSO, 2011)), para 10, Tables 1 and 3 show forecasted reductions in the volume of cases as a result of the legal aid reforms.

[55] See Appendix 3, Balmer and Pleasence (n 17).

[56] Written parliamentary answers by Shailesh Vara MP on 10 February 2015 in response to Parliamentary Questions 222961, 223099, 223066 and 223067.

children and young people, it has served a risible proportion of those whose cases have fallen out of scope since LASPO. Indeed, some legal aid providers specialising in working with children and young people have reported that applications for exceptional funding have become a waste of valuable time and that they no longer apply.[57]

The Impact of Legal Aid Cuts on Young People

Evidence and arguments to persuade the Coalition Government that they should reconsider the impacts of LASPO for young people, have centred around three main strategies: (i) to highlight the reduced accessibility of justice for children and young people in areas of greatest need; (ii) to demonstrate the inextricable links between their impaired health, wellbeing and lack of protection on the one hand and their inability to resolve their legal problems on the other; and (iii) to shift the access to justice debate to the international human rights arena, thereby highlighting the Government's failure to meet international commitments to young people under the UN Convention on the Rights of the Child (UNCRC). It is to the third of these strategies that we now turn.

A right of *effective* 'access to justice' provides the cornerstone for protection of the substantive enumerated rights in the UNCRC. For without the ability effectively to request, inform or challenge decisions, those rights cannot be secured and become meaningless. Thus, in September 2014, the Office of the Children's Commissioner (OCC) in England published its Child Rights Impact Assessment (with the aim of highlighting the impact of changes to civil and prison law legal aid implemented since April 2013) on the substantive rights of children and young people enshrined in the UNCRC.[58] The following potential impacts of the reforms on children and young people were identified in the report:

— Children and young people would be obliged to deal with decision-makers directly without support (including pursuing formal proceedings as litigants in person, or through an adult litigation friend); notwithstanding their reported feelings of intimidation when appearing unrepresented at hearings. The OCC report states that 'in these circumstances, it is very unlikely that a child or young person can effectively participate in the hearing nor that all relevant information can be put before the tribunal to enable them to make a decision fairly and in the child's best interests'.
— Children and young people would be obliged to seek alternative dispute resolution, including using complaints systems in which they had little confidence.

---

[57] See para 59, House of Commons Justice Committee, *Impact of changes to civil legal aid under Part 1 of the Legal Aid, Sentencing and Punishment of Offenders Act 2012*: Eighth Report (2014–15, HC 311), available at: www.publications.parliament.uk/pa/cm201415/cmselect/cmjust/311/311.pdf.
[58] OCC, *Legal Aid changes since April 2013* (n 1).

— Children and young people would need to look for legal assistance pro bono or from a voluntary sector provider that would be unable to cope with increased demand.
— Children and young people would be obliged to pay privately for legal advice, assistance or representation—an option that would only be available to very limited numbers of young people acting without adult support.
— Children and young people would give up trying to resolve their legal problems, leaving 'significant numbers' of children and young people with problems requiring resolution, which are no longer in scope for funding, and in respect of which alternative help is limited, resulting in 'a negative impact on them and their families'.

The OCC also concluded that a wide range of rights under the UNCRC are likely to be negatively impacted by the civil and prison law legal aid changes:

> These include both the rights enjoyed during proceedings—those under Articles 2 (non-discrimination), 3(1) (best interests to be a primary consideration), 12 (right to be heard) and the specific guarantees attached to specific proceedings (eg in Article 9 re separation from parents)—and substantive rights which are being infringed because of the legal problem that the child or their parent/carer is encountering. Therefore, we consider that urgent review and reform is needed in order to ensure that the Legal Aid system can adequately protect the rights of children and young people and that the Government's obligations under the UNCRC are met.

During the period under review, influential parliamentary committees repeatedly criticised the severity of the legal aid cuts in relation to their impact on children and young people's access to justice highlighting the Government's failure to comply with the UK's international legal obligations. In December 2013, the Joint Committee on Human Rights, in its report on the Government's 'Transforming Legal Aid' proposals—which included restrictions to judicial review, cuts to prison legal aid and a proposed 'residence test'—issued a clear reprimand to the Government for its failure to fulfil its duties to consider the specific needs of children and young people.[59] The Committee stated unequivocally: 'We do not consider that the removal of legal aid from vulnerable children can be justified'. Whilst commenting that it was 'sure that the Government does not intend vulnerable children to be left without legal representation', the Committee was clear that the Government had failed fully to consider its obligations under the UNCRC. It called for all children to be exempted from the residence test, and stated that cuts to prison law legal aid 'could leave young people vulnerable and deny them their rights'.

In March 2015, the House of Commons Justice Committee, in its report on the impact of LASPO's civil legal aid changes, expressed deep concern that the legal aid changes 'did not distinguish between children and adults' and about

---

[59] Human Rights Joint Committee, *The implications for access to justice of the Government's proposals to reform legal aid* (UK Parliament, 2013), available at: www.publications.parliament.uk/pa/jt201314/jtselect/jtrights/100/10002.htm.

evidence that 'children were facing particular difficulties in accessing legal advice and representation'.[60] The Committee concluded:

> Children are inevitably at a disadvantage in asserting their legal rights, even in matters which can have serious long-term consequences for them. We are particularly concerned by evidence that trafficked and separated children are struggling to access immigration advice and assistance. We recommend that the Ministry of Justice review the impact on children's rights of the legal aid changes and consider how to ensure separated and trafficked children in particular are able to access legal assistance.

Later in that same month, once again the Joint Committee on Human Rights strongly criticised the Government for its failure to fulfil its duties under the UNCRC, this time in even starker terms:

> The Government's reforms to legal aid have been a significant black mark on its human rights record during the second half of this Parliament ... the evidence we heard from the outgoing Children's Commissioner for England and from all the NGOs we took oral evidence from provides firm grounds for a new Government of whatever make-up to look again at these reforms and to undo some of the harm they have caused to children.[61]

As we have seen in the second part of this chapter, in addition to the important focus on binding international protections, campaigners and academic commentators have also relied on findings of a developing body of empirical research,[62] to argue that *any* reduction in access to legal advice and representation for vulnerable individuals would lead inevitably to increases in mental ill health, unemployment, homelessness and relationship breakdown.[63] It has also been argued that highly vulnerable children and young people already at risk of abuse and exploitation are bound to be disproportionately affected by legal aid cuts and that their inability to access legal support will leave them open to further abuse, exploitation and harm.[64]

Economic arguments have been no less compelling. Clear links have been established between young people's civil legal problems and crime; putting added pressure on the criminal justice system,[65] the NHS and social services, and costing local public services thousands of pounds per case.[66] Moreover, in light of evidence

---

[60] House of Commons Justice Committee, *Impact of changes to civil legal aid* (n 59).

[61] Human Rights Joint Committee, *The UK's Compliance with the UN Convention on the Rights of the Child* (UK Parliament, 2015).

[62] J Kenrick, *The Outcomes and Impact of Youth Advice—the evidence* (London, Youth Access, 2011).

[63] JustRights, *The effect of LASPO Act 2012 on children and young people* (London, JustRights, 2013), available at: http://justrights.org.uk/sites/default/files/The%20effect%20of%20LASPO%20Act%20 2012%20on%20children%20and%20young%20people.pdf.

[64] JustRights, *Legal Aid Cuts: Child Protection Implications* (London, JustRights, 2013), available at: http://justrights.org.uk/sites/default/files/Legal_Aid_-_Child_Protection_Implications_sept_2013_ FINAL.pdf.

[65] Clear links between young people's civil legal problems and crime were established in Pleasence (n 11). This study showed that 55% of 16- to 24-year-olds who have recently been arrested have reported experiencing at least one 'difficult to solve' civil justice problem.

[66] For a breakdown of costs identified, see Youth Access, *Youth advice: a mental health intervention?* (London, Youth Access, 2012).

from the Civil and Social Justice Survey data—that civil justice problems have a greater adverse impact on disadvantaged young people than on the general population, and that the receipt of professional advice has a greater beneficial impact on young people[67]—a powerful economic case can be made for dramatically rebalancing spending on legal advice services towards meeting young people's needs.

Indeed, even with little or no additional investment, there is manifest scope for improving young people's access to justice, by better designing services around their needs. Beginning with a basic level of democratic participation to which successive Westminster governments have been largely resistant, young people would be asked for their views on how existing services could be improved (indeed as required under Article 12 UNCRC),[68] after which in a well-functioning responsive twenty-first century democracy, government would listen to what they say, and where appropriate act on their advice.

Notably in 2014, Youth Access and JustRights undertook a participative study of exactly this kind with the object of discovering young people's views on the extent to which their rights are currently respected, and the changes they deemed necessary to ensure access to the information, advice and legal support needed to enforce their rights. Thus, working with hundreds of young people across England through focus groups, online consultation activities and a youth editorial board to create a manifesto entitled *Make Our Rights Reality*,[69] the two organisations have argued that this manifesto should be a starting point for any policymaker with serious intent to improve access to justice for this client group.

A Viable Solution: Getting Better Value from Existing Spending

Mindful of the long-term neglect of young people in the civil justice system, as the new Westminster government moves forward its programme of deficit reduction, youth advocates and campaigners in England and Wales no longer look to the reinstatement of pre-LASPO levels of expenditure as a means of addressing the continuing marginalisation of young people. Instead, consistent with Article 12 of the UNCRC, the focus has shifted to radical demands for the provision of dedicated interconnected services—legal information, advice and representation— measures that will begin to address the concatenation of problems surrounding their unmet needs. As highlighted by Balmer and Pleasence in 2012, the research evidence supports a cogent business case for such a radical approach: 'The survey findings highlight the importance of an advice model for this group that is

---

[67] Kenrick, *The Advice Needs of Young People* (n 6).

[68] Under Article 12 (Respect for the views of the child), when adults are making decisions that affect children, children have the right to say what they think should happen and have their opinions taken into account.

[69] *Make Our Rights Reality* (Youth Access and JustRights, 2014).

accessible to vulnerable young people and that acknowledges their high levels of mental illness'.[70]

Thus, it has been argued by the JustRights campaign that a new scheme should aim to build a network of expert lawyers for children and young people that is integrated with other relevant (non-legal) services and legal education. Moreover, departing from existing categories of law-based legal aid contracts, a client-focused 'Young people's law' fund for legal advice, assistance and representation, funded out of existing legal aid spending on children and young people's cases, should be established, encouraging an integrated approach to provision across social welfare, family and immigration law, whilst leaving room for specialist providers. It has also been suggested that providers would be selected based on their expertise in working with, safeguarding and representing this client group and might be quality-assured through some form of kite-mark for either practitioners or contract-holders that could be funded by the profession itself (as with the children's panel or mental health accreditation schemes).

Moreover, contracts for young people's law would: (i) give providers flexibility to meet the needs of vulnerable children and young people in what they judge to be the most efficient and effective way; and (ii) encourage co-location within services and institutions already attended by young people with the highest legal needs (such as youth advice agencies, prisons, immigration detention units, mental health institutions and Youth Offending Services). Furthermore, with the aim of facilitating seamless support across young people's wider needs (particularly their substantial and interrelated emotional and mental health needs), such specialist legal aid providers would work more closely in partnership with young people's information, advice and counselling services, that would be funded by local authorities and the NHS.[71] Finally, a national public legal education programme focused on young people would be established, led by youth advice providers and supported by the development of a single young person focused website where young people could access all relevant information about their rights in one place, with costs borne potentially by charitable trusts.

It is argued here that such a model would lead to vastly improved access, quality and outcomes at little or no additional cost through utilising existing spend far more effectively and drawing in co-funding from charitable trusts, the legal profession, the NHS and local authority commissioners. Moreover, its crucial advantage over the existing system would be that it would be responsive to young people's needs, rather than trying to fit them into an existing bureaucratic system designed around adult needs or, arguably, no one's needs.

---

[70] Balmer and Pleasence (n 17).
[71] The Department of Health's *Future In Mind* report (2015) recommends investment in Youth Information, Advice and Counselling Services as a key element of local youth mental health strategies, available at: www.gov.uk/government/uploads/system/uploads/attachment_data/file/414024/Childrens_Mental_Health.pdf.

Conclusion

Young people's legal needs are substantial, complex and all too rarely met: no child or young person should be required to navigate our complex legal system alone. Yet, the effect of government austerity policies in the UK, specifically of LASPO, has been to increase the number of children and young people abandoned in this way. This is not the place further to explore the complex institutional and political reasons for the marginalisation of young people in the UK justice system, or their lack of voice in other aspects of civil and cultural life. However, it is suggested here that ambivalence towards young people's rights and a pervasive lack of trust that they will use rights responsibly goes hand-in-hand with a 'culture of disbelief' in young people's capacity for development, that has permitted public authorities to ignore young people's persistent evidence of scandalous sexual exploitation of the kind most recently uncovered in the demographically disadvantaged communities of Rotherham, Rochdale and Doncaster. If young people as equal citizens are to engage fully in democracy, it is crucial that they view the legal system as existing for their protection, rather than merely for their punishment.

Appendix

Make Our Rights Reality

A manifesto created by hundreds of young people across England

Young people's difficulties enforcing their rights—in their own words[72]

Our basic rights—to housing, education, a reasonable standard of living, good health care and protection from abuse and exploitation—are enshrined in the United Nations Convention on the Rights of the Child. These rights matter to us. They are fundamental to our existence as equal citizens deserving of respect.

But rights mean nothing without the knowledge and means to enforce them. The Convention also sets out our rights to receive information, legal help and fair treatment under the law—and to be heard! Access to good quality information, advice, advocacy and representation is crucial if we are to understand our rights and responsibilities, deal with difficult problems in our lives and navigate our way to becoming confident and independent adults. However, many of us don't currently receive the help and support we need. This has to change!

---

[72] Extracted from *Make Our Rights Reality: a manifesto created by hundreds of young people across England* (JustRights/Youth Access, 2014).

We have had enough of:

— not being treated equally because of our age
— unfair and unlawful decisions being made that affect our wellbeing and quality of life
— our rights to housing and welfare benefits being ignored
— being taken for a ride by payday loan companies and employers
— being fobbed off by statutory services who are meant to be there to protect us, but who are more interested in saving money
— cuts to the services we desperately need, such as youth services, legal aid and mental health services
— getting passed around all over the place without anyone telling us what we're entitled to or where we can turn for help

We should always:

— be listened to, taken seriously and treated with the respect we deserve
— have our rights respected and upheld
— be treated as individuals, not as a problem
— get the help we need to enforce our rights and entitlements *before* we reach crisis point
— be allowed to participate in decisions that affect our lives

We want:

— to be able to help ourselves as far as possible—but we know that sometimes we need to access expert, independent advice, advocacy and representation to help us find our way through the system
— to receive help from workers we can trust, because they genuinely care about us, are skilled at working with young people, know what they're talking about, have only our best interests in mind and won't judge us

So that we can get the help we need, we call on the Government, local Councils and others to …

1. Make it easier for us to get the correct information

Contrary to popular belief, we don't always know our rights! And when we have a problem, we often aren't told by anyone what we're entitled to or where to go for help.

Information on rights and the law should be easier to find and clearer for all young people to understand. So that we can get hold of all of the relevant information we need in order to help ourselves:

— There should be ONE website where we can find ALL the information we need about our rights and services.
— All young people should be taught about their rights at school as part of the National Curriculum.

— All young people should be sent a pack of information about their rights in the post with their National Insurance number when they turn 16.
— Teachers, youth workers and social workers must actively help us find out about our rights.
— Some young people should be trained up to educate others about young people's rights.

2. Make independent advice services just for young people available in every local area

Our ability to make our rights a reality depends, above all, on being able to access a local advice service for young people, where we can have information and our options explained to us in terms we understand.

We want services to:

— be just for young people between the ages of 11 and 25
— allow us to just walk in off the street and ask anything, or nothing
— help us with a range of issues, including debt, employment, housing, homelessness, access to health services, education, family, relationships, welfare benefits, discrimination, crime, immigration and social services
— provide, or refer us on to, specialist legal advice services if our case is complicated and requires a lawyer
— provide advice alongside all the other services we need, particularly counselling and mental health services, advocacy, drug and alcohol support, help with finding work and managing our money
— respect our confidentiality and empower us to help ourselves
— be provided by charities that are genuinely independent from the organisations we have problems with (ie the Council, the Government, schools, employers)

The Government needs to recognise that access to these services is essential to our wellbeing. We find them helpful because we trust them—they are tailored to our needs, understand us, give us a voice and help us develop as individuals. Some of us are lucky to live in an area where services like this already exist, but cuts have forced some services to close. These cuts must stop!

3. Give us free access to solicitors who specialise in working with young people

Our inexperience and lack of knowledge of our rights make us especially vulnerable to exploitation and injustice. People in authority often don't take our rights seriously. To force these people to meet their duties towards us, we sometimes need a legal representative.

Legal aid cuts are making it impossible to find a lawyer who can help us. Many of us now get no specialist help with social services, homelessness, immigration, education, employment, money and family problems—leaving us in desperate situations! It is shocking that some children and young people even have to represent themselves in court.

— We need to have free access to lawyers who specialise in working with young people.
— We need to be able to see these lawyers in places where we feel comfortable and can get the other support we need, eg youth advice centres.
— The legal support we need must be properly funded. The Government must ask us what we think before making any more changes to legal aid that affect us.
— All lawyers who ever come into contact with young people should be trained in how to talk and listen to us.

4. Make Citizens Advice Bureaux young person-friendly

Many of us are not comfortable using services that are meant to be for everyone. We don't feel the CAB is for us—we don't expect to be taken seriously because of our age and are put off by all the waiting around.

Adult advice services should:

— have more flexible opening hours that suit young people, shorter waiting times and more friendly-looking reception areas
— employ advisers who can relate to us
— develop specialist services just for young people
— work more closely with youth organisations
— provide information that explains what they do and how they can help young people
— talk to us to find out what we want

If an advice service can't be bothered to do anything to make sure it is helping young people, it shouldn't carry on getting funding.

5. Tailor services to meet our individual needs

Services should be for all young people, but we are all different and must be able to get the support we need in the way we need.

Adults assume that all young people want services delivered online. Some of us do and many of us would use websites and apps to find information about our rights and the services available. But, when we need more in-depth advice and support, most of us want to see an adviser face to face.

— We need as many options available to us as possible—including online information and telephone advice—but **always give us the option of seeing an adviser in person.**

Some of us are particularly vulnerable because of disabilities or because of our background, circumstances or health needs. This may mean services need to develop a range of approaches to reach us.

— Where we need extra support—eg interpreters or people on our side to attend meetings with us—this should always be available.

6. Put our interests first—above those of the system

We find it difficult to trust the advice we receive from the official services—eg Social Services, JobCentre Plus and Councils' housing departments—that are meant to be there to uphold our rights and protect us. They often patronise us, make our situation worse and let us down when we need them most. They rarely refer us on to someone who can give us good advice about our situation—and sometimes they actively prevent us from getting independent legal advice!

It should be illegal to put the interests of the system above the rights and protection of young people.

Statutory services must:

— employ staff who actually like young people
— train all their staff in young people's rights—and to listen to us, take us seriously and show us respect
— be far clearer about what they can and can't do for us and what we're entitled to
— stop fobbing us off with bad advice that isn't in **our** best interests—and realise that this approach doesn't save money in the long-term!
— recognise that they are part of the same system that is causing our problems, so may have a conflict when giving us advice
— actively support us to access independent sources of advice and legal support—and be held to account when they don't
— have simple young person-friendly complaints systems—so we can speak freely when we are not getting a good service without worrying about it harming our rights or the services we receive
— refer us to an independent advocacy service if we might need help to get our voice heard or make a complaint

We also need the Government to sort out the problems in the system that are causing us to need advice in the first place:

— blatantly unfair benefit sanctions that leave us destitute
— rip-off payday loans that are targeted at young people and get us into a spiral of debt
— Councils who routinely turn us away when we're homeless—even when the law is clear that we should be rehoused and given ongoing support
— a hostile immigration system that's almost impossible to navigate and can leave young migrants and asylum-seekers destitute, mentally ill and cut off from society

We aren't asking to change the world! We just want to be given the help and services we need so that we can get on in life and become good citizens!

Part III

Alternative Approaches to Funding Legal Services

13

A Revolution in 'Lawyering'? Implications for Welfare Law of Alternative Business Structures

Introduction

Shortly before the beginning of the financial crisis in 2008, the UK Parliament passed the Legal Services Act 2007[2] which created a new regulatory structure for the legal professions in England and Wales, reorganised the complaints system and made it possible for entities providing reserved legal services to be owned by non-lawyers. This chapter is concerned with the possible implications of the last of these (known as Alternative Business Structures (ABSs)) for the provision of welfare law services in an era of austerity in which legal aid expenditure is being reduced, eligibility for legal aid curtailed, and expenditure from public funds to support not-for-profit organisations in providing legal advice to those on low incomes is being reduced. Some legal commentators have argued that the entry of ABSs will reduce the availability of welfare law (broadly defined) because they will 'cherry pick' the profitable areas of law undertaken by high street solicitors and deprive the latter of their ability to cross-subsidise welfare law work from this more profitable area of activity. Contrary to this view, it is argued below that because of their ability to achieve economies of scale and specialisation ABSs may be able to make welfare law profitable and indeed provide better advice than high street firms. The next section of the chapter outlines the changes introduced by the LSA 2007, focusing particularly on the permitting of outside ownership of providers of reserved legal services and arguing that the external involvement in entities providing legal services will lead to innovations in service provision which the prevailing system of regulatory competition could not. The third section of the chapter examines the 'cherry picking' critique of ABSs, and drawing on empirical

---

[1] I am grateful to Yseult Marique for comments on an earlier draft of this chapter. Any remaining errors or ambiguities are entirely the responsibility of the author.
[2] Hereafter the LSA 2007.

studies of the 'quality' of welfare law legal advice from high street firms and on the economies of specialisation open to consumer oriented ABSs, it argues that ABSs may be able to provide welfare law services of better quality, at a lower cost and more profitably than high street firms. A fourth section examines the role of the not-for-profit sector in the current regulatory scheme, arguing that similar economies of scale and specialisation could allow not-for-profit providers of welfare law services to overcome the reduction in public subsidy and enhance their traditional role. A final section concludes by summarising the arguments of the chapter.

The Legal Services Act 2007

The Legal Services Act 2007 (LSA 2007) was the legislative outcome of a review carried out by Sir David Clementi into the regulation of legal services in England and Wales.[3] This inquiry examined what had been described as a 'regulatory maze' and covered not only the regulatory framework and the complaints procedures of the legal professions, but also the restrictions on the form and ownership of the entities which were permitted to provide reserved legal services in this jurisdiction. A fuller discussion of the origins of the Act and the system of regulatory competition within legal services which developed in England and Wales as a result of government policy from the 1980s is provided elsewhere by the present writer.[4] The LSA 2007 introduced a new regulatory framework for the legal professions in England and Wales based on and extending the recommendations contained in the Clementi Review. The present section focuses on the reform of the regulatory system and the introduction of ABSs. The (then) regulatory system was regarded by Sir David as flawed because the governance structures of the front line regulators were 'inappropriate' and oversight of them was 'over-complex' and 'inconsistent'.[5] The LSA 2007 largely adopted the proposals of the Clementi Review for a new regulatory structure which involves both front line regulators which regulate individual professionals and an oversight regulator (Legal Services Board (LSB)) which has the task of ensuring that the front line regulators pursue the statutory objectives of the Act.[6] The self-regulatory bodies of the main providers of reserved legal activities automatically became front line regulators under the Act once they had separated their representative and regulatory functions.[7]

---

[3] D Clementi, *Review of the Regulatory Framework for Legal Services in England and Wales* (London, Department of Constitutional Affairs, 2004).

[4] F Stephen, *Lawyers, Markets and Regulation* (Cheltenham, Edward Elgar Publishing, 2013) ch 7.

[5] Clementi Review (n 3) 1.

[6] See F Stephen, 'Regulation of the Legal Professions or Regulation of Markets for Legal Services: Potential Implications of the *Legal Services Act 2007*' (2008) 19 *European Business Law Review* 1129.

[7] Following the Clementi Review and prior to the publication of the draft Legal Services Bill in 2006, both the Law Society and the Bar Councils separated their regulatory and representative functions through the creation of the SRA and the BSB respectively.

Thus, for solicitors the regulatory functions of the Law Society are now discharged by the Solicitors Regulation Authority (SRA) which is funded by members of the solicitors' profession. For barristers, the regulatory functions previously carried out by the General Council of the Bar are now discharged by the Bar Standards Board (BSB) which is funded by members of the Bar. Both the SRA and BSB have a majority of lay (ie, non-lawyer) members. The Council for Licensed Conveyancers was the third regulator which automatically became a front line regulator with the passage of the Act.

The present writer has argued[8] that Sir David's recommended regulatory structure (and that contained in the LSA 2007) can best be understood as enshrining regulatory competition in statute. Such a system had implicitly been promoted by the Administration of Justice Act 1985 and the Courts and Legal Services Act 1990. The former through the creation of the Council for Licensed Conveyancers inaugurated regulatory competition in the field of conveyancing which had previously been a monopoly of solicitors. The latter through giving the Law Society the power to designate appropriately experienced and qualified solicitors as solicitor advocates introduced competition in advocacy in the higher courts between solicitor advocates and barristers. However, prior to the passage of the LSA 2007 promotion of competition in legal services was not a regulatory objective imposed on the self-regulatory bodies. One of the main functions of the LSB can be seen as ensuring that the front line regulators do promote competition.[9] Anthony Ogus has argued that regulatory competition can be utilised to overcome the tendency of self-regulatory professional bodies to regulate the profession in the interests of the profession rather than in the public interest whilst retaining some of the advantages of self-regulation such as lower cost and utilisation of internal knowledge.[10] Under regulatory competition, it is suggested that, with more than one regulator, both consumers and producers have a choice. Consumers will have a choice of different forms of provision at different costs provided some public agency ensures that a minimum level of quality is maintained. Consequently, any attempt by one of the self-regulators to exploit their position will be counteracted by a move of consumers to suppliers regulated by another regulator. Firms or individual professionals will have the choice of different regulators who may offer different schemes in terms of educational requirements, practice rules and ethical standards. They will be able to choose the regulator which most suits their needs both in terms of business operations and value for money.[11] There will be a competitive tension between regulators which will tend to ensure no regulator exploits its position over either consumers or professionals.

---

[8] Stephen, 'Regulation of the Legal Professions' (n 6); Stephen, *Lawyers, Markets and Regulation* (n 4) ch 7.

[9] See further Stephen, *Lawyers, Markets and Regulation* (n 4) 114–16 for a discussion of tensions between LSB on the one hand and RSA and BSB on the other, on the importance of promoting competition.

[10] A Ogus, 'Rethinking Self-Regulation' (1985) 15 *Oxford Journal of Legal Studies* 97.

[11] Subject however to the minimum standard of service ensured by the public agency.

Stephen[12] argues that the LSB under the LSA 2007 performs the role of the 'public agency' identified by Ogus[13] in ensuring that competitive regulation does not result in a 'race to the bottom'. Fear of a race to the bottom (sometimes expressed as 'regulatory arbitrage') where there is competition between regulators was expressed by members of the Joint Committee of the Commons and Lords which scrutinised the draft Legal Services Bill in 2006 and by witnesses who appeared before the Joint Committee[14] including the (then) Lord Chief Justice and (then) Master of the Rolls.[15] However, it is possible that the focus of competition could be on service characteristics as well as fee, one self-regulator offering a higher 'quality' service than another. It could be argued that this is implicitly the form of competition which has existed between the Bar and solicitor advocates in the field of advocacy since the passage of the Courts and Legal Services Act 1990. The Bar holds itself out as providing higher 'quality' advocacy services arising from its specialised training. The entry of solicitor advocates into the market for higher court advocacy has challenged the Bar's monopoly and at the margin may have reduced fees. However, this process does not necessarily lead to an equalisation of barrister and solicitor advocate fees, but an equalisation of the quality/fee ratio at the margin, for example, if under the Bar's monopoly fees were high relative to the quality of advocacy at the margin, the entry of solicitor advocates would have reduced those prices or work would have moved from members of the Bar to solicitor advocates. The decision of the BSB to authorise self-employed barristers to conduct advocacy-related litigation and to apply to the LSB to become a regulator of entities suggests that in the future competition between the Bar and solicitor advocates will be more focused on the quality/fee trade off.

The move to allow members of the Bar to provide litigation services means that there is now regulatory competition in the three largest reserved activities: conveyancing (SRA and Council for Licensed Conveyancers); litigation (SRA and BSB); and advocacy (BSB and SRA). The business structures through which lawyers were permitted to provide legal services to the public prior to the LSA 2007 were restrictive in not allowing non-lawyers to be principals and in not allowing different lawyers to work together on an equal footing. The Clementi Review recommended that, in due course, non-lawyers be permitted to own suppliers of legal services. The LSA 2007 enacted provisions which permitted the LSB to authorise first line regulators to license ABSs which could be owned by non-lawyers. However, delays in the authorisation process meant the first front line regulator to receive authorisation (Council for Licensed Conveyancers) was not until May 2011.[16] It licensed

---

[12] Stephen, *Lawyers, Markets and Regulation* (n 4).

[13] Ogus (n 10).

[14] For details see Stephen, *Lawyers, Markets and Regulation* (n 4) 118–19.

[15] Joint Committee on the Draft Legal Services Bill, *Draft Legal Services Bill, Volume II: Evidence* (2005–06, HL 232-II, HC 1154-II) Q307–Q311.

[16] Prior to the LSA 2007 the Council for Licensed Conveyancers did regulate firms of licensed conveyancers owned by non-lawyers.

its first ABS in October 2011. The SRA was authorised to license ABSs in June 2011 but did not do so until March 2012. By July 2014, the SRA had licensed almost 300 ABSs.[17]

Building on the insight of Gillian Hadfield[18] that the traditional law firm model of lawyer partnerships together with the fact that lawyers were educated, trained and worked almost exclusively with other lawyers had contributed to the lack of innovation in the provision of legal services, Stephen[19] has argued that the licensing of ABS firms owned by non-lawyers will lead to the adoption of business models which will lead to a more dynamic form of competition between suppliers of legal services in England and Wales. The regulatory framework in place before the LSA 2007 restricted ownership of legal service providers to qualified lawyers. This created an environment in which the supply of legal services was supplier driven and was not consumer friendly. Because of the restrictions on who could provide legal service those running them did not have access to the business models developed by more consumer focused businesses. From an economic perspective this can be seen as a restriction on the technology being used by legal service providers.[20] The removal of the restrictions in ownership makes it possible for those with experience of a wider range of business models to adapt these to suit consumers of legal services. These innovations may in turn allow ABS firms to provide legal services more cost-effectively or provide clients with higher quality services at a given cost.

Daniel Muzio and John Flood point out that lawyers have not always lacked entrepreneurship and innovation.[21] During the nineteenth century (particularly in the railway boom) lawyers were not only developing new legal instruments, but were actively engaged with many of their clients as board members. However, the advancement of the so-called 'professional project'[22] in the twentieth century sought to insulate lawyers from the market and as a consequence removed the incentive to innovate.

Stephen also argues that ABSs linked to consumer service firms and membership organisations will build on the consumer orientation of the parent firms to develop a more client focussed provision of legal services.[23] Associating a supplier of legal services with a consumer service brand has implications for quality

---

[17] This compares with a total of 10,519 entities including ABSs and sole practitioners who were regulated by the SRA in May 2014.

[18] G Hadfield, 'Legal Barriers to Innovation: The Growing Economic Cost of Professional Control over Corporate Legal Markets' (2008) 60 *Stanford Law Review* 1689.

[19] Stephen, *Lawyers, Markets and Regulation* (n 4) ch 8.

[20] The term 'technology' is used here in a wide sense to include business model and not just information technology, see Stephen, *Lawyers, Markets and Regulation* (n 4) 128–31.

[21] D Muzio and J Flood, 'Entrepreneurship, Managerialism and Professionalism in Action: The Case of the Legal Profession in England and Wales' in M Reihlen and A Werr (eds), *Handbook of Research on Entrepreneurship in Professional Services* (Cheltenham, Edward Elgar Publishing, 2013).

[22] M Larson, *The Rise of Professionalism: A Sociological Analysis* (Berkeley CA, University of California Press, 1977).

[23] Stephen, *Lawyers, Markets and Regulation* (n 4).

assurance in the supply of legal services. Ogus' model of regulatory competition discussed above relies on a 'public agency' to ensure a minimum level of quality but sees difficulty in the communication of higher levels of quality to potential consumers.[24] Stephen argues that Ogus does not consider the role of established 'brands' in communicating quality standards.[25] The LSA 2007 by making possible the ownership of suppliers of reserved legal services by non-lawyers (including corporate organisations) makes it possible for the 'quality' of legal services offered by an ABS to be signalled by its association with a 'brand' whose quality of service is known from another field of activity. Any failure of the 'branded' ABS to provide an appropriate level of service quality will have a negative impact on the value of the brand more widely. The maintenance of brand name capital, thus, becomes an implicit guarantee of quality standards.

It should be noted that the need to maintain brand name capital works in both directions. Consumers of legal services provided by a banded ABS are likely to assume that the 'quality' of legal services provided by the brand will reflect the quality of service associated with the brand more generally. Consequently, the higher the reputation of the brand the more confidence consumers are likely to place in the quality and reliability of their legal services. On the other hand, a supplier of consumer-oriented products and services with a high reputation is unlikely to be willing to 'cut corners' in the provision of legal services because any adverse publicity associated with 'inadequate' legal services will have a negative effect on the brand more generally reducing income or profit elsewhere in the brand. A consequence of this is that the brand is unlikely to move into the provision of legal services through an ABS if it is not able to ensure that a commensurate level of service can be provided.

Among the ABSs licensed by the SRA is a small number of legal service providers associated with major brands. One of the first ABSs licensed by the SRA was Co-operative Legal Services which is a subsidiary of the Co-operative Group, a set of consumer-owned businesses, including a major supermarket chain, a bank, an insurance business and funeral directors. AA Law Ltd is owned by the UK's largest motoring organisation (the AA) which provides vehicle breakdown cover, car insurance, travel services, financial services and legal document services. AA is one of the largest membership organisations in the UK. Saga Law is owned by Saga a provider of insurance and travel services for the over fifties.[26] Admiral Law is owned by the car insurer Admiral and specialises in motor claims. DLG Legal Services is an ABS subsidiary of the major car insurer Direct Line Group, although its legal services will be provided by staff of Paribas.

Although such increased complexity of business model may lead to an increase in monitoring costs for the 'brand' it is unlikely that the brand will move into the

---

[24] Ogus (n 10).

[25] Stephen, *Lawyers, Markets and Regulation* (n 4) ch 8.

[26] Both Saga and AA had been owned by the same private equity company until shares in Saga were floated on the Stock Exchange in June 2014.

provision of legal services if the benefits of doing so do not exceed the costs. It should be noted that in some cases the ABS associated with the brand outsources the provision of legal services to an existing law firm.

The experience of ABS firms has not all been positive. Co-operative Legal Services has been reorganised within the Co-operative Group following significant losses. Senior executives have left the firm as a consequence. Christina Blacklaws has left Co-operative Legal Services where she was Head of the Family Law group. It is not clear whether the difficulties of Co-operative Legal Services are a consequence of the financial difficulties faced by the wider Co-operative Group. In a recent interview the Chief Executive of Co-operative Legal Services said that much of their loss was due to personal injury business and they had not been affected by the wider problems of the Co-operative Group.[27]

The Impact of the LSA (2007) on the Provision of Welfare Law Services

The present volume is concerned with access to justice in the age of austerity which the UK has encountered since 2008. The question addressed here is what, if any, are the implications of ABSs for access to justice? At the time of the passage of the Act and since, there have been a number of critics who have argued that ABSs will have a negative impact on access to justice because they will 'cherry pick' profitable areas of service which current providers use to subsidise unprofitable areas of law such as legal aid and welfare law advice. In this section of the chapter it is argued that this view is flawed on two grounds: first, ABSs may be able (by being more efficient in providing welfare law service than high street firms) to make welfare law cases profitable; and second, whereas research suggests that high street firms' welfare advice is often flawed, ABSs by operating at a higher volume can develop greater expertise in welfare law than many high street firms. The cherry-picking argument was articulated by a number of witnesses who appeared before the Joint Committee on the draft Legal Services Bill in 2006. For example, Richard Miller of the Legal Aid Practitioners Group said:

> My fear is ... Alternative Business Structures ... are more likely to go to cherry-pick the more profitable work ... [and] ... will undermine the economic viability of businesses currently providing legal aid services. I have my doubts whether, at least at current rates of remuneration these Alternative Business Structures would take on legal aid work.[28]

---

[27] 'Personal injury to blame for Co-operative Legal Services losses' (*Legal Futures*, 4 September 2014), available at: www.legalfutures.co.uk/latest-news/personal-injury-blame-co-operative-legal-services-losses.

[28] Joint Committee on the Draft Legal Services Bill 2006 (n 15) Q256.

In its written evidence the Legal Action Group stated:

> We think it is highly likely that there are some areas of legal work that can be com-
> moditised or carried out in high volume with efficiency savings, through ABS. In these
> circumstances we are concerned that the ABS will effectively cream off the work that
> currently subsidises legal aid.[29]

The Supplementary Memorandum submitted by Young Legal Aid Lawyers to the
Joint Committee declared:

> ABS firms will be attracted to work which can be profitably run by bulk methods ...
> These 'cherry-picked' legal services offend the notion that everyone has the right to legal
> representation. If a firm cannot rely on profitable work to support less profitable work,
> the disadvantaged will suffer reductions in access to justice.[30]

More recently in 2012 Lord Phillips of Sudbury in an interview in the *Times* said,

> if leading corporations get involved in ABSs they will not do the work that is complex,
> difficult and under-rewarded; they will cherry pick. And the diminishing number of high
> street solicitors' firms that are trying to service the whole population—and in particular,
> the less well off—will have the bits of work that are relatively profitable and relatively
> straightforward cherry picked by the ABS outfits. So what will they be left with? The
> difficult cases, with inarticulate clients, who can't instruct them in a straightforward
> manner.[31]

These views implicitly assume that work that is not profitable for high street firms
will also be unprofitable for ABSs. This is to totally underestimate the impact of
what Stephen describes as the 'technological revolution' in lawyering which may
be brought about by ABSs (see further above).[32] It also fails to appreciate that
since profit is the difference between price and cost, that profit can be increased
by reducing cost while price remains the same. If an ABS firm with an existing
national network of contact points which share overhead costs with other activities can use centralised legal expertise to provide expert advice on, inter alia, areas
of welfare law it may able to do so more expeditiously and at lower cost than high
street firms. This may make these areas of law profitable for ABSs even at legal aid
fees or fees which these clients can afford. Co-operative Legal Services (an ABS)
was able according to their website to provide legally aided divorce and family law
services before legal aid was withdrawn from these areas in April 2013.[33]

The significance of the cherry-picking argument is further undermined by
the evidence of a series of research projects examining the 'quality' of welfare
law advice. In his recent inaugural lecture at University College London, Richard
Moorhead has reviewed studies including some of his own on the quality of advice

---

[29] ibid, 140

[30] ibid, 359

[31] On 12 May 2012.

[32] Stephen, *Lawyers, Markets and Regulation* (n 4).

[33] See: www.co-operative.coop/legal services/family-and-relationships/breaking-up/Ways-to-pay-
for-our-service/public-funding-legal-aid.

given by solicitors to legally aided clients.[34] These studies shed light on the absolute level of quality of advice given and the quality relative to that of non-lawyer advice. The advice given was peer reviewed by experienced solicitors: 25 per cent of both lawyer and non-lawyer files were 'failed' by the reviewers; the non-solicitors were more likely to have given 'good or excellent' advice. In another study, specialist legal aid contractors in solicitors firms and not-for-profit agencies were reviewed by experienced peer reviewers. The failure rate of those in solicitors firms was more than twice that of those in not-for-profit agencies. It is likely here that the quality of advice given was related to the volume of this type of work being done by those in not-for-profit agencies. This was likely to be greater than that of the specialist legal aid contractors. This suggests that an ABS firm using centrally located specialist lawyers (dealing with a volume) are likely to out perform even specialists in high street firms and at lower cost because of economies of specialisation and shared overheads. It was also the case that the not-for-profit agencies provided a more holistic approach to problems than solicitors. Moorhead, Sherr and Paterson in drawing conclusions from these studies imply that part of the success of the not-for-profit agencies came from the fact that they challenged the traditional solicitors' preconception as to the nature of the service being provided to legally aided clients.[35] The characterisation of ABSs presented in the previous section suggests that ABSs entering this area of law similarly would bring innovation to this field and would also be likely to benefit from economies of scale.

The LSA (2007) and the Not-for-Profit Advice Sector

The research conducted by Moorhead, Sherr and Paterson discussed above found that the not-for-profit legal advice sector provided good quality legal advice on welfare law matters. Whilst this sector has a variety of organisational models, a common feature of many of them is that they have trained volunteers and employees working in collaboration with qualified lawyers under a management committee which may or may not include qualified lawyers. Although not commercial in nature, they have many similarities with ABSs (eg, specialist advisers dealing with significant numbers of similar cases). A crucial difference is, of course, that they are not in business to make a profit. Very often they are funded from public money either through legal aid contracts or by local authorities. Although legal advising is not a reserved activity there is sufficient potential for overlap for the draft Legal Services Bill 2006 to have contained provisions relating to the not-for-profit sector.

---

[34] R Moorhead, 'Precarious Professionalism—Some empirical and behavioural perspectives on lawyers' inaugural lecture (University College, University of London, 6 March 2014) 9.

[35] R Moorhead, A Sherr and A Paterson, 'Contesting Professionalism: Legal Aid and Non Lawyers in England and Wales' (2003) 37 *Law & Society Review* 765.

Witnesses giving evidence to the Joint Committee on the draft Bill sought to ensure that there was no ambiguity on the status for not-for-profits under the Bill. The Legal Action Group argued that there should be a clear statement of the regulatory requirements for not-for-profits and the Law Centres Federation stated that there should not be any 'substantially different standards of service and regulation between the two sectors'.[36] However, concerns were raised about the costs of regulation which would be imposed on the not-for-profit sector.

The LSA 2007[37] made provisions under which the not-for-profit sector together with other 'special bodies' such as trade unions were allowed to continue to provide reserved activities as before without being required to apply for licensing as an ABS. This was to be for a transitional period after which they would have to be licensed as ABSs. Only the LSB could recommend to the Lord Chancellor that these transitional arrangements be ended. The LSB has commissioned research on special bodies[38] and undertaken a consultation.[39] Although the transitional period was scheduled to end in April 2013, the LSB, following the consultation process, extended it until April 2015. However, LSB has subsequently reported:

> Transitional arrangements will stay in place for the time being and it is not anticipated that further work on the issue will be carried out until 2015. In practice this means that there would be an additional period after this date before the transitional protection would come to an end.[40]

Only the SRA currently licenses ABSs in the reserved areas of litigation and rights of audience which are the ones of interest to special bodies. The SRA currently insists that special bodies cannot charge fees to clients. This means that not-for-profit bodies cannot use fees from such services to subsidise other services without creating a fully fledged ABS. The LSB disagrees with this requirement. The LSB in its response to the consultation also criticised the SRA's separate business rule which prohibits an ABS being linked to an organisation providing non-regulated legal services. The SRA has in fact waived this rule on a number of occasions. This has been a major source of friction between the LSB and SRA. The former argues that frequent waiving of a restriction should call into question the restriction. The LSB considered that there was no front line regulator in a position to provide an appropriate regulatory framework for special bodies beyond the transition period.

At present special bodies are exempt from the entity regulation provisions of the LSA 2007. However, members of the legal professions working within and for them are subject to the practice rules/regulatory provisions of their profession. This would appear to be one of the sources of the SRA's prohibition of fee charging.

---

[36] Joint Committee on the Draft Legal Services Bill, *Draft Legal Services Bill, Volume I: Report* (2005–06, HL 232-I, HC 1154-I) 67.

[37] s 23.

[38] Frontier Economics, *Understanding the Supply of Legal Services by Special Bodies: A Report Prepared for the Legal Services Board* (London, Legal Services Board, 2011).

[39] Legal Services Board, *Regulation of Special Bodies/Non-commercial Bodies: Response to Consultation and Next Steps* (London, Legal Services Board, December 2012).

[40] Legal Services Board, *Annual Report and Accounts for the Year Ended 31 March 2014* (HC 122) 16.

Some of the not-for-profit organisations interviewed in the Frontier Economics research indicated that they might wish to charge fees in the future given the prospective reductions in public funding. Whilst this might not lead to a widespread use of the ABS structure until the introduction of a proportionate regulatory system which protects the interests of clients without imposing a heavy regulatory burden, some not-for-profit services have formed Community Interest Companies which have sought ABS status. Castle Park Solicitors is an ABS Community Interest Company in Leicester owned by a charity, Community Advice and Law Service. It carries out work in the field of family, employment and immigration law for a fee. Any profits are passed to Community Advice and Law Service. The ABS Ty Arian, based in Swansea, describes itself as a Social Welfare Law Centre specialising in welfare law and legally aided services.

Conclusion

It has been argued in this chapter that the Alternative Business Structures made possible by the passage of the Legal Services Act 2007 can provide the basis for innovation in the provision of legal services to the public which has been lacking in recent decades. Contrary to the view that ABSs will 'cherry pick' profitable areas of work to the detriment of high street law firms which subsidise their welfare law and legal aid services from their more profitable activities, it has been argued that large ABS firms may be able to so reduce the costs of providing welfare law services as to make them profitable. Evidence has also been presented which suggests that the 'quality' of welfare law services provided by some high street firms has been lower than that provided by non-lawyer providers. Finally, the difficulties faced by not-for-profit agencies in relation to the Act's transitional provisions for 'special bodies' have been examined.

14

CourtNav and Pro Bono in an Age of Austerity

PAUL YATES

Introduction

On 6 May 2011, Professor Richard Susskind gave a presentation, 'Access to Law and to Justice', as part of the ESRC funded seminar series, 'Access to Justice in An Age of Austerity: Time for Proportionate Responses'. In the presentation and in the lively discussion which followed, Susskind stressed—amongst other things—the potential for technologies which are already established, even routine, in other sectors to be used to great effect in the legal sector. It is a point he had developed previously, for example, in his *Times* column of 9 June 2011, 'The public needs an NHS Direct to provide legal advice—any takers?' which called for 'a second generation of online legal services in the UK', including 'automated document production'.[1]

Another major theme in the seminar series was the predicted surge in litigants in person as a result of the cuts in civil legal aid contained in the Legal Aid, Sentencing and Punishment of Offenders Act 2012 (LASPO), and ways in which the civil justice system might respond. My own experience of litigants in person comes in large part from the many years in which I have been an 'Honorary Legal Adviser' at the Royal Courts of Justice Advice Bureau (RCJ Advice Bureau): one of many volunteer lawyers who staff the face-to-face clinic at the Royal Courts of Justice on the Strand, giving procedural advice to litigants in person. Much, although by no means all, of the work at this clinic is routine: helping to fill out a court form, format a witness statement, comply with directions.

The potential for an online tool which could automate some of this work was obvious. Equally obvious were some of the potential pitfalls, particularly the ethical and tactical dilemmas which the LASPO cuts pose to any charity or pro bono initiative aiming to improve access to justice. Nonetheless, on 18 August 2011 I met RCJ Advice Bureau's CEO, Alison Lamb, and pitched to her the idea that

---

[1] Richard Susskind, 'The public needs an NHS Direct to provide legal advice—any takers?' *Times* (9 June 2011), available at: www.thetimes.co.uk/tto/law/columnists/article2992857.ece.

RCJ Advice Bureau, in partnership with Freshfields, should develop an interactive online tool to help litigants in person navigate the civil justice system. The choice of RCJ Advice Bureau as a partner for this project was obvious: they have unparalleled expertise and experience in dealing with litigants in person and specifically in providing them with procedural advice on their cases. And in 1996 Freshfields was one of a handful of City firms which helped RCJ Advice Bureau establish a very successful pro bono duty scheme, which now includes around 40 firms on its rota—Freshfields, for example, have around 30 litigators who regularly attend the clinic to provide procedural advice (face to face) to litigants in person. In this chapter, I will describe the initial development of CourtNav, as an example of a technological response to LASPO, but first I will set this example in the wider context of the dilemmas posed more generally to anyone developing pro bono in an age of austerity.

Pro Bono and 'The Gap'

Pro bono can be generally defined as 'free legal advice or representation for the public good'. In some jurisdictions there is more or less of an emphasis on pro bono work which directly meets the legal needs of impecunious individuals (which we call 'access to justice'), rather than providing free advice to charities or other NGOs. In the US or Australia, for example, pro bono is both relatively well developed within the legal culture and also focused relatively heavily on individuals, as reflected in the main US definition, maintained and policed by the Pro Bono Institute.[2] In Germany, by contrast, pro bono is much less established within the legal profession and is almost exclusively targeted at charities and other NGOs rather than at individuals. The UK is somewhere in the middle of these two extremes, with the Attorney General's 'Pro Bono Protocol' defining pro bono simply as 'legal advice or representation provided by lawyers in the public interest', but continuing: 'including to individuals, charities and community groups who cannot afford to pay for that advice or representation and where public and alternative means of funding are not available'.[3]

In comparing different approaches to pro bono in different jurisdictions, it is striking that overall average volumes of pro bono do not only go hand-in-hand with a focus on individuals as beneficiaries; both these measures are negatively correlated with levels of civil legal aid. It seems that in jurisdictions where the state does relatively little to ensure effective access to civil justice, the legal profession assumes some of this responsibility. And therein lies a central predicament for the pro bono sector (and for a charity using its resources voluntarily to give free legal

---

[2] See: www.probonoinst.org/wpps/wp-content/uploads/law_firm_challenge_commentary.pdf.
[3] See: http://lawworks.org.uk/pro-bono-protocol.

advice or representation): in trying to promote access to justice, we risk creating an argument for the state to cut publicly funded legal aid. If the private and charitable sectors will help people for free, a government might wonder, why should we spend scarce public funds on legal aid?

The UK Pro Bono Protocol attempts to navigate these difficult waters by reciting the official 'mantra' of the pro bono movement: 'Pro Bono Legal Work is always only an adjunct to, and not a substitute for, a proper system of publicly funded legal services'. But what does this mean in practice for the pro bono sector when considering whether—and if so how—to respond to emerging legal need created by cuts to publicly funded legal aid?

It is worth noting that the 'pro bono sector' is itself not a unified body. Data from the Law Society[4] and from TrustLaw[5] suggest that in the UK it is the legal aid and 'high street' firms which do proportionately the greatest amount of pro bono work, followed by the big 'City' firms, who do most of their pro bono work for charities; medium-sized firms do proportionately the least. In other words, when it comes to advising individuals, the firms with real expertise in the relevant areas of social welfare law (immigration, welfare benefits, housing, debt, and so on) already do a substantial amount of pro bono work (although they typically do not call it that) and have little or no capacity to do more; the large commercial firms generally lack expertise in these areas of law. Indeed, because of this expertise mismatch, most commercial firms operating social welfare law pro bono projects work in partnership with advice agencies which have the relevant specialisms and infrastructure to train and supervise—and sometimes insure—their volunteers. An unintended consequence of the legal aid cuts is therefore that, as not-for-profit advice agencies continue to shrink and close, there will be less opportunity—not more—for commercial pro bono lawyers to volunteer in areas of social welfare law.

These points and others have been clearly and repeatedly put to government by the City law firms to make sure it is understood that there can be no question of pro bono riding to the rescue of access to justice where legal aid is cut. But to the extent that big firms are still devoting a proportion of their pro bono contribution to access to justice issues, they will surely want to continue ensuring that their effort achieves the maximum social impact, and for that purpose the changing legal aid landscape cannot be ignored. I have argued elsewhere for three measures to be taken whenever a new pro bono or charitable legal project is established for individuals, to protect against the risk of unintentional harm: first, that any project is set up in close consultation with people who understand in detail the potential interactions with legal aid; second, that external evaluation is built in from the outset, to ensure wherever possible that data are collected to support the case for future investment in legal aid; and third, that training and processes

---

[4] See: www.lawsociety.org.uk/policy-campaigns/research-trends/research-publications/documents/pro-bono-work-in-the-solicitors-profession/.

[5] See: www.trust.org/spotlight/pbi14/.

are established to make sure pro bono lawyers can and do identify cases which could potentially be eligible for 'exceptional case funding'—and then refer them on to appropriate legal aid practitioners, with an offer of help with the application process.[6] The hope is to minimise the risk that pro bono work, whether by well-intentioned private practice or charity sector lawyers aiming to promote access to justice, inadvertently tip the scales of the policy debate about the extent of civil legal aid provision—and thereby score an unintended access-to-justice own goal.

This 'trap' is not confined to the policy arena but has also been set in the legal sphere. For, within the Council of Europe and the EU, because of Article 6 of the European Convention on Human Rights and Article 47 of the EU Charter of Fundamental Rights respectively, there is in principle a legally defensible core minimum when it comes to state-funded legal aid. This contrasts starkly with the position in jurisdictions such as the US and Australia where—with a few exceptions—receiving civil legal aid is a privilege and not a legal right in itself. However, the extent of this right to civil legal aid is not clearly defined and is influenced not just by other factors within the justice system (such as the complexity of the relevant substantive law and procedure) but also arguably by the availability of pro bono help itself.

The third paragraph of Article 47 of the EU Charter reads: 'Legal aid shall be made available to those who lack sufficient resources in so far as such aid is *necessary to ensure* effective access to justice' (my emphasis). This broadly reflects the approach the Strasbourg Court has taken on Article 6 cases. Whether legal aid is 'necessary' in any particular case therefore turns on the facts—a range of factors will be taken into account or, in the words of the Strasbourg Court:

> The question whether or not the provision of legal aid is necessary for a fair hearing must be determined on the basis of the particular facts and circumstances of each case and will depend, inter alia, upon the importance of what is at stake for the applicant in the proceedings, the complexity of the relevant law and procedure and the applicant's capacity to represent him- or herself effectively.[7]

But an additional potential factor should be at the forefront of the mind of anyone contemplating pro bono or charitable contribution to the access-to-justice cause: the provision or even perceived availability of pro bono help (whether from a charity or a firm) could on the face of it be relied on by a state to argue that legal aid is not 'necessary' for the purposes of Article 47 of the Charter and Article 6 of the Convention, since effective access to justice could be assured through other means. Such were the arguments put by the Government in the case of 'B', where the potential availability of free legal help, given on a voluntary basis, in this case by Islington Law Centre, was used as one of the reasons for refusing legal aid.[8]

---

[6] See: www.legalvoice.org.uk/2014/10/29/pro-bono-and-moral-hazard-first-do-no-harm/.

[7] *Steel and Morris v UK* (2005) 41 EHRR 22, 61.

[8] See *R (Gudanaviciene and others)* [2014] EWCA Civ 1622, 166.

This type of trap will be familiar to those with experience of giving charitable help to the destitute. Such safety nets as the state provides (such as, for example, the current asylum support system), usually require an applicant to prove his or her destitution to qualify for state-funded help. The rationale for this is obvious: to target scarce resources at only those who need it. But it has the unfortunate consequence of placing charities, religious groups and well-meaning individuals— who actually want to use their limited resources to give ad hoc help to someone presenting as destitute or street homeless—in the unenviable position of having to consider whether to stay their humanitarian instinct or risk undermining the case for more reliable publicly funded support of the very person they are trying to help.

In the case of *R (Adam, Limbuela & Tesema) v Secretary of State for the Home Department* [2005] UKHL 66, for example, the Government argued that the basic safety net provisions contained in section 55(5)(a) of the Nationality, Immigration and Asylum Act 2002 should not be available to people who might instead be able to rely on voluntary support from a friend or a charity.[9] And, indeed, in asylum support cases it is now routinely the case that a burden of proof is placed on an applicant to show that he or she is not able to rely on such voluntary support— for example, applicants in proving their destitution are routinely asked to provide evidence that they had unsuccessfully approached friends and local charities for support. And, naturally, anyone moved to offer such support on an ad hoc basis would in turn be justified in considering whether in voluntarily offering to help someone they are in fact jeopardising that vulnerable person's chance of ongoing state-funded support.

A system more corrosive of the natural impulse to help a fellow human in need is hard to imagine.

A possible solution to this problem of 'moral hazard' was introduced in Germany in 2014. There, the *Beratungshilfegesetz* (literally, 'advice help law') provides for publicly funded legal advice. One of the conditions to be satisfied under this law is that '*nicht andere Möglichkeiten für eine Hilfe zur Verfügung stehen, deren Inanspruchnahme dem Rechtsuchenden zuzumuten ist*' (no alternative options for assistance are available which it would be reasonable to expect the litigant to use)—section 1(1)(ii). This provision was amended in January 2014 specifically to clarify that '*Die Möglichkeit, sich durch einen Rechtsanwalt unentgeltlich oder gegen Vereinbarung eines Erfolgshonorars beraten oder vertreten zu lassen, ist keine andere Möglichkeit der Hilfe im Sinne des Absatzes 1 Nummer 2*' (the ability to consult a lawyer for free or on a CFA cannot be an 'alternative option for assistance' under section 1(1)(ii)). The perverse disincentive for would-be providers of charitable or pro bono assistance in the UK could be removed by an equivalent provision within LASPO, clarifying, for example, that the availability or potential availability of free legal services on a voluntary basis will be disregarded when considering whether the provision of services is 'necessary' or 'appropriate' under

---

[9] See Lord Hope's judgment, paras 35–36.

section 10(3) LASPO. In the absence of such a clarification, any well-meaning voluntary effort to improve access to justice—from private practice pro bono or from a charity—must consider the risk that in helping an individual, inadvertent damage may be done to access to justice at the systemic level.

CourtNav[10]

This is the legal, ethical and political maze through which the CourtNav project had to find its way. On the face of it, though, while it was undeniably conceived in part as a response to LASPO cuts, the aim was always for CourtNav to be an online extension of the existing face-to-face work of RCJ Advice Bureau. The Bureau has since 1978 provided procedural advice (that is, advice on civil procedure) to litigants in person within the Royal Courts of Justice and, since 1999, within what is now the Central London Family Court. The idea in moving part of that function from a face-to-face advice clinic to the internet was to allow the Bureau to achieve two things: first, to increase the reach of its services (from 'those who can travel to the Strand' to 'those able to access the internet'); and second, to enable those litigants in person who are most able to help themselves to do so (with assistance from the online tool) while concentrating face-to-face resources on those who need it most.

I say 'those who need it most' rather than 'those most in need' because the relationship between 'vulnerability' and the appropriateness of face-to-face advice is not straightforward. It is true that many litigants in person who present as the most vulnerable at a physical clinic may be the hardest to imagine being confident or capable enough to access online or other remote services. For example, they may need an emotional reassurance which is hard to give virtually, or they may need someone to physically work through a bewildering assortment of documents to even understand what their case is about. But, although by definition difficult to measure, there is another cohort of 'vulnerable' people who do not even present at a face-to-face clinic: people with mobility difficulties for whom travel or access to a physical clinic would be difficult or impossible; people with other disabilities— for example, visual or aural impairments—for whom online services are more accessible; people who happen to live far from a suitable advice clinic; people who for any number of reasons do not wish to be seen (by a partner or by others in their community) accessing legal advice, and so on.

The initial concept was clear: an online diagnostic tool which would present a simple question-and-answer interface to the user, hide complexity via a decision-tree architecture, and use the user's answers to auto-complete court forms and

---

[10] A video showcasing the CourtNav tool is available online at: http://play.buto.tv/tMnyS.

other documents. To move from concept to implementation, Freshfields' IT team ran a workshop on 30 November 2011, which teased out some key design choices which needed to be considered.

One example of such a decision was the question of how 'interactive' to make the tool: where to place it on the spectrum between a static, informative website and a full case management package. Both extremes have their place, but for litigants in person as a user group we believed there was significant value in being able to present an interface much simpler than the relevant court forms themselves (requiring a degree of interactive diagnosis in order to shield the user from aspects irrelevant to their particular case), while equally not adding so many bells and whistles that the interface itself became unwieldy for what would hopefully be at worst an occasional rather than regular user. A key inspiration from the outset was Shelter's online 'eviction rights checker', whose simple series of single questions masks a legal decision tree.[11] But a key additional feature of CourtNav is the ability to retain user answers in order to use them not just to tailor content, but to populate court forms automatically.

A second strategic decision concerned how the tool was to be accessed. One option was to make the tool publicly accessible to anyone freely over the internet. We opted instead to make access—at least at first—subject to initial 'triage' by RCJ Advice Bureau or an authorised partner agency. One advantage of this initial triage is that it allows the Bureau to be confident that only those who are suited to using CourtNav are given access. Initial data suggest this has been effective: of the first 100 clients to use the first module of CourtNav, only three did not go on to complete their forms—and these cases involved quite specific circumstances, such as the death of a partner or the need for face-to-face advice to tackle a complex issue in relation to children who were not part of the family. It also ensures that cases which could potentially qualify for legal aid—for example, in family cases where the potential user is a victim of domestic violence—are identified and referred out to appropriate legal aid practitioners as appropriate. For CourtNav users who are not entitled to legal aid and have experienced domestic violence, CourtNav will complete the C8 form for them automatically, which hides their current address from the respondent.

Similarly, a third choice, relevant to the end of the user journey, was whether to make automated document creation subject to any checks. We opted at least initially for a final requirement for solicitor review before releasing the pre-completed forms for user signature and issue at court. The trade-off here is between the resources required to carry out such checks and quality control. It was decided that within the court system the fact that a CourtNav form would be known to have been checked by a lawyer before being issued would act as an important quality mark. The scalability of this model is discussed below.

More generally, there were other interesting balancing acts to consider, such as the trade-off between simplifying jargon to present everything in plain English,

---

[11] See: http://england.shelter.org.uk/get_advice/downloads_and_tools/eviction_checker.

and empowering users by introducing them to the technical terms they would see on the completed form and hear if their case goes to court.

Finally, of course, there was the tactical decision of where to start. RCJ Advice Bureau's clear view was that the area where need was expanding fastest and there was the most room for CourtNav to have a meaningful impact was in applications for divorce and civil partnership dissolution.

Freshfields' involvement did not end with the initial suggestion of developing an interactive online tool for litigants in person: continuing input into the design and strategy has been complemented by financial support and a range of other in kind contributions. For example, after running the initial workshop, Freshfields' IT team created a wireframe prototype to be used as a 'proof of concept' for funding purposes. The PR team gave pro bono advice on external communications, and came up with the 'CourtNav' name, and the IP team gave pro bono advice on branding and trademark protection. For Freshfields, the project is a natural extension of the long-running face-to-face clinic staffed by its litigators, and also an example of the innovative and practical approach the firm brings to all client work.

Following a funding commitment from the Ministry of Justice, an IT developer (Electric Putty) was selected and contracted to deliver the first pilot module, centred around the D8 petition (the eight-page form required to apply for a divorce or civil partnership dissolution). This module seeks to replicate so far as possible the approach of a face-to-face adviser. It takes the user through a series of pages, each presenting a few simple questions. Answers are selected in a variety of ways: some are binary choices or multiple choice tick boxes; and some are free text entry (eg, name and address).

In terms of the 'user experience' there are several key advantages of an interactive tool such as CourtNav over a physical court form. Most simply, checks can be automated to reduce the likelihood of simple human error—for example, the validity of UK postcodes can easily be checked, and the sex of both parties can be checked against the date of the marriage or civil partnership and the type of application (that is, whether a divorce or civil partnership dissolution is sought). If divorce between two people of the same sex is applied for, but the UK 'wedding' was in 1995, then CourtNav will prompt the user to double-check the date and/or sex and/or application sought.

More far-reaching value is added by shielding the user from complexity through the structure of the question set. A physical court form has to include all questions potentially applicable to any applicant, along with the associated guidance; with the right structure, an online tool can lead the user on a much shorter journey with much of the complexity never even visible. A good illustration of this principle lies in the treatment of 'jurisdiction' in the pilot CourtNav module. This is the most legally complicated section on the D8 form, with many technical terms to grapple with, plus a series of similar sounding but subtly different alternative 'gateways', through any one of which an applicant must pass. See the extract from the D8 form below (Figure 1).

The court has jurisdiction to hear this case under

☐ Article 3(1) of the Council Regulation (EC) No 2201/2003 of 27 November 2003

or

☐ the Civil Partnership (Jurisdiction and Recognition of Judgments) Regulations 2005

or

☐ The Marriage (Same Sex Couples)(Jurisdiction and Recognition of Judgments) Regulations 2014

on the following grounds

☐ The Petitioner and Respondent are both habitually resident in England and Wales and/or

☐ Other (please state any other connection(s) on which you wish to rely)

```



```

or

☐ The court has jurisdiction other than under the Council Regulation on the basis that no court of a Contracting State has jurisdiction under the Council Regulation and the ☐ Petitioner ☐ Respondent is domiciled in England and Wales on the date when this application is issued

or

☐ The court has jurisdiction other than under the Marriage (Same Sex Couples) (Jurisdiction and Recognition of Judgments) Regulations 2014 or under the Civil Partnership (Jurisdiction and Recognition of Judgments) Regulations 2005 on the basis that no court has, or is recognised as having jurisdiction as set out in these regulations, and

either:

☐ the ☐ Petitioner ☐ or the Respondent is domiciled in England or Wales

or

☐ the Petitioner and Respondent registered as civil partners of each other in England or Wales or in, the case of a same sex couple, married each other under the law of England and Wales and it would be in the interests of justice for the court to assume jurisdiction in this case.

Figure 1: Extract from the Jurisdiction section of the D8 court form

The experience of RCJ Advice Bureau is that the great majority of applicants fit through the 'habitual residence' gateway (the fourth box on the form). So by asking a yes/no tick-box question first—'Are you and your ex-partner both habitually resident in England or Wales?'—over 70 per cent of users never even see any other options. CourtNav's in-line guidance notes explain what habitual residence means. It is only if the user answers 'no' to this first question that the next potential gateway is revealed, and so on. RCJ Advice Bureau has found that it does not receive queries on jurisdiction even from the CourtNav users who have married outside the UK.

Another advantage over a physical form is that guidance relevant to a particular question can be available adjacent to the question itself, rather than on a separate sheet of guidance notes.

RCJ Advice Bureau's experience of using the initial module has been very positive. CourtNav has enabled the Bureau to support some clients online and staff have been surprised by the diversity of people confident in using CourtNav. Staff and volunteer solicitors find CounrtNav checking can take minutes compared with the much longer time it takes for a face-to-face interview. Clients appreciate the fact that they can now download not only the completed D8 petition, but also the completed EX160 fee exemption form (and completed C8 if needed for victims of domestic violence). RCJ Advice Bureau has used its pro bono volunteers to carry out the checking of forms, alongside their face-to-face advice sessions. The project won the inaugural 'Access to Justice through IT' award at the Legal Aid Lawyer of the Year Awards 2015. At the time of writing, discussions are under way to explore with Citizens Advice a national roll-out of the divorce module, involving a second-tier subscription model.

With further funding granted to RCJ Advice Bureau by foundations including the Legal Education Foundation and the Money Advice Service to develop Court-Nav further, work is also under way to add other stages of the divorce process (such as arrangements for children) to the system, and the development of further modules dealing with bankruptcy, fee exemption and applications in county court possession proceedings, the latter to be piloted in late 2015.

As the tool develops we will ensure that it continues to be used both to gather evidence on the impact of legal aid cuts and to identify and refer out cases potentially eligible for legal aid.

5

15

The French Approach
to Access to Justice

AUDREY GUINCHARD AND SIMON WESLEY

The French government website 'vie publique.fr', similar to the English 'gov.uk' website, introduces access to justice in the following terms:

> Access to justice is recognized as a *fundamental right*. *Various mechanisms* ensure its *effectiveness*. The right to go to courts ... [to be implemented effectively] is guaranteed by a system of *legal aid* ['aide juridique'] allowing the poorest to access fully the law and the courts (our emphasis).[1]

Thus, in France access to justice, especially access to courts is a fundamental right. In its decisions no 88 248 DC of 17 January 1989 and no 96-373 DC of 21 January 1996, the French Constitutional Court, the Conseil constitutionnel, has held that the existence of *effective* access and recourse to justice are essential components of the Constitution based on the 1789 Declaration of the Rights of Man and the Citizen which stated in its Article 16 that 'where rights could not be guaranteed there would be no constitution'.[2] The right is also enshrined in various European and international instruments, which Article 55 of the 1958 French Constitution makes directly applicable.[3] Access to justice covers both access to courts and access to legal advice, even when there is no litigation involved. Its effectiveness depends on financial solidarity,[4] at the heart of which lies the Government's legal

---

[1] See: www.vie-publique.fr/decouverte-institutions/justice/definition/garanties/comment-acces-justice-est-il-garanti.html.

[2] For further details, see S Joissans and J Mézard, 'Aide juridictionnelle: le Temps de la Décision' *Rapport d'information fait au nom de la commission des lois du Sénat* (Report for the Sénat Commission des Lois (the Sénat is the Upper House of the French Parliament and is referred to as Senate Law Commission in this paper) no 680 (2 July 2014), available at: www.senat.fr/rap/r13-680/r13-680.html, 13; S Guinchard, F Ferrand and C Chainais (eds), *Procédure civile. Droit internet et droit communautaire* (Paris, Dalloz, 2008) 116–19 on the right to access courts (*droit d'agir en justice*); T Renoux, 'Le droit au recours juridictionnel' La Semaine (1993) I *Juridique: Juris Classeur Periodique* 3675.

[3] See P Gosselin and G Pau-Langevin, *Rapport d'information en vue d'améliorer l'accès au droit et à la justice, Assemblée nationale* no 3319 (6 April 2011) 9–13; Joissans and Mézard (n 2) 11–13.

[4] The word 'solidarity' is enshrined in the Constitution of 1946 which the Conseil constitutionnel considers as part of the constitutional texts (1946 text); Guinchard, Ferrand and Chainais (n 2) 116; Gosselin and Pau-Langevin (n 3) 8, 85–86, 134.

aid budget. Regulated by statute, mainly by Loi no 91-647 of 10 July 1991,[5] the provision for legal aid reflects the breadth of institutional responsibilities involved in access to justice, stating that legal aid, identified as *aide juridique*, comprises three components. First, *l'aide juridictionnelle*, or aid to access the courts, covers assistance and representation in court proceedings.[6] Second, *l'aide à l'accès au droit*, or access to law, covers initial information and orientation on legal matters where no litigation before the courts is involved, assistance with various formalities and procedures outside court, legal consultations, and assistance for drafting legal deeds and documents. Third, *l'aide à l'intervention d'un avocat dans les procédures non-juridictionnelles*, or aid for a lawyer's intervention outside courts, covers various interim procedures such as advice at the police station when the person is detained as part of the *garde-à-vue* (preliminary police investigation), retention of foreigners and criminal mediation.

The Government's budget for legal aid to access the courts, we will see, is the main—albeit not unique—source of funding for legal aid. This budget was recently described in an official report to the Ministry of Justice, as a crucial aspect of a public service, dedicated to facilitating access to law and justice.[7] The Government's budget was substantially increased from €56 million in 1991 to €187 million in 1998,[8] €197 million in 1999[9] and €305 million in 2005,[10] to reach €347 million in 2014.[11] To that must be added the cost of legal aid to access law, in which the Government partially participates.[12] Overall, the forecast government budget for legal aid in 2014 was €368 million of which 94 per cent should go to the first and third components of legal aid described above. In 2015, it was raised to €379 million,[13] approximately £273 million, compared with the approximate £2 billion in 2014 in England and Wales.

---

[5] Its implementing Décret is no 91-1266 of 19 December 91 amended by Décret no 2003-300 of 2 April 2003. The Loi was notably amended in 1998, 2001 and 2007, and most recently in 2014 by Loi no 2014-1654 of 19 December 2914.

[6] A *'juridiction'* is a court in French.

[7] J-Y Le Bouillonnec, 'Financement et gouvernance de l'aide juridictionnelle. A la croisée des fondamentaux. Analyse et propositions d'aboutissement' *Rapport pour le Premier Ministre* (October 2014), available at: www.ladocumentationfrancaise.fr/rapports-publics/144000610, 5.

[8] Y Détraigne, *Rapport fait au nom de la commission des lois du Sénat sur la proposition de loi relative aux contrats d'assurance de protection juridique, et sur la proposition de loi visant à réformer l'assurance de protection juridique* no 160 (7 January 2007), available at: www.senat.fr/rap/l06-160/l06-160_mono.html, 16.

[9] Commission de réforme de l'accès au droit et à la justice, *Rapport* (April 2001), available at: www.ladocumentationfrancaise.fr/var/storage/rapports-publics/014000368.pdf, 5.

[10] Joissans and Mézard (n 2) 16.

[11] *Les chiffres-clés de la Justice* 2014, available at: www.justice.gouv.fr/art_pix/1_stat_livret_final_HD.pdf, 6.

[12] Conseil national de l'aide juridique, *Rapport triennial Mars 2010–Mars 2013*, available at: www.justice.gouv.fr/art_pix/rapport_CNAJ_mars2010_mars_2013.pdf, 18–19.

[13] Le Bouillonnec (n 7) 33.

However, despite such considerable increases over the last 25 years, the system is recognised as being seriously underfunded, 'rationed' in French discourse, and has variously been described in 2007 by the Sénat, the French upper House in Parliament, as being 'on its last legs' (*à bout de souffle*) or 'on the edge of implosion' (*un système au bord de l'implosion*).[14] The serious inadequacies of the current system were reiterated in a detailed report of the Assemblée nationale parliamentary enquiry in April 2011,[15] whose conclusions have been examined further by a current Sénat Law Commission (Committee for law reform). The subsequent report, published early in July 2014, has a revealing title: 'Legal Aid: The Time for Decision',[16] and sets out propositions to improve the French system of access to law and justice. Recent strikes by the Bar throughout France, in October 2013 and June/July 2014 led the Minister of Justice, Christiane Taubira, to commission a report to MP Le Bouillonnec. Presented in October 2014, on 16 December the report triggered the commissioning of four further reports, yet to be published.[17]

Thus, we see that despite a strong political will to reduce central government expenditure in the context of economic crisis and calls for austerity measures, the French approach to legal aid can be characterised as a continuing commitment from government, political parties and the legal professions to the constitutional principle of access to justice.[18] Moreover, as we will further demonstrate, it appears unlikely that legal aid provision will be reduced, although some governments have made efforts to do so. It is also noteworthy that despite the difficulties of underfunding, and the serious tensions between lawyers and successive governments on the subject of legal aid, various public and private resources have contributed to maintaining the system. Thus, there are signs of willingness from government and all other stakeholders to keep the system operating as far as possible, despite the pressures of the economic downturn and austerity.

It could be argued that one of the reasons underlying this approach is that legal aid as a means to achieving access to justice is embedded in a culture where access to law and the courts has a social function that cannot simply be reduced to the provision of state financial support to the poorest. It is true that historically, access to justice can be traced back as far as the eighth century, with the kings instructing their judges 'to decide the cases of indigents and elderly without delay and without cost'.[19] The images of St Louis, the thirteenth-century king giving justice under an oak tree and accessible to all his subjects including the poorest and lowest,

---

[14] R Du Luart, 'L'aide juridictionnelle: réformer un système à bout de souffle', *Rapport d'information fait au nom de la commission des Finances, du contrôle budgétaire et des comptes économiques de la Nation sur l'aide juridictionnelle*, Sénat, no 23 (9 October 2007), available at: www.senat.fr/rap/r07-023/r07-023_mono.html.

[15] Gosselin and Pau-Langevin (n 3).

[16] Joissans and Mézard (n 2).

[17] See Ministère de la Justice, 'Réforme de l'aide juridictionnelle' (16 December 2014), available at: www.justice.gouv.fr/la-garde-des-sceaux-10016/reforme-de-laide-juridictionnelle-27737.html.

[18] Le Bouillonec (n 7) 6.

[19] George A Pelletier, 'Legal Aid in France' (1967) 42 *Notre Dame Lawyer* 627.

continue to permeate French legal culture and imagery.[20] The role of the Bar was, and remains, crucial as well. It was customary for the *avocats*, French lawyers, to provide advice without a fee, and St Yves, the fourteenth-century lawyer helping '*la veuve et l'orphelin*' ('the widow and the orphan') is today the patron saint of the *avocats*.[21] In the seventeenth century, under Louis XIV, one of the established rules of the Paris Bar was that every week, nine *avocats* of the Paris Bar would meet in order to provide free advice to the poor.[22]

Nevertheless, affordable and fair access to justice has always been at the heart of the often fraught relationship between French citizens and their governments. Indeed, access to justice, or rather the lack thereof, was not only one of the many complaints that triggered the 1789 Revolution, but also the reason for the willingness of the National Constituent Assembly, composed at the time of 322 lawyers and judges (about 27 per cent of the Assembly),[23] to offer access to courts and to law at no cost.[24] Thus, a right first inscribed by the 1789 National Assembly in Article 16 of 1789 Declaration of the Rights of Man and the Citizen, became the text upon which the Conseil constitutionnel based its decisions of 1989 and 1996 cited above.

A series of reforms to simplify the legal system and give citizens access to the corpus of laws enacted by the National Constituent Assembly then followed. However, despite the numerous reforms of the French legal system that have taken place over the past two centuries, in principle, the overarching objectives of the 1789 National Assembly have not been challenged.

Against this background it should be no surprise that the 2013 report on *The Courts of the 21st Century* commissioned by the Minister of Justice Christiane Taubira not only proposed changes in the organisation of the courts, but also had a whole chapter dedicated to improving access to law, alternative dispute resolution solutions, and access to courts,[25] in addition to improving legal aid. There is continuing recognition that a guarantee of effective access to justice requires

---

[20] The image is a staple of French primary school books, although St Louis did not decide the cases himself, but heard them before referring them to his courts. See, eg, J Le Goff, 'Saint Louis invente la justice—propos recueillis par Emilie Lanez' (Le Point, 16 December 2010), available a: t www.lepoint. fr/societe/saint-louis-invente-la-justice-16-12-2010-1278821_23.php. The King's reputation for justice led Henry III and his barons to request his arbitrage in a dispute opposing them in December 1263. St Louis gave his sentence on 23 January 1264 in Amiens in favour of Henry III.

[21] See the blog post by M Jean-Louis Charvet, on the blog held by former Professor J-M Doucet, renowned in France for his work in criminal law, (6 November 2005), available at: http://ledroitcriminel. free.fr/dictionnaire/noms_propres/biographies/saint_yves.htm.

[22] Pelletier (n 19) 627.

[23] Edna-Hindie Lemay, 'La composition de l'Assemblée nationale constituante: les hommes de la continuité?' (1954) *Revue d'histoire moderne et contemporaine* 341, 345.

[24] D Soulez-Larivière, 'Overview of the Problems of French Civil Procedure' (1997) 45 *American Journal of Comparative Law* 737.

[25] Working Group chaired by Didier Marshall, 'Les juridictions du XXIe siècle. Une institution qui, en améliorant qualité et proximité, s'adapte à l'attente des citoyens, et aux métiers de la Justice' *Rapport à Mme la garde des sceaux, ministre de la justice* (December 2013), available at: www.justice.gouv.fr/ publication/rapport_Marshall_2013.pdf, 24–30.

attention to this set of institutional and organisational concerns. Nevertheless, one of the recurring themes of French justice, and not simply legal aid, is its lack of funding. The forecast justice budget was €7,824.12 million in 2014,[26] about £646 billion compared with the £8 billion of the UK justice budget.[27] This discrepancy between the vision for access to justice as enshrined in law and embedded in legal culture, and the financial means to achieve it, permeates the French justice system and the main features of legal aid.

Setting the Scene: Overview of the French Justice System and Legal Professions

There are some very significant differences in the way the French legal system and lawyers operate, for example, compared with England and Wales. Among relevant distinguishing features of the French system, the following can be highlighted for present purposes: the organisation of the legal professions; and the public service of justice.

The Legal Professions

One of the distinguishing features of the French legal system is the division of lawyers into a number of regulated and distinct professions: *avocats* (equivalent to solicitors and barristers as the *avocats* can appear in court); *notaires* (public notaries); *avocats au Conseil* (advocates admitted to plead before the Supreme Courts for administrative law—the Conseil d'Etat—and civil and criminal law—the Cour de cassation); *huissiers* (bailiffs); *greffes du Tribunal de Commerce* (commercial court clerks and company registrars); and *mandataires et liquidateurs judiciaires* (creditors' representatives and insolvency practitioners). Each profession specialises in certain types of legal work in accordance with the monopoly that they have been granted. How much they charge can also be regulated.

Lawyers' Monopolies

The regulated legal professions benefit from a legal monopoly of giving legal advice, with some very limited exceptions.[28] Furthermore, some have a monopoly for certain types of legal work, with the corresponding obligation to use their

---

[26] Le Bouillonnec (n 7) 6. The French justice budget represents only 2% of the general budget.

[27] Ministry of Justice, *Annual Report and Accounts 2013–14* (HC 23), available at: www.gov.uk/government/uploads/system/uploads/attachment_data/file/323308/moj-annual-report-2013-14.pdf.

[28] Eg, if accountants can give legal advice, they can only do so for work ancillary to their accountancy practice.

services only. For conveyancing, succession and real property work, one must use the *notaires*. For service of process, it is the *huissiers*. For insolvency, one of the liquidators or receivers with a local monopoly has to be appointed by the court.

Outside those specific areas, the assistance of an *avocat* is obligatory in most cases in the Tribunal de grande instance, the Cour d'assises (equivalent, in England and Wales, to the Crown Court with a jury for criminal cases only), and the Tribunal pour enfants (youth tribunals). On appeals on the facts and/or law, before the civil and criminal Cours d'appel as well as before the Cours administratives d'appel, the *avocat* also represents the litigant. For appeals on points of law to the French Supreme Courts, litigants must use the services of an *Avocat au Conseil* who are *avocats* specially admitted to the two French Supreme Courts, ie, the Cour de cassation for civil, commercial, employment and criminal matters, and the Conseil d'Etat for administrative and public law, tax and social security matters.

In terms of numbers and turnover, *avocats* and *notaires* are the two main professions. The 58,224 *avocats*, as lawyers admitted to plead in most courts, are organised in 161 Bars[29] on a local basis and membership of a local Bar is compulsory for practising *avocats*. The central representative organisation called Conseil National des Barreaux (CNB) represents the local Bars vis-a-vis the French Government. Over one-third of French *avocats* are sole practitioners and many operate in small firms. In 2008, the annual turnover of the profession was €3.5 billion. By contrast, the *notaires* had a turnover of €6.5 billion annually.[30] They employ more lawyers and clerks in-house (*clercs de notaire*) than *avocats*' firms.[31] Yet, on 1 January 2015, there were only 9,651 French *notaires*, of which approximately 2,000 were sole practitioners.[32] The *notaires* have a central national Conseil Supérieur du Notariat with regional notarial organisations responsible for discipline and representation with local authorities.

Avocats are the main providers of legal aid services in France. They provide close to 93 per cent of legal aid services related to access to courts[33] and of the €3.5 billion turnover cited above, some €236 million was income from the legal aid system. The 2014 Senate Law Commission (Committee for law reform) report on legal aid indicates that the typical law firm structure dealing with legal aid work would be a firm of two to three lawyers, usually women, specialising in legal aid work, which probably constitutes 80 per cent of their workload.[34]

Besides the *avocats*, the other legal professions also have to provide legal aid as stated in Article 25 of the 1991 Loi. Their contribution to *aide juridictionnelle* (access to courts) remains small, reflecting the fact that in most situations, the

---

[29] Le Bouillonnec (n 7) 10.

[30] See the official website of the *Notaires*: www.notaires.fr/fr/le-notariat-en-chiffres.

[31] See M Richard Ferrand, 'Professions réglementées. Pour une nouvelle jeunesse' *Rapport auprès du Ministre de l'Économie, de l'Industrie et du Numérique* (October 2014), available at: www. ladocumentationfrancaise.fr/rapports-publics/144000657, 10.

[32] Statistics on the official website of the *Notaires*, available at: www.notaires.fr/fr/le-notariat-en-chiffres.

[33] Joissans and Mézard (n 2) 45.

[34] ibid, 31.

avocats are the main providers of legal services linked with litigation: 4 per cent for the judicial experts; 1.5 per cent for the *huissiers* (bailiffs); 1.7 per cent for mediators; and 0.2 per cent for other professions like the *notaires*.[35] The *notaires*' role, however, is more important when it comes to access to law. Their presence at the Maisons de justice et du droit is noted in the statistics given in the 2010 *Report on Maisons de Justice et du Droit*.[36] Furthermore, *notaires* are remunerated in accordance with fixed or scale fees established by the Government, and in practice families tend to go to their *notaires* to plan their inheritance and sale of real estate property, both legally and fiscally. In many places the *notaire* also provides ancillary legal advice in family matters without charge and in certain areas, particularly rural ones, acts as an informal social mediator. There is little quantitative evidence of what this involves, but it is a reality of French life.

Lawyer's Charges, Outside Legal Aid

With the exception of the *avocats*, the legal professions' remuneration for legal services is strongly regulated, with mainly fixed fees for the transaction or legal act involved. As noted in the 2014 report on the regulated professions, the fees are not indexed to counteract inflation and hardly ever cover the economic costs of the work done. Furthermore, the re-evaluation of the fees follows no particular plan or strategy.[37] The report recommends increasing the fees to better reflect economic costs and introduce their review every five years.[38] However, the report warns that the re-evaluation should not result in thwarting access to justice for the poorest and that a balance must be maintained.[39] To give an example, for the authentication of a will by a couple, the authentication being necessary for the validity of the document, the *notaire* would currently receive €320 after having provided legal advice, assessed the parties' ability to consent, and checked all identity documents the testators have to provide.[40]

One-third of *avocats*' firms in France are sole practitioners and there are many small firms with minimum equipment and staff. As a result, many law firms charge significantly less for their services than in the UK. It is estimated that the break even point for small firms is approximately €75 per hour before remuneration of the lawyer. Typical hourly rates range from around €100 to €600 depending on the size and activity of the law firm. Furthermore, one must bear in mind the

---

[35] ibid, 45.
[36] D Baux, 'L'activité des Maisons de Justice et du Droit et des antennes de Justice en 2010' *Rapport au Ministère de la Justice* (December 2011), available at: www.justice.gouv.fr/art_pix/2_stat_MJD_2010.pdf, 11–14.
[37] Ferrand (n 31) 29.
[38] ibid, 32–33.
[39] ibid, 32.
[40] Official website of the *Notaires*, available at: www.notaires.fr/sites/default/files/Notaires_testament%20authentique_0.pdf.

courts' practice when awarding legal costs (see below), and the fact that *avocats* representing clients before the courts are participants in the 'service public de la justice'.

The 'Service Public de la Justice'

In France rendering justice is an integral part of the 'service public de la justice' whose organising principles centre notably on equality, free access and neutrality (impartiality). The concept therefore informs the structure and functioning of the courts as much as the drive to provide for unmediated access to legal information.

The Courts

Access to justice was at the heart of the French Revolution whose work 'can be summarised as an ongoing attempt to further streamline the judicial system'.[41] As soon as the Declaration of the Rights of Man had been adopted in August 1789, the National Constituent Assembly started working on the new judiciary and the principles underlying its organisation. Its aims were to rationalise the messy court system inherited from the Ancien Régime so that justice would be easy and affordable. The result was the Loi of 16 and 24 August 1790, which abolished all courts of the Ancien Régime and created the key features of the current French civil and criminal justice systems. Among those characteristics, two deserve mention.

First, citizens have a right to appeal in fact and in law without filtering.[42] Moreover, although the right of appeal has not acquired constitutional status,[43] citizens can exercise it for most decisions at first instance and, as we will see, legal aid also covers appeals. Second, the 1790 Loi aimed to establish a simple justice system geographically close to its users, a '*justice de proximité*', the object of which was to manage conflict resolution through mediation and equity judgments.[44] The resulting *juges de paix* (justices of the peace) lasted until 1958, before being replaced by the Tribunaux d'instance (equivalent of local county courts), complemented in 2002 by the *juges de proximité* (local justices of the peace mainly for civil matters).[45] Nonetheless, in essence, today as before, the role of these courts remains that of conciliation; with the twofold aim of achieving speedy resolution of low cost conflicts and the avoidance of appeals wherever possible.

---

[41] Soulez-Larivière (n 24) 741.

[42] The only notable exception was, until 2000, the Cour d'assises, the decisions of which could not be appealed.

[43] Conseil constitutionnel, Décision no 2004-491 DC, Loi complétant le statut d'autonomie de la Polynésie française du jeudi 12 février 2004, considérant 4.

[44] J Perelman, 'Legal Aid in France: A Survey', edited for the Bellow–Sacks Project 2004, available at: www.law.harvard.edu/academics/clinical/bellow-sacks/papers/Perelman/Final/Draft.doc, 6.

[45] See: http://vosdroits.service-public.fr/particuliers/F2289.xhtml. The *juges de proximité* may be abolished in 2017.

The importance of the 1790 Loi cannot be underestimated, since it has also been recognised by the Conseil constitutionnel as the progenitor of two distinct judicial orders: the 'judiciary' (*judiciaire*) order, comprising civil and criminal law matters, and the 'administrative' order mainly pertaining to judicial review. Nevertheless, the citizens of France had to wait another century for a formalised and fully independent administrative court system: the administrative courts were fully recognised for the first time in 1873. Thus, today each order has first instance and second degree courts (Cours d'appel). Each order also has its own supreme court: the Cour de cassation for civil and criminal law cases, the Conseil d'Etat for administrative law. Both courts can now refer questions of constitutionality to the Conseil constitutionnel, the French Supreme Constitutional Court, because of the introduction of the *Question préjudicielle de constitutionnalité* (preliminary question of constitutionality) in 2008.

This established system of courts is part of the French *service public de la justice* whose governing principles are equality, gratuity and neutrality (or impartiality).[46] It is in this *public service* context that members of the judiciary and the prosecutors, who are all civil servants,[47] and have seldom practised law, operate. Therefore, when we come to consider judicial responses to the threat of austerity in France, it is not only important to remember the prevailing public service ethos, but also the institutional fact that courts and prosecutors have a key role in the local administration of legal aid and access to law at the level of the *département*, which corresponds very roughly in size to a county in the UK, although there are 95 *départements* within continental France. Thus, whereas access to law issues are dealt with by a Conseil Départemental de l'accès au Droit (CDAD), the Bureau d'aide juridictionnelle (BAJ) attached to the Tribunal de grande instance,[48] filters applications for legal aid to access the courts and appoints lawyers for the 8 per cent of cases where the person concerned has not found their own lawyer.

To put the courts' and prosecutors' involvement in legal aid into further context, it is important to highlight their own underfunding, and their practice when awarding legal costs. The following account concentrates mainly on the civil and criminal courts.

A Justice System Chronically Underfunded

Despite a central Ministry of Justice (Ministère de la Justice), the court system is largely one of decentralised justice, with local High Courts (Tribunal de grande instance and Tribunal administratif) and regional Courts of Appeal, in addition to two central Supreme Courts for appeals on points of law.

---

[46] See official website Vie publique, 'Quels sont les grands principes d'organisation et de fonctionnement de la justice?' (31 August 2012), at: www.vie-publique.fr/decouverte-institutions/justice/definition/principes/quels-sont-grands-principes-organisation-fonctionnement-justice.html.

[47] The prosecutors are '*magistrats*' and belong to the judiciary, but do not perform the function of judging.

[48] There is at least one TGI per département.

The number of judges and courts has hardly evolved since the nineteenth century in spite of very significant increases in population and litigation activity. For many years the court system in France has been in urgent need of additional resources in terms of judges, court clerks as well as probation officers and specialist social workers. One of the main consequences of this is severe delay in delivery of justice. For example, the 'Livre Blanc' (White Paper)[49] published in 2010 by the Union Syndicale des Magistrats, one of the leading unions of the French judiciary, as well as their communiqués of 20 September 2012[50] and 12 June 2013[51] recalls the severe paucity of means available to the French court system. The more left-wing Syndicat de la Magistrature does not mince its words, claiming in 2012, that the public service of Justice was on the verge of collapsing.[52] Both publications confirm the 2010 Council of Europe report (European Commission for the Efficiency of Justice)[53] and have been followed by various international reports from the World Bank Doing Business database, and the OECD on judicial systems.[54]

Against this background, the French Government in 2007 launched a politically sensitive programme to reform the judicial map with regard to first-instance courts. The project had cost €413 million, more than the budget for legal aid of €379 million. It had resulted in the abolition of 341 courts (of which 178 were Tribunaux d'instance),[55] and was deemed to have led to a better use of resources in terms of staff and buildings[56] *and* to decisions of higher quality as noted by the Cour des comptes, the French Audit Court for public institutions, in 2015. Interestingly, in accordance with the French institutional approach to access to justice, the Cour des comptes considered that the reform had improved access to justice,[57] despite noting that it had not led to a decrease in the use of legal aid.[58]

---

[49] Union Syndicale des Magistrats, *Livre blanc 2010—l'état de la justice en France*, 2010, available at: www.union-syndicale-magistrats.org/web/p361_livre-blanc-2010-l-etat-de-la-justice-en-france.html.

[50] Communiqué, 'Comparaison des systèmes judiciaires européens', available at: www.union-syndicale-magistrats.org/web/p484_comparaison-des-systemes-judiciaires-europeens.html.

[51] Communiqué, 'La justice en faillite', available at: www.union-syndicale-magistrats.org/web/p580_la-justice-en-faillite.html.

[52] 'Rentrée 2012: vers l'effondrement du service public de la justice', *Lettre ouverte à la garde des Sceaux sur la situation des juridictions*, published 13 July 2012, updated 17 July 2012, available at: www.syndicat-magistrature.org/Rentree-2012-vers-l-effondrement.html.

[53] European Commission for the Efficiency of Justice (ECEJ), 'European Judicial Systems. Efficiency and Quality of Justice, Edition 2010 (data 2008)', available at: www.coe.int/t/dghl/cooperation/cepej/evaluation/2010/JAReport2010_GB.pdf (it was updated in 2014).

[54] See OECD, 'What makes civil justice effective?' OECD Economics Department Policy Notes, No 18 (June 2013), available at: www.oecd.org/eco/growth/Civil%20Justice%20Policy%20Note.pdf.

[55] Cour des comptes, 'La réforme de la carte judiciaire: une réorganisation à poursuivre' (2015), available at: www.ccomptes.fr/content/download/79155/1980528/version/1/file/122-RPA2015-reforme-carte-judiciaire.pdf, 37.

[56] ibid, 44–46.

[57] ibid, 36.

[58] ibid, 52.

Awards of Legal Costs by French Courts

The Loi no 77-1468 of 30 December 1977 states that issue of process and procedural steps at court in litigation are free. Today, this is not completely true as some court fees and taxes are still charged[59] yet, this principle affects significantly the question of the legal costs more generally in that they remain relatively low. Whilst the French Code of Civil Procedure gives the court discretion on awards of legal costs, costs usually follow the event. However, the awards habitually bear no relation to real levels of legal costs or lawyers' charges. Typically awards of legal costs in civil or commercial matters will be limited to anything between €1,000 and €3,000, higher amounts being the exception. This can be explained partly by lower levels of legal costs and charges in France, but also by the fact that the French judiciary are career judges who have not practised as lawyers, and are to some extent traditionally reluctant to award significant amounts of legal costs.

In the employment tribunals and commercial courts, the judges are locally elected trade union officials, employers' representatives or local business people. They are unpaid for their work as judges. Whilst there is little empirical research, it is probable that this also colours their approach to awards of legal costs, although it is said in legal circles that commercial court judges are more 'realistic' about legal costs.

Leading lawyers also admit that *avocats* have been reticent about requesting higher amounts of legal costs and providing full details of legal charges and costs. This is apparently due to ingrained professional attitudes about client confidentiality and disclosure of fee levels and charging methods.[60] The result is that courts have also been deprived of properly detailed information about real levels of legal costs.

Unmediated Access to Law and Legal Information

As we have noted above, French central and local government officials have a strong tradition of 'public service'. Many ministries and departments operate detailed information systems, information points and websites accessible to the public, such as 'Vos droits -service public.fr', 'vie publique.fr', or 'Legifrance'. The latter, for example, is called the 'service public de la diffusion du droit' (public service for the dissemination of law) and is far more complete than its English counterpart 'legislation.gov.uk' as it includes case law and constitutional texts.

Historically, as well as today, access to law meant free access to the statutes. From 1790 onwards, the Lois were published in the *Bulletin des lois*, superseded later by the *Journal officiel*, the latter published on the noticeboards of the local *mairie*

---

[59] Guinchard, Ferrand and Chainais (n 2) 1298–309.
[60] See M Charrière-Bournazel, a former head of the Paris Bar, 'L'imputation des honoraires de l'avocat en droit français' (18 April 2005), available at: www.charriere-bournazel.com/limputation-des-honoraires-de-lavocat-en-droit-francais/.

(the parish), and since 1999 on the web,[61] with equal binding force between the printed and electronic version of statutes (Article 1 Civil code). Even the entry into force of the Lois was adapted to the geography of France so that access to legal information meant the ability for the citizen to physically read the statutes. As stated in original Article 1 of the Civil code, the effect of the promulgation of the Lois was delayed by one day outside Paris, ie, the time it took for the journal to reach by horses the smallest *mairies* of France. With the development of the web, the impact of the geographical difference between Paris and the rest of France upon the citizen's access to law disappeared and thus, Article 1 of the Civil code was amended in 2004 and the delay disappeared.[62]

Access to justice also means easy access to the comprehensive corpus of laws, thanks to the enactments of various codes, and notably the Civil code, now on the web on Legifrance. The Civil code was considered in 1804 to be the 'civil constitution' of France because all citizens should know their rights by reading the code and without the intermediary of a lawyer and the related costs involved.[63]

Furthermore, access to justice means access to case law, with access historically, first, to the Supreme Court's decisions, and increasingly, thanks to the internet, to the Courts of Appeals' decisions.[64] To summarise, the debates about access to justice in France cannot be reduced to debates about legal aid. The approach is far more holistic and the structure of the courts, as much as the costs of using the services of the legal profession, are viewed as other means to achieve affordable justice. Nevertheless, this broader approach is not always matched by appropriate funding, despite recent reforms notably to rationalise the first-instance courts in civil matters. The real economic costs of justice are not always recognised. This paradox is even more acute when it comes to legal aid.

The Main Features of the Legal Aid System in France

State financial assistance for persons with low incomes and financial resources was established in 1851 to facilitate their access to courts. The system of *assistance judiciaire* did not work well, despite numerous reforms in the first half of the twentieth century.[65] It was estimated that in 1971, before the significant reform of 1972, only 6 per cent of civil courts' users benefited from legal aid.[66] Furthermore,

---

[61] By comparison, legislation.gov.uk was launched in 2010: www.nationalarchives.gov.uk/news/732.htm.

[62] For the text of Article 1 in its original version and its 2004 version, see: Legifrance.gouv.fr.

[63] Doyen Carbonnier, 'Le Code civil en tant que phénomène sociologique' (1981) *Revue de la Recherche Juridique: Droit Perspectif* 74 et seq; Doyen Carbonnier, 'Le Code civil' in P Nora (ed), *Les Lieux de mémoire* t II, *La Nation* vol 2 (Gallimard, 1986; reed, Quarto, 1997).

[64] Private publications publish lower courts' decisions, but the web allowed for the publication of printed and unprinted decisions.

[65] The 1851 Loi was amended in 1901, 1903, 1907, 1956, 1958 and 1960. See Pelletier (n 19) 626.

[66] In French, Guinchard, Ferrand and Chainais (n 2) 1312, para 1896; in English, Perelman (n 44) 6.

the 1851 statute did not cover legal aid before administrative courts as these courts operated (and still operate) separately from the civil and criminal courts.[67] Legal aid for administrative law matters was dealt with by the Ministry of Justice's use of '*circulaires*' (detailed ministerial instructions) that have only interpretative authority and thus no legal binding force,[68] until the Loi 1972 integrated procedures before administrative courts into the scope of legal aid.

Substantially revised in 1972, legal aid included civil and administrative law cases, as well as ex parte applications (*juridiction gracieuse*). Criminal law matters remained governed by previous legislation.[69] The aim was for the state to subsidise lawyers in private practice to represent legal aid clients. Yet, the system, underfunded, did not achieve its objectives. In 1989, the Bar went on strike and as a result the Ministry of Justice created a Commission on Legal Aid Reform chaired by the Conseiller d'Etat Paul Bouchet[70] who was a member of the French administrative Supreme Court—the Conseil d'Etat—and had been the *bâtonnier* or head of the Lyon Bar.[71] The subsequent report entitled 'Legal Aid: For Better Access to Law and Justice' led to parliamentary adoption of the Loi of 1991 cited above.[72] Since then amended in 1998, 2001 (following strikes by the Bar), 2007 and 2014, the 1991 Loi remains the main text governing the aid for accessing the law, the courts, or a lawyer in specific matters. As noted above, in 2015, the Government's budget for legal aid was €379 million,[73] approximately £273 million. Compared with the approximate £2 billion in 2014 in England and Wales, this appears to be a very low figure. Indeed, the delivery of legal aid services is notoriously underfunded. If one were to stop there, it could be said that access to law and justice in France is severely rationed and that the constitutional principles are not attained. However, as will be suggested below when explaining the funding of legal aid, there is a different and perhaps slightly better picture of access to justice in day to day reality, but which is wearing very thin.

The Delivery of Legal Aid

As explained in the introduction, legal aid comprises access to the law and access to courts. For those different services, the French government fixes the fees, with little leeway for an increase for the *avocats* who do 93 per cent of the legal aid work.

---

[67] '*Judiciaire*' in French legal language refers to matters before the civil and criminal courts only, and thus excludes matters before the administrative courts.

[68] Pelletier (n 19) 626, fn 10.

[69] For details of the 1972 legislation, see P Herzog and B Ecolivet-Herzog, 'The Reform of the Legal Professions and of Legal Aid in France' (1973) 22(3) *International and Comparative Law Quarterly* 462, 483–90; see also Perelman who states that appeals before administrative courts were included only in 1988 (n 44) 7.

[70] Perelman (n 44) 7.

[71] Guinchard, Ferrand and Chainais (n 2) 1312, para 1897. Paul Bouchet also reported in 2001 on reforms in legal aid, see Joissans and Mézard (n 2) 8.

[72] For the details, see Perelman (n 44) 7.

[73] Le Bouillonnec (n 7) 33.

The Various Services

Aide à l'accès au droit (Free Legal Advice Outside Litigation)

The Conseil Départemental de l'accès au Droit (CDAD) or Departmental Council for Access to Law[74] coordinates the various services offering free legal advice and defines a local policy for access to law/legal aid provision. Its members include representatives of the local High Court (TGI), local authorities, government, the local Bar and local charities.

Its budget does not derive solely from government and involves financing by various local authorities, the local Bars, and other legal professions as per Article 68 Loi 1991. In 2014, the Government's contribution to access to law represented 6 per cent of the €368 million making up the legal aid budget.[75]

Free legal advice, where no litigation before the courts is involved, is mainly available locally through advice sessions organised at town halls and at specific centres—the Maisons de justice et du droit (MJD) and Antennes de justice (ADJ) existing since 1998. The MJD are part of the French judiciary.[76] Access to law advice counts for about 69 per cent of their activities. The other activities of the MJD involve matters that are related to criminal and civil proceedings, as the MJD and ADJ are involved in the follow up of convicted offenders and persons on probation. Furthermore, the Médiateur de la République, who deals with matters involving difficulties with the justice system and government bodies, is also present at the MJD and this activity represents about 2 per cent of the MJD's overall activities.

The Ministry of Justice's report of 2011 on the activities of the national network of Maisons de justice et du droit and Antennes de justice shows that in 2010 there were 127 MJD, with only 74 out of 181 TGI having a MJD in their jurisdictional area.[77] On 1 January 2014, this number increased slightly, as there are now 134 MJD.[78] The MJD and ADJ employ just over 200 permanent staff each, the majority being seconded from the courts (public prosecutors, court clerks, accounting for 55 per cent of the hours provided), charities (around 40 per cent) and lawyers (around 8 per cent).[79] Lawyers are present on average only 8 per cent, ie, about 23 hours per month on average, of the total time the MJD are open for business. In 2010, 704,578 people were assisted in various ways,[80] and 427,518 actions were in the field of 'access to law' of which 23 per cent were in the field of family law.[81]

---

[74] Loi no 98-1163 of 18 December 1998, replacing the original provisions of Loi no 91-647 of 10 July 1991.

[75] Le Bouillonnec (n 7) 5.

[76] Thus, their organisation is in Title 3 of the Code de l'organisation judiciaire (Code of the Judiciary Organisation).

[77] Baux (n 36) 5. See also Conseil national de l'aide juridique (n 12) 16–19.

[78] According to the government website vie publique.fr: www.vie-publique.fr/decouverte-institutions/justice/fonctionnement/modes-alternatifs/que-sont-maisons-justice-du-droit.html.

[79] Baux (n 36) 11–13.

[80] ibid, 19.

[81] ibid, 27; confirmed in Conseil national de l'aide juridique (n 12) 16.

The running costs of the MJD are covered by central government (estimated at 38 per cent) and local government (estimated at 62 per cent). The central government budget for the MJD in 2010 was of the order of €6 million.[82] The 2011 parliamentary enquiry refers to chronic underfunding of this system of 'access to law', which it characterises as alarming.[83]

Outside this network of MJD and ADJ, in many towns, the local Bar also provides free consultations either at the offices of the Bar or at the local High Court or Tribunal de grande instance (TGI).

For example, in Lyon, provision of legal aid and assistance by the *avocats* is organised around nine Maisons de justice et du droit or 'Points d'Accès au Droit', with one session organised each week or month depending on the location. The local town halls provide premises for these purposes and each sends out a call for tenders to local lawyers. The Lyon Bar is also involved in consultations in the prisons, and gives advice to small businesses, the consultation being organised and paid for by the local small business federation (la Chambre des Métiers).

The Lyon Bar provides free consultations by telephone. The telephone reception is provided at the cost of the Lyon Bar based at the TGI which provides the facilities. In 2012 there were 19,000 calls, and 6,131 consultations (limited to a quarter of an hour) on specific matters with an *avocat* were organised in a room provided at the TGI. Most of the work concerns family, employment, administrative, tax, landlord and tenant, protection of adults, consumer and some commercial matters.

Aide Juridictionnelle (Including Aide à l'intervention d'un Avocat)
(Legal aid for Proceedings and for the Intervention of an Advocate)

Legal aid to access the courts covers all procedures, civil, criminal and administrative, as well as mediation processes[84] and enforcement of judicial decisions (Article 10 Loi 1991). Legal aid also covers the costs of lawyers when the litigation ends with a settlement out of court. Legal aid is available on appeal for the citizen who is the defendant (Article 8, Loi 1991); if the person benefiting from legal aid wants to appeal, then she or he will have to apply and the request will be examined upon its own merits.

Legal aid is organised by the CDAD and the BAJ at each Tribunal de grande instance in permanent coordination with the local Bar. The local BAJ, or Legal Aid Office, decides whether to admit applications for legal aid and maintains the record from which the statistics on legal aid (*aide juridictionnelle*) are drawn.[85] Presided over by a member of the local judiciary, it comprises representatives from tax, social security, the local Bar and a lay representative.[86] The local Bars deal with

---

[82] Gosselin and Pau-Langevin (n 3) 105.

[83] ibid, 104–06. For the details, see also Conseil national de l'aide juridique (n 12) 19.

[84] Since 1901, Guinchard, Ferrand and Chainais (n 2).

[85] *Annuaire de la Justice. Edition 2011–12*, 292.

[86] For a full list of the BAJ members, see Loi 10 July 1991, art 16—Decree 19 December 1991, arts 12 and 14.

the day to day administration of legal aid. The various responsibilities between the BAJ and the local Bar are often set out in protocols as per Article 91 Decree 1991, a practice the extension of which the Senate Law Commission (Committee for law reform) recommended in 2014.[87]

For example, a detailed triennial protocol 2013–15 has been signed between the Lyon Bar and the local Tribunal de grande instance setting out the means to be used to organise legal aid within the local jurisdictional area, including numbers of duty *avocats* and legal aid rates. The protocol details, in particular, the various judicial institutions and prisons in the Lyon area and the available numbers of lawyers enrolled with the Lyon Bar who are volunteers for legal aid work and on permanent standby: between 100 and 424 lawyers depending on the type of work involved. The legal work includes such activities as urgent criminal hearings, criminal investigations by the investigating judge (*juge d'instruction*), juveniles, and immigration cases. The resources made available by the Lyon Bar for the administration of the legal aid system pay for a permanent team of six people employed by the Bar.

The protocol also provides that the lawyers should be specifically trained for the various types of work and sets out the specific legal aid fees payable to the lawyer for each type of matter, with a slightly more favourable application of the legal aid fee tariff than the standard legal aid rates in certain cases. The courts undertake to make certain facilities and documents available to the lawyers to enable them to accomplish their role.

Furthermore, the protocol sets out the various types of intervention undertaken by the Lyon Bar and its members, within the scope of the legal aid system, but outside the terms of a specific protocol with the court. This includes: duty lawyers at police stations with over 300 volunteers; foreigners detained on entry to France (eg, at Lyon airport) with 39 volunteers; EU arrest warrants; prisoners' disciplinary hearings at the local prison; juveniles; free legal advice consultations; and mental health internments.

Legal Aid Fees

Avocats are poorly remunerated for the work done for legally aided clients.

For advice given at the local MJD and ADJ (access to law), fees are established with the local authority. In Lyon, which is France's second largest city in economic terms, the *avocats* at the local MJD are remunerated for their assistance, which can last for several hours, at around €61 per session. The work on the telephone is slightly better paid as the *avocat* is paid €61 for a two-hour stint.

Regarding work for access to courts, in its 2014 report, the Senate Law Commission (Committee for law reform) indicated that 90 per cent of legal aid work is accomplished at a loss for the lawyer concerned.[88]

---

[87] Joissans and Mézard (n 2) 50–51.
[88] ibid, 31–33.

The amount per case is regulated at a national level, with very limited latitude for adjustment. The fees are not usually based on time spent, with some limited exceptions, for example, for extra days at a trial before the Cour d'assises, which is the equivalent to the English Crown Court for serious criminal cases. Experienced lawyers are paid at the same rate. Because of this, litigants or an accused will not always have access to senior specialists. This being said, a number of well-known specialists, particularly in the criminal field, are prepared to take high profile cases on legal aid, where she or he will be paid the usual legal aid rate. It is possible for the legally aided client to agree to top up the legal aid fees, but an agreement has to be drawn up within certain guidelines approved by the Bar.

The examples given in the 2014 Sénat Committee for legal reform report indicate the following typical remunerations for handling a case: €593 for a civil court trial in the Tribunal de grande instance (roughly equivalent to the High Court in England); €1,250 for a divorce by mutual consent where the *avocat* represents both spouses; €180 for cases before the Tribunal correctionnel, which handles the equivalent of a mix of Crown Court and magistrates' court work in England; €2,000 overall for a lawyer advising and representing a client on legal aid for a Cour d'assises criminal trial, including the detailed judicial investigation phase which may last a couple of years.[89]

The consequence has been to concentrate legal aid work in a small number of firms which can benefit from a volume effect. In 2011, the Law Committee for the Assemblée nationale, the French equivalent of the English House of Commons, reported that only about 400 *avocats*, out of the 45,000 *avocats* admitted nationally, deal with the majority of legally aided cases.[90] However, the real figure may be significantly higher. Indeed, a recent article about the Nantes TGI quotes a figure of 25,000 *avocats* doing at least one legally aided case each year.[91] Similarly, in Lyon, almost half (1,033) of the 2,700 lawyers at the Lyon Bar were voluntarily registered to do legal aid work in 2012. Thus, the statistics belie a wider commitment of *avocats* to legal aid, and many accomplish some legal aid work, if irregularly.

Statistics on Users and Volumes of Cases

According to the 2014 report from the Senate Law Commission (Committee for law reform), 14.3 million people are entitled to legal aid, with 7.4 million

---

[89] ibid, 32. For lively comment on what it means for an *avocat*, see the post of 18 July 2005 on the well-known blog by Maitre Eolas, available at: www.maitre-eolas.fr/post/2005/07/18/161-rediffusions-laide-juridictionnelle. More recently, a number of strike movements by the *avocats* in 2013 and 2014 highlighted the difficulties of making a living out of legal aid, S Mouillard, 'Les Avocats inquiets pour l'aide juridique aux plus pauvres' (*Libération*, 17 September 2013), available at: www.liberation. fr/societe/2013/09/17/les-avocats-inquiets-pour-l-aide juridique aux plus pauvres_932496; F Béguin, 'Les avocats en grève: L'aide juridictionnelle rembourse à peine nos frais de secrétariat' (*Le Monde*, 26 June 2014), available at: www.lemonde.fr/societe/article/2014/06/26/les-avocats-en-greve-contre-une-aide-juridictionnelle-proche-du-benevolat_4446297_3224.html.

[90] Gosselin and Pau-Langevin (n 3) 8.

[91] A Coignac, 'L'aide juridictionnelle: le grand parcours du combattant' (*Dalloz actualité*, 21 July 2014).

earning less than €937 net before tax per month,[92] entitled to full legal aid, and 6.9 million—who earn between €980 and €1,404 per month –entitled to partial legal aid.[93] These numbers are unlikely to vary much following the slight increase of 0.5 per cent in this threshold from €937 to €941 in 2015.[94] For reference purposes, the French Government statistical office INSEE estimated that in 2012, 8.7 million people were earning the equivalent of or less than the poverty threshold per household which in 2012 was an income of €987 per month.[95] The minimum monthly wage is €1,128.79 and INSEE estimates that half the population in France has a monthly income of less than €1,629. Some estimates suggest that about 40 per cent of French households are entitled to legal aid.[96]

Regarding the number of legally aided cases, the admissions to legal aid have increased from 688,637 in 2002 to 915,563 in 2012,[97] with 821,777 full legal aid and 93,786 partial legal aid. The breakdown in 2012 was 8,700 cases heard by the Cour de cassation;[98] 374,737 criminal cases (Cour d'assises, Tribunal correctionnel, Tribunal de police); and 540,493 civil cases including 26,688 employment tribunal cases, 43,141 administrative court cases, and 24,330 'other' including commercial court and TASS (Tribunal des affaires de sécurité sociale) social security tribunal cases (in which 86,473 cases were completed in 2012).[99]

These numbers of legally aided cases can be compared with overall volumes of contentious matters in 2012: 2,647,813 civil and commercial cases completed in 2012 in all courts (the number of new cases in 2012 was comparable); 1,251,979 criminal cases where the courts rendered a decision. Approximately 500,000 appeals from decisions of social security organisations were heard by the Commission de recours amiable de la sécurité sociale in 2010.[100] The procedure is on documents only with a possible appeal to the TASS and from there on appeal to the administrative courts. Legal aid is available for the assistance of a lawyer before the TASS and on appeal. On a very rough and ready basis this gives about five million contentious matters of which about 18 per cent benefit from the provision of legal aid. Approximately 465,000 cases settled out of court with advice and assistance provided by legal protection insurers.

---

[92] Most households would not be paying income tax at this level of income. There is an uplift for dependants, and certain social security benefits are excluded from the calculation.

[93] Joissans and Mézard (n 2) 22.

[94] Article 2, Loi de finances of 2015 no 2014-1654 of 29 December 2014.

[95] INSEE, *Niveau de vie en 2012*, available at: www.insee.fr/fr/ffc/ipweb/ip1513/ip1513.pdf.

[96] Détraigne (n 8) 17.

[97] Joissans and Mézard (n 2) 15, based on the Ministry of Justice statistics published each year in 'Les Chiffres clés de la Justice', available at: www.justice.gouv.fr/budget-et-statistiques-10054/chiffres-cles-de-la-justice-10303/.

[98] Also on the Cour de cassation website, *Activité 2012 du bureau d'aide juridictionnelle*: www.courdecassation.fr/publications_26/rapport_annuel_36/rapport_2012_4571/livre_5_activite_cour_4623/bureau_aide_juridictionnelle_4632/bureau_aide_26451.html.

[99] Joissans and Mézard (n 2) 15.

[100] Cour des comptes, 'Le fonctionnement des commissions de recours amiable dans les organismes de sécurité sociale' (September 2010), available at: www.ccomptes.fr/content/download/1467/14511/version/1/file/Rapport_securite_sociale_2010_septembre_2010_chapitre_9.pdf.

The Financing of Legal Aid

In its 2014 report on the efficiency and quality of justice, based on 2012 data, the European Commission for the Efficiency of Justice for the Council of Europe indicated that France devotes €57 per head to the justice system, well below most other European countries. France was thus ranked twenty-eighth out of 40.[101] Indeed, the legal aid system is notoriously inadequate and underfunded, despite being increased to €379 million in 2015. It has not been reduced in the last few years, although some governments have tried to adjust the payments to lawyers, whereas the number of admissions to legal aid for representation in courts has increased consistently since 1991, from 49,601 in 1991 to 105,379 in 2006.[102]

Governments, both on the right and left of the political spectrum, remain committed to the provision of legal aid, even if there has been no progress in improving remuneration of lawyers willing to take on legal aid work. As noted in the introduction to this chapter, we are still awaiting four reports commissioned in December 2014.

Meanwhile, French legal aid remains financed in the following ways: central government funding and provision of legal personnel; local government funding and support; and funding and support from the French Bars and some charities.

Central Government Funding

The annual legal aid budget is determined by government, and is administered by the Ministry of Justice which delegates the function to the local Bars in coordination with local courts and local government. As seen above, the Government budget for legal aid regarding access to the courts 'has increased significantly', a fact that the Cour des comptes does not criticise.[103] Rather, the Court worries that the Maisons de justice for access to law remain seriously underfunded, and thus unable to fulfil their legal obligations.

Avocats cannot hold client monies which have to be placed with an independent organisation administered by the local Bars (CARPA). Legal aid budgets are also allocated to CARPA which organise payment of fees and expenses to lawyers through the local Bars, the latter supervising the allocation of fees to lawyers in each case.

The amount of the fees has been a bone of contention between the French Bars and the Government for some years. The Government has been attempting to reduce the fees (or at least limit any increases) as part of budget restrictions. However, there is considerable attachment among *avocats* in general to the principle

---

[101] European Commission for the Efficiency of Justice (ECEJ), 'European Judicial Systems. Efficiency and Quality of Justice, Edition 2014 (data 2012)', available at: www.coe.int/t/dghl/cooperation/cepej/evaluation/2014/Rapport_2014_en.pdf.

[102] Du Luart (n 14) 28.

[103] Cour des comptes (n 55) 52.

of access to justice. Article 10 of the 1971 statute on the profession of *avocats* provides that all lawyers have a professional duty to assist those in need.[104] There have been regular strikes and demonstrations, very often by a majority of the members of the Bar, not just lawyers doing legal aid, to obtain better legal aid fees for the profession. This came to a head again in June 2014 with proposals by the current Government and its Minister of Justice, Christiane Taubira, to tax the legal profession to increase the legal aid budget. After a day's strike and protest marches across France by the *avocats*, the Prime Minister undertook to engage in negotiations with the legal professions and dropped the proposal.[105]

Other Public Funding

Finance or other support, in the form of personnel and premises, is also made available for various legal aid services by local and central government authorities. For example, this takes the form of the participation and presence of public prosecutors and court staff at the local Maisons de justice et du droit and the Antennes du droit, as well as provision of support staff and premises by local authorities for the Maisons de justice et du droit and Antennes du droit.

Financial and Other Support from the French Bars and the Notaires

The French Bar contributes considerable resources to legal advice and assistance through its local Bar institutions and individual *avocats*. As will be seen below with the example of the Lyon Bar, the legal professions provide financial support to legal aid in various ways, which include financial support in the form of dedicated teams administering the legal aid system, payment of fees to duty lawyers, and time spent by lawyers without payment to support the legal aid system. Lawyers give their time in various ways, through Bar commissions assisting with organisation and coordination in liaison with the local courts and Maisons de justice; and individual lawyers providing services which are unremunerated or remunerated, frequently at rates not covering office costs, whether this is a legally aided matter or pure pro bono.

For example, the Lyon Bar estimates that in 2012 it contributed a net sum of €166,000 of Bar funds (financed out of obligatory annual subscriptions paid by the Lyon *avocats*) to the provision of free legal advice and assistance. The Lyon Bar employs a permanent team of six people to administer legal aid and access to justice.[106] There is a specialised Commission Accès au droit with lawyers who give up some of their time to report to the Bar on this topic, and assist management with the legal aid schemes in Lyon.

---

[104] Loi no 71-1130 of 31 December 1971 as modified by Loi no 91-647 of 10 July 1991.

[105] See 'Aide juridictionnelle: une concertation pour modifier le financement' (*Le Monde*, 9 October 2014), available at: www.lemonde.fr/societe/article/2014/10/09/une-concertation-va-etre-engagee-sur-le-financement-de-l-aide-juridictionnelle_4503105_3224.html.

[106] Simon Wesley, interview in 2014 with Véronique Delorme, who heads the Lyon Bar and who kindly provided information about the Lyon Bar's activities in this field.

Furthermore, *notaires* offer a hotline service and/or individual consultations, and also provide consultations at the Maisons de justice et du droit. *Huissiers* also offer some support to free legal consultations. And, for example, in Lyon, the local small business federation (Chambre des métiers) organises and pays for consultations of *avocats* by small businesses.

Some Solutions and Attempts to Improve Access to Justice

Various proposals to improve access to legal aid and access to justice have been made in the various parliamentary and other reports mentioned above. These include such measures as increasing taxes on business transfers, taxing the legal professions and legal protection insurance, taxing litigants who lose their cases, increasing legal aid thresholds, increasing the unit value of legal aid services of lawyers, increasing legal aid remuneration for Bars which subscribe to certain targets, simplification and computerisation of procedures, reinforcement of the role of legal protection insurance subject to certain safeguards, and developing ADR. Some have been implemented; others are just suggestions.

In the short space of this chapter, it is difficult to analyse in detail these very diverse solutions. Nevertheless, there seem to be three trends: rationalising the use of the current system; increasing the budget for legal aid by various means including rationalisation; and redirecting claims and legal assistance outside the system of legal aid.

Rationalising the Use of the Legal Aid System

The 2011 Assemblée nationale report and the 2014 Sénat report suggested extending full legal aid to those earning less than the legal minimum wage. The Senate Law Commission (Committee for law reform) has calculated that the cost of extending full legal aid to those earning up to the minimum legal wage would simplify the system and its administration and would not add significantly to the cost.[107] The parliamentary reports also indicate that recovery of legal aid costs against unsuccessful parties in litigation is insufficient, whereas this could be an additional source of finance for the legal aid system.[108]

In the same spirit of rationalisation, the Senate Law Commission (Committee for law reform) suggested a proper review of financial resources, with increased involvement and checks by tax and social security services, and an assessment of

---

[107] Joissans and Mézard (n 2) 43–45.
[108] ibid, 40; Gosselin and Pau-Langevin (n 3) 58.

the likelihood of success of claims to be made before the granting of legal aid. The Senate Law Commission (Committee for law reform) indicates that even though the statute on legal aid provides for a review of the merits of claims before legal aid is granted, this is not done in practice. The grant of legal aid is determined solely on the basis of financial resources. The Senate Law Commission (Committee for law reform) recommends that the legal aid commissions should review claims on their merits before agreeing to grant legal aid. This would confine legal aid to cases that genuinely deserve to be funded.

This rationalisation of the system, however, does not extend to the reintroduction of the claim form fees. In 2011, the Government introduced a tax of €35 on many proceedings issued in the courts and €150 to file a notice of appeal. This was vigorously challenged on the basis that it reduced access to the justice system. The Ministry of Justice statistics quoted in the parliamentary law commission report suggest a reduction of about 13 per cent in the number of new cases introduced between 2011 and 2012. The fact that the tax was withdrawn in January 2014 and that the Sénat report of July 2014 does not recommend reinstating this tax, indicates that rationalising legal aid should not be confused with deterring individuals from accessing justice and the courts in particular.

Increasing the Funding of the Legal Aid System

The Senate Law Commission proposes a slight increase in taxes on property, inheritance, shares and business transfers. For example, it indicates that an increase of just 0.09 per cent of the current tax of 2.6 per cent on business transfers would produce the equivalent of the 2014 government legal aid budget of €368 million.[109]

Similarly, the report suggests a slight increase in the tax on legal protection insurance, a proposal partly implemented by the Loi des finances of 29 December 2014 for policies covering non-criminal law matters. The increase is of 2.6 per cent, from 9 per cent to 11.6 per cent and it is estimated it will raise €25 million within the next three years.[110]

However, the 2014 Sénat report considers that funding by the legal profession is inappropriate given the various contributions of the legal professions and low levels of remuneration for legal aid work.[111] It thus rejects the report to the Minister of Justice of February 2014 by a senior member of the judiciary.[112]

---

[109] Joissans and Mézard (n 2) 55–56.

[110] See: http://cnb.avocat.fi/Loi-de-finances-pour-2015-nouvelles-dispositions-relatives-a-l-aide-juridique_a2126.html.

[111] Joissans and Mézard (n 2) 54.

[112] A Carre-Pierrat, 'Note à Mme la Garde des Sceaux Ministre de la Justice: l'accès au droit et à l'aide juridictionnelle. Solidarité et responsabilité' (10 February 2014), available at: www. conferencedesbatonniers.com/images/rapports/aide_juridictionnelle/Reforme_financement_AJ_2014/RAPPORT_CARRE-_PIERRAT_-_AJ_f%C3%A9vrier_2014_201406301324.pdf. Carre-Pierrat is Honorary Advocate General (Avocat Général Honoraire) of the Cour de cassation.

The future Loi on the regulated professions, passed on 9 July 2015, but yet to be validated by the Conseil constitutionnel, adopts the proposal of a tax on property and rights transfers when the transaction reaches the threshold of €300,000. The tax will be between 0.05 and 0.2 per cent and will fund an 'interprofessional fund for access to justice and the law' which aims to redistribute the money so as to cover all regions of France and all aspects of legal aid. If the Conseil constitutionnel validates the Bill, the tax will be applicable by 1 January 2016.[113]

Moving Beyond Legal Aid

We will consider the two main features of the French legal system alleviating, partially or totally, the recourse to legal aid: legal protection insurance; and mediation and ADR.

Legal Protection Insurance as a Means of Access to Law

The Loi 1991 established the principle that a person covered by legal protection insurance for the type of matter concerned could not be entitled to legal aid. Whilst bringing an important contribution to access to law and justice, this type of insurance, despite being regulated,[114] has been criticised as it does not cover all types of legal matter (eg, cover for criminal matters is usually limited to automobile accidents) and does not sufficiently involve lawyers.

Nevertheless, legal protection insurance provided by the French insurance industry is becoming of increasing importance in enabling access to law and justice, including out-of-court solutions to disputes. The French insurance industry estimates that about 45 per cent of French households hold legal protection insurance of various kinds.[115] The Senate Law Commission (Committee for law reform), in its 2007 report prior to the vote of the Loi 2007 regulating these contracts, referred to average policy premiums of between €60 per annum for individuals and €250 per annum for small businesses.[116]

The insurers provide a telephone hotline advice service and where needed, more detailed advice and assistance for legal proceedings including representation by a lawyer. The Senate Law Commission (Committee for law reform), in its 2007 report, estimated that approximately 35,000 cases were handled by some 4,000 lawyers registered with insurers under legal protection policies. This represents a

---

[113] Future articles: Loi no 444-2 and Loi no 462-2-1 Commercial code, as in 'Projet de Loi pour la croissance, l'activité et l'égalité des chances économiques' (9 July 2015) 56–57. For a summary of the different aspects of the project, please see Legifrance at: www.legifrance.gouv.fr/affichLoiPreparation. do?idDocument=JORFDOLE000029883713&type=general&typeLoi=proj&legislature=14.

[114] See Loi no 2007-210 of 19 February 2007 portant réforme de l'assurance de protection juridique (Statute reforming legal protection insurance).

[115] Détraigne (n 8) 15.

[116] ibid, 11.

small proportion of the cases dealt with by insurance companies. In 2007, there were approximately 500,000 claims per year under legal protection insurance policies, of which around 70 per cent were settled by out-of-court discussion.[117] Fees paid to lawyers are approximately double those paid by legal aid. The 2014 Senate Law Commission (Committee for law reform) considers that insurers will tend to encourage settlement which means that the insured will probably recover less than if the matter had gone to court.

The parliamentary law commission which reported on the subject has recommended establishing complementarity between legal protection insurance and legal aid as has been done in other countries such as Germany, the Netherlands and Sweden. Premium income from this type of insurance in France is estimated at approximately €958 million, which is almost three times the national legal aid budget. The reports suggest that France was ahead of the UK in terms of legal protection insurance cover, but significantly behind Germany where the use of such insurance is more widespread. It proposes increasing the tax on legal protection insurance policies as a way of financing legal aid.

Mediation and ADR

Conciliation is provided for in the French Code of Civil Procedure which empowers the judge to attempt conciliation, although this is not widespread in practice. Where mediation is used, the costs of mediation are usually shared equally, particularly where one of the parties is legally aided, unless the judge determines otherwise. There is an obligatory conciliation hearing in the employment tribunal but rates of success are low. Family mediation ordered by a judge or criminal mediation initiated by the Public Prosecutor may be financed by legal aid.[118] The 2011 Assemblée nationale report[119] recommended developing and extending legal aid for mediation procedures. However, this has not been reiterated in the latest Sénat report of 2014.[120]

In addition to this form of mediation, in 2013, 233,472 cases were submitted to the '*Conciliateurs de Justice*' who are empowered to deal with small claims, especially property matters.[121] This demonstrates a healthy demand for ADR with a 59 per cent rate of successful resolution. This seems, however, to be the exception since mediation has not developed more generally in the way that it has in the UK.

The attachment of the French people to access to justice and to a judge is perhaps one of the reasons why mediation has not taken off as rapidly as in other countries, even though in the fields of family law and less serious crime, mediation

---

[117] ibid, 15–16.

[118] See Ministry of Justice information note, 'Médiation Familiale' 'Médiation Pénale', available at: www.vos-droits.justice.gouv.fr/fiches-pratiques-telechargeables-11760/.

[119] Gosselin and Pau-Langevin (n 3) 43.

[120] Joissans and Mézard (n 2).

[121] From the official website of the *Conciliateurs*: www.conciliateurs.fr/Les-chiffres-temoignent-de-la-vitalite-de-la-conciliation.

has been successfully introduced. Whilst mediation is felt to be positive and broadly successful, it is still viewed in some quarters (including by some lawyers and judges) with some suspicion, as a form of 'private' justice. This is in spite of the fact that experiments, such as that carried out in the employment chamber of the Grenoble Court of Appeal, notably when Mme Béatrice Brenneur presided over the chamber, have been successful. The Cour de cassation has reported in detail on the subject and France has implemented the EU Directive on Mediation. Senior figures in the French judiciary actively promote mediation with, for example, the activities of the Groupement des Magistrats Européen pour la Médiation (GEMME).[122]

Another factor reducing the attraction of ADR is the low levels of legal costs and legal costs awards by the courts. Parties have less incentive than in other countries to seek out-of-court solutions or use ADR. However, the Paris Court of Appeal recently refused to award costs to a successful party where no attempt at mediation was made. This is probably the beginning of a new trend. The latest figures published by the Centre de Médiation et d'Arbitrage de Paris indicate that mediation is on the increase.[123] New mediation centres are opening in the provinces, for example, the CIMA in Lyon.

Conclusions

There are various ways of measuring access to justice understood as access to law as well as to the court system. We have touched upon a few: constitutional protection of access to justice; the level of public services' provision of advice and assistance in various forms including conciliation and mediation mechanisms as a contribution to access to law; the budget of the justice system and of legal aid; financial factors such as legal costs, court costs, legal aid fees, legal protection insurance and recovery of legal costs; access to legal dispute resolution mechanisms (including access to legal protection insurance, conciliation schemes at the employment tribunal and with public and tax authorities); as well as the participation of lawyers and Bars (in France this includes the *notaires*) including provision of legal advice and legal representation services at cost or below cost. This brief report has *not* attempted to deal with other factors that can give indications of the effectiveness of access to justice, such as the location of courts, obtaining decisions within reasonable time, the standing to bring legal actions, the legal time limits and limitations, and the level of redress and effective remedies.

---

[122] See: www.gemme.eu/fr.
[123] For the latest statistics, see the Centre's website at: www.cmap.fr/Qui-sommes-nous/Nous-Connaitre-49-fr.html.

Yet, this short chapter suggests that the features of the legal aid system in France are as much shaped by the embedded French legal culture of and commitment to affordable and easy access to justice as by the limitations of a legal aid budget restricted to barely 20 per cent of the legal aid budget in England and Wales.

Legal aid and the justice system in France are seriously underfunded (rationed) compared with many other countries. This situation has existed now for many years and perennial protest by lawyers and the judiciary have failed to move successive governments, both right and left, to significant reform or increases in funding or support. The legal aid fees paid to lawyers are based essentially on a single fixed rate for each type of matter, which is mostly unrelated to actual time spent, complexity or seniority of the lawyer engaged, with some limited exceptions and adjustments taking account of the duration of the trial and other matters. It is widely considered that the legal aid rates do not really cover lawyers' real costs. So whilst many lawyers will do some legal aid work, most of it is carried out by a small number of dedicated small firms which can just about cover costs and earn limited remuneration, through volume handling of legal aid cases. Although 40 per cent of households are estimated to have some form of access to legal aid, it is also recognised that large numbers of the population whose resources are not low enough to qualify them for legal aid are probably not able to access law or justice without using legal protection insurance or the assistance of consumer organisations. The difficulty is to some extent attenuated by pro bono or similar free advice services from *avocats* and *notaires*, but this is not sufficiently widespread to make a significant difference.

In spite of the above difficulties, governments, lawyers, the judiciary and public civil servants both at national and local levels remain committed to the provision of legal aid services to those in need. The various participants try to find other solutions to finance legal aid and ensure access to law and justice in the face of persisting government austerity and lack of finance in this field. The recent parliamentary reports point the way to a variety of feasible solutions, notably the fact that very limited increases in certain types of business taxation could easily double funding for legal aid in France. The question of increasing taxes even by small amounts is, however, very sensitive politically at present. It is therefore difficult to predict at the moment whether any government would be in a position to take such a measure.

Furthermore, legal protection insurance which comes with most householders' insurance policies could be extended, clarified and made complementary to legal aid as envisaged by the recent parliamentary reports. This would potentially improve access to legal advice and assistance for approximately 60 per cent of the population. The extension of legal aid to mediation in areas other than criminal and family litigation would certainly be beneficial. Mediation where used in France has developed very similar levels of success for dispute resolution as found in other countries such as the UK. France already has in place suitable legal frameworks for mediation which should avoid some of the risks affecting mediation in some jurisdictions such as California.

The current government is currently investigating lawyers' monopolies with a view to opening up competition and accessibility in the field of legal advice and assistance. For example, there is nothing like 'Tesco law' in France at the moment. The legal professions have been combating new types of legal service providers (eg, online), on the basis of the current legal monopoly of providing legal advice reserved to *avocats* and *notaires* and certain other professions.

Finally, new technologies and expert legal systems can certainly bring a significant contribution to resolving standard or recurrent legal questions at low cost (eg, consumer disputes). No one in France has yet written a book similar to Richard Susskind's book *The End of Lawyers?* The difficulty would be though financing their installation in small law firms which have very limited resources. The Bars could perhaps consider establishing a shared facility in the cloud for example.

6

16

How Scotland has Approached the Challenge of Austerity

SARAH O'NEILL

Introduction

Scotland has in recent years faced similar challenges to those experienced elsewhere, with increasing pressure on public finances in the face of rising demand for public services. The current Scottish Government has sought to manage expenditure on publicly funded legal services largely through the implementation of wider reforms to the justice system, as part of a strategic approach across government, accompanied by a range of efficiency measures. Its declared ambition is: 'to maintain a fair, high quality and equitable system which maintains public confidence at an affordable and sustainable level of expenditure'.[1]

Scotland has long had its own civil and criminal justice system and institutions, which remained separate from those of England and Wales following the 1707 Acts of Union. This separation was maintained in the Scotland Act 1998, which devolved the power to legislate on justice issues[2] to the Scottish Parliament, including legal aid provision.

While Scotland has had its own legal aid system for more than 60 years,[3] however, it took a very similar approach to that followed in England and Wales until devolution:

[T]he two systems were pretty much alike: overwhelmingly judicare; overwhelmingly concentrated in the areas that the profession felt most comfortable in supplying: criminal,

---

[1] Scottish Government, *A Sustainable Future for Legal Aid* (Edinburgh, 2011) para 1, available at: www.scotland.gov.uk/Resource/Doc/359686/0121521.pdf.

[2] With the exception of tribunals dealing with reserved matters in Scotland. Following the recent Smith Commission report, the UK Government has proposed that the management and operation of all currently reserved tribunals (but not the underlying substantive rights and duties) is to be devolved to the Scottish Parliament.

[3] Legal aid was first introduced in Scotland in 1950 by the Legal Aid and Solicitors (Scotland) Act 1949 for civil cases in the sheriff courts and Court of Session. Criminal legal aid was introduced in 1964.

family and personal injury; overwhelmingly demand led; and considerably more expensive in per capita terms than the rest of Europe.[4]

Since the late 1990s, there has been a marked divergence between the two systems in their approach to the provision of publicly funded legal services. While south of the border, successive reforms have led to the introduction of a cap on civil legal aid expenditure, reductions in the scope of legal aid, and reduced eligibility limits, Scotland has taken a very different approach. It has retained its open-ended legal aid budget; there have been no reductions in scope; and eligibility limits have actually been increased.

As one former senior civil servant described it: 'Put simply, the preferred approach is to make the system work more efficiently and therefore reduce demand on legal aid, rather than to reduce legal aid to curtail demand in the system'.[5] In other words, Scotland's approach seeks to address the underlying causes of demand on the legal aid budget, rather than its symptoms.

The purpose of this chapter is not to compare the Scottish system directly with that in England and Wales, although it is worth noting that the differences are not explained by higher levels of expenditure in Scotland. Direct comparisons are difficult, given the wider differences between the two jurisdictions, not just in terms of their different justice systems, but also their respective public policy contexts and other factors such as patterns of criminal activity. Professor Alan Paterson has set out elsewhere in detail some of the possible underlying reasons for the different approaches of the two systems.[6] That said, a 2014 European research report found that legal aid expenditure per capita in England and Wales was €39, compared with €29 in Scotland.[7] Net expenditure on civil legal aid in Scotland in 2013–14 was only around 6 per cent of that in England in Wales, suggesting that Scotland's civil spend is proportionately lower in terms of population.[8]

This chapter aims to provide an overview of the strategic approach which Scotland is taking to address the challenges faced by those responsible for providing publicly funded legal assistance in the current climate, in order to ensure that those who need it most are able to access justice. While nearly two-thirds of legal

---

[4] A Paterson, *Lawyers and the Public Good: Democracy in Action?* (The Hamlyn Lectures) (Cambridge, Cambridge University Press, 2012) 66–67.

[5] C McKay, 'The Scottish Government Response to Austerity', paper for the ESRC Access to Justice Seminar Series, Seminar 2, *Revaluing a Market Based Approach to Legal Services* (14 July 2011) 2.

[6] See Paterson (n 4).

[7] HiiL, *Legal Aid in Europe: Nine Different Ways to Guarantee Access to Justice?* (2014), available at: www.hiil.org/data/sitemanagement/media/Hiil%20Legal%20Aid%20in%20Europe%20Nine%20 Different%20Ways%20to%20Guarantee%20Access%20to%20Justice.pdf.

[8] Scottish Legal Aid Board, *Annual Report 2013–14*, available at: www.slab.org.uk/common/ documents/Annual_Report_2013_2014/A_-_Annual_Report_2013-14.pdf; Legal Aid Agency, *Annual Report and Accounts 2013–14*, available at: www.gov.uk/government/uploads/system/uploads/ attachment_data/file/323366/laa-annual-report-accounts-2013-14.pdf. Note: Scotland's population size is roughly 9.3% of that of England and Wales combined. Source: Office for National Statistics: www.ons.gov.uk/ons/guide-method/compendiums/compendium-of-uk-statistics/population-and-migration/index.html.

aid spend in Scotland goes on criminal cases, the primary focus of this chapter is on civil legal assistance.

Background

The Scottish Government has overall responsibility for legal aid policy in Scotland. The Scottish Legal Aid Board (SLAB), a non-departmental public body, is responsible for administering and managing the legal aid fund. Its other roles include advising the Scottish Government on the availability and accessibility of legal services in Scotland; developing and grant funding targeted advice services; and researching and analysing trends in legal aid and their impact on the wider justice system.

The current Scottish Government views legal aid as a vital public service; it seeks to strike a balance in ensuring wider access to justice, while at the same time recognising the need for a system which is efficient, affordable and sustainable. This is particularly challenging, given that the legal aid fund in Scotland remains non-cash limited and demand-led, which means the Scottish Government will provide funding for any case which meets the statutory (merits and financial) tests.

Successive Scottish governments have also resisted introducing restrictions in the scope of legal aid along the lines of those which have occurred elsewhere. Its scope remains very wide in Scotland, with some form of legal aid available for virtually all types of civil disputes and criminal matters.[9] The Scottish Government's current legal aid strategy states: 'The Government's view remains that wholesale reductions to scope can have a damaging impact on access to justice and can have adverse consequences for other parts of the justice system as well as wider society'.[10]

Recent proposals by the Law Society of Scotland to remove areas of law such as debt, employment, housing and personal injury from the scope of civil legal assistance[11] provoked considerable criticism from law centres and third-sector organisations.[12] SLAB has estimated that if implemented, the proposals would take more than 24,000 people out of scope each year, leaving them 'facing complex

---

[9] There are currently three categories of legal aid provision: Advice and Assistance (criminal and civil); Assistance by Way of Representation (ABWOR) (civil only); and legal aid (criminal and civil).

[10] Scottish Government, *A Sustainable Future for Legal Aid* (Edinburgh, 2011), available at: www.scotland.gov.uk/Resource/Doc/359686/0121521.pdf.

[11] Law Society of Scotland, *Legal Assistance in Scotland: Fit for the 21st Century* (2014), available at: www.lawscot.org.uk/media/391321/legal-assistance-in-scotland-discussion-paper.pdf. Note: the discussion paper states that these proposals 'must be taken in the context of the development and maintenance of a strong network of advice agencies and the implementation of reforms to costs and funding and access to justice'.

[12] See, eg: www.journalonline.co.uk/Magazine/59-12/1016767.aspx#.VK6dn2ByZ2s; http://scotland.shelter.org.uk/news/january_2015/legal_aid_changes_will_deny_most_vulnerable.

civil problems without access to specialist legal representation and potentially lead to higher costs in other parts of the justice system'.[13] Following publication of the Society's proposals, the then Cabinet Secretary for Justice reiterated in the Scottish Parliament the Scottish Government's continued opposition to the removal of any subject areas from the scope of legal aid.[14]

It therefore seems unlikely that there will be any reductions in the scope of legal aid in Scotland in the foreseeable future. This, together with the unpredictability of a demand-led budget, raises significant continued challenges in ensuring that there is sufficient funding available to meet the costs of publicly funded legal assistance.

While a package of reforms and efficiency savings designed to reduce legal aid expenditure has resulted in significant savings in recent years,[15] legal aid spending is currently exceeding the allocated budget. In 2013–14, the Scottish Government had to allocate an additional £10 million from other funds to meet legal aid expenditure, over and above the £138 million initially allocated.[16] SLAB has forecast a total shortfall of £39 million for the three-year period from 2014 to 2017.[17]

The Move from Judicare Towards a 'Planned Complex Mixed Model'

In the early 2000s, various consultation papers and policy reports recognised that in order to best meet the complex and varied needs of those with 'justiciable' problems, there was a need for a shift away from a judicare-based legal aid model focused on lawyers' traditional practice areas towards a 'planned complex mixed model' for the provision of publicly funded civil legal assistance, which could provide advice and support in other areas, such as social welfare law.[18] Progress in

---

[13] Scottish Legal Aid Board, *Response to Legal Assistance in Scotland: Fit for the 21st Century* (2015), available at: www.slab.org.uk/common/documents/news/2015/SLAB_response_to_LSS_Discussion_paper.pdf.

[14] Scottish Legal Aid Board, 'News release: Cabinet Secretary for Justice responds to questions on the legal aid system' (2014), available at: www.slab.org.uk/news/articles/Cab_Sec_on_legal_aid.

[15] The Scottish Legal Aid Board has reported that the savings measures already implemented delivered around £12 million of savings in 2011–12, rising to nearly £20 million in 2013–14—Scottish Legal Aid Board, *Corporate Plan 2014–17*, available at: www.slab.org.uk/export/sites/default/common/documents/about_us/whatwedo/Corporate_Plan_2014-2017.pdf.

[16] Scottish Legal Aid Board, *Annual Report 2013–14* (n 8).

[17] Scottish Legal Aid Board, *Corporate Plan 2014–17* (n 15).

[18] Scottish Executive, *Review of Legal Aid, Information and Advice Provision in Scotland* (2001); Scottish Executive, *Justice 1 Committee Report on Legal Aid Inquiry* (Edinburgh, Scottish Parliament, 2001); Scottish Executive, *Strategic Review on the Delivery of Legal Aid, Advice and Information: A Report to Ministers and the Scottish Legal Aid Board* (Edinburgh, Scottish Executive, 2004); Scottish Executive, *Advice for All: A Consultation Paper* (2005).

taking this vision forward was slow, however: SLAB had limited powers under its founding legislation, the Legal Aid (Scotland) Act 1986. It was unable to employ solicitors directly until the necessary legislative changes were brought forward in 2001;[19] nor could it award contracts to voluntary sector organisations until 2007.[20]

The primary model of delivery remains the traditional 'case by case' model: 90 per cent of total legal aid expenditure in 2013–14 went on payments to solicitors, solicitor advocates and advocates.[21] The Scottish Government has stated its commitment to ensuring that the legal profession is fairly remunerated, while ensuring value for money for the taxpayer.[22] The Law Society of Scotland has called for legal aid rates to be uprated, arguing that current rates are unsustainable.[23] SLAB has countered this by pointing out that there has been an increase in recent years in the number of firms and solicitors registered to provide both civil and criminal legal assistance, which suggests that they are neither unwilling nor unable to provide assistance at legal aid rates.[24] It is likely, however, that as the economic situation improves, some of those firms will move away again from legal aid towards more profitable private work.[25]

There has been an increasing shift towards other methods of provision over the past 15 years or so. First, SLAB runs seven Public Defence Solicitors' Offices (PDSOs) across Scotland, which employ salaried solicitors to provide advice and representation in criminal cases. Secondly, it has four Civil Legal Assistance Offices (CLAOs) across Scotland,[26] which employ solicitors in order to address unmet legal need based on either geography or thematic area of need.[27] The offices work in partnership with each other and have strong links with local advice agencies and legal firms. They are intended to provide a service to complement existing local provision; they offer a second-tier support service to local advice agencies, and refer clients who are eligible for legal aid to a solicitor in private practice who is willing and able to take the case. If such a referral is not possible, the CLAO will take the case on itself in some circumstances.

Third, since 2007, SLAB has used its grant funding powers to develop a 'targeted legal assistance' approach through a number of grant funded programmes, as further discussed later in this chapter. Given the increasing emphasis on prevention and on outcomes for users, as further discussed below, the shift towards alternative forms of provision seems likely to continue.

---

[19] With the commencement of Part V of the Legal Aid (Scotland) Act 1986.

[20] s 68 Legal Profession and Legal Aid (Scotland) Act 2007 gave SLAB powers to provide grant funding to such organisations.

[21] Scottish Legal Aid Board *Annual Report 2013–14* (n 8). Note: an advocate is the Scottish equivalent of a barrister.

[22] See *A Sustainable Future for Legal Aid* (n 10).

[23] See *Legal Assistance in Scotland* (n 11).

[24] See *Response to Legal Assistance in Scotland* (n 13).

[25] See Scottish Legal Aid Board, *Annual Report 2013–14* (n 8).

[26] These are located in Inverness, Lochgilphead, Aberdeen and Edinburgh.

[27] The Inverness and Lochgilphead offices provide a general civil service across the Highlands and Islands and Argyll and Bute respectively. The Aberdeen and Edinburgh offices are focused on the needs of those affected by the economic downturn.

A Strategic Approach

The current approach in Scotland is distinctive in the sense that policy relating to publicly funded legal services is being taken forward as part of the Scottish Government's wider priorities for Scotland as a whole. The Scottish Government's National Performance Framework[28] sets out its stated purpose, which is 'to focus Government and public services on creating a more successful country, with opportunities for all of Scotland to flourish, through increasing sustainable economic growth'. Beneath this overarching purpose sit five strategic objectives and sixteen 'national outcomes', which are intended to support the achievement of this aim.

In 2012, the Scottish Government published its *Strategy for Justice in Scotland*,[29] which views the justice system[30] as contributing both directly, and in partnership with other areas of government responsibility, to the delivery of one of its strategic objectives: a Scotland that is 'safer and stronger'. The strategy identifies three key national outcomes as being particularly relevant to the justice system. These are:

— We live our lives safe from crime, disorder and danger.
— We deliver strong, resilient and supportive communities where people take responsibility for their own actions and how they affect others.
— Our public services are high quality, continually improving, efficient and responsive to local people's needs.

The strategy goes on to set out a series of eight 'contributory justice outcomes' which the Scottish Government aims to achieve:

1. We experience low levels of crime.
2. We experience low levels of fear, alarm and distress.
3. We are at a low risk of unintentional harm.
4. Our people and communities support and respect each other, exercising both their rights and responsibilities.
5. We have high levels of public confidence in justice institutions and processes.
6. Our public services are fair and accessible.
7. Our institutions and processes are effective and efficient.
8. Our public services respect the rights and voice of users.

These outcomes are intended to support the Scottish Government's vision of

a justice system that contributes positively to a flourishing Scotland, helping to create an inclusive and respectful society in which all people and communities live in safety and

---

[28] See: www.scotland.gov.uk/About/Performance/scotPerforms.
[29] Scottish Government, *The Strategy for Justice in Scotland* (2012), available at: www.scotland.gov.uk/Resource/0040/00401836.pdf.
[30] Including civil, criminal and administrative justice.

security, individual and collective rights are supported and disputes are resolved fairly and swiftly.[31]

In order to achieve this vision, the strategy focuses on the need for prevention and early intervention; greater partnership working and integration of services; and increased innovation and use of digital technology. It exemplifies a clear focus across Scottish government on the importance of collaboration in order to achieve its desired outcomes.

First, the strategy recognises that publicly funded legal assistance must be considered within the context of the wider justice system, in order to maximise resources and because changes within other parts of the system will impact on it, and vice versa. Second, there is a clear recognition that the wider justice system itself cannot be viewed in isolation, and that effective reform will require collaboration across the public sector. This system-wide approach, facilitated by Scotland's size and scale, allows for a more focused and coordinated strategy for justice reform, which aims to achieve a series of clear, shared outcomes.

A key aspect of the strategy is the Making Justice Work Programme,[32] which brings together a range of organisations working across civil and criminal justice in Scotland. Its aim is to ensure that 'the Scottish justice system will be fair and accessible, cost-effective and efficient, and make proportionate use of resources. Disputes and prosecutions will be resolved quickly and secure just outcomes'. In addition to legal aid reforms and the strategic coordination of publicly funded legal assistance, the programme encompasses structural and procedural court reforms, reform of tribunals and administrative justice, and developing legal capability and alternative forms of dispute resolution.

This approach allows legal aid reform to be considered in the context of wider justice reforms which are likely to have an impact on legal aid. There have been a number of major reviews and reports in Scotland in recent years, including Lord Gill's review of the civil courts,[33] the reports of the Administrative Justice Steering Group chaired by Lord Philip,[34] the final report of the Civil Justice Advisory Group chaired by Lord Coulsfield,[35] and Sheriff Principal Taylor's review of expenses and

---

[31] See *The Strategy for Justice in Scotland* (2012) (n 29) 13.

[32] See: www.scotland.gov.uk/Topics/Justice/justicestrategy/programmes/mjw.

[33] Report of the Scottish Civil Courts Review (2009), available at: www.scotcourts.gov.uk/about-the-scottish-court-service/the-scottish-civil-courts-reform.

[34] Scottish Consumer Council, *Options for the Future Administrative and Supervision of Tribunals in Scotland: A Report by the Administrative Justice Steering Group (2008)*, available at: http://ajtc.justice.gov.uk/docs/Tribunals_in_Scotland.pdf; Consumer Focus Scotland, *Administrative Justice in Scotland—The Way Forward: The Final Report of the Steering Group* (2009), available at: www.consumerfocus.org.uk/scotland/files/2010/10/Administrative-Justice-in-Scotland-The-Way-Forward-Full-Report.pdf.

[35] Consumer Focus Scotland, *Ensuring Effective Access to Appropriate and Affordable Dispute Resolution: The Final Report of the Civil Justice Advisory Group* (2011), available at: www.consumerfocus.org.uk/scotland/files/2011/01/Civil-Justice-Advisory-Group-Full-Report.pdf.

funding of litigation.[36] All of these will have an impact on the way in which publicly funded legal assistance is provided, as discussed further later in this chapter.

Current Legal Aid Priorities

In line with wider current public policy priorities, there is a strong focus on prevention, in an attempt to avoid civil justice problems arising in the first place, and on early intervention to prevent the escalation of such problems where they do arise. The aim is to secure better outcomes for both the individuals who receive assistance and support, and for the wider community. Providing such support to those who need it at difficult times in their lives, can, for example, help them to preserve their financial security, or prevent them losing their job or their home. By doing this, legal aid helps to prevent wider social problems such as poverty, debt, homelessness and ill health, which can impact on the cost and provision of other public services, such as health and housing. In addition to improving outcomes for individuals and communities, prevention and earlier intervention should lead to savings within the justice system, including legal aid costs.

The Scottish Government's current approach to legal aid is set out in its legal aid strategy, *A Sustainable Future for Legal Aid*, which was published in 2011.[37] An updated strategy, taking account of developments since then, was awaited at the time of writing. It is anticipated that the forthcoming strategy will continue to follow the same broad approach.

The present strategy has four key themes:

1. Focusing legal aid on those who need it most.
2. Ensuring wider access to justice—the right help at the right time.
3. Maximising the value of legal aid expenditure.
4. Making the justice system more efficient.

Focusing Legal Aid on Those who need it Most

First, there is an emphasis on ensuring that those who are able to pay for at least some of their legal costs do so. An estimated 75 per cent of people in Scotland are currently eligible for civil legal aid, following a substantial increase in the financial eligibility limits in 2010. There is, however, a sliding scale system of contributions, which means that some people may have to pay for most or even all of the cost

---

[36] *Review of Expenses and Funding of Civil Litigation in Scotland* (2013) report by Sheriff Principal James A Taylor, Edinburgh, available at: www.scotland.gov.uk/Resource/0043/00438205.pdf.

[37] See *A Sustainable Future for Legal Aid* (n 10).

of their legal assistance. An award of legal aid can still offer significant advantages for those in this situation. They may be able to spread the costs by paying these in instalments; legal aid rates are generally much lower than solicitors' private rates; and if they were to lose their case, they would not run the risk of being responsible for the other party's legal expenses.

At present, contributions are not payable in respect of criminal legal assistance. Despite opposition from the legal profession, legislation has now been passed, but not yet implemented, which will introduce such contributions for those who are able to pay towards the costs of this,[38] in order to target assistance towards those who need it most.

The Scottish Government is also currently considering possible alternatives to public funding in civil cases, in keeping with its declared intention to move towards a system where the legal aid fund becomes the 'funder of last resort' for civil litigation.[39] In the wake of the Jackson review south of the border, the Scottish Government established an independent review of the costs and funding of civil litigation in Scotland chaired by Sheriff Principal Taylor. The final report of the review was published in September 2013,[40] and at the time of writing the Scottish Government is consulting on proposals to implement the review's recommendations on matters such as speculative fees, damages based arrangements and qualified one-way costs shifting.[41]

Second, initiatives such as SLAB's grant funded programmes and its Civil Legal Assistance Offices focus on particular areas of need, where there is no or insufficient existing provision, whether in relation to subject matter or geographical area, with the aim of ensuring that people can obtain the type of assistance and support that they need. There is a clear emphasis across the grant funded programmes on encouraging partnership working between different organisations in order to identify particular areas of law and/or groups of people who might benefit from targeted advice and assistance. At the time of writing, SLAB is managing three such programmes, which cover a total of 108 different projects across Scotland:

1. The Making Advice Work Programme, which is due to run until March 2015, supports people across Scotland who have been affected by welfare reform and debt-related problems. This programme is funded by the Scottish Government and by the Money Advice Service, as part of its UK debt advice funding partnership. A total of 72 services are currently funded through this programme, with a particular focus on: (1) projects that can provide advice, information and representation for people across a geographic area; (2) advice for tenants of social landlords; and (3) assistance for people with disabilities and those experiencing domestic abuse.

---

[38] Scottish Civil Justice Council and Criminal Legal Assistance Act 2013, Part 2.

[39] See *A Sustainable Future for Legal Aid* (n 10).

[40] See *Review of Expenses and Funding of Civil Litigation in Scotland* (2013) (n 36).

[41] Scottish Government, *Expenses and Funding of Civil Litigation Bill: A Consultation* (2015), available at: www.scotland.gov.uk/Resource/0046/00469240.pdf.

2. The Economic Downturn Programme, which also runs until the end of March 2015, funds a further 20 services across Scotland. It is focused primarily on (a) assistance and representation for those with debt issues who are facing court action for mortgage or tenancy repossession and (b) information, advice and signposting for people with small claims or other civil court cases, in order to increase their ability to navigate the court process or enable them to resolve the matter at an early stage.

3. From October 2014, the Scottish Government has provided funding for the Tackling Money Worries Programme, to run until 2016. This programme funds 16 projects focused on debt advice and preventative financial capability work to assist low income families with children facing a change in their circumstances. This is a clear example of the coordinated approach that is being taken across the Scottish Government—the programme aims to contribute to achieving the priorities and outcomes of the Scottish Government's revised Child Poverty Strategy by improving outcomes and opportunities for low income families and children.

Since 2011, SLAB has also had a duty to monitor the availability and accessibility of publicly funded legal services in Scotland, and to provide advice to Scottish ministers about this.[42] SLAB gathers intelligence on potential problems with access to and/or availability of legal services on an ongoing basis through analysis of its own data on supply and demand trends; data collection from other sources within the justice system; and seeking the views of stakeholders across the justice system.

SLAB's most recent monitoring report to the Scottish Government concludes, for example, that there is a medium probability of a systemic access problem in specific areas of Scotland for mortgage repossession cases, which should be kept under review; and that there are systemic access problems in three particular local authority areas in relation to mental health law.[43] This type of intelligence can be fed into ongoing work on the strategic coordination of advice services across Scotland.

Ensuring Wider Access to Justice: The Right Help at the Right Time

There are a number of strands to the work in this area, which are being drawn together within the Enabling Access to Justice Project, a key project under the Making Justice Work programme, which is being led by SLAB. The project's aim is 'to help people to resolve their problems earlier, with the right advice at the right

---

[42] s 141 Legal Services (Scotland) Act 2010.

[43] Scottish Legal Aid Board, *Third Report to the Scottish Government on the Monitoring of Availability and Accessibility of Legal Services* (2014), available at: www.slab.org.uk/export/sites/default/common/documents/about_us/policy/2014_monitoring_reportxa_FINALx.pdf.

time, outwith the formal court and tribunal structures where possible, but with effective access to representation where that is needed'.[44]

This work builds on the recommendations of the Civil Justice Advisory Group chaired by Lord Coulsfield that the civil justice system should follow a 'triage' approach, which would help to inform and guide people, helping them to identify the most appropriate route to dealing with their civil justice problems at each stage of their 'journey' through the system.[45] It also builds on work done by the former Consumer Focus Scotland,[46] and now being taken forward by SLAB, in the area of 'legal capability'. The idea behind this is to consider ways of 'legally empowering' people to equip them with the knowledge, skills and confidence they need to help them avoid experiencing legal problems in the first place, to recognise when they have a legal problem and to deal with such problems when they occur.

Other ongoing areas of work which fall within the ambit of the Enabling Access to Justice project include consideration of how alternative methods of dispute resolution might be used to resolve disputes at an early stage,[47] and looking at new ways of delivering services, including through digital technology.[48] SLAB was also involved in the development of the Scottish Government's Digital Strategy for Justice,[49] which aims to use technology to broaden access to justice, improve quality of service and safeguard the rights of citizens and users.

As part of the Enabling Access to Justice project, SLAB has also been taking a lead role in work on improving the planning, coordination and delivery of publicly funded information, advice and representation services across Scotland. Its 2014 *Landscape Review of Publicly Funded Legal Assistance*[50] examined the current pattern of funding and planning of such services across Scotland, including local government, Scottish Government and SLAB funded provision, with the aim of assisting those who plan and fund advice and representation services to better understand the complex planning and funding environment. This was recently followed by a framework for public funding of advice in Scotland,[51] produced

---

[44] Source: www.scotland.gov.uk/Topics/archive/law-order/17822/EnablingAccesstoJusticeProject.

[45] See *Ensuring Effective Access to Appropriate and Affordable Dispute Resolution* (n 35).

[46] Consumer Focus Scotland, *Facing up to Legal Problems: Towards a Preventative Approach to Addressing Disputes and their Impact on Individuals and Society* (2012), available at: www.consumerfocus. org.uk/scotland/files/2012/12/Facing-up-to-legal-problems-Full-report.pdf.

[47] SLAB is currently carrying out a series of research exercises in this area in collaboration with the Scottish Government. Its most recent publication on this topic is Scottish Legal Aid Board, *Overview Report of Alternative Dispute Resolution in Scotland* (2014), available at: www.slab.org.uk/about-us/ what-we-do/policyanddevelopmentoverview/AlternativeDisputeResolution/index.html.

[48] See, eg: www.slab.org.uk/search/results.html?index=SLABSiteOnline&searchPage=1&matches PerPage=10&displayPages=10&query=digital+strategy&search=+.

[49] Scottish Government, *The Digital Strategy for Justice in Scotland* (2014), available at: www. scotland.gov.uk/Resource/0045/00158026.pdf.

[50] Scottish Legal Aid Board, *Landscape Review of Publicly Funded Legal Assistance* (2014), available at: www.slab.org.uk/export/sites/default/common/documents/about_us/research/Patterns_Supply/ PFLA_landscape_review_FINAL.pdf.

[51] Framework for Public Funding of Advice in Scotland (2015), available at: www.slab.org. uk/about-us/what-we-do/policyanddevelopmentoverview/Planningandcoordination/Funders Framework/index.html.

by SLAB in partnership with the Scottish Government and the Improvement Service[52] which sets out a series of good practice principles for those who fund advice services, focusing on the best outcome for the client facing a problem and value for money for the public purse, by minimising duplication and overlap, encouraging referrals, and a joined-up, strategic approach between funders and providers.

Maximising the Value of Legal Aid Expenditure

A variety of reforms and efficiencies have been put in place in recent years in order to achieve this goal. As noted earlier in this chapter, however, while significant savings have been achieved, there is still a gap between legal aid expenditure and the money allocated by the Scottish Government to pay for this. Despite SLAB having taken on significant new responsibilities and an increased workload in the past few years, its administrative budget has been reduced significantly, representing a real terms cut of almost 30 per cent from 2007/08 levels by 2014–15.[53]

SLAB and the Scottish Government are continuing to look at new ways to make savings. These include an ongoing series of best value reviews by SLAB in specific subject areas, looking at possible efficiencies. There is currently a specific focus on family cases, which accounted for 61 per cent of total civil legal aid expenditure in 2013–14.[54]

Proposals to introduce a contractual model for criminal legal assistance are also currently in development: detailed proposals were submitted to the Scottish Government by SLAB in late 2013, following a consultation process with organisations across the criminal justice system.

Making the Justice System More Efficient

In addition to short-term efficiency measures, this theme encompasses many of the ongoing justice reforms resulting from major reviews such as Lord Gill's review of the civil courts and Lord Philip's review of the administrative justice system. For example, the reforms to the civil courts which are due to be implemented from this year following the Gill review include the transfer of all cases with a value of less than £100,000 from the Court of Session to the sheriff court,

---

[52] The Improvement Service is a partnership between the Convention of Scottish Local Authorities (COSLA) and the Society of Local Authority Chief Executives (SOLACE). It works with Scottish councils and their partners to improve the efficiency, quality and accountability of local public services by providing advice, consultancy and programme support.

[53] See Scottish Legal Aid Board, *Corporate Plan 2014–17* (n 15).

[54] See Scottish Legal Aid Board, *Annual Report 2013–14* (n 8).

and more active case management by the courts.[55] These changes should result in reduced legal aid expenditure.

A new group of 'third-tier' judges are also to be introduced, who will be responsible for dealing with cases with a value of up to £5,000 under a new simple procedure. The intention is that this will be more inquisitorial, informal and accessible to party litigants and non-lawyer representatives than the current small claims procedure. Legal aid is not currently available for representation in small claims cases (claims of under £3,000), although advice and assistance may be available. It is not yet clear what the legal aid position will be as regards the simple procedure, but there is scope within the legislation to provide for this in certain categories of case. If, however, the new procedure is, as intended, more accessible and inquisitorial than the present system, there may be less need for party litigants to obtain legal representation. At present, many such litigants access advice and support from non-lawyer advisers, such as the SLAB funded in-court advisers who operate across a number of Scotland's sheriff courts.

Meanwhile, a programme of tribunal reforms is currently under way, with the aim of creating a new tribunal structure for Scotland. As part of this, private rented sector housing cases currently dealt with in the sheriff court are to be transferred to a new specialist tribunal in 2016.[56] Concerns have been expressed by the legal profession that legal aid may not be available for representation at the tribunal, as it currently is in the sheriff court.[57] It can be argued, however, that there is less need for legal aid in the traditional sense within a more inquisitorial and specialist tribunal than in a court. While many people who find themselves involved in tribunal processes may need advice and support, whether from a lawyer or other adviser, representation may be less crucial. Research with tribunal users has found that pre-hearing advice was more important than representation in the outcome achieved, with overall success rates for those with pre-hearing advice almost as high as those who were represented, and in some cases actually higher.[58]

In relation to both courts and tribunals, specialist non-lawyer advisers may often be better placed to provide advice, support and even representation than some solicitors, who may be less familiar with a particular process or category of case. This was recognised in the Homeowner and Debtor Protection (Scotland) Act 2010, which introduced new rights of audience for accredited non-lawyer advisers in mortgage repossession cases. Projects employing such advisers have been funded by SLAB under its grant funded programmes.

---

[55] Courts Reform (Scotland) Act 2014.

[56] Housing (Scotland) Act 2014, Part 3.

[57] See, eg, the written submissions made in relation to the Housing (Scotland) Bill to the Capital Infrastructure and Investment Committee of the Scottish Parliament by the Legal Services Agency, available at: www.scottish.parliament.uk/S4_InfrastructureandCapitalInvestmentCommittee/14.01.16_ Legal_Services_Agency.pdf, and the Law Society of Scotland, available at: www.scottish.parliament. uk/S4_InfrastructureandCapitalInvestmentCommittee/14.02.10_The_Law_Society_of_Scotland.pdf.

[58] M Adler, 'Tribunals Ain't What They Used to Be' *Adjust Newsletter* (March 2009), available at: http://ajtc.justice.gov.uk/adjust/articles/AdlerTribunalsUsedToBe.pdf.

As recognised in the Scottish Government's current legal aid strategy, another example of how the efficiency of the justice system might be improved would be to encourage both public bodies and private organisations to observe the principle of 'getting it right first time' wherever possible, as recommended by both the Administrative Justice Steering Group and the Civil Justice Advisory Group.[59] This could lead to fewer cases being taken to a court or tribunal in the first place, resulting in improved outcomes for parties and savings to both the justice system and the organisations involved.

Conclusion

To date, Scotland has been largely successful in continuing to provide legal aid to those who need it, without introducing a cap on expenditure, or major reductions in scope and/or eligibility. Moreover, it is likely that the targeted forms of assistance and strategic approach to advice that are being developed have already resulted in improved access to justice for many people.

There is a clear commitment from the current Scottish Government to maintaining the current approach, but this is certainly not without its challenges. There is at present a shortfall between the allocated legal aid budget and the projected spend, and this looks set to continue at least in the short term. This means that government will need to find cash from other budgets in order to maintain an open ended fund with a wide scope.

While the Scottish Government and SLAB continue to look for ways to further reduce costs, there must come a point beyond which further efficiency savings are very difficult to find. Other ways must therefore be found to balance the books. At the time of writing, a new legal aid strategy is awaited, and this may have some of the answers. Proposed reforms such as the introduction of criminal contributions should have a noticeable impact. Some of the other changes outlined in this chapter, such as the civil court reforms which are due to be rolled out over the next year or two should also lead to reduced costs, but it may take some time before the impact of these on legal aid expenditure become apparent. Meanwhile, other current initiatives, such as the work on early intervention and legal capability, are likely to be longer term in nature—the impact of these may not be seen until some years down the line.

Finding ways to balance the budget will be an ongoing challenge. While demand for legal aid may reduce in some areas—there are signs of a slight downward trend in civil legal aid, for example, which is likely to continue as the economy picks

---

[59] See: *Options for the Future Administrative and Supervision of Tribunals in Scotland* and *Administrative Justice in Scotland* (n 34); and *Ensuring Effective Access to Appropriate and Affordable Dispute Resolution* (n 35).

up—it is likely to increase in others at the same time, such as the recent rise in criminal legal aid applications as a result of targeted activity by Police Scotland.

Demand for legal aid will always fluctuate, depending on a variety of external factors at any given time. While this results in a budget which is volatile, that budget also has flexibility, which allows it to respond to changing needs. There will be a need for constant vigilance and monitoring in order to keep abreast of relevant changes on the horizon—whether these come from within other parts of the justice system, such as the changes which will result from the current Criminal Justice (Scotland) Bill, or from elsewhere, such as the forthcoming UK welfare reforms—and the impact these are likely to have on the fund. SLAB already tries to take account of such changes in its forward planning and forecasting of future expenditure, although there will always be unexpected developments from time to time. The strategic and collaborative approach which is being taken across government in Scotland can only assist with such strategic planning.

In the longer term, the investment which is being made now by the Scottish Government, SLAB and other partners in working towards preventative and innovative approaches, targeted assistance, and strategic coordination and delivery, together with the eventual impacts of wider reforms within the justice system, could reap rewards in terms of both the legal aid budget and access to justice for the people of Scotland.

INDEX

Acas:
  Code of Practice, 182
  early conciliation scheme, 177–78, 184–85
  fixed time periods for conciliation, 182
  role, 187, 191
  statutory disciplinary and grievance
    procedures, 182
access to justice, 1–2
  administrative law and justice and, 69–72
    Coalition government reforms, 82–102
    future, 102–03
    pre-Coalition, 80–82
    remedies, 72–80
  alternatives, 19–22
  current position, 14–15
    consequences, 15–18
    government attitude, 18–19
  descriptive aspect, 28
  ECHR, 53–56
  employment disputes, 192–95
    impact of fees, 178
  EU law, 56–58
  European case law, 58–60
  European legislation, 60–65
  family justice:
    legal aid, 201–05
  France, 259–85
  housing disputes, 159–74
  immigration and, 106–14
    legal aid, 114–22
  meaning, 27
  normative aspect:
    equal access, 28–30, 31–35, 36
    pragmatic interpretation, 30, 35–36
    relationship with social rights, 30, 31–35
  Scotland, 287–301
  tribunal justice, 135–41
  welfare entitlement and, 135–41
  young people:
    impact of legal aid cuts, 221–29
Adler, M, 100, 143–44
Administration of Justice Act 1985, 239
Administrative Justice and Tribunals Council
  (AJTC), 82
  abolition, 83
administrative law and justice:
  advice, assistance and representation:
    Citizens Advice Bureaux, 79

    declining availability, 99–102
    lawyers, 79
    local authority advice services, 79
    non-lawyers, 79–80
    trade unions, 79
  austerity policies, impact of:
    community care, 93–95
    costs, 87–88
    failure to address lack of remedies, 93
    failure to pursue holistic approach, 82–83
    fees, 88–89
    legal aid, 88
    minor procedural defects, 87
    planning cases, 86
    removing right of appeal, 90–92
    undermining judicial review, 83–86
      criticisms of, 89–90
    weak cases, 87
  future of access to justice, 102–03
  good decision-making:
    discretion, 72
    legality, 70–71
    standards, 71–72
  government role, 13
  justice and law distinguished, 69
  nature of administrative decisions, 71–72
    individualised decisions, 71
  pre-Coalition government:
    complaints procedures, 80–81
    court appeals, 80
    judicial review, 81
    ombudsmen, 81
    remedies, 80–82
    tribunal appeals, 80
  remedies, 70–71, 72–73
    adjudication in ordinary courts, 73, 74
    adjudication in tribunals, 73, 74
    availability, 95
    internal complaints and review processes,
      73, 75, 80–81
    new obstacles, 95–99
    ombudsmen, 73, 74–75
    pre-Coalition government, 80–82
    public inquiries, 73
    welfare benefits appeals, 95–99
advice, assistance and representation:
  administrative justice and law
    Citizens Advice Bureaux, 79

declining availability, 99–102
lawyers, 79
local authority advice services, 79
non-lawyers, 79–80
trade unions, 79
benefits of advice, 151–52
case study, 152
future, 154–55
Independent Advice Project, 149–50
Islington Law Centre, 147–48
Islington Schools Advice Project, 148–49
outcomes, 151–52
response to welfare reform, 153–54
Three Advice Projects, 150–51
form-filling, 151
pre-hearing advice, 143–44
Airey v Ireland, 53–54, 55
alternative business structures (ABS), 237–38
branding, 241–43
impact on welfare law services, 243–45
Legal Services Act 2007, 237, 238–43
licensing, 240–41, 246
alternative dispute resolution (ADR):
employment disputes, 182
family justice, 202
France, 279, 282–83, 284
housing disputes, 160, 164
immigration disputes, 116
Asylum and Immigration Tribunal
asylum disputes, 111–12
asylum disputes, 19
Asylum and Immigration Tribunal, 111–12
legal aid cuts, 223
provisions on legal aid, 60–65
reception conditions Directive, 61–62
Upper Tribunal (Immigration and Asylum
Chamber), 112
young people, 213–14
austerity measures, 1–2, 18–19, 176–77, 261
see also legal aid

Bar Standards Board (BSB), 239–40
'bare minimum', 30, 34–36
benefit appeals, *see* social security benefit
appeals
Beveridge Report, 18
Blunkett, D, 14, 23–24, 84–85
immigration, 108–09
ouster clause, 109
Bowman report, 78

Cappelletti, M:
development of access to justice, 31–32, 34
child poverty:
Islington (case study), 145–46
welfare reforms and, 145, 147
Child Poverty Act 2010, 145
Children Act 1989, 117, 165, 197, 201, 207

Children and Family Courts Advice and Support
Service (CAFCASS), 16, 209
Citizens Advice Bureaux (CAB), 2, 216
employment disputes, 177, 188, 194–95
family justice, 205
housing disputes, 169
pro bono work, 21
Scotland, 3
welfare issues, 79
young people, 217
citizenship, 18, 42
equal access for justice, 29–30
immigration disputes, 114
types of citizenship, 32
citizens' remedies, 70–71, 72–73
adjudication in ordinary courts, 73, 74, 78
adjudication in tribunals, 73, 74, 77
historical development, 75–77
Bowman report, 78
Leggatt inquiry, 77, 80
Woolf report, 78
hybrid remedies, 75
internal complaints and review processes,
73, 75
ombudsmen, 73, 74–75
impact of devolution, 77–78
public inquiries, 73
Civil Legal Assistance Offices (Scotland), 291,
295
civil right of access to justice, 30–35
CMVMC O'Limo v Spain, 59
Coalition Government:
administrative law and justice, 82–102
fiscal planning, 4–5
impact, 5
immigration disputes, 108
restricting judicial review, 108–09
judicial review policies, 83–86
community care:
administrative law:
inadequacy of remedies, 93–95
welfare benefits appeals, 95–99
comparative law, *see* France; Scotland
complaints procedures, 69, 70
administrative law, 73, 75–76
pre-Coalition government, 80–81
Legal Services Act 2007, 238
conditional fee agreements:
housing disputes, 167, 170–71
costs, 4–5
administrative law:
impact of austerity policies, 87–88
judicial review, 86, 87–88
European Court of Human Rights (ECtHR):
security for costs, 54–55
France:
awarding legal costs, 269
impact of austerity policies on, 87–88

judicial review, 86, 87–88
mediators v lawyers, 208
social entitlement tribunal:
  no costs regime, 137
Council for Licensed Conveyancers, 239, 240–41
county courts, 15
  counter services, 171–72
  housing disputes, 161–62
    warrants of possession, 165
  impact of cuts, 171–72
  possession proceedings, 258
  small claims procedure, 79–80, 99
CourtNav:
  development, 255–56
  extending RCJ Advice Bureau reach, 254
  funding, 256
  RCJ Advice Bureau experience, 257–58
  supporting litigants in person, 254
  user experience, 256
Courts and Legal Services Act 1990, 239, 240
Courts and Tribunals (Scotland) Act 2014, 78
cross-border disputes:
  EU Directive, 63

DEB case, 58–59, 60
Denvir, C:
  use of remote access by young people,
    220–21
Dicey, AV, 29–30, 39
domestic violence, 17
  see also family justice
  evidential burden, 17–18
  family justice, 197–98, 255, 258
  immigration disputes, 115–16
  prescribed evidence, 17
Dublin III Regulation, 62, 65
Dworkin, R, 51

employment disputes:
  see also Acas; Employment Tribunal
  case study, 175–77
  collective dispute resolution:
    decline, 180
  current reforms, 177
    Acas Early Conciliation scheme, 177–78,
      184–85
    fees regime, 177
    unfair dismissal claims, 177
  industrial action:
    decline, 180–81
  recommended reforms:
    enforcement of awards, 194–95
    independent forum for adjudication, 193
    introducing a regulatory mechanism, 193
    simplifying the system, 192–93
    supporting litigants in person, 193–94
  trade union role:
    decline, 180–81

Employment Tribunal:
  fees, 178–79
    impact of introduction for workers,
      179–80, 183–84
  numbers of cases, 182–84
  review of system, 184–86
    deregulation of employment law
      framework, 183
    increased use of ADR, 181–82
    worker experiences of, 186–87, 190–92
      CAB's role, 188
      case study, 189–90
equal access to justice, 30–33
  attainment, 36
    socialisation of legal advice and assistance,
      36–37
      advantages, 37–38
      disadvantages, 38
  failure of policy, 33, 35–36
EU law, 53
  case law, 58–60
  e-justice, 65
  EUCFR, 56–58
  human rights protection:
    Art 6 TEU, 56
    ECHR, 56
    EUCFR, 56–58
  provisions on legal aid:
    cost allocation, 63–64
    Dublin III Regulation, 62
    immigration and asylum, 60–65
    legal aid for pre-judicial assistance
      Directive, 63
    legal aid in cross-border disputes
      Directive, 63
    maintenance obligations in cross-border
      disputes, 64
    procedures Directive, 60–61
    reception conditions for asylum seekers
      Directive, 61–62
    returns Directive, 63
  state-funded legal aid, 252
European Charter of Fundamental Rights, 56
  explanations, 57–58
  general provisions, 57
  legal aid, 57
    effective remedy, 57
    fair and public hearing, 57
    state-funding legal aid, 252
  limitation and interpretation, 57
  relationship with ECHR, 57
  scope of application, 57
  state-funded legal aid, 252
European Convention on Human Rights
  (ECHR), 18, 53–56
  case law, 53–56
  EU law and, 56
  family law, 65

legal aid, 53–56
  state-funded legal aid, 252
European Court of Human Rights (ECtHR), 35
  case law, 53–56
  libel and defamation, 55–56
  member state discretion, 56
  no right to legal aid in civil proceedings, 54
  right to a fair trial, 54
  security for costs, 54–55
European Court of Justice (CJEU):
  case law, 58–60
exceptional case funding:
  family justice, 200
  immigration disputes, 120–22
  young people, 224–25
Ewing, K, 185–86

family justice, 197–98
  arbitration, 198
  arm's length negotiations, 206–07
  civil status and, 205
  cost effectiveness, 197–99
  direct dealing with parties, 206–07
  domestic violence, 17
    evidential burden, 17–18
    family justice, 197–98, 255, 258
    immigration disputes, 115–16
    prescribed evidence, 17
  exceptional case funding, 200
  finance and, 205
  human rights and, 199–200
  legal aid changes, 201
    closure of mediation services, 202
    expansion of IT services, 203
    reduction in lawyer case load, 203
  matrimonial disputes, 19, 21, 49, 197, 203–06
  mediation, 198–200
  mediators v lawyers, 201, 203–05
    arm's length negotiations, 206–07
    costs, 208
    direct dealing with parties, 206–07
    facilitating proposals, 207
    legal framework, 207–08
    taking instruction, 207
  personal safety cases, 199–200
Family Justice Modernisation programme, 199
Family Justice Review, 199
fees:
  administrative law:
    impact of austerity policies, 88–89
    judicial review, 86
  austerity policies, impact of, 88–89
  employment disputes, 177
    Employment Tribunal, 178–79
    impact of introduction for workers,
      179–80, 183–84
  France, 274–75
  immigration disputes, 122–23

France, 259–60
  access to law and legal information:
    case law, 270
    Civil code, 270
    Journal officiel, 269
    parish noticeboards, 269–70
  aide à l'accès au droit, 260, 272–73
  aide juridictionelle, 260, 273–74
  commitment of government, 261
  funding, 260–61, 277
    central government, 277–28
    French Bar, 278
    huissiers, 279
    notaires, 279
    other public funding, 278
  increasing the legal aid budget,
    280–81
  judicial orders, 267
  justice de proximité, 266
  justice system:
    legal profession, 263
      avocats, 264–65
      charges (non-legal aid), 265–66
      huissiers, 264
      lawyers' monopolies, 263–65
      notaires, 264, 265
    service public de la justice:
      access to law and legal information,
        269–70
      awarding legal costs, 269
      courts, 266
      delays, 268
      underfunding, 267–68
  legal aid, 270–71
    aide à l'accès au droit, 272–73
    aide juridictionelle, 273–74
    delivery, 271
    fees, 274–75
    funding, 277–79
    users and volume of cases, 275–77
  legal history, 261–62
    reforms, 262
  rationalising use of the system, 279–80
  redirecting claims and legal assistance,
    legal protection insurance, 281–82, 284
    mediation/ADR, 282–83, 284
Franks Committee, 76, 99, 138

Garth, B:
  development of access to justice, 31–32, 34
Gibbons, M:
  review of Employment Tribunal procedure,
    182
Gill review (Scotland):
  judicial review, 78
  reform of civil courts, 78, 293, 298–99
GREP case, 60
Gudanaviciene case, 121–22, 134

Hampshire, S, 44, 47
Health Service Commissioner, *see* Public Service
   Ombudsman
health services:
  compared to legal services, 41
  decommodification of services, 43, 45,
    50–51
  differences:
    extent of individual's exposure to law/
      medicine, 49
    positional outcomes of legal disputes,
      47–48
    remedies in law v remedies in medicine, 48
    supply of services, 49–50
  financial barriers, 43, 45, 50–51
  similarities:
    access to qualified professionals, 45–46
    priority setting, 47
    rationing, 46–47
    removal of financial barriers, 45
    search for remedy, 46
  universal access, 42
    financial barriers, 43
    quality of services, 43
    range of services, 43
housing disputes, 157–60
  advice providers:
    CAB, 167
    not-for-profit agencies, 167–68
  case studies, 157–59
  conditional fee agreements, 170–71
  county court counter cuts, 171–72
  features, 160
    complexity of housing law, 160–63
    lack of ADR/mediation, 164
    number of crisis applications, 164–66
    number of hearings/applications for
      possession, 163
  impact of LASPO, 170–71
  impact of legal aid cuts, 166–70
  Jackson reforms, 170–71
  Law Commission recommendations:
    advice and assistance, 172
    ADR, 172
      pre-action protocols, 172–73
    duty adviser schemes, 173
    jurisdictional reforms:
      county courts and tribunals, 173
      procedural rules, 173
    problem-solving courts, 174
  litigants in person, 170
  possession claims, 163
    warrants for possession, 164–65
  problem clustering, 162–63, 169
    ill health, 165–66

Immigration Act 2014, 91
  rights of appeal, 123–27

immigration disputes, 19, 106–08
  challenging decisions, 110–11
    Asylum and Immigration Tribunal, 111–12
    judicial structure, 113
    Upper Tribunal (Immigration and Asylum
      Chamber), 112
  Coalition policies, 108
    restricting judicial review, 108–09
  exceptional case funding:
    ECHR and, 120–22
    LASPO and, 121
  foreign criminals, 126
  judicial review, 91–92, 107
    legal aid restrictions, 129–31
    limitations, 91, 108–09
  legal aid, 114
    impact of LASPO, 114–16
    impact of legal aid cuts, 116–17
    post-LASPO, 129
      judicial review cases, 129–31
    unrepresented appellants, 118–20
  ouster clause, 109
  residence test, 131–33
  rights of appeal, 90–92, 124
    fees, 122–23
    family visitor appeals, 122–23
    future of, 127–29
    Immigration Act 2014, 123–27
    Joint Committee on Human Rights
      criticisms of government policy, 125
    role of Lord Chancellor, 109–10
Independent Advice Project, 149–50
Independence Review Service for the Social
  Fund, 75
Islington Law Centre, 144, 147–48, 152
  funding, 152
  future of, 154–55
  Independent Advice Project, 149–50
  Islington Schools Advice Project, 148–49
  outcomes, 151–52
  response to welfare reform, 153–54
  Three Advice Projects, 150–51
Islington People's Rights, 149
Islington Schools Advice Project, 148–49

Jackson review, 159, 167, 170–71, 295
Joint Committee on Human Rights, 117–18
  immigration disputes, 121
    criticisms of government policy, 125,
      131–32
  young people:
    criticisms of government policy, 126–28
judicial review:
  administrative law, 73, 75
    Coalition austerity policies and, 83–86
    consultation papers, 85
    pre-Coalition government, 81
  Bowman report, 78

costs, 86, 87–88
criticisms of reforms, 89–90
fees, 86, 88–89
immigration disputes, 91–92, 129–31
  limitations, 91
legal aid, 86, 88
minor procedural defects, 87
planning cases:
  time limits, 85, 86
pre-Coalition government, 81
rights of appeal, 90–92
Scotland:
  Gill review, 78

Kreuz v Poland, 54–55

Land Registry, 44
Law Commission:
  housing dispute recommendations:
    advice and assistance, 172
    ADR, 172
      pre-action protocols, 172–73
    duty adviser schemes, 173
    jurisdictional reforms:
      county courts and tribunals, 173
      procedural rules, 173
    problem-solving courts, 174
Law Society:
  alternative ways of practicing
    Practice Note, 20
    proposals, 23
  rule of law, 24
  solicitor advocates, 239
Law Society of Scotland, 179
  criticism of, 289, 291
lawyers:
  alternative ways of working, 20
  mediators compared:
    arm's length negotiations, 206–07
    costs, 208
    direct dealing with parties, 206–07
    facilitating proposals, 207
    legal framework, 207–08
    taking instruction, 207
  'unbundling' of legal services, 20
legal aid:
  asylum disputes, 223
    statutory provisions, 60–65
  budgetary controls, 14–15
  EU law, 53
    legal aid for pre-judicial assistance
      Directive, 63
    legal aid in cross-border disputes
      Directive, 63
    state-funded legal aid, 252
  European Charter of Fundamental Rights, 57
    effective remedy, 57
    fair and public hearing, 57

state-funding legal aid, 252
European Convention on Human Rights
  (ECHR), 53–56
  state-funded legal aid, 252
European Court of Human Rights (ECtHR):
  no right to legal aid in civil proceedings, 54
family justice, 201–05
France, 270–71
  aide à l'accès au droit, 272–73
  aide juridictionelle, 273–74
  delivery, 271
  fees, 274–75
  funding, 277–79
  increasing the legal aid budget, 280–81
  rationalising use of the system, 279–80
  redirecting claims and legal assistance:
    legal protection insurance, 281–82, 284
    mediation/ADR, 282–83, 284
  users and volume of cases, 275–77
immigration, 114–22
Scotland:
  background, 289–90
  divergence in English and Scottish
    approaches, 288–89
  Law Society of Scotland proposals, 289–90
  'planned complex mixed model', 290–91
  rates, 291
  priorities:
    ensuring wider access, 296–98
    focusing legal aid on those who need it,
      294–96
    increasing efficiency of the system,
      298–300
    maximising value of expenditure, 298
  strategic approach, 292–93, 299–300
    Economic Downturn programme, 296
    Making Justice Work programme, 293,
      295
    priorities, 294–300
    reviews of justice systems as a whole,
      293–04
    Tackling Money Worries programme,
      296
young people:
  impact of cuts, 221–29
Legal Aid, Sentencing and Punishment of
  Offenders Act 2012 (LASPO), 1–6, 197–98
  advice, assistance and representation, 101–02
  consequences, 15–17
  exceptional case funding, 120–22
  housing disputes, 166–67
  Jackson Reforms, 170–71
  immigration disputes, 114–16
  impact on court-based remedies, 101
  post-LASPO access to legal aid, 222–24
    family law cases, 223
    immigration and asylum cases, 118,
      129–33, 223

social welfare law cases, 222–23
  young people, 222–24
scope, 15, 101
welfare benefits, 101–102, 144
young people, 212, 221–22
  post-LASPO, 222–24
Legal Services Act 2007, 237
  alternative business structures:
    impact on welfare law services, 243–45
  Clementi Review, 238–39
  not-for-profit advice sector, 245–47
    regulation, 246
    trade unions, 246
  reform of regulatory system, 238–39
Legal Services Board (LSB), 238
  promotion of competition, 239
  'public agency', as, 240
Leggatt inquiry, 77, 80, 99–100, 119, 136, 138, 140
Lewis, P, 200–01
litigants in person, 16, 100
  CourtNav, 254
  disadvantages, 16–17
  employment disputes, 193–94
  housing disputes, 170
  online tools, 249–50
    CourtNav, 254
  procedural advice, 249
Local Government Ombudsman, *see* Public
  Service Ombudsman
Lord Chancellor, 18, 87–88, 200, 246
  role in immigration disputes, 109–10
Lord Mackay of Clashfern, *see* Mackay JPH

Mackay, JPH, 14
MacKenzie friends, 21
Make Our Rights Reality manifesto, 230–34
Marshall, TH, 32–33
matrimonial disputes, 19, 21, 49, 197, 203–06
  see also family justice
mediation:
  see also alternative dispute resolution
  family justice, 198–200
    mediators v lawyers, 201, 206–08
  France, 282–83, 284
  housing disputes, 164
mediators:
  lawyers compared:
    arm's length negotiations, 206–07
    costs, 208
    direct dealing with parties, 206–07
    facilitating proposals, 207
    legal framework, 207–08
    taking instruction, 207
mental health:
  correlation with legal problems:
    young people, 217–19
Moorhead, R, 244–45

Nationality, Immigration and Asylum
  Act 2002, 91
Norgrove, D:
  Family Justice Review, 199
Northern Ireland Ombudsman, 77
not-for-profit advice:
  see also Citizens Advice Bureaux (CAB)
  housing disputes, 167–68
  Legal Services Act, 245–47
    regulation, 246
    trade unions, 246

Oestreicher, P, 24
Office of the Children's Commissioner
  (OCC), 255
  impacts of legal aid reforms on human rights
    of young people, 225–26
Ogus, A:
  self-regulation of legal services, 240, 242
ombudsman:
  administrative law remedies, 73, 74–75
    pre-Coalition government, 81
  devolution and, 77–78
  Northern Ireland Ombudsman, 77
  Public Services Ombudsman for Wales, 77
  Scottish Public Services Ombudsman, 77

Parliamentary Ombudsman, *see* Public Service
  Ombudsman
Paterson, A, 28
Police and Criminal Evidence Act 1984 (PACE),
  14
Posner, R, 34
poverty:
  child poverty, 145
  indicators, 146–47
  Islington (case study), 145–46
  welfare reforms and, 145, 147
pre-judicial assistance Directive, 63
preventive law, 44
pro bono work, 20–21, 250–54
  City law firms and, 251
  Pro Bono Protocol, 251
  setting up new projects, 251–52
provision of alternative legal services:
  see also alternative dispute resolution;
    mediation
  MacKenzie friends, 21
  pro bono work, 20–21
  unqualified legal providers, 21–22
Public Administration Committee:
  abolition of AJTC, 83
Public Bodies Act 2011, 82
Public Defence Solicitors (Scotland), 291
Public Service Ombudsman, 77–78
Public Services Ombudsman for Wales, 77

Q v Q, 16–17

R *(Public law project) v Secretary of State for Justice*, 133, 134
regulatory issues, 20
  competition:
    advocacy, 239–40
    conveyancing, 240
    litigation, 240
remedies:
  see also citizens' remedies
  administrative law, 70–71, 72–73
    adjudication in ordinary courts, 73, 74
    adjudication in tribunals, 73, 74
    availability, 95
    internal complaints and review processes, 73, 75, 80–81
    new obstacles, 95–99
    ombudsmen, 73, 74–75
    pre-Coalition government, 80–82
    public inquiries, 73
    welfare benefits appeals, 95–99
  community care:
    inadequacy of remedies, 93–95
  immigration control, 90–92
  impact of LASPO on court-based remedies, 101
  remedies in medicine compared, 48
representation in tribunals, 143–44
responsibility for fairness:
  general public, 23–24
  government, 24
  legal profession, 23
rights of appeal:
  immigration control, 90–92
Royal Courts of Justice (RCJ) Advice Bureau:
  CourtNav:
    extending RCJ Advice Bureau reach, 254
    RCJ Advice Bureau experience, 257–58
rule of law, 24–25, 28–29
  equal access for justice, 29–30

Scotland, 3–4, 287, 300–01
  Civil Legal Assistance Offices, 291
  devolution, 287
    divergence in approach, 288–89
  Gill review:
    judicial review, 78
    reform of civil courts, 298–99
  Homeowner and Debtor Protection (Scotland) Act 2010, 299
  legal aid rates, 291
  non-lawyer advisers, 299
  'planned complex mixed model, 290–91
  priorities:
    ensuring wider access, 296–98
    focusing legal aid on those who need it, 294–96
    increasing efficiency of the system, 298–300
    maximising value of expenditure, 298

Public Defence Solicitors, 291
publicly funded legal assistance:
  background, 289–90
  divergence in English and Scottish approaches, 288–89
  Law Society of Scotland proposals, 289–90
  'planned complex mixed model', 290–91
Scottish Public Services Ombudsman, 77
strategic approach, 292–93, 299–300
  Economic Downturn programme, 296
  Making Justice Work programme, 293, 295
  priorities, 294–300
  reviews of justice systems as a whole, 293–94
  Tackling Money Worries programme, 296
tribunal reform, 299
Scottish Legal Aid Board (SLAB), 3, 289
  Economic Downturn programme, 296
  Enabling Access to Justice programme, 296–98
  Making Justice Work programme, 293, 295
  Tackling Money Worries programme, 296
  targeted legal assistance, 291
Scottish Public Services Ombudsman, 77
Smith, R, 31–32
social entitlement tribunal, 136–37, 141
  case management, 137
  challenges:
    benefits reforms, 140
    cuts in advice provision, 140
    increase in appeals, 140
    statutory reconsiderations, 141
  enabling/inquisitorial function, 137–38
    consequences, 138–39
  no costs regime, 137
social policy:
  community care:
    inadequacy of remedies, 93–95
    welfare benefits appeals, 95–99
social right of access to justice, 30–35
  civil right distinguished, 32–33
social security benefit appeals, 96–97
  decline in number, 97–98
    concerns, 98
socialisation of legal advice and assistance, 36–37, 38–39
  advantages, 37–38
  disadvantages, 38
solicitor advocates, 239
Solicitors Regulation Authority (SRA), 239
Steel and Morris v UK, 55
Stephen, F:
  competitive regulation of legal services, 240, 241–42
Straw, J, 14
Susskind, R:
  use of technology, 249

technological advances, 20
   CourtNav, 254–58
   vulnerable young adults, 219–21
Tolstoy Miloslavsky v UK, 54
Treaty on European Union, 56
Tribunal Procedure Rules:
   case management, 137
tribunals, 135
   see also social entitlement tribunal
   representation and, 143–44
   welfare benefit appeals, 96

'unbundling' of legal services, 20
United Nations Convention on the Rights of the
   Child (UNCRC), 211–12
   UK government's failure to meet
      commitments, 225–28
unqualified legal providers, 21–22
   concerns:
      lack of compensation to protect
         customers, 22
      lack of complaints procedures, 22
      lack of professional indemnity insurance,
         22
      lack of qualification, 22
      lack of regulation, 22
      no overriding duty to the court, 22
   MacKenzie friends, 21
Upper Tribunal (Immigration and Asylum
   Chamber)
   asylum disputes, 112

VP Diffusion case, 59

Welfare Reform Act 2012, 141
welfare reforms, 143
   Beveridge Report, 18

child poverty, 145
current reforms, 19
Legal Aid and Advice Bill (1948), 18
local response to (Islington), 153–54
Welfare Reform Act 2012, 141
Woolf report, 78

young people, 211–12, 230
   advice needs:
      adolescent transition, 212–13
      cognitive behaviour and neurological
         development, 213
      nature of need, 214–15
      prevalence of need, 214–15
      problem triggers:
         asylum seekers/refugees, 213–14
         leaving education, 213–14
         leaving home/care, 213–14
         victims of crime, 213–14
      severity of need, 214–15
      social exclusion, 213
   failure to meet UNCRC commitments,
      225–28
   impact of legal aid cuts, 225–28
   LASPO, 221–22
      exceptional case funding, 224–25
      post-LASPO access to legal aid, 222–24
   Make Our Rights Reality manifesto, 230–34
   marginalisation in civil justice system,
      215–16
      civic engagement, 216
   mental health issues, 217–19
   NEET status, 218
   provision of dedicated services for young
      people, 228–29
   social isolation, 218
   technological advances and, 219–21

Lightning Source UK Ltd.
Milton Keynes UK
UKHW02f2324180418
321314UK00005B/115/P